# Scattering
# the Ashes

# Bilingual Press/Editorial Bilingüe

*General Editor*
Gary D. Keller

*Managing Editor*
Karen S. Van Hooft

*Associate Editors*
Karen M. Akins
Barbara H. Firoozye

*Assistant Editor*
Linda St. George Thurston

*Editorial Board*
Juan Goytisolo
Francisco Jiménez
Eduardo Rivera
Mario Vargas Llosa

*Address:*
Bilingual Press
Hispanic Research Center
Arizona State University
P.O. Box 872702
Tempe, Arizona 85287-2702
(602) 965-3867

# Scattering the Ashes

María del Carmen Boza

Bilingual Press/Editorial Bilingüe
Tempe, Arizona

ISBN 0-927534-75-4

Library of Congress Cataloging-in-Publication-Data

Boza, María del Carmen.
    Scattering the ashes / María del Carmen Boza.
       p.    cm.
    Includes bibliographical references.
    ISBN 0-927534-75-4 (alk. paper)
    1. Boza, María del Carmen.  2. Cuban American woman—Biography.
  3. Cuban Americans—Biography.  4. Exiles—United States—Biography.
  5. Suicide victims—United States—Biography.  6. Cuban Americans—
Social conditions.  I. Title.
    E184.C97B69   1998
    973'.04687291—dc21                  98-5512
                                              CIP

PRINTED IN THE UNITED STATES OF AMERICA

*Cover design, interior design, and typesetting by John Wincek, Aerocraft Charter Art Svc.*

*Back cover photo by Kurt Kuss.*

# Contents

| | |
|---|---:|
| The Wake | 1 |
| I | 2 |
| II | 67 |
| III | 101 |
| | |
| The Realm of the Hungry Ghosts | 125 |
| I | 126 |
| II | 163 |
| III | 185 |
| | |
| Girón | 211 |
| I | 212 |
| II | 245 |
| III | 276 |
| IV | 313 |
| | |
| Memorial | 351 |
| I | 352 |
| II | 356 |
| III | 366 |
| | |
| *Appendix A:* | |
| Selected Genealogy | 371 |
| *Appendix B:* | |
| Chronology of Elected or Appointed Cuban | |
| Administrations and an Intermission | 375 |
| *Appendix C:* | |
| Fathers and Sons and Sundry Other | |
| Public Men Mentioned in the Text | 377 |
| *Bibliography* | 385 |

For my parents, in life or death,
and for Kurt.

# Acknowledgments

Among the many to whom I am indebted, I wish especially to thank my husband, Kurt Kuss, for his steadfast patience, sweet companionship, good writing instincts, and amazing bloodhound nose for sources. And my mother—for information that she must have found painful to be asked for yet delivered readily, with warmth, and without complaint.

Many thanks go to Gary D. Keller who, as general editor of the Bilingual Review/Press, demonstrated faith in me from the start of my writing career. I received good advice and generous encouragement from Howard Norman, Joyce Kornblatt, and Neil D. Isaacs at the University of Maryland, for which I am grateful.

For their friendship and support I thank Barbara Bjanes, Kip Brunk, Cathleen Cooper, Sherri Schaefer, Pamela Thompson, Connie Monfiletto Uchida, and Celeste.

*What Exile from himself can flee?*
*To zones, though more and more remote,*
*Still, still pursues, where'er I be,*
*The blight of Life—the Demon Thought.*

—George Gordon, Lord Byron
*Childe Harold's Pilgrimage*

*Hell hath no limits, nor is circumscribed*
*In one self place; but where we are is hell,*
*And where hell is, there we must ever be.*

—Christopher Marlowe
*Doctor Faustus*

# The Wake

*It's a contemptible thing to want to live forever*
*When a man's life gives him no relief from trouble.*

—Sophocles, *Ajax*

My father, Ramiro Boza, loved Cuba above all other things, animate or inanimate, real or imagined, remembered or forgotten. Therefore, he walked away one day from human company and forced himself to climb the desolate summit of Nebo, a place where exiles go. His body was exhausted by old age and leached by decades of dust. He stopped every few steps to catch his elusive breath with his bent body. When breath came, he heard himself sound like a man being strangled by his windpipe. The ascent took my father longer than he would have hoped or guessed, but through the climb he kept vibrant in his mind the idea of the land of his devotions, the country that had been the foremost goal for his people, even through decades of exile, and for no one more insistently than for him, day and night in all his thoughts and in every action, even to the turning of his arthritic hand in the socket of his wrist.

When my father could walk uphill no more, he threw himself upon the cleft of a sharp outcropping to view the extent of his lost land, the land he had promised to see again before the final darkness enclosed him—but not like this, from the distance. He looked nevertheless toward her.

At first he was blinded by the black glare of sun upon the water. But when his eyes adjusted to the light, he descried the caiman-shaped Pearl of the Antilles in her turquoise sea, in her turquoise and emerald sea—and in the sapphire-colored deep water, sharks forming a ring in the sea. And he saw her, the loved one: what he loved most about her, her fresh green country where people seemed more freshly born than others and hills and val-

leys sprouted royal palms, gray columnar women whose dark
green fronds scratched and combed the sunlight; red earth, the
mother, growing green-brown tobacco; breeze-waved, enslaving,
sweet cane fields; a vast mangrovey swamp, treacherous foothold;
rocky, inletted edges trolled for life and left for new lives; post-
card beaches, for which he had never arranged time, poxed with
oiled aliens sipping rum colas; and poinciana-littered cities with
the plaster of gracious histories turning to dust in streets where
people with crossed arms stood in barely moving lines. This was
his pain, this Cuba. Like Moses, he died as destiny had made
him: an exile.

It was 1989. In a few months Communism began to tumble
with European walls, and Fidel Castro, who for thirty years had
had possession of our country, began calling his own generals by
the name of traitor. For the first time during this exile, our Long
Exile—our history has been one of exile—the Cuban Diaspora
began to think with excitement about packing to return home.

My mother and I did not consider return a possibility. We
knew that the Cuba for which our compatriots reached was like
the phantasmal light of a star that has exploded many light years
before yet appears sharply clear in our earthly night. But exiles
feed on empty dreams of hope, Aeschylus wrote. When the
dream disappears, you get old men so desperate to die they will
not wait for nature to take them.

A short time into our exile, I—perhaps no more than ten—
wrote a poem in Spanish on So Near and Yet So Far, a theme that
recurred among us wherever Cubans spoke or wrote. It felt mine
in the poem. I drew a Cuban flag upon the page. My father
approved of the flag and of the poem.

The telephone call came on a Friday afternoon, the call that must
one day come. For nineteen years I had dreaded it—since I left
my parents' home—but I had always imagined it would have a

different shape. In my mental rehearsals it was usually brought on by a failure of simple organs—at worst, by a traffic accident. My father was eighty years old. I was thirty-seven.

At about two or two-thirty that Friday I awakened from a nap. I had allowed myself the luxury of an afternoon's sleep because the day before I had turned in my last paper of my first year as a graduate student at the University of Maryland. I had been ill since February with stress-related viruses and fatigues. "Now I can rest," I had said. I imagined a week of indolence before beginning my efforts to find summer employment. "Now I can rest."

The moment I heard my mother's voice, I knew. *"Mi hijita,"* she said, "I have terrible news to give you." She paused to weep long enough for me to think, My father is dead. So I was surprised to hear her continue, "About an hour ago your father attempted to commit suicide." The reflexive verb in Spanish, *suicidarse,* establishes a direct connection; the doer does to himself, as in real life. "You say he attempted," I said, but what already haunted me was the fact of suicide.

My mother's eyes are three-quarters green and one-quarter brown. They are the windows of an unusual soul. My mother, even under the calmest of circumstances, does not tell stories linearly. She plays hopscotch with facts on a sidewalk of such cosmic scale that the finite listener frequently cannot detect the pattern. It has always been my role in conversation to pepper her with questions that might clarify the connections. I have sometimes detected some resentment from her about my logic-bound intrusions, which, I admit, have not always been made without perceptible irritation. During this telephone call we both tried our best, she to make sense, I to treat her with compassion despite my urgency.

My father had used his gun—He had been taken to Jackson Memorial Hospital—As my mother lay in the bedroom taking a nap, my father had gone into the bathroom with the gun and he had shot himself—

That morning he had gone next door to the offices of the Colegio. He went every morning. But that day he had taken his hard-sided briefcase. "He had a real mystery with that briefcase today." When he returned home he kept it with him. When my mother had lain down for a nap, he had seen his chance.

As my mother described it, sputteringly, disconnectedly, briefcase this and briefcase that, I pictured this: My father had taken the briefcase into the bathroom. He had taken out the gun, leaving the case's only other content, the suicide note. The briefcase lay open on the floor of the bathroom, proclaiming to all the absoluteness of its owner's final focus.

The gunshot exploded. My mother rushed out of the bedroom, which was right next to the bathroom. She saw my father lying in a pool of blood, gasping for air.

"Where did he shoot himself?" I asked.

"On the head," my mother told me. "But the man from the rescue squad said that he had missed the important part, that he would live."

"Then they'll put him in the psychiatric ward after his medical treatment. They always put people who attempt suicide in the psychiatric ward," I said, thankful to know the procedure, to feel I had some control of facts.

I should have remembered the time my father was rushed to the intensive care ward with wild cardiac arrhythmias. On the phone my mother had ascribed his problems with breathing to a cold. But, uncharacteristically unskeptical that afternoon in 1989, I clutched at the comfort of her underestimation of danger: my father would live and he would finally get psychiatric care for his bone-deep depression, his strange delusions, his tormenting obsessions.

"I didn't touch anything," my mother told me. "On detective programs on television they always tell you not to touch anything. I went next door to my neighbor Isabel."

My parents lived in a government-subsidized residence for people of limited income, a building full of elderly Cuban exiles.

No one knew to dial 911. As my father lay on the floor gasping and bleeding, neighbors attempted to find someone who knew what to do in an emergency. Finally, someone was located who could call the rescue squad; she was a kind of visiting health aide, also Cuban, who made weekly visits to a woman with heart disease.

A rescue squad came, but two cops from the Miami Police Department homicide squad also came. The two men spoke Spanish. They asked my mother many questions.

My mother asked me, "Was your father's Valdés with an *s?*"

"Yes," I said to her, surprised that anywhere in the United States, even in Miami, a government official would be concerned about the second surname, the one we derive from our mother, the one we are forced to discard when we come to this country.

"Then I told them wrong. I told them with a *z*," my mother said. I was wounded by this, though I knew that my mother's mind became severely muddled when she was under stress. But she had been married to my father for forty-six-and-a-half years.

She had not touched him. As he lay on the bathroom floor, she had thought about evidence and the police. Or she had not thought, rather, she had reacted, and her instinct had been to leave no traces on the man with whom she had lived through four decades of pain. Jackie Kennedy in Dallas had knelt on the back seat of the limousine and reached for the piece of her husband's skull that had been torn off by a gunshot, and, as if this could save him, she had held the bloody fragment to the top of the head of Jack Kennedy, who had humiliated her. My mother in her shock could not attempt even the lightest touch on a body so helpless, an old husband turned bloody infant. At the wake, a sweet-faced lovely woman who worked next door to the apartment building would embrace my mother and weep in her arms, and when she walked away my mother would say, "She kissed your father's face as he was being wheeled into the ambulance."

The police took my father's suicide note. The logic for their action was that it was written to the police. In English. It was almost unbearable—his last words, in English, a tongue foreign to him, and he a man who lived by words. As if the Miami Police Department could not find someone to read Spanish. He must have been crazy. The cop told my mother in Spanish what the note said, and she remembered it well. It said that no one should be blamed. "He didn't want the police to blame me," she said. "He said that he was sick. That he loved me. He asked to be cremated and for his ashes to be thrown into the sea." She wept loudly as she told me.

"Did the police tell you if they would return the note?" I asked her.

"They didn't say."

Everything was desolation.

"I'm going to the hospital now," my mother told me. "I'll call you when I can."

I knew this meant that she would wait until she was at a private telephone, and that trying to explain to her how to make a long-distance call from a public telephone at the hospital would be worse than useless. She gave me the phone number of her next-door neighbor, a stranger to me, whom I could call for updates.

Kurt. As soon as my mother hung up, I rang Idle Time Books. When my call reached the store, my husband had just stepped out to make a bank deposit, but there was so much urgency in my voice that, without my asking, a coworker ran down Eighteenth Street to get him.

"My father tried to commit suicide; he shot himself in the head," I told Kurt. What a thing to say or hear in the middle of a sunny day.

It would take Kurt some time—too long a time—to drive home from Adams-Morgan to Silver Spring. I had to do something. I stood naked under the raging shower, a waterfall in a warm country, where I could listen to my litany of discernments and still feel I was purifying something. My father's hatred of life, so extreme that he would choose a violent death. The rejection of my mother. The rejection of me. My inability and unwillingness to make his life better. His anger, his shooting himself, his shooting himself in the room next to where my mother slept. His English note to a faceless police. My anger that might eat me up if I did not weep and weep into the jets of water that coursed down my head like my father's blood. I then remembered the much-repeated words of *el cabo* Chávez.

Long before I was born, when my father was still a young man of twenty-six, he was summoned to take the interrogation chair before *el cabo* Chávez, a member of the national police who had chosen to become my father's enemy. The corporal was in his own headquarters, at his own desk, with his gun at his holster and other guns around him. If sergeants were a rising class in Cuba—and they were (Fulgencio Batista had quickly scrambled up from sergeant stenographer to untitled ruler of the nation)— then the hour of the corporal could not be far behind. Chávez sat back contemptuously, sizing up my father, setting the scene for the interview. It was his way with suspects to remind them of their weaknesses.

Ramiro Boza, on the other hand, while possessing an intrinsic hatred of oppressive authority, was not a man to be easily rattled into rash statements. His will to survive and succeed tempered his intemperateness. He knew he was in a match for his life. When he was a boy, it had been his great pleasure to box. His hungry skinniness had gotten him classed as a featherweight, but he could hit hard with his bony fists. And with words he could hit harder. And with his nimble wits he could dance away from corners and ropes.

Many in Cuba found themselves in similar confrontations. La Huelga de Marzo, the political strike of March 1935 against ever tightening control by Batista and his servant president, Carlos Mendieta, was being crushed. The last bit of oxygen was being squeezed out of the great, betrayed Revolution of '30. But in this last gasp the country had been brought to a standstill. Students, teachers, public sector and government employees, railway workers, and physicians joined the strike. In perhaps the greatest threat of all because of the Cuban economy's dependence on one sweet crop, striking workers took over several sugar mills.

That was my father's crime, bringing the strike to El Central Hershey in Santa Cruz del Norte, where he worked. But Corporal Chávez decided, for the sake of argument and the warrant later to be issued, to accuse my father of a more specific act. Every battle for Cuba, since the first sugar planting, has taken place to the crackle and smoke of burning cane fields. In this instance, a cane field belonging to the large, powerful Hershey mill had been set on fire. It seemed to the corporal that my father was responsible. My father informed the corporal that he had been nowhere near the field at the time in question.

"Ah," the corporal explained, "but you don't have to be in a field to set it on fire. You can collect rats in a sack and get on a train. Then as you are passing a cane field, you can light the rats' tails and hurl them from the train. As the rats run through the cane, they set it on fire."

My father was unfamiliar with the method. It seemed far-fetched. "How do you make sure the rats run in the direction that you want? If you ask someone from the countryside—and I am from the countryside—he will tell you that when you disturb a nest of rats, they flee in every direction."

My father knew that the corporal and his superiors would not need evidence of proximity to fields or rats or fire. They were satisfied that he spoke to large gatherings in a loud, passionate voice and that the thoughts he spoke were dangerous. Batista had commanded that order be restored through any means necessary. Pedraza, the chief of the national police (another ex-sergeant) had been given new, sweeping powers as military commander of the province of Habana.

The authorities would finally settle on charging my father with being the "intellectual author" of crimes committed at the Hershey sugar mill—these being agitation, I suppose, and the setting of fires through mysterious agencies. *"Detenido. No presentado,"* the warrant decreed. In other words, the court ordered my father detained but not kept alive long enough to be presented before it.

Many of the revolutionaries of 1935 would be pursued and killed, while my father would escape to live too long. He was lucky. That night in the *cuartel* under yellow light and rhythmic shadows cast by the blades of a ceiling fan, *el cabo* Chávez was not yet ready to charge my father. He wanted only to make a mark, to give my father a threat or a warning.

Chávez leaned forward toward my father and made a pretense of sniffing the air around my father's head. "Your hair smells of gunpowder," the corporal said.

My father, as any other Cuban would, tried to joke the threat away. "No. Gunpowder!" my father said. "Maybe it smells of soap or brilliantine. But not gunpowder."

"Be careful," Corporal Chávez said.

Months later, when my mother met my father at the home of her friend Haydée, she noticed that he skulked. He came in through the back door and left also by the back door after peering in every direction. She did not know that the man with the teasing sense of humor and the threadbare jacket and the missing teeth was a fugitive. Haydée and her sister Nata, who had given their cousin Ramiro refuge, did not act as if they entertained visitors under unusual circumstances. And the man himself, when not near doors, sat calmly and talked affably and looked motherless because of his shabbiness, but not like a hunted thing.

Through the safety of time, my father transmuted his encounter with *el cabo* Chávez into that precious metal, the favorite story. But despite frequent repetition, he seems not to have caught the significance of the words. He did not heed the prophecy of gunpowder in the hair. Only an enemy gazes upon our faults with the advantage of magnified definition, undistracted by consideration of amiable virtues. And our faults, unchecked, can kill us.

After showering, I thought up a project for Kurt and me to undertake to channel our anxiety: we must find the cheapest way to get to Miami within a reasonable time. I was still operating under the spell of my mother's fantasy that my father's shot had missed the brain; we were going to Miami to be with my mother during a trying time and to visit my father in the psychiatric ward once he got transferred there. So Kurt and I even called the railway company. We made a reservation—I do not recall whether on plane or train—that would get us to Miami on Sunday. When I called my mother's neighbor, I wondered about the wisdom of trusting my mother's version of events. The neighbor asked me baldly, as if she talked of hours, "When do you come?"

At ten o'clock my mother called me again. She was gathering up some things because her brother Mario's wife was going to take her to their apartment to spend the night.

My father was not expected to live through the night, she told me. "He lost too much blood." She sounded much calmer than in the afternoon, resigned. I called up an airline and booked a ticket for the next morning.

Kurt and I gathered up baskets of clothes to take them to an all-night laundromat. We did not have the right clean clothes for funerals in hot places, though I owned a lot of black. I had begun buying black clothes in the fall of 1981 when my father ended up in intensive care. On that occasion he had developed arrhythmias because he had planned to have drinks with a psychiatrist friend and had, in preparation, suddenly stopped taking the Inderal that had been prescribed to him after a heart attack several years before. Since then, I had felt it necessary to be in a state of reasonable sartorial readiness for my father's death. By the time we got to bed, it was 2 A.M., twelve hours since my life had changed.

We got up around 6 A.M., not that had I slept. All night I had pictured my father floating in a hospital bed tied to life by a thin silver cord. I periodically tested my pain and found it undiminished, like the ache in a tooth whose nerve is inflamed. Upon rising, my first order of business was to find out if my father still existed. I like to define, clarify. But I did not want to make the telephone call myself. I asked Kurt to call the hospital. The receptionist at Jackson Memorial, the one who usually gives out the status of patients, transferred the call to the intensive care unit. I knew then my father must be dead. I could tell from Kurt's side of the conversation that he was reluctant to answer the nurse at the I.C.U. with a compelling claim to knowledge about my father's condition. He finally answered her questions with, "I'm a family member." He was asked to be more specific about the degree of relation. "Close?" Kurt seemed uncertain. He offered, "I'm married to his daughter."

I was screaming, "You're his son-in-law! I'm his only daughter. Tell them! I'm his only daughter!"

Kurt, the close relation, had never met my father. Despite my screams, I could hear Kurt saying, "Oh. He did? Thank you," with a somber voice. When he hung up, he hugged me and said, "He died at 3:25 this morning." Like me, Kurt jots down what he hears on the telephone.

Epinephrine propelled me. I rushed about in a frenzy Saturday morning gathering everything I might need, as my mind leaped ahead forming lists. At the twenty-four-hour supermarket I bought black pantyhose for mourning and flesh-colored pantyhose for I knew not what and travel toiletries because, although my mother would in fact have soap and toothpaste and Miami offered these for sale besides, I wanted to control my brands; I wanted to control something.

As Kurt drove me to the airport, our Pontiac nearly hit a van when Kurt failed to see a confusing lane marking that he had always negotiated before. I imagined trying to calm the angry driver of the van, "I'm sorry but my father shot himself in the head yesterday and my husband is driving me to the airport so I can attend my father's funeral." I imagined having to call a taxi and abandon the scene, because I must not miss my plane.

We arrived at the Baltimore-Washington airport early and I caught my flight—alone, because Kurt had to stay behind for a day to deal with loose ends. I hoped no strangers would speak to me, that I would not be asked if I traveled for business or pleasure, and that I would not cry. Mercifully, I rode the airplane anonymous in my condition. Amid the people dressed for Caribbean cruises and the business travelers, I with my heavy burden did not stand out. I wondered how many others might be on the same flight rushing to news of an emergency. We all ate—or refused—food from identical plastic trays.

At Miami International, my mother looked calm as she waited for me at the gate. But I know not to trust that. As she embraced me, she began to weep, saying, "I didn't want to tell you because you were coming, but your father died this morning."

"I know," I said. "We called the hospital."

She looked surprised and uncomfortable. I was on my guard. She turned to the people next to her, "This is my daughter. You may not remember her because she does not come to Miami very often."

"This is the Mariñas family," my mother said to me. "Mariñas was a very good friend of your father's."

Of course, I knew that—that he was a good friend, not that the people before me were the Mariñas family. I had always imagined my father sharing seafood dinners with a Manolo Mariñas whose skin was very pale and pink, his scarce remaining hair straight and white, and his body quite rotund. I was wrong on all counts. The family that stood before me was of African ancestry. I could not have known it without seeing them because to my father it was unacceptable (unthinkable, really) to refer to the race of friends.

The Mariñases were dark more in the way that southern Subcontinent Indians are dark, with a pale ochre glow, than the way Africans are dark. They were all tiny, the husband, the wife, the daughter, as if they had dropped down from a world built to a different scale. I wondered how they had found each other, the tiny husband and the tiny wife; were they cousins? Their thin daughter—in her twenties?—could not have been anyone else's. They were all very solemn, barely speaking. I did not know if this was due to the gravity of the occasion, to a feeling that there was nothing appropriate to say when such devastation had been wrought by someone close to all of us, or if they secretly blamed me for not being enough of a daughter, for leaving my father in his pain and my mother in her isolation.

"We'll go get the car," Mariñas said, and he walked away from us with some physical difficulty. His daughter went with him.

Even though Mariñas did what my father would have done, I felt an acute pang of nostalgia for my father's height. I felt abandoned by my father's height. He had been about five-nine before the departure of his youth left him to bend; he said five-ten, but it could not have been so, even though details were his preoccupation. At that airport, he would wait at the end of the concourse, his arms crossed. He hated to wait; I hate to wait. My mother would be standing next to him, but it was for his head that my eyes scanned the crowd with some dread. Immediately he would begin taking care of things, even insisting on doing so after he had shrunk within his old age and weakness had overtaken him, and I had to fight him to let me carry my own bags. He had been the kind of man who, before his women were ready to go on an outing, had already checked the level of the oil in the car and the state of the tires.

My husband is five-nine-and-a-quarter and he takes care of things too. "I can go get the car so you don't have to get wet," and I won't let him. Or "Of course, I'll go pick you up, babe." Or "Let me do that." I would have to live through a day without the comfort of my husband.

Mariñas's wife, my mother, and I stood curbside at a ramp waiting for the car. My mother said oddly cheerfully, "They know the airport well because their son, who is a doctor and lives in Atlanta, visits very often. Every chance he gets he comes." I had last been in Miami in May 1987.

My mother and I were soon alone in what, I reminded myself, I would now have to think of as my mother's apartment, no longer my *parents'* apartment. I had never been inside it. They had moved into it since my last visit. As soon as we had arrived, my mother took me to the bathroom, as she would on any visit to show me which towels are mine.

"This is where it happened. There are still stains that I could not get out," my mother said, pointing to a spot in front of the sink. In the grout between the beige tiles of the bathroom floor were two dark brown stains. "When I left for the hospital, Finita said, 'Don't worry, I'll clean for you,' but she only got the thick stuff." I knew of Finita as some sort of bureaucrat who had helped put through the paperwork for my parents to get this apartment. "I had to scrub the floor this morning. I didn't want you to see that. The bathroom was filled with blood," she said, gesturing with her right arm in a circle around the bathroom.

My mother's neighbor Isabel came for a visit. We talked about her interests. On the day of my father's death, we sat talking with someone I had just met about the rudeness of people in government offices (state and local) and the politics of legalized abortion—I for, the neighbor, priest-ridden. My mother did not speak the opinion about abortion I knew she held—I am used to being the public radical, my mother having been brought up to soothe, not irritate—but she did offer up her disgust about the negligence of those with a public charge. It was strange. There are people who think that distracting the bereaved from their pain is constructive.

Eventually my mother and I were alone again. I sat in a rocking chair in the living room with my back to the little hallway that leads to the bedroom and the bathroom. But nothing in that small apartment is far from the bathroom. My mother had changed into one of the sleeveless housedresses she likes to wear at home in hot weather, which in Miami takes up most of the year. She sat with her back propped against a pillow that rested on an arm of the couch, her legs stretched out on the seat. We were truly alone together, she and I, for the first time in my life. I was afraid of how we would treat each other without my father at the center of our relationship. If the anger she displayed at the airport was any indication, she might turn on me permanently. I knew that she must fear I would abandon her. When I was a little girl in Cuba, I was my father's joy. My mother was jealous of me then. But circumstances had long changed. As an adult, I was not as my father would have me be. He was not as I could stand for him to be. We had failed each other. My mother had not noticed.

But one thing my mother had found easy to do with me since I was an adolescent was to talk. Her talk would come in sporadic bursts, as if she were freeing herself from an enormous pressure of containment. During her brief verbal excursions, before the silence again enclosed her, she told me about her terrible female experience, her servility, her isolation. In these matters I feared to reciprocate. I saw my role—I think, accurately—as sympathetic listener, rational counsellor, information imparter. I did not let her see my feelings.

This role I carried out as my mother told me from the sofa about my father's last months, and about her last months with my father. He was obsessed with colon cancer. He was sure he had it despite having undergone tests that revealed his intestines free from any abnormality other than the diverticulosis he had known about for years. The imagined state of his bowels was a constant worry, although he had real diseases enough. One thing is certain: he had an unreliable heart. He had suffered myocardial infarction. He could have let his heart, rather than a bullet, kill him. Who, if given a choice of weapons, would not choose the swift neatness of a heart attack? But he had had to invent some other internal enemy to choke his living. He was burdened with severe, and worsening, shortness of breath. This was imputed by one doctor to mild emphysema. Maybe he did have emphysema, though he did not suffer from bronchitis and he had only smoked uninhalable cigars—and not one since January 1959. Sometime in the 1960s a doctor discovered, through an X ray, scar tissue in one of my father's lungs; without knowing it, early in life he had probably had a bout of the tuberculosis that had taken his mother. At least that is my interpretation. My parents never dared ask doctors questions, and doctors try to get away with saying as little as possible. The nature of their afflictions I had to try to discern through distance and the scrim of my parents' purposeful confusion about medical matters.

In the last few months he had been getting dizzy when he stood up. He sometimes called my mother and she would run to the easy chair to catch hold of him. His orthostatic hypotension was probably yet another symptom of old age or a side-effect of one or several of the many medications he took in his effort, on the face of it contradictory, to stay alive. To my parents the dizziness was another sign of doom. They should have told me; I could have looked it up. But I was not informed about most of my father's deterioration.

*"No te me enfermes, vieja,"* my mother now told me he had said. That is: don't get sick on me, *vieja.* "He felt he would not

be able to help me," my mother said. "Lázaro told me that Ramiro told him that he would not make me suffer," she sobbed.

I wondered when my father's friend Lázaro had told my mother this. "What did he mean?" I asked.

"That he would not put me through a long illness."

I let there be a pause, and then I said with the soft, even voice of a psychotherapist, "And he made you suffer anyway."

"And he made me suffer anyway," my mother said with a sharp cry into her Kleenex.

"It had to happen. I don't know how anyone could stand to live like that," my mother told me. "No one can stand that constant torment that he poured on himself." For the first time since the news of my father's suicide attempt, I was given an explanation for his actions that made sense, that in fact cut through my anger like light.

My father had been deeply depressed, my mother said. "Do you think I should have insisted your father see a psychiatrist?" she asked with the tone of a little girl who fears being punished.

"He knew that psychiatrists exist. A friend of his is a psychiatrist. He had to decide that himself," I said.

"And who was to say to Ramiro Boza that he should see a psychiatrist?" my mother said.

I told her that psychotherapy only works for patients who want to change. "Antidepressants might have helped him but I am allergic to tricyclics and he might have been too."

I did not know about new antidepressant therapies, though otherwise I considered myself something of an expert in the field of mind treatments. By the time this conversation took place I had been undergoing some kind of psychotherapy, with only brief respites, for nineteen years. I had had a dozen therapists; I cannot say it without laughing. "And I am much better," I assured my mother, "but look how long it's taken me. Psychotherapy is not an exact science." I spoke as if I were a member of the profession passing along scientific observations. "Don't blame yourself," I told her.

"And he would abuse me verbally," she said.

It was such a problem, the combination of my father's impatience and my mother's distance from anything he might try to explain. He must have feared for her ability to carry out even minor transactions after his departure. Death was the only way out of that worry. Abusive criticism had been its provisional manifestation. That was his way of improving us—crushing our faces into the ground.

I explained to my mother that I too had seen increasing irrationality in my father's behavior. I am not sure how many things I actually told her about. I know that I did not mention the letter he had written to me on the occasion of my wedding. Kurt and I had married on 9 December in the simplest possible civil ceremony at the Annapolis courthouse. We had had to take a number as if we were at a delicatessen. Kurt's parents and two women friends of mine were our only company. Actually, the courthouse looked beautiful, decked as it was in winter holiday greenery and in the first snow of the year, which had fallen that morning as we drove. I had informed my parents by letter of the upcoming wedding only a month before the occasion. I waited because I did not want them to come up for it. I could not have dealt with their presence. Unbeknownst to my parents, Kurt and I were living together. We would have had to rearrange all our belongings.

My parents were startled by the news of my impending marriage. I thought that my mother should not have been so surprised; I had told her I was seeing someone and that I was happy. But my father I had not told. He responded in a letter. When I think of the letter, I see a bright light that blinds me to the contents of the page. I encountered in the text evidence that my father had disconnected from shared reality to an alarming degree. I cannot say what evidence. The links in his sentences had come undone, but, then again, his syntax had always been tortuous. He seemed to be addressing someone other than me, but that was not new. I do not know what I saw, but it terrified me, and contrary to my lifelong practice, I threw away the letter shortly after receiving it. I still tremble to think of it.

I remember one sentence, in which he conveyed to me that he was thinking about my past error: "I utterly reject that common saying that a person will trip over the same stone twice." I had been married before, to a man with manic-depressive disorder, with whom I spent eleven years. He had told me of his illness from the start, when I was nineteen. The union had ended so disastrously that my father had had to travel to Maryland to help me move out while my husband was away at work. I hired a moving company—three nervous guys with a truck—that specialized in very quick, stealthy moves; "separation moves" they were called. The saying that my father alluded to was his own frequently repeated joke: "Man is the only animal stupid enough to trip over the same stone twice." My father assumed that I would fail.

The sole relief I derived from the letter was that in it my father agreed that it would not be a good idea for him and my mother to come up for the wedding. He claimed to be worried about *la vieja*. That was my mother. For as long as I could remember, he had called her *la vieja*, "old woman," or more affectionately, *viejuca*, even though she was more than eight years younger than he was. Assigning worry to or about *la vieja* was his cover when he did not want to admit to something, did not, for example, want to call a hesitancy his own. As if he had not made his plans not to travel clear enough, he scheduled cataract surgery for the day before my wedding.

Later my father did not seem to believe that I really had married. One day when my mother called, Kurt answered. When Kurt had put me on and she had given the phone over to my father, my father said, "A male voice answered the phone. It scared your mother."

I said, "My mother knows I'm married."

My father said, "You tell us that you're married and we believe you." Meaning of course that he did not.

He was eager to form a poor opinion of Kurt. In a card that we had sent to my parents, Kurt had signed himself "El Guapo," roughly, "The Tough Guy." I had thought the joke would flatter my father because he had often referred to himself that way. It would be endearing, I also thought, that Kurt was trying to learn Spanish. Rather than laugh, my father expressed acute reservations about my marriage to a man who considered himself to be El Guapo. He wondered about my safety in private and about Kurt's actions toward others in public places. I considered it beneath my dignity to tell my father that the only time Kurt had been involved in a fistfight, he was in fifth grade and the other kid had it coming to him because he had sent Kurt's basketball flying to the top of a roof. I knew that my father would not want to believe that Kurt is a sweet man. My father had a double satisfaction: something new to worry about and further confirmation that I would continue to screw up my life. He did not let go of it, but referred to it again and again.

I did not read any of these actions as the behavior of someone whose strange reworkings of reality might lead him to harm himself or his constant companion. I concentrated on their significance for myself.

Sitting before my mother after the fact, I did tell her that my father had said something I should have recognized as a sign of his plans. The Sunday before my father's shooting was Mother's Day, so I called my parents. My father answered the phone. He said, "Where are you calling from?" I was startled. I was indeed calling from somewhere other than home, from Kurt's parents' apartment in College Park, which had been left conveniently vacant that weekend. I explained to my father that we had had to sleep there the previous night because our upstairs neighbors had made it impossible for us to have any peace. These people, whose very footsteps caused our thin ceiling to shake, were in the habit of holding parties that began after eleven at night. One had begun at two in the morning. "That's solved with a forty-five pistol," my father startled me by saying. "That's solved with a forty-five pistol."

"I should have recognized it," I said to my mother. "He was thinking about using a pistol."

"That's how he talked," my mother said. "How could you have known?"

My father had owned a gun for several years. He bought it when his large old car got vandalized one night. Someone punctured the tires and threw black paint over the roof. The incident frightened my father because the car had been parked right outside his and my mother's supremely accessible first-floor bedroom window a few steps from Southwest Fifth Avenue, next door to the decrepit stucco edifice that had been our dwelling during our first ten years of exile.

The vandalism was all the more frightening to my father because some very strange things had happened among exiles in Miami during the mid-1970s—in the Watergate aftermath, during investigations of past intelligence practices by select committees in the House and Senate. One man who had been involved in some CIA activity—a man who had had access to too much secrecy and was expendably Cuban to boot—had died in his own living room when someone had stepped up to the window, aimed calmly (my father added this detail), and shot. Cubans were being deadly to each other as well; frustrated, unventable hatred toward Fidel had found more accessible targets. My father wanted to be ready in case he was lucky enough to hear the approaching rustle of the men who did not like him or his past or the contents of his head. He bought a gun. I do not know what caliber. He kept it near him while he spent his nights in insufficient rest.

Whenever I went to visit my parents in the Fifth Avenue apartment, my father moved into the second bedroom, the one he used as an office, so that I could have his more comfortable bed. He took the gun with him. He placed it on top of the timeworn, naphtha-scented, brown art deco highboy my parents had rescued from our first apartment in Miami. During the day I would enter the spartan room, stand at the foot of the narrow, flimsy bed, and

to the death itself. As my mother lay in the bedroom that
night, I scouted out my father's liquor. He did not drink
anymore but people still gave it. I could not have slept at
out my father's Johnnie Walker.

day morning I was awake as soon as I heard my mother
o the bathroom. I busied myself with folding the living
uch on which I had slept. I had a bowl of cereal. My
made herself some coffee. Life seemed to be as usual.
mother asked me what dress I was wearing. I showed her
black cotton broadcloth dress I had brought. My moth-
ht out the ironing board. "I'll iron it for you," she said.
n do that."

I'll iron it," she insisted.
asked me if I usually pressed in a crease at the top of the
admitted that I did not usually iron it. The broadcloth
seemed to hang well enough by itself. "No, you don't iron
other said, not lightening, this morning, her reproach.
y going-away gift for college my mother gave me a
steam iron with easily replaceable parts. This was the
on my mother apparently thought I would need for aca-
rigorous Barnard College. Few other mothers had
hat way, and my iron was popular among the other girls
ormitory floor. They used it more than I did. I had
eans and wrinkled shirts as a sign of liberation from my
he Lifelong was still my only iron. I did use it, although
mechanism no longer worked. I kept meaning to get it
eday, but that would probably cost more than my
aid for the whole thing in 1970. I wanted to tell my
is somehow, but there was too much pain behind her
I just asked her please not to iron my black jacket; it
of silk crêpe de chine.
other surprised me with her own outfit. She wore a
ormal polyester black skirt and a white blouse. But she
her arm an amazing bright, white polyester jacket on
m fat black-and-white amoebas. The pattern gave me

stare at the black gun, mesmerized, paralyzed. I was certain some-
day it would go off.

I tried to shake myself loose from my guard by reminding
myself of the story of Juana la Lista, Joan the Quick-Witted, that
my mother and her sister Nena, my second mother, told me when
I was small. Juana la Lista was sent down to fetch rope from the
basement. When she got there, she saw a hatchet hanging from
two pegs on the wall. "Oh, what if that hatchet should fall and kill
someone!" she exclaimed to herself, and she sat down to weep.
After a long time had passed and Juana had not returned with the
rope, her mistress went down to see what was the matter. She
found Juana la Lista wailing wretchedly.

"Juana, what's the matter with you? Why do you cry?"

"*Señora*, it's just that I saw that hatchet hanging from those
pegs on the wall, and I said to myself, 'What if the hatchet falls
and kills someone?'" at which her mistress sat down beside her
and began worrying and weeping too. Then the mistress's hus-
band came down, and he too was caught in the spell of worry—as
was the rest of the household, as each member successively came
down and became entangled in an obsession of possibilities.

When I managed to tear myself from my stillness before my
father's gun, I moved softly, in case the merest movement would
trigger its blast. When I left Miami, I still worried, so I wrote my
father about the need to make sure guns were registered and had
their safety catch on. Perhaps my mother and I should instead
have sat before the metal monster and wept and worried. One
day the gun did go off, intentionally, in my father's hand. He had
no need of strangers aiming through windows. The homicide
squad took the gun away.

Telephone calls punctuated our afternoon and evening after the
death. Organizers of the next day's wake—or Cuban *velorio*—
called to exchange information with my mother. On such

occasions my mother seemed to possess an almost businesslike efficiency. But there were other calls. People expressing sympathy and wanting to know what arrangements we were making. "We are asking people not to send flowers," my mother said repeatedly. "*El velorio* will be held at Rivero Funeral Home on Calle Ocho between ten in the morning and midnight. No, there will be no burial. He wanted to be cremated."

There were calls from people unable to believe; these my mother supplied with the details on which to base belief.

Before my arrival there had been one reporter's call—that is, a reporter acting as a reporter, not a friend placing a call. My mother had been so befuddled by events and was so startled by the call that she could not supply the reporter with my father's past for the obituary and had to refer him to the Colegio de Periodistas de Cuba en el Exilio, the journalists' association that had been the center of my father's life since his retirement. The tactless caller wrote for the good newspaper with the absurd Spanglish gryphon of a name, *El Nuevo Herald,* for which one added *o* would have worked wonders. Because the reporter was employed by a *yanqui*-connected paper, I was able at least to explain to my mother, who was so shaken by the intrusion at a time of intense grief, that the guy may have been Cuban but that he practiced journalism in the United States where standards about privacy were minimal. I may have added something about being glad I was not a journalist in this country. My father had always wanted me to be one.

Contrary to U.S. tell-allism, however, the *Nuevo Herald* reporter did not mention the cause of death. In fact, none of the many Spanish-language newspapers that carried the often eulogistic notices of my father's death mentioned its cause, though my mother and I never hid it. When a particularly dense elderly man asked us at the wake, "What did he die of, his heart?" my mother answered him rather more loudly than was necessary, "*¡Se suicidó!*"

*Diario Las Américas,* whose social notes frequently chronicled the events of the Colegio, came closest to naming the

unnameable with "ceased to exist
manner," from which discreet phr
assume my father had been the vi
tion. *Diario Las Américas* further
the wake would last from ten in
two hours. "That would be an
when someone informed her. The
ial for Monday. At least the intrus
of the wake right.

I rejected journalism as a car
been a comfort to me: the Mediev
the influence of Zoroastrianism o
omy of primates, the psychology
and the sacramental power of w
mation underneath me: the ti
valediction of forbidden flowers.

No flowers, she had said ov
accept. A woman at the wake sai
mitted flowers, this place would
it had been up to me, we woul
viewed—and my father had vie
wasted on someone who could
comforts to the living. They wer
ditures they saw people with lim
of respect, at the many funerals
in the United States is older tha
expensive. There may have been
tion of pomp. Almost no one
mother, but despite a Roman (
cose father had spent several ye

I was still too stunned to drea
I was more curious than appre

was due
Saturda
alcohol
all with

Sun
walk int
room c
mother

My
the loose
er broug
"I ca
"No
She
sleeve. I
material
it," my n
As
Lifelong
preparati
demically
thought
on my d
adopted
destiny.
the steam
fixed son
mother p
mother t
reproach.
was made

My
perfectly
slung ove
which sw

a twinge of seasickness. The combination was, she explained, her going-to-burials outfit. My mother despises wearing somber colors, but especially black. She always steered me away from it. She complained bitterly when her sisters decided to wear mourning for their mother. After my father's wake she would return to normal dress.

All the arrangements for my father's wake were made and paid for by the Colegio de Periodistas. My father was their *decano ejemplar,* or exemplary dean. He had taken over the Colegio in 1983 when its affairs were in disarray—" in moments of crisis and confusion," said the Colegio's declaration following his death. The account books had been in shambles; my father straightened them. Although exiles had founded their branch of the Cuban journalists' association in Miami as long ago as 23 July 1960, no one had yet filed for official nonprofit status. My father got the Colegio nonprofit status. Furthermore, the Colegio had gone for more than twenty years without publishing a newsletter with which to keep the membership informed and interested. Therefore, my father started publication of *Papel Periódico,* which, all things with us being historical, was named after Cuba's first newspaper, founded in 1791.

When my father's two-year term was over, he was asked to run again for the office, but he declined. "He did not wish to continue, because it was necessary that the wheel should always be driven by different efforts," said the declaration. That was part of it; he did not believe in reelection. But it was also true that he was exhausted. Few want to be *decano.* It is a post for old people who have no job and can support themselves with Social Security checks; it takes too much effort and pays nothing.

The old men and women who formed the faithful core of the Colegio were so grateful for what my father had done that they knew they would be forever grateful, and so they gave him his title of exemplary dean in perpetuity. "Exemplary must be he whose life had always been exemplary," the declaration had said—thus did colleagues think of him. One obituary referred to his "cult of friendship," and another, employing the double meaning in Spanish of *caballero* as "gentleman" and "knight," called him a "*caballero* of friendship and *compañerismo*." Mariñas, in a very loving eulogy published in *Diario Las Américas,* drew images of him as both gladiator and knight, one whose "combatant's shield bore the following inscription: anti-Communist *caballero,* rational and emotional." Others, in other obituaries, called him a gladiator and a soldier. One notice, written by a friend in Belle Glade, said, "We wish to take the opportunity in these lines to extend our deepest sympathy to his widow Carmen, as well as to his daughter, whom he always mentioned with much love." I must admit that I was touched, surprised, and skeptical.

Although my father's extremes had made my adult self cringe, I had been proud of him at least one time in adulthood. When Channel 23 still cared about Cuban matters, my father was a regular member of a press panel in a Spanish-language "Meet the Press." One day when I was spending the summer working in a discount store in Miami after my freshman year of college, I turned on the television to watch my father. My mother usually did not. The guests that day were two young Cuban men who aspired to create in Cuba (after the ever-stipulated Big When) a party that would promote the principles of Swedish-style social democracy. Most of the press panelists were doing the reactionary exile thing of equating social progressiveness with Communism and were peppering the poor guests with hostile questions. But not my father. To begin with, my father considered himself too old to be in need of asking questions of those younger than himself. Whenever his turn came, he made a speech. This embarrassed me, but at the same time what he said heartened me. He defended the young men in passionate rhetoric that went beyond the young men. He stopped only long enough to half ask, "Because I assume that you oppose Castro and you would not seek to establish a government until Communism was rooted out," and to watch the young men begin hurriedly to nod their heads and murmur assent before he continued his theme's arc: that all Cubans must work together toward that overriding goal of overthrowing bloodthirsty Communism from our native land and establishing democracy; that other differences did not matter; that all sincere Cubans must be allowed to make their contributions. Within the counterrevolution, everything. He was a "man of cohesion," one of the obituaries said. People in restaurants and on the street came up to tell him that he spoke for them. "Hit them, *viejito*," they said.

My father probably received as much from the Colegio as he gave. He did not know how not to work. He was driven by his industriousness, by his desire for efficiency of methods and depth of scope and excellence of product. It was the curse he passed on to me, and he saw it in me and recognized it as a curse. We do not know how to rest; we cannot ever feel that we have done enough. Employers took advantage of my father and he knew it—but he also could not stop. And when he had to retire from Channel 23 because of the toll that power struggles were taking on his psyche—because the corporation asked him to accept a system that violated his sense of patriotism—he had the Colegio to turn to. He still wrote occasional articles and for a while made regular guest appearances on radio station WQBA. But he needed a job to go to every day. And so did the other old men who gathered in the Colegio's offices on Southwest First Street in a building that once had been a Baptist church. In those offices they could talk journalism and politics and Cuba gossip, and they could tend to their book collection. There they could feel a connection with their profession's history and tap the moral force of Juan Gualberto Gómez, *mulato* champion of independence, underneath the portrait of Pepín Rivero, most admired newspaper editor, renowned for his stylistic purity. And, of course, there was Martí, who from within a frail body attempted everything for his country. Everything was expected of everyone.

My father shot himself on 19 May 1989. He died on 20 May. I commemorate the two days differently. Nineteen May is the day of violence, the day when his pain and anger reached a point of obliterating thought of everyone else, of my mother and me and the bloodstains he would leave on all of us. Twenty May is the day on which he was released by merciful death. I have a day to mourn and a day to express thanks. So have those two days been among Cubans this century. Nineteen May is the day of national mourning for the death of José Martí, journalist, innovative poet, founder of the Partido Revolucionario Cubano, organizer and inspiriter of the last War of Independence, *el Apóstol de la patria*. Twenty May is our Day of Independence, celebrating the day in 1902 when Cuba became a nation.

Of course, my father chose 19 May because of Martí's death. How could he not have, when he thought about him and, like him, about Cuba, Cuba, all the time like a mistress, an obsession apart from which there could not be a life? And Miami too remembers. Every year patriotism is stirred and attention is demanded as the May commemorations approach. People give speeches. Events are organized, sometimes semi-celebratory events for a 20 May that reminds everyone of the tenuousness of independence, of the exigencies of nationality. Tony Varona, who now is dead too, through his Junta Patriótica always organized a well-attended dinner. But in 1989 my father told my mother in advance that they would not be going. He had chosen his time, as had Martí.

José Martí set an unmeetable standard. He dedicated his time, his passion, and his poet's voice to the cause of a self-determining Cuba that was but a bold dream. He wrote, "On the cross died the man in one day; but one must learn to die on the cross every day." But then that did not suffice. He insisted on joining the army of independence for which he had raised much financial and moral support and on fighting the colonial government not with the weapons that he mastered but rather with the gun that he did not. He left the safety of the land of exile and joined the Liberation Army. And then mere fighting did not suffice. He had written, "All great ideas have their great Nazarene." José Martí must sacrifice his existence, must offer up to the nascent nationality of Cubans a martyr around whom we could form ourselves, as a pearl does around the pain in an oyster. On 19 May 1895, he propelled himself toward the rifles of a Spanish squadron. He had tuberculosis. He found something constructive to do with inevitable death.

The old men and women of the Colegio, over whom the image of Martí hung as a burden of example, had, like Martí, been cast upon a country whose language was foreign—and words were their tools. So they had established their own conduits for their Castilian words and Cuban thoughts. There were some scurrilous scandalmongers and cesspool stirrers and outright crackpots. But many had waged a relentless word fight for Cuba; word fights are only internally effective, and they had seen no political results even though Martí had written, "Honoring one's country is another way of fighting for it." The effects were seen rather on their bodies that showed loose skin over more prominent bones. In pictures of Colegio de Periodistas events my father looks like an old sea turtle, all skull and concave bite and furrowed eye sockets. In the end, my mother says, he could no longer write. He could not discipline his mind to think orderly thoughts. How could he contemplate living?

> The years of our life are threescore and ten,
> or even by reason of strength fourscore;
> yet their span is but toil and trouble;
> they are soon gone, and we fly away.

My mother arranged for us to be driven to the funeral home by Laurentino Rodríguez, who had been *decano* after my father. We waited for him downstairs. He and we were punctual, intent on our mission to arrive at the funeral home at the very beginning of the wake. Laurentino was businesslike as he opened the doors to the back seat for us.

A short way into our ride uptown, my mother said a startling thing, something she had not brought up to me the day before, "I would like to have a Cuban flag to drape over Ramiro's casket. He always wanted a Cuban flag as a *sudario.*"

I thought she had misused *sudario,* which is "shroud," a cloth with which to wrap the body of the dead. I usually trust the old to be better acquainted than I with the language of death. I worried because it was Sunday. I wondered if any stores likely to sell objects of patriotic devotion would be open. Laurentino mumbled something about seeing what could be done. I sat aghast, because I am good at taking care of details if I am informed on a day when I can turn my attention to the task. My duty that day was by my father's coffin.

I finally allowed myself to wonder how my father's coffin would look, if it would be uncovered, if vain efforts by funereal cosmetologists would underline all too plainly the accusatory violence of the wounds of his face.

We drove into a large, almost empty parking lot adjacent to a building that had the flat, modern, antiseptic appearance of new Miami offices both outside and inside. The final stroke of the *R* in Rivero Funeral Home swept in a curve below the other letters; the *R* in a tie-tack he had in Cuba; the *R* on one of his monogrammed handkerchiefs. Ramiro. In the lobby, a board just like an office building's announced the corporate suite in which Boza was to be found. Immediately next to it, the elevator stood ready to convey us to our appointment.

Two men in their mid-forties got on the elevator with us, said *"Buenos días,"* and pressed the button for our floor. They were well dressed. They looked like Cuban journalists. Ignoring our presence in the elevator, they continued a discussion already in progress. "You are not going to tell me," said one who had a mustache, "that he did not have every detail planned, as meticulous as he was. He must have thought of everything." I was appalled, scandalized by this conversation in front of us. The worst part was that I wanted to argue with the men, to tell them that the act was committed in a fit of madness, to tell them that my father would not rationally design to cause his head to explode in the room next to where my mother lay resting.

The elevator released us into a large parlor with sofas and armchairs where Roberto Pérez, the recently invested (now deceased) *decano* of the Colegio, already awaited us. Into this large, deeply carpeted hall issued two smaller rooms. One was closed with a screen. The other one, open, was identified by the sort of portable sign that identifies the topic of a hotel conference room's lecture during a meeting of scientists. Boza. Laurentino led us in.

The two longer sides of the small room were lined with chairs. I vaguely remember chrome among them. Against the wall opposite the room's entrance stood a closed, brass-colored metal coffin on a pedestal. "So there he is," I thought, as my heart leaped. "He is really dead." I felt tears gather in my eyes. But was he there? My mother took it as a given that the solid metal box contained the body of my father. I wondered if now that we had arrived, the casket would be opened. I did not feel I had sufficient evidence of his corpse's presence, but I did not say anything. As if my mother had read my thoughts, she quickly foreclosed the possibility of a viewing. "Remember him as he was when he was well," she said, and she began to sob as she lowered herself onto the chair that was closest to the coffin's feet. I sat down next to her unable to control my own weeping. We must instinctively have chosen the chairs intended for the next of kin, for I do remember that they were the most padded.

For years, I had harbored an angry fantasy—that I remained resolutely tearless at my father's burial. The men, his friends, who so admired him because they had never had to live with his inflexibility and his intolerance of imperfection and his dark moods, praised him for the things that men deem important. His camaraderie. His love of ensnaring, obsessing, goddamned Cuba. And I would resist their tug at tears. Knowing the fuller truth about my father, nursing my rejections at his hands, I would remain unmoved, standing straight in my black dress. I had never been to a burial, so I had to extrapolate the scene from U.S. films and Cuban attitudes. The day was always hot and clear, as was this day that we spent in an over-air-conditioned dimly lit room in which I could not hold back my eyes' treacherous floods next to my mother. Not that I would not have cried on my own, but since my adolescence, my mother and I have answered each other's weeping with weeping of our own. It is almost a physical response, like the milky release of a lactating mother's breasts at the sound of an infant's cry.

It was good to be in that room from the beginning of the wake, not just because it was our duty, but because it was quiet and the air was smokeless and my mother and I could be alone with something that, to my surprise, I still thought of as someone, my father, who was dead and only a few feet from me, a cadaver dying further every second. It sent chills through me. And yet a corpse was not all he was. I felt the urge to talk to another presence, a consciousness that lingered next to the body it had been joined with for eight decades. And I asked it mentally, for that was all I felt I need do, *"¿Por qué, papá, por qué?"* And I neither expected nor received an intelligible answer, for nothing worth having, my father taught me, ever comes without hard work. His only reply then seemed to be the muteness of a bulletlike coffin so metallically impermeable that it must have been built to withstand the nuclear blast of any Communist bomb. And yet while my father's familiar frail bones and transforming flesh lay encased against our interference—even our sight—they would afterwards be lifted out by the arms of strangers hired to handle what we could not. And what would be done with the coffin? Were metal coffins reused, could they be easily scrubbed, like stainless steel pots? Did Rivero keep special ones for the few Cubans who chose cremation, to be donned by successive hermit-crab-like cadavers before they faced the fire? I hoped there was no waste.

I was touched that the men of the Colegio had ordered a solid brass casket—or solid-brass-seeming—for the wake. Obviously they had insisted on nothing but the best. It was a sign of the respect they had for my father, and of respect too for my mother and me. But that elegant ensconcement was so unlike my father, who took pleasure in being a cart driver's son, who left his jacket off whenever he could get away with it, who drove old heaps (*chatarras,* we say), a man whose only affectation was his conviction that he could remain an intact peasant seventy years away from the soil.

"I told them that your father would not want any religious ceremony, that Ramiro was not religious," my mother informed me soon after we sat down. Yet we must gaze for the long hours upon the incongruous sight of a crucifix that flew at an angle from the coffin's lid, like a Gothic flying buttress that held up nothing. It was a part of the lid, soldered onto it and in the same golden color. The intention was perhaps to give the impression that Jesus Christ, still attached to his cross but miniaturized, had, spritelike, descended upon the coffin. There was perhaps a compensatory purpose to the lid: an effort to let a symbol of forgiveness mitigate the starkness of my father's—in ecclesiastical eyes—final sin.

It was unfortunate that my mother's irreligious orders had not reached the funeral home. The staff had also supplied the coffin with a faldstool. It constituted an invitation to devout Roman Catholics to kneel and say their prayers. The sight of the men and women—more women than men—who took this invitation and knelt a few feet from my mother and me unsettled me. I felt sorry for my father as he endured helplessly in death the humiliation of having his soul prayed for publicly. And I squirmed in my chair for other reasons. From my angle near the foot of the coffin, the iconography of the scene was disturbing. These pious women and men seemed to be bowing before my father, seemed to be praying to my father, and I wanted to tell them most forcefully that my father was not a god. I dreaded what my father's Protestant cousins, who knew his history, would make of the display when they arrived.

In an attempt to please my traumatized mother, who still fretted over the absence of a flag, the men of the Colegio ordered a spray of flowers for the coffin lid. "Because you requested no flowers we did not order any," they said by way of explanation, as they brought in the spray.

"Ramiro did not like flowers at wakes. He wanted a flag," my mother said.

The florist had sent a spray of anthuriums. They looked, as do all anthuriums of their peculiar species, like yellow, partly aroused simian penises rising from flared, scarlet testicles. A white-shirted employee of the funeral home or the florist shop draped the bobbing phalluses over the lid just below the flying crucifix. The two adornments provided a kind of balance to each other, pagan strangeness counterpoising Christian strangeness. "That is not the flag I asked for," my mother said to me.

Eventually a large Cuban flag did arrive. It was made up of red, blue, and white flowers. We placed this standing wreath behind the head of the coffin. The flag arrangement had been ordered by my father's provident friend Pancho Carrillo. When my mother thanked him for it, he just said, "I knew from all those burials we had been to together that that's what he liked: a flag."

The flag wreath made my mother feel a little calmer, though years later she blamed herself for not having had a cloth flag on the coffin. "I should have remembered that Onelia had a flag," she said to me suddenly in a conversation. "But I was confused. My mind was in limbo." Then, as if I had not been present at my father's wake, she informed me, "Do you remember Pancho Carrillo? Well, he gave us a wreath in the shape of a Cuban flag." My meticulous father who bothered to put a request for a flag into his will should have bought his own goddamned flag since he knew what he was up to.

Some other flowers had arrived earlier, a wreath from the telephone workers' union that had been led by my father's deceased friend Vicente Rubiera. They had not gotten the no-flowers message, I guess. But I tell you, I did not mind a bit. We placed this wreath at the foot of the coffin.

The people came all day, and many stayed all day. Some, mostly relatives and nonpolitical women, took turns sitting with us in the small room. They chatted among themselves and with us. Some male relatives read newspapers. Because I left Miami when I was eighteen, I had not seen many of our companions, some of them related by blood or by marriage, for twenty years or more. We all looked a little older, but not enough for any of us to suspect that things were not much the same, though things could not possibly be much the same.

For fourteen hours people—and the past many brought in tow with them—paraded before my mother and me. As a disciplined stream, they passed before the coffin and offered their respects to us. If friends or relatives sat to my left, they were assumed by visitors to be part of the reception line. If a woman sat to my mother's right in the first but uncomfortable seat, though she be my father's second cousin Onelia or my mother's sister-in-law Olga or an old neighbor we had not seen for many years, she was accorded by those who did not know us the most profound professions of sorrow until my mother at long last set the visitor straight and, motioning to her left, said, "This is my daughter."

"My daughter" was the simplest thing for my mother to call me. At my birth, my parents named me María del Carmen. They had no idea that one day we would live in a foreign country where time is short and spaces on forms even shorter. My parents perhaps never themselves planned to call me María del Carmen except in the most formal occasions. My formal teachers in my formal school in La Habana and my fellow students did it day to day, and I liked it; I was a person in my own right. At home I was Carmencita, a diminutive of my mother's diminutive, Carmita. When I entered my first class in the United States, my teacher, Mrs. Tuttle, dubbed me Carmen because there were too many Marías for the senescent Floridian's taste. "Carmen" made me uncomfortable because it made me sound older than my mother, who was still stuck in her diminutive. In the next grade, Mrs. Meyer asked me what I wanted to be called. I told her that my name was María del Carmen. "María," she said and wrote it down—of course, without the acute accent—in her book.

Since then, I have been Carmencita or Carmita to those who know me through family ties or friendship with my parents. I have been María to the rest of the world. After a while my mother, ever flexible, gave in to the pressure of circumstances. She calls me whatever seems most practical at the moment. My father, on the other hand, never forgave my abandonment of my mother's name. He included it in the long list of my perfidies when my adolescence produced in him fits of rage; having cut my hair (at my mother's urging) was another. I do not know what name to call myself. I cannot identify myself to others with a sense of accuracy or without a twinge of pain.

"I unite myself to your pain," strangers and near-strangers said. *"Me uno a su dolor."* It was a strange formula, without logical sense if you examined it. And presumptuous in a way: as if they could, as if they possibly could know. "If you need anything, let me know," they said because they were well brought up.

When journalists did not know us, they were often brought in by one of the past, present, or future *decanos* of the Colegio to be introduced. After the first quiet time of our arrival, the two overly talkative men from the elevator were guided toward my mother and me by Roberto Pérez. They were aghast at the sight of us. They turned to each other. They turned back to us, finally speechless, except that the mustachioed man muttered, *"Pero, pero, pero . . ."* "But, but, but . . ." They extended their hands nervously to us. I did not feel sorry for them, because they should have known better, in the elevator, with us going to the same floor, at that early hour.

Nearly everyone came. Those who did not read of the death in the newspaper heard it broadcast on the radio. My father's wake was a political event. Political had his life been. And both his death and life brought to my mother and me the steady stream of strangers I so despised. But so it had to be now to fit him.

Once in the evening when I was crossing the parlor after answering a telephone call, a thirtyish man stopped me to ask if this was the wake of X, some other name. I said, "No, this is Ramiro Boza's wake. You might try the other room," which had by then been opened.

"Ramiro Boza is dead?" the man asked me with surprise.

"He died yesterday morning," I assured him, and restrained myself from asserting the authority with which I spoke, because I could not make "He was my father" not sound melodramatic under the circumstances.

Later, the man showed up before my mother and me. "I was coming to the wake next door. Then when you told me it was Ramiro Boza's wake, I decided to come because I knew him. I just hadn't heard." I felt he was my very own guest. He was my contemporary and he had spoken to me.

The politicals made a brief pass through the coffin room and headed quickly away from the isolating intensity of our grief and into the parlor, which by mid-afternoon was full and smoky and loud. They perhaps did not find us interesting, the ones who had some prior acquaintance with us, or they did not want to contaminate themselves with sorrow, or they did not want to irrupt into our privacy with their public personas and fling irrelevancies of exile power struggles into the concerns of life and death. In the outer parlor people sat on the few sofas or they stood gesticulating at each other's chests, defining, I suppose, the shape of Cuba's future, each as different as a crystal's, and talking about who was saying what about whom *en el exilio*.

All the people at my father's wake, in the large parlor and the small room, politician and peasant and neighbor woman, were exiles forever. We had survived a history of revolutions, executions, and suicides to enter into a state of eternal expectation. We were exiles over the entire earth but the one place that was most dangerous to us. And those of us who had grown up away from Cuba would be exiles there too. And those who had come as adults from Cuba would find it had changed beyond bearing. It was a terrifying day, the one when we woke up alone and realized that we belonged nowhere. If we were noisy and talked of things that had nothing to do with death and took the opportunity of visiting with people we had not seen in an age, it was in part that we could not help for a funeral to be part celebration: one of our number had been released from exile.

A future U.S. congresswoman, Ileana Ros-Lehtinen, signed the guest register with her father. But the day belonged to the past. There were old confederates from the Consejo Revolucionario Cubano (or Cuban Revolutionary Council) with whom my father had shared the friendship of its president, José Miró Cardona, long gone from the earth but still felt by many of us as part of our destinies, like one of our bones. Two of these friends from the Consejo days were Mariñas and Pancho Carrillo. They had watched my father bear restlessly the burden of "mute and impotent witness"—as Mariñas wrote—about the Bay of Pigs and the Missile Crisis and the dissolution of the Consejo and the vanishing of Cuban exiles' power to influence their fate.

And there were friends too from the long, frustrating years that followed, like Lázaro Asencio and his wife Lidia. Lázaro had been a fighter in the second Escambray front, a rebellion that arose in the mountains near Cienfuegos against Fidel Castro's government. But my father had not explained that. As an adolescent, I had heard stories in Lázaro's house of Escambray fighting and had assumed they were set during the revolution, when there had been a first front. And my father did not tell me about Mariñas's past. For one thing, I had imagined him a doctor, not a lawyer. If I wanted a context, I would have to provide it.

Some political women did spend time with us in the small room. One was a member of the Colegio who described herself as a *poetisa,* a poetess. She had wavy black shoulder-length hair. She stood her very small frame in front of my father's casket and told us of her life. Her poetry had been read by someone in China very long ago. She had served as a senator in Cuba for the Liberal Party. Yes, okay, she admitted it, as loudly as she possibly could in that wake full of *antibatistianos,* she had been a *batistiana.* She still was a *batistiana.* She knew my father from the Colegio banquets.

"He was always so simple. He dressed so simply and so neatly," she said, gesturing down the front of an invisible neat shirt.

My mother and I were temporarily brought out of our small-room purdah into the big parlor sometime around noon. Finita, the tall, corpulent woman who had helped my mother mop up my father's blood, got us some take-out chicken noodle soup, the near-universal comforter.

Finita spoke to my mother as if the latter were an invalid child. Underscoring their size difference, Finita reduced everything connected with my mother into a diminutive. She cooed over her with little pet names like *"mi vidita"* and *"mi amorcito."* She said, "Carmen, *mamacita,* you must bundle yourself up. Don't let yourself get cold," as she tucked my mother's jacket over her chest and lap.

Certainly my mother would now like to eat some *sopita, mi amorcito.* Finita dramatically helped my mother out of her seat, made her put on the black and white jacket, and half-carried her to one of the parlor couches, my mother's body leaning against her as if it had sustained an injury from my father's gun. I tagged along behind, thankfully propelled by my own leg muscles. The parlor was not yet very full. My mother and I sat facing each other on two sofas. Finita hovered over my mother. "*Mi amor,* here put this on so you won't splash on your little blouse." She tucked a napkin under my mother's chin, like a bib. Finita asked me how my *sopita* was and I admitted that my *sopa* was just fine. However, I did not feel fine about it. The fact is that I was terrified to be eating soup in an area just outside my father's coffin room.

In eleventh grade in Miss Castiñeira's French class I had read *L'Étranger.* I borrowed a paperback copy of the book from Nely, a friend and neighbor from the childhood phase of my exile. Her sonorous name, Nelia de la Milagrosa Hernández, is still inscribed on its title page. I kept it, I confess; I think she said that was all right. Her elderly parents surprised us by coming to the funeral home, although we had not seen them for many years.

I remembered only one element from my long-ago reading of Nely and Camus's book, but I remembered that well: at Meursault's trial the strongest piece of evidence against his character was testimony by a witness that at his mother's wake he had drunk *café au lait.* Finita offered to bring me some *café con leche* and I said no thanks. With horror, I watched my mother drink hers with the innocence of a child.

Soon a very thin, dainty woman with hair dyed blue walked up to my mother. They tearfully embraced. They were friends from the 1950s, when they worked at the Caja de Retiro. My mother reintroduced this friend of hers—hers alone, from when she had a job of her own—as someone very precious to her. Of course, I remembered the name Lala, knew I had met her many years before back in Cuba, a world away. Lala was accompanied by a son who was older than I was. I felt I needed to explain why we were not with my father but did not know if snacking would sound like a good excuse.

I would not feel comfortable with food all day. Later, around ten o'clock at night, my cousin Marta Fuentes, née Salas, went out for *croquetas preparadas* and *cafecito,* which we consumed right in the coffin room. I bit into the thick sandwich with meat croquette and cheese and various other things, knowing I was biting off more than I was prepared for. I attempted to swallow the existentialist ghost of Meursault along with the feeling that to eat in a coffin room is to eat the dead symbolically. I also fought with an instinctive, visceral revulsion at eating anything so close to a presumably rotting cadaver. The sight and smell of rotting, fly-blown *jutías* and other, indeterminate dead things in the grassy lots of La Habana and in the green Cuban countryside invaded my mind. No one else seemed fazed, especially not my mother, who bit into the large sandwich, as into most other food, with direct, animal appreciation. I was probably the only one to wake up with fever and diarrhea the next morning.

Benito, the husband of one of my father's cousins, drove me to the airport. I got there early. Moreover, Kurt's 4:15 flight from Baltimore was delayed. Coping with the frenzy of Miami International Airport requires energy. I had none, so I went directly to the assigned gate, which fortunately turned out to be almost empty. It was a good place for me. I took out a set of spiral-bound index cards in order to write down some phrases that had been going through my head at the wake. They came out forming a whole.

> *You are earth now*
> *earth that wants to be ocean*
> *You were my father once*
> *I hoped to see again your hands*
> *before they became simply*
> *molecules of burnt earth*
> *to be mixed with ocean*
> *The earth's pulse never sufficed you*
> *you preferred to beat to your shaking*
> *You are only earth now*
> *the brother of mountains*

*swimming in the sea toward Cuba*
*swimming toward the Arctic*
*Your heart was always Cuba's*
*our caiman-shaped earth mother*
*no human bond could equal*
*the attachment of molecule of*
*dust to dust*
*while we beat our wings, merely human.*

*You didn't know you were earth*
*Your voice of fire misled you.*

Others' phrases had also gone through my mind, over and over as if they were attached to a wheel. *Je suis un cimetière abhorré de la lune.* And sometimes: *Je suis un cimetière abhorré de la lune / Où, comme des remords, se trainent de longs vers.* But I remembered no more of it. They were dismal enough.

The gate was still fairly deserted. I was afraid that the gate assignment might have been changed. I thought that I might go explore elsewhere, when suddenly people started pouring in through the gate. A gateside ticketer softly announced the plane's provenance; it was not Baltimore. I thought I should stay and make sure because one never knew.

Suddenly Kurt, my beloved husband, stepped into the waiting area. My heart leaped up. He had trimmed his dark beard so as to minimize any possible offense to a community with bad memories of revolutionary *barbudos.* Its neatness emphasized the compactness of his body, like a shortstop's. Because he was going straight to the funeral home, he wore the pants from his only suit—a midnight blue wool one he had bought for his younger brother's wedding—and a thin blue-black tie and a white shirt whose sleeves he had, of course, rolled up. He carried his suit jacket and luggage. He was dashing and strong. He smiled as soon as he saw me, and, as is his way, he saw me soon. Nothing on this earth had ever looked as good to me in so many ways. He was my home. Amid desolation, there was someone who would take my part, a piece of the vast, alien world that was my own.

We had been so busy with the upheavals of our lives that we had not had much time to worry about how Kurt would fare at a wake of Cubans, other than my casual pondering over how we would enter inconspicuously with Kurt's bags and where we would stash them. My real apprehension set in as we were about to step into the elevator. I wondered what theories of my father's suicide I would be forced to listen to now. Inside it, a woman with very black hair stared at me, and as I began to shift nervously from foot to foot, she asked me, "You are Ramiro's daughter, aren't you?"

"Yes," I said, surprised.

"I thought you must be," she said.

I was spared by the sphinx.

As we approached the coffin room, my anxiety increased and made a knot in my throat. The moment we entered, my mother rose and crossed the room. She extended her hands and soon was holding Kurt's. They met, my husband and my mother, in the center of the room in front of my father's coffin. I have no idea what they said to each other. The next day, my mother would say to Kurt flamboyantly in English, "You may call me Carmen, like the opera." But there in that funereal cubicle, I know that my mother was sweet and welcoming and English-speaking and that Kurt was sweet and full of condolences— *"Lo siento,"* Spanish condolences, he tells me—and that my mother wept, but I was too overwhelmed to remember what was said, too full with this introduction of my husband to my family when my mother was a freshly grieving widow and my father a tacit presence in a metal box.

Room was made for us next to my mother. Kurt found himself in a noisy hall full of strangers speaking a language of which he knew only a few words, sitting next to the only person he knew, who could speak his language but who was spoken to by all the unknown others in the unfamiliar language and who was, at any rate, so distracted by grief that she was distant from him. In the midst of exiles, Kurt felt exiled; he was a foreigner in his native country. Because he was sitting in the place for the immediate family and because my mother introduced him as her son-in-law, he was included in professions of sympathy of which he could barely understand the particulars, even as he could decipher the likely sentiment; he was not obviously un-Cuban.

Kurt's great savior was Ernesto Pino, my father's former colleague at the Associated Press, where they had monitored Cuban radio broadcasts, kept logs, and performed other uninspiring but steady work. When Miró resigned from the Consejo, reporter Ted Ediger offered the job to my father with embarrassment at the low salary, but it was equal to my father's salary at the Consejo, where he could not remain. "Who do I have to kill?" my father said by way of acceptance.

Pino told Kurt that he had begun monitoring La Habana radio from a listening post in Key West before the operation was moved to Miami. He spoke about his very good first wife, whom I had known, and his very good second wife and what a fortunate man he was that after one had been taken away, he had been provided with the other. Monseñor Román had given him the second wife's telephone number. "Call her," the priest had said. Pino sat serenely telling his stories, looking not very different from when I had known him—still the small black mustache perched on a large, round face—but using a cane as a result, he explained to Kurt, of a knee operation. Kurt was very grateful to have met him. One night, Pino escaped quietly into death, in his sleep, without a sound to stir his good second wife, having been shown again the mercy of God, who plucked him from the pain that bone cancer would have brought him.

Although Kurt missed much else that was said at my father's Cuban wake, he was able to understand keenly the essential elements of the Battle of the Boat, even as the action occurred. Strong emotion carries universal cadences.

Apparently, as soon as my father had died, my mother had set about finding a way to comply with my father's request in his suicide note and (I did not know it then) in his will that his ashes be "thrown to the sea." At the wake my mother informed me when she returned to her chair after one of her trips away, "A friend of Lázaro's has a boat. Lázaro says that he will take the boat out to throw the ashes into the sea. I don't want to go, it would be too difficult for me. But Lázaro says he will do it. Finita will go with him." I was shaken by these words, or rather, by what had been omitted from them. I was still my father's only daughter and I had not been consulted, I had not been asked if I wanted to help dispose of my father's ashes.

I sat in silence trying to collect myself before I spoke to my mother. "Mamá," I finally said, "I want to go to dispose of Papá's ashes."

My mother seemed genuinely surprised. "*¿Sí?* Then let's go tell Lázaro that he should take you."

We walked swiftly toward the parlor where we found Lázaro. "*Mire, Lázaro,*" my mother said—she addresses most people by the formal second person, even if they are younger than she is and even if they do not return the formality. "She wants to go throw Ramiro's ashes."

Lázaro thought a moment. He was next to Finita. He said that, yes, we would make arrangements, that the cremation would not be completed for another three days. Then he turned to Finita and said by way of explanation, "She is my wife's god-daughter."

Lidia Asencio had been my sponsor when I was confirmed at fourteen, but to me the most compelling reason for my inclusion was that I was Ramiro's DAUGHTER. I could see resistance to my request, and for the life of me I did not understand why.

My mother and I returned to the coffin room where I filled Kurt in on the discussion in the parlor and my nervousness over the hesitation I saw about allowing me to assist with the scattering of my father's ashes. We therefore started making plans of our own. We could rent a boat. With what money we did not know, but we would do it. We would take control of the process.

Finita then came into the coffin room and stood before my mother and me. She said, "*Mi amor,* Lázaro thinks that there isn't enough room for all of us on the boat." The type and dimensions of the boat would never be made clear.

I stood up. "Then I should go," I said simply.

My mother piped in with, "Lázaro has been a friend of our family for many years." At the time I thought that this was beside the principal point, but on further reflection I realized that she was probably trying to underscore the fact that Finita was not.

Finita, ever ready to seize a cue, replied, "Oh, yes, I know that you were friends since Cuba, since she [meaning me] was a baby." This was humorous. We did not know them in Cuba; Lidia was not my *baptismal* sponsor.

Then Finita made a very big mistake. She forgot that I was Ramiro Boza's daughter. She said to me as if I were a very young child, "I just thought that it would be best for you to stay with your mother."

I said to her very slowly, enunciating clearly with a voice that came from my chest, there, as I stood in front of my father's coffin, in the presence of the other mourners, "*I* will be the judge of what is best for me."

Finita recoiled.

My mother surprised me by saying to her, "*¡Vas a hundir el bote!*" That is, "You're going to sink the boat!"

Finita walked out of the room.

When I sat down, I tortured myself with trying to understand how this woman dared assume that her claim could supersede mine in carrying out the last wishes of my father. She had not been a family friend—and, so what, even if she had

been? What had made her think that she could behave so pre-
sumptuously? Was my status as daughter considered so tenuous
by the community in Miami? Was my long absence so adamant-
ly held against me? Had my father complained about me to his
acquaintances? I formulated a question for my mother and tried
to level out the hurt in my voice when I delivered it, "I am the
daughter. What makes Finita think that she can go instead of
me?"

My mother snorted sardonically. She said, "It's that Finita
wants to go on a boat ride."

Despite a few moments of acute vision, my mother seems to have
experienced a different wake from the rest of us—or from me, at
any rate. She thought later that Roberto Pérez had driven me to
the airport instead of Benito, whom she herself had suggested as
driver. She assumed I had seen Alfredo Izaguirre Riva. But I did
not see him. He must have come while I was at the airport.
"Don't you remember how he fought to get out the words but
could not?" my mother asked. He had survived seventeen years
of prison and torture, had come to Miami, and then had been
brought low by a stroke that mocked his newfound freedom of
speech with a physical inhibition of it. No, certainly I would have
remembered someone so significant to my life.

When my mother's friend Lala died of the colon cancer that
had not invaded my father, my mother wept into the telephone,
saying, "What I regret the most is that I did not introduce her to
you at your father's wake." I must suppress the urge to scream
when my mother speaks to me as if I had not been with her. She
said to me once, "You know, I never told you that I went into the
wrong room in the funeral home." Jesus.

As the wake had progressed into evening and I was returning
from the lavatory, I noticed that the other mourning room that
gave out onto the parlor had been opened. It was of the same

dimensions as ours and immediately to the left of it as one looked toward them from the parlor. Although the rooms were identical in configuration, their contents were not. The new room had a white coffin whose top's tricky, smaller lid had been opened to reveal only the corpse's face, which had belonged to a white-haired old man with hawklike features. I could see him that clearly from the parlor. The room, unlike ours, was full of flow-ers. Whereas our room was dim, this room, because of the white of the coffin and the flowers—and maybe even because of a stronger lamp—was vibrant with light. I thought to myself, "I hope later arrivals know which room to go to."

After her next trip to the restroom, my mother walked into the bright, neighboring vigil room. I was told this by a very agi-tated woman who came to fetch me so that I could go help my mother, who had collapsed into a sofa in the parlor. Before I could make my way to the doorway of the coffin room, my father's psychiatrist friend ran excitedly in with Lázaro. The psy-chiatrist hysterically asked me, "Do you know what's wrong with your mother? We have to make sure she is not having hallucina-tions. We must watch this confused mental state."

I had known my mother for thirty-seven years. I was not caught by suprise. "Simply, she walked into the wrong room," I said to the concerned doctor.

My mother was more shaken than I had ever seen her, as if she had just found my father's bleeding body again. I and some other women supported her back to our own coffin room and into her chair. She was still wiping tears and sweat off her face as she explained to me, with a voice full of nervousness and unsuc-cessful starts and crying, what had happened to her.

She had gone to the bathroom and thought she was walking back into the room where my father's remains were laid. But the coffin had been opened. Who had dared commit such an act of disrespect, who had dared do this without her permission? She walked up to the coffin just to see what my father looked like in death. But the man there looked nothing like my father. She ran out into the parlor. "You can imagine how upset I was." She told Lidia Asencio and others that someone had opened my father's coffin without permission. She wanted to know who had committed such an injury.

The other coffin was white and my father's gold, I pointed out to her.

"I didn't remember the color."

But what of the flowers, I asked her.

"I thought that someone had brought them," she said.

But what of the fact that Kurt and I were not there?

"I thought you had felt offended when the coffin had been opened and that you and Kurt had left. That upset me so much. Thinking of how offended you must have been."

"We wouldn't leave you alone," I said.

"I thought you had been offended," she said crying.

But the man in the coffin did not resemble my father.

"I thought the undertakers had changed his appearance. I thought they had had to do that."

My mother had looked for the face of the man she had lived with for forty-seven years and had not recognized that the one before her was not his. All was pain and desolation. My mother could not discern between husbands or between *salas*.

My mother's family name was Salas—that is, "rooms" or "halls." Upon arriving in the United States, she had been forced to give up her surname by the U.S. authorities who judged that all women should carry their husbands' names. I know from her testimony that this had pained her deeply. At once she had been forced to leave both her Salas family and her Salas name.

While my father's nostalgia was for an idea of Cuba, my mother missed the Salas family gatherings and my baby pictures, which had been left behind because we did not know that we would stay away. It might have been difficult for us to act as we

*My first birthday party.*

needed to act had we known our fate. How could we have developed the resolve, she and I, in August 1960 to bid good-bye forever to the Salas siblings, and the spouses of the Salas siblings, and their offspring? How could we have accepted that we would no longer lose ourselves in dreams together? The Salas family is dreamy-eyed, but I could call its members back when I wanted to, and they would turn their attention, not seeming to mind, most of them, that they had been interrupted in their ethereal journey. Marriage had, for the most part, been good for the clan. It introduced people who were alert.

After the death of my mother's beloved brother Óscar Salas in late 1982, his widow Dulce Delgado sent us a photograph of my first birthday party that my uncle had kept. My father, who had liked the Salas clan before politics divided us, had several halftone prints made. He knew that my mother and I regretted our lost photographs—and maybe he himself regretted them and knew it was his fault that they were not brought, for he did not tell us with adequate clarity that we would be staying in the United States when he called us out. He talked happily of having these *ampliaciones*. When I visited him and my mother, he allowed me to pick the one I liked best. My mother framed the original. It is little and has beige tones and jagged edges. Dulce must have had to cut the photograph to get it to fit inside the envelope. Or perhaps its corners had been conscientiously glued into an album. Jagged edges and all, it was a generous gift, especially considering how deeply Dulce had loved her husband Óscar and how precious every single image of his would have become after she could see him in the flesh no more.

Óscar and Dulce were at my first birthday celebration, as were, judging from the photograph, many other members of the Salas family by blood or marriage: my grandmother; aunt Nena (whose legal name is Pilar); uncle Rafael; and cousins Elsa, Mayito, Marta, and Oscarito. There were friends too and our housekeeper. In Cuba my parents threw me big parties.

I may not have been entirely enthusiastic about that on my first birthday. In the photo my eyes are wide and my mouth is an inverted bow. I look confused and bewildered, and more than a little rebellious. Kurt laughs now when I look like my first birthday picture, which is not infrequently. In the picture the immediate object of my frightened curiosity seems to be the plastic swan hanging from a flowered arch on top of my two-tiered birthday cake. My father, however, is there to protect me. He holds my left arm in the tight, crooked grip of his long fingers. His right hand is behind my right shoulder. His lips are curled and his mouth is open with speech (of course: he is being photographed). As he looks down at me, he is doubtlessly attempting to cajole me into not being afraid.

Even amid my mother's family, my father's strong, broad-shouldered presence dominates my first-birthday picture. How could I not turn to him as my salvation and my rock? The hair of his head and eyebrows is jet black, his mustache gray. He would later cut off his mustache because its gray made people think that he colored his hair.

Standing next to my father at my first birthday—which was her own thirty-sixth, I having been a birthday gift—my lovely sylphid mother looks as if she has just touched a poisoned spindle and is falling under a spell of sleep. She looks twenty and has the delicately chiseled chin and mouth of a princess in a picture book, the prize bride of a powerful king.

At Rivero Funeral Home my uncle Mario Salas kept watch independently. He sat in a corner of the coffin room reading a newspaper, looking as if he did not want to be disturbed. He went out into the parlor to work on his death—on the lung cancer and emphysema that would kill him nine years later. He stomped back into the coffin room, perplexed. "A man said hello to me and I don't recognize him. Could I know him from somewhere?" For a long time, he could be seen to ponder.

Mario, whom my mother called El Neno, immediately preceded her in birth order. He looked nothing like her. He was Cuban javelin champion for a time, and he was so much taller than my mother that a neighbor in Miami broke down laughing when she introduced him as her brother. In coloration they were each other's photographic negative. When still youthful, my mother had almost-black hair and light skin; Mario had olive skin and light brown hair.

He was the only one among my mother's siblings to go into exile. Some of the other Salas siblings stayed because they approved of the revolution. My uncle Óscar, who did not, seemed able to put aside political disagreement and to keep on seeing the family he had always loved. It was difficult. It had been difficult before we left, even as the mother of them all lay dying.

Mario came to the United States with his family by boat. His sons would eventually be of military age, so the risk of crossing the Florida Straits in a small vessel seemed worthwhile. We saw them soon after their arrival and then rarely after. In Cuba they had been frequent Sunday visitors to my grandmother's house, where my mother and I would always be found on weekends. But in exile, just when you would think we would draw most closely to ourselves those few relatives still allowed to us, we kept them at a distance. Mario and Olga sometimes visited us, but I recall my father initiating only two visits; in our nuclear family, only my father had the power to initiate visits. In our last, Olga made the mistake of revealing to my father that a young man was driving her twenty-year-old daughter Marta to choral practice. My father came away fuming because Mario and Olga allowed their daughter to be alone with men without a chaperone. The sons were even wilder, interested in music and the theater. At the wake, Mayito said to Kurt, "We rarely saw each other because her father did not approve of us." I felt pained that they knew. Actually I thought they had turned out to be very fine.

The rediscovery of my cousins was the only happy excitement I derived from those awful death days. I did not get to talk to Oscarito as much as I would have liked. (He would probably prefer I call him "Óscar.") As a child, I played with him rather than with his siblings because he was my age. They all look like their father, but I suspect that in Oscarito the resemblance extends to a tendency toward taciturnity. I thought how different he must be with his drums.

Marta had been an awkward number of years older than I when I watched her, mostly from a distance, in our grandmother's house. She was too much older to find me stimulating and not old enough to find me cute. She was tall and quiet and dignified and I was shy, so we barely spoke then. Now she talks for a living. She is a clinical social worker who obviously takes her vocation and family obligations seriously enough to sit down next to my mother at the wake and attempt to comfort her by asking her about my father's mental state the last few months, by explaining depression to her, and in general by providing my mother with the supports of kinship and understanding.

Mayito was the biggest surprise. I was afraid of him at my grandmother's house. He was much stronger than I was, and I was terrified of roughness, actual or potential. He grew to be a gentle, candid man who demonstrated a lively curiosity about Kurt and me, our lives, and what we had gone through. He told us that he was deeply involved with the Hispanic theater of Miami and that he composed music. He wanted to hear about my writing and Kurt's poetry. I told him I had written a story about a family who manufactured kites, as the Salas family had done, and he was excited because he had never heard about this enterprise. He,

Marta, and I spoke about the sorts of books we liked. At one point Mayito came back to where we were sitting and said, "I think I remember a birthday party that you had in which there was a clown." And I did not remember a clown but only a magician I had disliked. It felt good, the fleeting illusion of family.

There were relatives from my father's side with us at Rivero, my father's cousin Onelia Boza and her husband Juan Pérez and their daughter Milla who is now a grandmother. Because I did not know them in Cuba, even if in exile we saw them much more frequently than my Salas relatives, they seem more abstractly related to me. What they carried with them that seemed familiar, if not quite familial, was the countryside. In fact, they brought with them Artemisa, the big town near my father's poverty-stricken native hamlet of Las Cañas. In their speech and in their movements I heard the *guajiras,* the peasant songs that my father had so loved, especially when sung by Guillermo Portabales. The short white shirtsleeves of the men allowed me to feel the breezes of palm stands. Like my father, they felt entitled to live only if they were engaged in hard work. The Pérez Boza family is so industrious that they create for themselves a whirlwind of activity wherever they go. Onelia is the calmest, but idleness does not suit her, and so she changed seats a lot during the ten hours she must have spent in the funeral parlor away from her sewing. Juan is incapable of remaining still for more than five minutes. My memory of him at the wake is of his rushing in and out of the coffin room, sometimes carrying a newspaper.

The Pérez family may have a more common name than ours, but in Artemisa they were the big landowners, and the Bozas, the eaters of dirt. Despite hard times, or perhaps because of them, the children of the *municipio* named after the noble city of Artemisa remained loyal to their mother soil and in exile formed an association through which they could remember her and themselves. My father attended some of their reunions despite having left Artemisa for the greater opportunities of La Habana at about age ten.

At the wake, Juan was with his *artemiseño* friend El Negro. He was a jovial man whose Caucasian features were covered by nut-brown skin and outlined by bushy white hair, some of which was formed into a thick and well-tended mustache. He had the same compact and taut musculature as Juan, but I do not think they were relatives. El Negro was more relaxed. He told me that at one time he had courted my father's niece Olga Madrigal. I wondered how he had done this, for she had grown up in La Habana and he still looked pure Artemisa. Neither of us mentioned that she had ended up having three husbands and becoming a Communist.

El Negro was a gallant. He smiled at me and looked at my face as if trying to read me, as if trying to figure out what one says to a creature so exotic. He seemed to want to offer me something, and eventually he thought of the right thing. He stood before me and said, "I don't know if you have seen this," and he placed into my hands as if it were an aquamarine or a pearl the obituary from *Diario Las Américas,* torn out, not cut in straight lines. I knew that my mother would want to keep her copy so I eagerly accepted it and put it in my purse, whether he actually meant for me to keep it or not—in a less selfish state I would have asked—though I assume he did mean it as a gift, for he looked pleased to have been of service.

Olga Madrigal, who had remained in Cuba, was the daughter of my father's sister, María Boza Valdés, a bitter, ill-tempered, shrunken prune of a woman whose loyalty to Castro's revolution was so fanatical that she wrote insults to my father after he left Cuba. *Gusano* was among the characterizations with which she graced him. She was even angrier and more punishing with her son Fernando for leaving her and the revolution. Fernando had married very young and it turned out to be a very good thing that he left for exile, because he fathered conscriptable son after conscriptable son.

We had seen Fernando much less frequently in exile, even though, as his father was dead, my father was his patriarch by default. Fernando looked after himself financially fairly well. He is an electrician, a skill highly sought after in the United States. In particular, in 1972, the White House Plumbers sought after it. At the wake Fernando told us of keeping a low profile during the Watergate revelations and hearings. Whatever he may have done—and that remains a mystery—he was never indicted by the U.S. government. My father did indict him, though not for foolishly believing at such a late date the promises of cloak-and-dagger skulkers whispering emissarial messages from powerful Washington addresses. My father simply did not approve of the way Fernando conducted his life. There was some point to this— some of it involving alcohol—but my father had such an absolutist way of rejecting the sinner along with the sin as to make it a wonder that the rejected bothered to pay respects to his corpse. This too is family, I know.

Because of my inexperience in wakes, I was not prepared for a custom that had evolved in exile: those who could not, or would not, make the trip to pay their respects in person called the family of the deceased at the funeral home to extend their condolences and, where applicable, their excuses for not being present. The funeral home staff paged the family—"call on line two for the Boza family"—as if we toiled in an office. My mother forced upon me the execrable secretarial duty of responding to the pages. I had my own grief, I felt. I had my own need for privacy, I felt. But I could think of no one else to deputize to the task. I have never as intensely regretted being an only child. With decreasing energy and good cheer I answered each page by getting up from my chair in the coffin room, crossing the coffin room, crossing the wide parlor, and picking up one of the in-house telephones on the far wall. It was difficult to talk because I did not want to talk and because with each incoming phone call my civility was increasingly strained. If they had not called, I would not have missed them, and if they had written notes I would have noticed, in the peace of privacy, the delicacy of their statements of sympathy.

I was favorably excited by one call because it was for me. The call was from Daisy Pérez, who had formed part of my group of friends in high school—and heaven knows that a strange, bookish girl like me had needed friends. But here the isolated phones of that far wall again let me down. I had no writing materials with which to note down her address and her married name— she had changed her name, not I, not the first time, not the second. She had her first husband still and her energetic mother who lived with her and several children and a high engineering post with a big corporation. I did not bother telling her about all my years of psychotherapy. I asked her to call my mother in a few days to ask for my address and telephone number, but she never did. And it took me a year to write to Mayito, and then he answered once. Pasts are difficult lawns to maintain.

I was understanding as well with telephone calls from great distances. From San Juan, Puerto Rico, Nena Pérez, José Miró Cardona's secretary of many years, telephoned. She was another person I knew, one as forceful in appearance as in personality. I had watched her move tensely, leaving ripples of energy in her wake and more than occasionally a bad word, through the offices of Miró Cardona when there was still something to do about Cuba. Her body was wiry and her hair chopped and prematurely gray as if all that mattered was her secretarial efficiency. She now wanted explanations from me—what happened? why did it happen? I described the shooting. I told her about my father's depression and his physical obsessions. I told her more than other people because she showed interest in more.

"I will say a Mass for him. May God forgive him," Nena Pérez said.

I felt angry at what I thought was her blinkered, Roman Catholic insistence on the church's dogma that suicide is a mortal sin, an offense against the Paraclete from which there is no opportunity for repentance. What I needed was comfort. But then I felt as if she gripped my hand when she said, "I know what you're going through. My father did the same."

One summer I had spent several mornings with Nena's sweet, elderly, Spanish-born mother Niní, who coddled her gentle miniature dachshund Lucha—which means Struggle—and vainly attempted to teach me how to knit. They seemed an indefinably lonely threesome despite the engulfing extension of Miró's family, which had drawn them in. I had attributed their aloneness to the divorce in Nena's past; as a devout Catholic, she could not remarry.

Standing at the telephone in Funeraria Rivero, I saw them differently. And to my surprise, I found myself wondering how much similarity Nena had meant by "did the same." Had her father too shot himself in the head? Had he shot himself elsewhere? Had he killed himself, but by other means? And I saw in her life a rosary of Masses said in the hope that God, at least, would forgive her father.

My mother's insistence on barring religious ceremonies from my father's wake made some of his friends and colleagues in attendance very nervous. Not the relatives, of course; they knew, and some even shared, his nature. Especially disconcerted was Mariñas, whose love for my father had kept him at Rivero the whole day. He came to my mother with a woman journalist who had a suggestion for organized prayers—or, better yet, perhaps a priest should be called. My mother said no. My mother never thought to inquire about my feelings in the matter; for one thing, she still assumed me to be an atheist because I had been one my last two years of Catholic high school. Mariñas and the woman went away to the parlor. A while later he came back. Would my mother mind if members of the Colegio performed a guard of

honor before the coffin? My mother gave permission for that sec-
ular-sounding ritual.

Mariñas and a group of five others, both men and women,
marched in two ranks into the coffin room. At the coffin,
Mariñas and his five colleagues stood at attention, turned toward
each other, and lowered their heads. After a while of standing in
this manner, the journalists filed out in formation. Perhaps honor
guards are always peculiar except among uniformed persons, but
performing one seemed to calm the uneasiness of those who felt
an urge to do something.

A woman past sixty who had not heard that we had request-
ed no flowers be sent approached my mother very humbly and
told her that she had not been able to afford flowers. She instead
had gotten a card announcing my father's inscription as one of
those for whom prayers would be said in perpetuity by a clerical
order. We were sorry indeed that she had gone to any expense;
my mother had tried to prevent expenditures by people in her sit-
uation especially. For my part, I hoped that the order existed, that
the woman had not been taken advantage of by empty pious
promises. I later looked it up; it exists. My father is probably
being prayed for in New Jersey.

If some of my father's friends thought that we were denying
him rites he would have wanted, it was his own damned fault.
"We Catholics . . ." he would say to someone at the other end of
the phone who had no reason to know any better, and he would
wink at me as he said it. From the stories he told me, it was obvi-
ous that "Protestantism," as he had generically labeled it, had
gotten under his skin the way that his maternally-imposed
Roman Catholicism had not. But irreligion had won; it was to
him as an irreligious man that my mother was faithful.

At my father's wake people were free to say their silent
prayers, of course, but the idea of imposing a particular set of
prayers on everyone, and of having them imposed on her and on
my father's remains, did not make my mother comfortable. To
me spoken prayer would have been permissible—all spoken

prayer. All true religions being of equal value, if it had been up to me, I would have allowed—not initiated, not imposed, but allowed—incense and rosaries and Kaddish and gongs; and chants to Siva the Destroyer, who dances upon the flames that consume the world; and drummings to Changó, ruler of fire and thunder and swords and sudden death; and the poems of a Sufi who longed for the divine homeland; and, interwoven, sage reminders from liturgical Christianity: remember, human, that you are dust, in the midst of life we are in death. I would even have permitted the rebellious, inspired ghost of George Fox to shout us down into silence and from that sobered stillness, one by one, draw us, at last, to speak the contents of our broken hearts.

Late in the evening a black-cassocked Roman Catholic priest approached us. He had eyeglasses with thick frames perched on his hooked nose. The frames were as black as his hair. He looked like every other Spanish-speaking priest I had ever heard rail against immoral acts, missing Mass on Sundays, bad children who entertained bad thoughts—and I had to admit to myself that he was not much older than I was. He had obviously been speaking to some people in the parlor; in fact, I suspected he had been called by them. He said, "*Señora,* would you permit us to say a few prayers?" My mother said no.

There were certain enjoyable ironies to this religious war over my father's farewell. In times past and present, Christian ministers have denied religious rites to suicides. Yet here was an anxious insistence on providing a Christian send-off not to a usually faithful son of the church, but to a proud apostate.

Probably Monseñor Agustín Román, the auxiliary bishop of Miami, came of his own initiative, though I have sometimes imagined a panicked call from the parish priest to Román, the auxiliary bishop, "They won't let me do a thing!" The priest brought in Monseñor Román. "Monseñor Román has arrived," he announced to my mother and me, preceding the older priest like a herald strewing imaginary palm fronds on the road to Jerusalem, hosanna. Monseñor Román walked briskly, stopping only very briefly to express his condolences to us and to say to my mother, "I knew him," and for my mother to say, "Yes, I know." To his statement of "We are going to gather here," made while pointing to my father's coffin, my mother, to my surprise, said, "Yes." We had never had much choice, really. Monseñor Román had seen the tear that my father's violent rejection of the world had made in his community and he was going to perform his duty of attempting to repair it. My father did not belong only to my mother and me.

My mother hurriedly explained, for things were moving very rapidly, people having started to congregate from the moment of Monseñor Román's arrival, "He knew your father. As a child he heard him speak in the countryside."

We got up and walked into the middle of the crowd. I wondered which speeches of my father's the good priest had heard in his youth. Because irony provides me with much pleasure, I hoped that perhaps they were my father's Quaker speeches inciting others to God, Quakers in Cuba being the evangelizing sort. But I learned otherwise much later, when among my mother's papers I ran across the text of my father's inaugural speech as *decano* to the Colegio in a copy of the first issue of *Papel Periódico* that bore a label with an old address of mine and had never been mailed to me. In that speech my father thanked Monseñor Román, who had given the convocation at the inauguration, and explained that Román had heard my father's fiery speeches "reclaiming justice for the most humble and forsaken class, during wanderings undertaken by us [meaning my father and his colleagues] to establish the Federación de Campesinos, so that we could count with a combative organization that would put an end to the abuses with which they were victimized, which I suffered in my own flesh, because I am of the most humble extraction, son of an agricultural worker from the small settlement of Cañas, in the municipality of Artemisa, Pinar del Río." The son of a cart driver, he usually described himself. *"Era orador de agitación,"* my mother explained to someone who later asked about the connection. My father had been very proud of being the kind of orator who got sent in when there was need to get a crowd inspired to do battle. Son of thunder.

For the first time since the wake's beginning there was silence. With his right hand Monseñor Román held the knife-edge of his left. "When I was a boy," he said, "my father would take me to hear Ramiro speak in the fields. I don't remember the words that he uttered but I remember their beauty. And such beauty must surely be a manifestation of God."

He continued, "The view from heaven, that of God and the Blessed Virgin and the saints, is different from that on earth. We see but a slice of time and space. The view from heaven is complete. From earth, we cannot know what God and the saints know." With humility, without mentioning either judgment or humility, Monseñor Román declined to judge my father. Without mentioning charity, he anointed my head with a balm that dripped such merciful love as I wished were possible to obtain from God. I wept then and later as I recalled his words. I wept with gratitude for their kindness and with heartache at the rarity of his actions among humanity in general, and among priests of his church, which used to be my church until I could bear it no longer.

The nettling part of the ceremony was the formulaic prayers and responsories. Others knew the new words, the expected responses, but I did not, and neither did my mother. Most disconcertingly, I could not say with the others even the words of the most frequently intoned of Christian prayers, the Paternoster, *el Padre Nuestro* in my first language of prayer. During my absence the church had gone and changed even that.

Excluded, I thought instead about Monseñor Román's words about the view from heaven. A smile rose in my chest, for in his comforting speech the priest had lit up a scholar's darkness. The week of my father's suicide I had finished working arduously on a paper on Chaucer's great story of love betrayed and private lives caught in war, *Troilus and Criseyde.* I would wager a large sum that Monseñor Román had never read the medieval English *Troilus,* but through his words he explained to me the critic-picked palinode from the eighth sphere. For upon his death from Achilles' spear, the risen soul of Troilus seems to reject the struggles that had weighed with such consequence in his living days. In a blessed state from which he can look at once upon all stars and hear the music of the spheres, he sees our earthly strivings as but futile, blindly sought pain in a world that "passeth soone as floures faire."

Monseñor Román withdrew from his black suit's breast pocket a plastic bottle that looked as if it might contain contact lens solution. Instead it contained holy water, which he squeezed onto my suicide father's crucifix-bearing temporary coffin. I had long ago abandoned my child's view of God. At the age of sixteen, I had become convinced that God, whatever God was, did not punish humans according to the rules set down by any church. Standing in the funereal room, I did not ascribe condemnation and forgiveness to divinity. These were human concerns. Now that my father was dead, what rage the universe still held toward him was my mother's and mine. It was left to us to forgive. I could not do so then. I knew that, living, I would have to strive toward my own eighth sphere and do more than Troilus: forgive Criseyde, the Trojans, and the Greeks.

Monseñor Román's ceremony ended a short time before midnight, and many people took the opportunity to begin to bid good-bye to us and to one another, to ask us if we needed rides home. People brought us the remaining *recordatorios,* the memorial cards that had sat next to the guest book. The memorial cards had on the cover a reproduction of a watercolor of a tower mirrored in a pond surrounded by tropical foliage. For some enigmatic reason, I look at the picture and every time I think, "Augustine of Hippo." *E.P.D.,* the *recordatorio* said above my father's name on the third page. Even the decoding of that euphemistic alphabet I had learned from my father. I first saw it in a political cartoon. Liborio, the personification of Cuba, wept over a tombstone that read "*E.P.D.* Freedom of the Press." My father explained the general usage of the abbreviation. "You'll see it here in English as 'R.I.P.'," he said. "It's one of these *hipocresías* we must commit." Only if the wish is insincere.

On the second page, the *recordatorio* bore an exotic translation of Psalm 23, praising *Jehová* rather than *el Señor*. *Thy rod and thy staff they comfort me.* The words mocked my father's pain. One psalm away lay the description of my father's last months. *My God, my God, why hast thou forsaken me? Why art thou so far from helping me, from the words of my groaning? O my God, I cry by day, but thou dost not answer; and by night, but find no rest. I am poured out like water, and all my bones are out of joint; my heart is like wax, it is melted within my breast; my strength is dried up like a potsherd, and my tongue cleaves to my jaws; thou dost lay me in the dust of death.*

Hard upon midnight, as the last people were filing out, I walked up to the coffin, as I knew all along I would do, and I put my hand on the solid cover as if my hand could melt a channel in the metal and touch my father's skin. I was too afraid to lift the lid; he might not have been prepared. There would be no farewells said broken heart to broken face. *"Adiós, papá,"* I said to him in my mind. It was final. I would walk out of the door and he would be dead forever. *"Adiós, papá,"* I thought, but I did not mean good-bye.

My cousin Marta had stopped at the doorway of the coffin room to watch like a psychological sentry for signs of distress in my mother and me. When I turned from the coffin, I saw her. She was looking at me with sympathy, and when I had finally torn myself from the place that held my father, she hugged me. I had not wanted to be seen. Marta read something noble into my action, but there was nothing noble in it. I simply could not accept that after I walked away, my father would be burned and all that would remain would be a handful of nothing and a pain like this.

## II

After a death, one keeps busy, as Emily Dickinson observed. It seemed to my mother natural that we should fill our days as if Kurt had come down just so that I could show him Miami. We went to the Seaquarium to see the tropical reef fish and the performing dolphins two or three days after the wake. Like a child taken for an outing, my mother let us pay for the steep admission tickets and all the overpriced sodas and ice creams. Our finances were in the dirt, but she did not know that, and she had had to assimilate too much too quickly for me to dare tell her. Therefore, she persisted in her dependency wherever we went. She wanted recompense for her pain, she wanted to be taken care of in her time of trouble. She enjoyed the leaping dolphins. We tossed a ball with one of them. We were surrounded by tourists.

Then we tried to deal with the real. Perhaps it was too soon. But my mother felt an urgency about taking my father's name off the safe deposit box and off the checking account. After all, he was dead. One could not pretend fiscally that he was not. So we went, all three of us, to the tall tower of Southeast Bank in downtown Miami. Southeast Bank had been my father's, and therefore my parents', bank for almost three decades. My father felt confidence in Southeast Bank and thought that Southeast Bank, because of his loyalty and his impeccable record of financial responsibility, felt a corresponding confidence in him. In other words, my father thought the bank had noticed him.

For the downtown outing, Kurt put on a Hawaiian shirt that his older brother John in New Hampshire had gotten rid of. Its background was black but from it jumped large pink hibiscuses. I felt offended by the sight. We were, after all, supposed to be a family in mourning. Yet with my typical Cuban reticence to point out the offensiveness of an act and my bad habit, inherited from my father, of assuming that the action's noxiousness is evident to the perpetrator, I said nothing.

When we arrived in downtown Miami, we looked for parking near the Dade County Courthouse, on whose sky-scraping ziggurat top, to my delight since childhood, buzzards perch—waiting, said my childhood imagination, for those sentenced to death. On one side of the courthouse was an official sign saying "Media Parking."

Kurt asked me what it meant. *"Media,"* he said, "does that mean a half hour?"

"No, media," I said, "as in CBS and the *Washington Post.* The sign is not in Spanish."

We parked where we could, and we walked the few blocks to the bank. As we got to its doors, Kurt said that he had an errand to run, that he would meet us in the bank's lobby later.

My mother and I approached the service counter designated for deposit box transactions. As we waited, my mother startled me by breaking down in sobs.

"I'm afraid they'll make me move," she said through her sobs. "I've heard that they make people who are living alone move to an efficiency. I don't want to move. I think the last move is what broke your father."

I put my arm around her but felt myself drawing emotionally distant. I was a teenager again and my mother was embarrassing me once more with her social ineptness. I tried to fight my feelings of anger but I could not, especially when she committed one of her typical reversals of logic, reminding me of how difficult it had been to be her daughter. She said with nostalgia and more weeping, "In Cuba the wakes were held at home, and then people moved because of the memories."

She wailed, or so it seemed to me. I rubbed her shoulder and wished fervently to be elsewhere. The two middle-aged Cuban women behind the counter came up to us. One of them limited herself to looking sympathetic. The other, more forceful one, the one with the right form in hand, ordered my mother to compose herself. My mother, consistent with her new habit, seemed to welcome the arrival of a parent.

"You must overcome this sorrow," said the woman.

She and her associate asked questions to see what tack might prove most fruitful. "You have a daughter. You have grandchildren probably."

"No."

"Your daughter lives near you?"

"In Maryland."

"You have family here in Miami?"

"One brother."

"Look, you have such a pretty daughter. Live for your daughter," the forceful woman said with finality.

My mother looked at me with irony. We both recognized the painful absurdity of the proposition.

My father's name was taken off the form that named the owners of the safe deposit box. My own name was added. I was given a key. The milder woman took us back into the safe deposit room so that my mother could show me the contents of the family box. Among them was the chunky gold jewelry we had brought to hock for cash in the United States because Castro's government restricted to $100 per person the currency we could take out of the country. My mother resumed her sobbing.

Our business transacted there, we stopped off at the counter, where my mother stated that she also wished to remove my father's name from the checking account. As my mother wept, her new confidantes informed us that that operation must be transacted in another office.

I said to my mother, "Let's go. I think this is all too hard for you. It's better to do this another day," and I hugged her around the shoulders. I did not see how she would get through a second procedure, nor did I see how I would. We might not find such sympathetic personnel in the checking accounts department.

Before we got ready to leave their counter, the women of the safe deposit box section, in a heroic act of Cuban politeness, invited my mother to stop by again if she needed to talk to someone.

In the lobby Kurt sat wearing a new shirt, a somber gray short-sleeve. "Let's go," I said, and I blessed the extreme heat and sunshine of the street.

Several months after my return to the Maryland that was so far off, my mother informed me that she was considering putting either Mario or Lázaro down as the other person on her checking account.

I exploded. "How could you do this to me? How could you complicate the matter of inheritance so much?"

"You wanted to leave the bank. I didn't think you were interested," my mother said.

A couple of weeks after our conversation my mother told me that she had gone to the bank and put my name down. I asked her if they would send me a signature card or if they needed my Social Security number. She said they had told her that they needed no further information on me. I dread the day, assuming I outlive my mother, when I learn what the bank records actually show.

In 1991 Southeast Bank, with its tall tower and numerous branches, failed. It was taken over by another bank. We who had felt so frail in its lowest story outlasted it, as did the patient ladies at the safe deposit counter. My mother visits with them whenever she goes to the bank with the changed name.

My mother was most efficient and determined about clearing memories out of her apartment. She despised the hospital bed that took up a third of her bedroom, the hospital bed that my father had had to use because he could not breathe if he lay flat. She announced that she would have it removed.

My father's clothes hanging in his closet also irritated her into action a mere few days after the disappearance of a body to fill them. She became a whirlwind of housekeeping inside the walk-in closet that opened onto the living room. She brought out shirt after shirt, offering them to Kurt, "Do you like? Do you like?"

She liked Kurt. At the time, she liked Kurt more than she liked me. The day after the wake, as she looked in one of the many books my father had left, she spotted a reproduced photograph in which Martí had a seriously receding hairline. "Your head is like Martí's," she said to Kurt. Among Cubans it is a compliment to be compared with Martí, even if the point of comparison is one's baldness. When Kurt helped her repot some plants, she wept, saying, "What a shame your father never knew Kurt. He would have liked him." I wondered why she tortured herself with this might-have-been that never actually could have been. My father would have found it impossible to accept Kurt. My mother's acceptance of him was enough of a boon for me.

Therefore, because Kurt was a nice son-in-law and because she had her own frantic need to drive out the presence of the man who had hurt her, she offered garment after garment that had ridden close to my father's skin during his last years of turmoil. Kurt wore my father's shirt size. We sat captive, giving each other questioning looks. There was something eerie about either accepting or refusing a dead man's possessions. Death might cling to them like the dust of moths. Guilt might follow the rejection of something that had belonged to a parent. We were confused, among other things, about the etiquette of the moment. How does one refuse a dead man's shirt, not to one's taste, offered by a grieving widow? I kept trying to guess whether Kurt liked or disliked a garment so that I could help him with his response. I would go up to him and ask him softly. Kurt had professed not to like short-sleeved shirts, so I was surprised when he said yes to many. When something was just not to his liking, I said to my mother, "It has too much polyester. Kurt is not comfortable in polyester." After that, she looked at the fabric content before handing over a shirt on its hanger to Kurt.

My mother brought out a cheap little pocket knife, the sort
that is displayed near the register in small plastic buckets at the
five-and-dime.

"Do you want it?" she asked Kurt. To her it was a man's object.

Kurt smiled and said, "María likes that kind of thing."

I am fanatical about Swiss army knives. I hungrily took the
little knife with a dull blade and a fingernail filer and bottle cap
remover. Something of my father's was mine.

My mother brought out the ties too. At one time my father
had owned a nice collection, for he liked ties. In the 1970s,
unfortunately, he had bought a lot of the strange, fashionably
wide ties of the decade. Some of these remained in his closet. I
was sorry to see that he had not bought ties for a long time; some
of the normal width ones were worn with age. My mother
showed me a gray silk tie I had given him. He had gotten a stain
on it and she had washed it. Predictably, it had come out wrin-
kled from the washing. My father could no longer wear it.

Then my mother brought out a silk tie in mint condition. Its
maroon background was scattered with tiny blue-edged cream-
colored paisleys like raindrops.

"You sent this to your father," my mother said to me.

Ah, yes, I then recognized it. I had hunted at a department
store for a tie that was pleasing to me and yet conservative.

"Your father never wore it," my mother informed me. "He
received it, and he started thinking, 'A red tie. If I put it on, peo-
ple are going to say I'm a Communist, wearing a red tie.' He
didn't like red. So he never wore it."

The tie was boardroom maroon. To see Communism in this
red required an odd perspective. It would have taken a strange
perspective too not to see the rejection in my mother's words;
perhaps the rejection was intended. Kurt accepted the tie; at
least, this man I loved would wear it.

After dispensing my father's clothes, my mother thought I
should see my father's will. She knew exactly where it was, in the
top right-hand drawer of their dresser. She handed it to me to

read. My father had gone to a Cuban lawyer a few months before and in the parenthesis-columned form of legal documents had put down that all his worldly goods should go to his wife and that a Cuban flag should be present at his funeral and that his body should be cremated and scattered in an ocean. His carcass here and in the suicide note overwhelmed other concerns.

The will contained no acknowledgment of my existence. He had reserved for me not a book, not a thought, not a thin lock of steel-gray hair, not the writing of my name. My mother had given me the document without comment and without comment I handed it back to her. She had meant to wound me, I believed, and I would not let her see that she had succeeded.

I would have to depend on my mother's generosity to get anything of my father's. Possessing no clue about how my mother would respond, I said to her, "Could I have my father's Colegio de Periodistas lapel pin?"

"Yes," she said, and with eagerness to please, she set off to look for it.

She brought out the pin that I knew, the one with the dark blue inkpot and gold old-fashioned quill pen on a white scroll with the dark blue initials C.N.P. It was not the original but a close exile approximation of the pin I ran across in my explorations of my father's cuff-links box in Cuba. Like this one, that past treasure had had a little wheel on the back screw to keep it in place.

"But he was given a new pin," my mother said. "I don't know where it is."

With agitation, she looked on his sports jackets and in the dresser. I told her that the pin she had given me was absolutely fine. But she was determined to find the new one. After more searching, she gave up. "I wonder if he was wearing it," she said.

"May I take this one?" I asked.

"Of course," my mother said, as if my question were ridiculous.

There were duties that cried out to be performed before necessity forced us to return to Maryland. Foremost in our minds was the disposition of my father's ashes, by borrowed or rented boat or by standing at the water's edge. Lázaro had said at the wake that a strong current ran in Biscayne Bay beside the Ermita de Nuestra Señora de la Caridad del Cobre, the Shrine of our Lady of Charity, the patroness of Cuba. It did not matter much to us how we got to the sea just so long as we did so with my father's ashes.

Yet there were no ashes. We had been told there would be a wait of seventy-two hours before cremation could take place. The time had passed and still my father's body lingered uncremated in a refrigerator. The men of the Colegio inquired on our behalf. Unfortunately, it seemed, Rivero Funeral Home did not have its own crematorium. They accepted bodies for cremation but they shipped them out to other funeral homes that had incinerators. My father's cadaver must wait in line for a slot to open at a crematory facility. It might take ten days, we were told. By then Kurt and I would be back in Maryland. If we delayed working, we might not be able to pay our rent. My mother could not rest, she said, until she had fulfilled my father's request.

I was lucky. I got a summer job on my first call. A week after our return home, I was working. The criminal justice research organization at which I had held a temporary assignment the spring and summer before my first semester of graduate school needed help. Because I lived near the Silver Spring metro station, the commute from Washington was uncomplicated.

It was Tuesday, 6 June, the evening after my second day of work. By the time the ABC network news began at 6:30 P.M., I had stretched out on the futon. I was anxious for news about China. One of the signs of my father's detachment had been his indifference to the massive pro-democracy protests in Tiananmen Square. And one of the signs of my determination to hang on to a sense of the world outside our tragedy had been my insistence on watching news, some news, in Miami despite my mother's current repugnance for anything journalism-related. When we at last bought a *Herald* and I was able to read the news of the rebellion in hard-line China, I felt more nearly myself again. For a while I took hope from events. When the violent onslaught of the government-ordered troops began, inexorably, to crush the rebellion of spring, I thought not so much of the repressive machinery of totalitarian government, but of young soldiers, one by one, pulling triggers, driving tanks, leaving behind, in proliferative array, in thousands of people's lives, the trauma that my father had left in mine.

The most startling news on the evening of 6 June was not of the latest repressive measures by the Chinese government. The source this time was Iran. I sat suddenly very far forward when images of the Ayatollah Ruhollah Khomeini's funeral began parading along their bizarre route on my television screen. Fanatical throngs pressed toward the dead, old, fanatical leader's bier. Some frenzied mourners pulled at the dark shroud that covered the body so that they might take with them as relics pieces of the cloth. The ayatollah's naked feet, stiff, helpless before indignity, were exposed. The body was pulled partly off the bier and then somehow pushed back on, like a cow carcass that had started to slip off the butcher's table.

The telephone rang. It was my mother. "We finally did it today. We went to throw the ashes," she told me. "Now I can rest."

"How was it done?" I asked.

"Well, I went with Lázaro and Finita to the Shrine of Our Lady of Charity. You know where that is?" I had attended Immaculata-La Salle High School, blessedly situated on the bay, right next to the shrine's future site. "And Lázaro threw the ashes into the sea. There was a current," my mother said simply.

But I wanted details. What container did the ashes come in? "They came in a cardboard box. The ashes were in a plastic bag inside the box. The bag had one of those twisted strips to hold it

shut," my mother answered. Like a Baggie? "Yes, like a Baggie."
What was actually done? "Well, I took the bag out of the box. I
undid the strip. Lázaro took the plastic bag from me. And he
threw it into the water."

In my mind, I was picturing the actions as my mother
described them: my mother took out the Baggie, she undid the
twisted wire fastener, Lázaro threw the Baggie. "He didn't scatter
the ashes? He just threw the Baggie?" I asked.

"He just threw the bag. He threw it far and there was a
strong current. It wouldn't take long for the bag to sink. We'd left
it open at the top. The water could get into the bag. Because of
the delay in the cremation, the flag made out of flowers wasn't
saved. It would have wilted by now. It's a pity."

I would later learn from the cremation certificate issued by
Grove Park Facilities that my father's body had been cremated on
2 June. My mother had endured a second delay.

"But for me it is a great relief. That is done," my mother said.
Was anything else done? "No, nothing else. We left," she said. I
said that, yes, for her it must be a great relief.

After hanging up the telephone I returned to the bedroom. I
was in time to watch the beginning of the CBS News broadcast
at seven and again the attempted burial of the imam of Iran, the
ayatollah, that most successful former exile, who had accom-
plished the ultimate political exile's dream of triumphant return,
leadership, and transformation. He had done what Moses could
not, and the world was worse for it.

Yet again the old ayatollah's lifeless mannequin of a body was
thrown about. And I thought with horror that, just a few hours
before, my father's ashes, fragments of my father's carbonized
bone, all that was left of his physical presence among us, had
been tossed unceremoniously in a Baggie like a stale sandwich
into Biscayne Bay. I wondered what I could possibly do to atone,
to my satisfaction, for an act of such daunting disrespect. The
concept surprised me. It had been a long time since I had
thought about atonement.

I realized that I was basing my harsh judgment on the testimony of an unreliable witness. No disrespect would have been meant by any of the three. Perhaps they had not wanted to burden my father—or my mother—with unwanted prayer. Perhaps they had paid respects anyway, silently, embarrassed by a situation for which they had received no training. Two acquaintances had done my mother a favor. The pressure on her shoulders had lightened. But: "he threw it far." The image of my father getting tossed like the first ball at the opening game of the baseball season would not leave my mind. My despair first came out in spurts like water from a newly tapped well; then it flooded.

As I watched again the crowd's lunging toward the dead remains of what had been the ayatollah, I marveled at the mourners' lack of fear of contagion by death. I was repelled by their primitive hysteria, but I was more revolted by my own civilization's fanatical efforts to disconnect from the implications of death and the duties of death—in Cuban Miami, in the United States, in the West. The Parsis, remnants of ancient Persia who more than most fear death's contagion, isolate the bodies of the dead on great towers of silence to be picked clean by vultures so that death will not defile fire, air, water, or earth—but they do so to the accompaniment of days of ritual. We, on the other hand, have fabricated such a careless civilization, a morality of convenience in an age of exiled death.

Does it require love to overcome our revulsion toward the human end enough to dig into a pile of ashes that were once someone we knew and get his death all over our hands? If love is required, then we will continue to wrap death in tight plastic packages until our civilization crashes under the burden of the discarded heaps.

I wore black, gray, and other austere colors for several weeks; my mother ceased to do so after the wake. The restricted palette dramatically limited my already few business attire possibilities, but I persisted; whether or not anyone noticed or cared, I felt I owed my father that outward sign of respect.

One day when I had worn the black dress of the wake to work, I ate lunch at the office's kitchen table with my friend and coworker Connie, who had happened to wear black that day too. A researcher walked into the kitchen and said loudly, as a joke, "You look like you're in mourning!" I told him I was. His face fell. I told him details of my father's suicide. I made explicit the death I carried with me. And I wished silently that the symbols of mourning were still recognized, without explanation, as warnings that those who bear them require special delicacy, special care, and that we lose everything to death.

My mother can seal her emotions against leakage into consciousness. She has so circumscribed her world that it is not difficult to know what is important to her. Photographs are important, the snapshot record of a life that is gone. While we were still in Miami a few days after my father's death, my mother sought to show Kurt two photographs of me in Cuba, two of the priceless few that had made it out of the country. "You will see. She was so cute," my mother said. But she did not know where the pictures were.

I was about two when the photographs were taken. In one, a close-up, I wore a large polka-dotted bow on top of my head and exhibited the Boza fierceness. In the other, the "cute" one, I wore a plaid bow and a jumper as I danced the flamenco—I am attempting to snap my fingers—in front of a rocking chair. The photos smelled of leather because my father had carried them for decades in his wallet. They were worn thin, too, like well-used leather. Now and then I would ask my father to take them out so that I could see myself in that long-gone time in which I possessed so much charm that I was his chief joy. The last time I had seen the pictures, however, my parents were living in an awful HUD building on Mundy Street, and my father extracted the photos from his briefcase, not his wallet.

*Ramiro Boza at work.*

I told my mother this, in case it might help her look for them. She pulled out all the cards in his wallet. The picture in his last driver's license showed him shrunken like a dried fruit; it was proof that he was not up to what the license permitted. She looked through his briefcase—the one in which he may have hidden the gun—but she found nothing of significance there. I thought that perhaps he had taken the photographs with him when he shot himself, that he had pinned the elusive, fabled new pin of the Colegio on his collar and stuffed my baby pictures into his shirt pocket. Maybe the clothes had been discarded by the hospital as too bloody, or they had been burned up with him. I did not know, but my mother did not find the snapshots.

A short time after Kurt and I had returned to Maryland, my mother told me in her weekly telephone call that she had dropped my father's photograph and the frame had shattered. My father's photograph had sat for many years unscathed in its

easel-type frame on top of the television set. She had picked it up
every few days and dusted it, and never, until after he had forced
her to witness the sight of his blood-covered, dying body, had it
slipped through her fingers. *"Se me cayó,"* she said. The photo-
graph, a close-up of my father, showed him when he was sixty.
His hair was dark gray still and slicked back. His lower lip pro-
truded in challenge. He was in his element: he was at work.

The shattered frame had contained another, very disturbing
object. Father's Day had followed soon after my father's hospital-
ization with arrhythmias. Overcome with guilt and thankfulness
at his survival, I had purchased a blue-bordered card that pre-
tended rather cartoonishly to be an official document. It read:

### THE I-CAN'T-THANK-YOU-ENOUGH
### FOR-BEING-SUCH-A-WONDERFUL-FATHER CERTIFICATE

*This certifies that although I will never be able to thank you
enough for being such a wonderful father, I'd sure like to try.*

There was an official-seeming line for my signature. I dated it
June 13, 1981.

My father had been so happy to receive the card, so full of
jubilant vindication—as if I had reassured him, through the
agency of the postal service, of something he had doubted—that
he had framed the card next to his picture. When on a future visit
I saw the garish object sitting in a prominent place, I regretted it.
I was nauseated by my act of weakness, my attempt at cheap con-
solation and expiation. Through it I had betrayed myself and my
experience. Its public display mocked me. Whatever I might do
that might seem the act of an unloving daughter could be
demonstrated to be born of an independently acquired perversi-
ty. My father had been a wonderful father; I had signed an
attestation to the fact. I hoped at least that in adopting a new
frame, my mother would see fit to divorce the Father's Day card
from my father's photograph.

My mother told me that she had gone to a far-off photogra-
phy shop to buy a new frame, that she had forgotten that Luria's

catalogue shop was two doors away. She had taken a long bus ride during which she had been confused about where she was going. She had gotten very hot. Once at the shop, she had broken down and wept and told the man what she had come for. She had told him her story. I cringed, remembering my mother sobbing uncontrollably at the bank. I felt embarrassed once again.

Yet I should have understood, for I was having a difficult time finding people willing to hear me talk about death. My psychotherapist, Dr. N., upon my return from attending to the immediate aftermath of my father's suicide, wanted me to discuss not my loss, but rather why I had not warned Kurt that people do not wear Hawaiian shirts in Miami. This clinical psychologist had been behaving very erratically the last few months, getting up every few minutes to kill invading ants with a gizmo called, he said, a Bug Vac, which emitted a loud whine and drowned out whatever a patient was saying or even thinking. I had long suspected that he would be terrible at helping me with my father's death (in my mind, always preceding my mother's) because he viewed all sadness as sickness and neurosis. The final straw came during one session when he said, laughing the loud laugh that used to fill and rattle the office, "So why do you want to feel bad about your father's death? He was dead already anyway. Him shooting himself was like shooting a dead dog on the highway." He laughed with stentorian glee at this comparison, "A dead dog on the highway!" I stopped seeing him soon after, though it would have been more satisfying to rip out his laughing throat.

My grieving mother told the man at the photography shop her story and he sold her a frame. When she got it home, however, she realized that it was the wrong kind of frame. She wondered how he could have gotten it wrong because she explained to him what she needed. The one he gave her did not have an easel back. It had a bracket for hanging from the wall. She would not be able to put my father's photograph back on the television set. She would have to put it on the wall above it. But there was already another photograph hanging on the wall, just above the television set.

My mother will tell visitors with complete confidence that I was fifteen when the photograph was taken, but I was not. I was eleven, my last good year until thirty-six. I had already developed a young woman's body, which is one reason why my mother is confused about my age. A sales agent from a photography studio had gone door-to-door through the apartment building giving out certificates for one free black-and-white portrait ("of your daughter, so pretty"). As is usual with such inducements, when we arrived to have the free photo of me taken, the photography studio staff attempted, successfully, to sell my father a whole series, including small, card-encased black-and-whites to send out to relatives and the "color" enlargement that had hung in my parents' living room since. I arrived at the photo session wearing a blouse with a print of mustard- and brown-petaled flowers scattered on a white ground. The photographer did not like that at all. He said it would not be good for the photograph. He urged my mother to take me home to change into a solid-colored blouse, but my mother refused, and, grumbling, the photographer proceeded with the session. When we saw that the enlargement was hand-tinted rather than shot with color film, my mother said, "Ah, so he didn't want to do so much work." Unfortunately, when telling this story years later to Lidia Asencio, my mother said, "The photographer wanted her to take her blouse off, but I said no." Lidia's jaw dropped and my heart sank, while my mother continued placidly with her drink and hors d'oeuvre.

"The frame is for hanging," my mother said to me on the telephone. "I'm going to have to take your photograph down." She might as well have just struck me across the face. "Maybe I can find another frame for your picture. But it's so big. Maybe I can cut it."

She had two otherwise empty walls in the living room from which to hang pictures of me, my father, and all her siblings, alive or dead, had she possessed their likenesses. It was pointless to say to my mother, "You are so enraged with me." I tried to explain, with a voice that I was trying very hard to keep from screaming at her, that there was enough room on her wall for two photographs, if she wanted them both to be up, if she wanted them. She then asked me how one went about hanging something from a wall.

I spent a year without knowing if my mother had purged my puberal likeness from its place of honor. When Kurt and I next visited, we found that she had framed a color snapshot of the two of us and had put it on her étagère. And she had found, after all, that her wall provided ample space for loved ones. There hung my hand-tinted portrait, in its old place, in its old frame, with my father's newly framed picture next to it. Unfortunately, in purchasing the replacement frame, my mother had been careful to include in the dimensions enough room for the blasted Father's Day card.

Times of illness, crisis, or personal loss are the worst in which to deal with the health care system. Its practitioners tell you that your father is no more than a dead dog on the highway and/or they send you a very large bill. My mother was besieged by bills from Jackson Memorial Hospital. One was for $10,000. I wondered why Medicare was not taking care of it.

"I don't know," my mother said in her tone of confusion. "They don't cover everything. I've asked Lázaro to look into it. He knows people at the Pan American Hospital." Note that the Pan American Hospital is not the Jackson Memorial Hospital. "Finita said that I should pay nothing. I gave her the bill. She said she would investigate."

What was the bill for, I asked.

"Neurosurgery. He spent several hours undergoing neuro-surgery."

Neurosurgery on an old man who had attempted to die. It seemed ridiculous, this blind following of the medical imperative. Even though I too would have called the rescue squad, I recognized a logical disjunction in performing heroic acts to save the life of someone who had violently rejected it. Surgery in such a case was a violation of the will, not just an invasion of the body. *O let him pass, he hates him that would upon the rack of this tough world stretch him out longer.*

"Neurosurgery on someone who wanted to die," I said sardonically.

"Just so," my mother said. "And you know what else is strange?" she continued. "That night they had him on intravenous penicillin. And he was very allergic to penicillin." She said this as if this medical fact about my father could have escaped me. From childhood I had heard him tell of his dramatic swelling the first and last time he was injected with the antibiotic.

"Of course, I knew about his allergy to penicillin," I said. "And you knew about it and you were sitting right outside the operating room. And they never asked you?"

"They never asked me," she said.

"Mamá, if the hospital tries to collect from you again, threaten to sue them for malpractice. My father was very allergic to penicillin. Having massive doses of a substance that was toxic to him could have finished him." Merciful penicillin, delivering my father in the night from a world that was only pain. I found this unintentional poisoning a far kinder act than the intentional surgery.

"I am not going to sue," my mother said.

We both wanted resolutions, periods at the end of sentences. "I know you're not going to sue. Just say you are. He was allergic to penicillin and they didn't ask you. It says right there on the bill that they administered the penicillin, doesn't it?"

"Yes."

"Well, send me a copy of the bill."

"I don't have it. I gave it to Finita."

"Couldn't you ask for it back? It's your bill," I insisted.

"I suppose so. If she still has it," my mother said uncertainly.

Hospital billing, the subject of several more telephone conversations, was rendered all the more frustrating for me because I was not sent copies of any paperwork; others, my mother said, were looking into it. I could not verify that the bill contained a charge for penicillin. I did not know how my mother was going to pay a bill for $10,000. My guilt and helplessness over my mother's financial predicament made it difficult for me to treat the problem rationally: I was terrified that if I became involved, as other next of kin, I would be sent the bill for $10,000.

Now and then, however, my mother came up with something so irrational that my love of logic kicked in. My father had supplemental health insurance through his retirement from the Associated Press. My mother was despairing of being able to file a claim for the expenses of his last hospitalization.

Why? "Because the form requires a signature and there will not be a signature," my mother explained.

"Mamá, even insurance companies have probably accepted the fact that dead men can't sign," I said with the unkindness I usually employ when I am struck, unprepared, by such monumental lack of reason.

The matter of the bill from Jackson Memorial was resolved when either the billing computer or the hospital staff made a connection between my father's age and the probability of my father's being eligible for Medicare. The hospital sent my mother a form asking her to specify my father's Social Security number. It seems that in the confusion of the admission, this simple identifier, necessary in order to bill Medicare, had gone unrecorded. Once she sent in the nine digits, my mother's troubles with Jackson Memorial were over.

My mother was reluctant to trust me to get things done. Perhaps she saw me as unconnected and therefore as lacking all possible power to influence an outcome. Regardless, I made it my mission to get a copy of my father's suicide note. The importance of possessing it seemed patently obvious to my mother and me. My father meant something to us, not to the Miami Police Department, which held it. Without his suicide note our hands felt empty. Without seeing it, his handwriting could not speak to us, could not tell us through the shape of letters and lines on paper what my father suffered during his last moments of unbearable consciousness—or what he meant us to know. Without it, his last message to my mother was as vapor before the leaden evidence that contradicted it. The obvious, however, was either not obvious or not compelling to the homicide detective handling my father's case—what there was of it to handle. At the suicide scene he had given my mother his business card. Heaven knows what for, judging from his subsequent behavior. Perhaps it was just departmental procedure.

Detective Tony Rodríguez was ever polite on the telephone. I called him a couple of days after the shooting to ask him if he could possibly send us a copy of the suicide note. He said, "I can read it to you." And he did. But—I insisted with the elaborate politeness through which I attempt to reconcile my reluctance to disturb someone by a request with my absolute determination to see it fulfilled—it was important to us to have an actual photocopy, even if the police must keep the original. The original was written to the police, Detective Rodríguez punctiliously insisted. Yes, I knew, but my father's last words were important to us.

"Would you like me to drop it off at your mother's apartment?"

"Oh, no, no, that will not be necessary," I said, scandalized that I would put someone so much out of his way. "If you would mail it to us, that would be fine."

I called him again a couple of days later, so it is not as if he could have forgotten about our existence. I called to ask if my father's cremation was being held up by a police investigation. He said, "No, this is such a clear-cut case. We have nothing to do with the delay. It's probably the funeral home." I reminded him of the suicide note. He said he would take care of it.

What we could do directly by applying at a counter in the lobby of the Miami Police Department headquarters was to obtain a copy of the incident report filed by the other cop who answered the call, Officer Roberto Santiago González. It was not our principal interest. Getting my father's note still was. But it was information, and easily obtained at that.

Cops know the incident report number instantly at the scene; they were able to leave it with my mother. This turned out to be a good thing, for I never would have traced it through my father's name. The incident report that the young woman at the counter printed for Kurt and me from her computer attested that my father's surname was Valdez and his first and middle names Ramiro Boza. It sought to inform me that my father was a female born on 1 September 1928, rather than 1908, as had always been supposed, and that "she" was therefore sixty years old.

Based on this case of gross misrepresentation, I resolved henceforth to be skeptical and to encourage others to be skeptical of Miami Police Department statistics. I wondered what huge percentage jump my father's death was creating in the number of sixty-years-old-or-over women who attempted to commit suicide in Miami by a gunshot to the head. Three years later, when preparing to write about the incident report, I noticed the presence of a UCR code on the page, a sign that the report was probably the medium used to transmit crime statistics to the Federal Bureau of Investigation's much quoted Uniform Crime Reports.

Three years after the event I also finally read the narrative contained in the report. I had thought I had read it upon receipt. But I did not do so with understanding. This came to me as an unsettling surprise. I like to think that while others around me may become hysterical, I at least retain control intellectually. But apparently I too had limits to what I could absorb. This is how the incident report narrative reads:

Person reporting Boza advises her husband
Ramiro had been complaining about his health
and in the past has been mentioning committing
suicide. Person reporting stated that her hus-
band's mental state has been deteriorating and
today as she laid on her bed she noticed her
husband was sitting at the dining room table
writing a letter. Ms. Boza advises she was
awaken by a loud noise and upon checking the
apartment discovered her husband had shot him-
self and was laying on the bathroom floor. Ms.
Boza asked neighbors to call police. Note: a
suicide note was discovered on the dining room
table, witness states it is her husband's
handwriting in English. Projectile was found
inside bath tub. Revolver was found on vic-
tim's right hand. The police was called by
neighbor's cleaning lady Zaida Alvarez.

Events had been significantly different from the way I had
envisioned and replayed them time after time over the years.
They were not as I had described them to others in careful, con-
cretizing detail. My mother had seen my father writing his
suicide note at the table. His back was to her. He wrote a lot, so
nothing seemed unusual. It would be like someone seeing me
writing, an act so commonplace that the person could drift
peacefully to sleep at the sight. Contrary to what I had under-
stood from my mother's anguished telephone call, my father did
not go into the bathroom with the gun hidden in his briefcase.
What a risk to take. How did he conceal it? He would have had
to walk within sight of the bedroom to get to the bathroom. My
mother thinks he left the briefcase in its usual place on a dining
chair. So he got up from the table, leaving the suicide note in
plain sight on the dining table; I had imagined the note at risk of
getting spattered with blood in an open briefcase on the bath-

room sink. My father had a way of arising from a table by turning his hands in, palms down, so that the fingertips of each hand approached those of the other parallel to the table's edge in front of his chest. He then concentrated his force on the palms as he leaned forward holding his upper arms nearly parallel to the table edge, his bony elbows jutting out. He walked to the bathroom in his short shirtsleeves risking detection. His anxiety must have been acute as he snuck past my mother to do something he should not.

The cops, upon reading the note, must have asked my mother if my father had been complaining about his health, to which she would have said, "Yes," and they must have then asked, "Has he been talking about committing suicide?" to which she would have said, "Yes," probably without a hint of irony. There may have been a time, in Cuba, when my father did not speak of suicide. Once when I was seven or eight he poured his wrath on me, calling me an ingrate and threatening to beat me, when I repeated what I had heard from adults, with a great sigh, "I wish I were dead." Yet one afternoon in our living room in Miami in my eleventh year or so, my father said to me, "If it weren't for you and your mother I would have committed suicide a long time ago." He did not say it as if he were grateful to us, but rather as if our existence presented a huge burden of responsibility that kept him from fulfilling his fondest wish. Now and then, through the years, he repeated the reproof. I never said anything, but I always wondered if I should apologize.

For my father to overcome his feelings of responsibility to my mother, to leave her without the protection that he had felt it his duty to extend to her through all the difficult years, his state of mind must have been at an extreme of pain or confusion or detachment—all the more important, then, that I obtain a copy of his suicide note so that I could attempt to understand. I knew that the longer the time that passed the farther back into the police department's files my father's case would recede. I feared that my father's note might become irretrievable.

At first my mother had told me not to worry, that Finita knew people and she was trying to get it. I admit to feeling competitive, to finding her presence in the picture a goad to push ahead with my efforts. I did not want to be beaten out by Finita. If I had had all my wits about me, I would have realized there was no competition at all to get the note. After weeks without results from her quarter, my mother told me, "Finita says these things are very difficult."

I sent Detective Tony Rodríguez a letter dated 6 June that began thus: "I am the daughter of Ramiro Boza. I was very heartened when I spoke with you two weeks ago and you agreed to send us a copy of my father's last note. I realize that the note was written to the police and not to my mother or me, but it does contain a message to my mother, and as it is the last one we will ever have from him, it would mean a lot both to her and to me to have a copy of it in our hands." I ended with: "This is a very painful matter for me, and an even more distressing one for my mother. The sooner we can tie the remaining loose ends, the sooner we will be at peace. Your help will be greatly appreciated." In between I dropped the not-so-subtle warning that for the next two months I would be working at a criminal justice research organization, whose name, I believed, should have been recognizable enough to him to let him know that I did have some connections. I also took the opportunity to point out the errors about my father's name, age, and gender that had appeared in the incident report. I enclosed a self-addressed stamped envelope.

I had one last telephone conversation with the detective. I wrote the following note for my file:

> On 21 June 1989 (3:25 p.m.) I spoke with Detective Rodríguez about my letter requesting a copy of my father's suicide note. He said he'd been out of town a few days, but, as soon as his meeting ended, he would put the note in the mail. He noted that I had sent a self-addressed envelope.

His meeting must have been long. I did not receive a response even though all the guy had to do was take the one page out of my father's file, make a photocopy of it, and put it inside the envelope I had provided.

I had wanted Tony Rodríguez to have a chance to do the right thing. However, I had no peace and I ran out of patience. I worked in the office of the well-connected president of the criminal justice organization. When the staff returned to work on 5 July from the Independence Day holiday, among them the president, freshly mourning the loss of his mother, I told him about my problem. He asked me to place a call to Perry L. Anderson, Jr., the chief of police in Miami, whom he knew. The president participated in the image game of not dialing telephones himself—and for once I would be a party for my own benefit. The police chief was not in but his executive assistant was. The president talked to him, black ex-cop to black cop. The man at the other end engaged him in small talk. The president said atypical things like "How you doin', brother?" Eventually he gave a brief description of my difficulties. I clearly heard him ask that a copy of Ramiro Boza's suicide note be sent to María Boza at our office marked "Personal." When he got off the phone, he assured me that a copy would soon be on its way to me. Although I never trust things to happen until they happen, I began to feel a bit calmer.

I took off a few days at the end of the following week to move. When I returned to the office on 17 July, I asked the president's executive assistant, for whom I worked as a kind of sub-secretary, if she had noticed whether my father's note had come. With profound embarrassment she said that it had, that it had come addressed to the president, not to me, and that it had not even been marked "Personal," and that, as she did with all his mail, she had opened it. She had held my father, naked and pain-racked, in her hands; I apologized for the shock she must have received.

"You don't owe me an apology," she said. "I owe one to you."

But she did not owe me an apology. When the president came in, he asked me into his office and shyly handed me the letter, apologizing for its having been opened. Such embarrassment about doing me a favor and then getting incidentally spattered with my father's blood. I could not thank them enough.

The envelope, postmarked 11 July, had been stamped as received by the president's executive assistant on 13 July. By the time I got the letter, it felt like an afterthought. I had memorized the text from my first conversation with Tony Rodríguez. Holding the envelope in my hands, I wondered if I should dare look at it in my office cubicle where anyone might wander past and see me weep, see me break down. But I looked. I cannot resist looking. And I discovered that I felt detached from the object in front of me. I read it. And I skimmed the strange cover letter to the president, signed by someone else for the chief of police of Miami, who was out of town—a cover letter in which my father's last description of lethal pain is referred to as "the information requested." A message at the bottom of the letter, hand-written by the police chief's executive assistant, sends the president the chief's regards. To the Miami Police Department I still did not exist.

I made two copies of my father's suicide note, one for my mother and the other as back-up. I folded it and I put it away in my briefcase. As soon as I got home, I called my mother to tell her that I had received it and she would soon receive her copy. My mother, I think, wanted the original copy sent by the Miami P.D., and even though I realized that there was something ridiculous in coveting the first photocopy, I did not want to part with it. I did not want to be at a greater remove. She would only put it away in a drawer and look at it no more anyway. I was vague in how I described what I was sending, "I will send you the copy." I assured my mother that I was keeping one for myself. I had, after all, obtained it.

I felt powerful, even if the power I held was derivative. I was not defenseless. I knew someone who knew someone. And I had proven it to my mother and to Detective Tony Rodríguez of homicide.

*Miami Mayo 19, 1989*

*To the Police:*

*Nobody be blamed for my death. I decided to kill my self. I am tired and very sick. I beg that my body be cremated and the ashes thrown to the sea.*

*My beloved wife Carmen forgive me. I have loved you very much.*

*Good bye.*

I told people, "It was strange. My father was so detached. The note is in English, not Spanish. And the handwriting was not his. It was as if in trying to make himself perfectly understood by the police, he had adopted what he thought would be a more legible style." I noticed the tall looped *t*s, *d*s, and *b*s that strove for legibility. Not finding my father in the photocopy of his note, only someone who had removed himself from himself and others, I put it away in its Miami P.D. envelope inside a file folder for three years.

The handwriting is absolutely my father's. The words are written large across the unruled page with barely a margin, gigantic letters as if words of lesser size could not contain the powerful emotion behind them. He thought he had terrible handwriting, yet I always found it legible. I did not try to imitate it, having been warned about its defectiveness, but as I got farther and farther away from third grade penmanship instruction and from him, my handwriting got wilder and bigger so that it came to resemble his in style if not in the specifics of form. If I am really impassioned, and untamed by ruling, I can only get four words to a line. But he did things with letters I would never do. He put an extravagant curlicue on the first *M* of his note. The other letters are shaky.

The handwriting is incontrovertibly his. I am stunned that I told myself the contrary when I first viewed it. Perhaps I was reacting to the barrier he had erected through the use of English, a language he employed only for the transacting of business, the language of a country of which he had requested refuge and despised, the foreigners' tongue. His English was a wall, his address to the police a firm rejection. Yet in that last message to an unknown police in alien language, he had embedded the only direct statement of affection I ever remember him making to my mother. It seems, because of its context, a public statement for the record, such as a political candidate might make. It seems intended to help exculpate my mother in the eyes of the world. It was perhaps meant to create a fact by virtue of its being stated. He got up from the writing of it to leave my mother to deal with brains on the floor.

He wrote the note in English, but Spanish slips in with *mayo.* Or perhaps he had not yet chosen English, though the placement of month-day is the common U.S. form. And, contrary to Spanish-language practice, the month appears to be capitalized, though I cannot be certain that the initial *m* is not just a large, forceful lower case initial letter.

His lack of punctuation after "My beloved wife Carmen" is not like him. But then, he says he has decided to "kill my self." His signature is an eerie testament to his determination to destroy that self. The signature has the appearance of having been introduced by a secretary who was not a skilled forger. His normal official signature, the one he used on checks and documents and correspondence, was a *garabato,* a doodle, but an elegant and consistent one. He would begin a baroque upward curve of the *R* of his first name and on it he would inscribe the initial *B* of a surname that would end in a squiggled fury that doubled back under the rest in an underline. The signature on the suicide note is that of someone who had knowledge of these elements but could not succeed in the particulars of their execution. The *B* is not his; the surname, someone else's. The hand trembled. The great circle of the *R* is a wobble. His heart must have wanted to pound its way out of his chest. The note would be finished, all preparation would be accomplished, with one last uncertain statement of identity.

Two hours before his death at Dos Ríos on 19 May 1895, José Martí delivered a stirring speech to an encampment of *mambises*. "I want it to be known that for the cause of Cuba I allow myself to be nailed to the cross." Much of the insurgency's leadership was gathered at one place—a catch beyond price, therefore, for a Spanish column that apprehended a nervous, talkative young man on his way to buy supplies for the rebels. The *peninsulares* advanced toward the insurgents with the advantage of woods and higher ground. Experienced *mambí* generals ordered a retreat. Martí seized his longed-for moment. In defiance of sense, Martí sped his white horse toward the Spanish column in a wild charge. Bullets struck him; one was fatal. It was one o'clock in the afternoon.

The police report on my father's shooting gives the dispatch time as 1:49 P.M. We must allow fifteen to twenty minutes for my mother to seek help, for neighbors to search through the building for an able caller and, before that, for my father to make certain that my mother was safely napping. The evidence is sufficient for me to suspect that my father closely timed his self-immolation on 19 May 1989 to coincide with the Apostle's.

In the dappled sunlight of the lush Cuban countryside, Martí ate a meal with his brothers-at-arms without knowing that the next hour exactly would be his death hour. "The lunch hour" would later be my mother's most precise timing of my father's. Did my father eat lunch before, at noon, like a condemned murderer awaiting the voltage of the chair, as Jesus, who seemed to know his fate, ate his Last Supper? Did he stop to enjoy the tastes as never before, the usual strawberry gelatin, the canned peach or pear half, maybe even a soda cracker?

Perhaps I was numbed to my father's suicide note by my move. I hate moving. It calls up all my worst demons of rootlessness. With the exception of the condominium at Río Mar, my parents and I have never owned one spot of the earth. We have been renters, passing through.

The tall Río Mar, where my parents and I lived from late 1955 or early 1956 till after the Revolution, represented a new idea in housing, a building where one bought the inside of one's apartment but did not own one's ceiling or floor, because the latter was someone else's ceiling and the former, a neighbor's floor. The new phenomenon was called *propiedad horizontal,* that is, "horizontal property"; "condominium," by comparison, is deficient in descriptiveness. It was a bizarre concept to my father, buying a dwelling and owning only its internal air.

My father groused for years about having been rooked into buying into this weird arrangement by his boss Alfredo Izaguirre Hornedo, who was one of the building's owners.

"Alfredo told me, 'You can have a completely furnished apartment with a view of the sea,'" my father complained, shaking his head, partly in disapproval of himself.

Alfredo's family could look around in all four cardinal directions, for they had the luxurious penthouse *(el penthouse).* We got neither furniture nor a view of the sea. Instead our balcony jutted out over the car ramp on which rebel guards would one day keep their watch. My father, who was suspicious of politicians, was easily deceived by his supposed friends.

We had apartment 333. This generated for my mother and Tía Nena some sarcastic fun. In the Chinese lottery, 33 is the vulture. And I did, in fact, frequently see from our windows *auras tiñosas* soaring in groups, especially when the sky became abruptly dark gray and the air smelled of wet earth. It looked to me almost, though not quite, as if they brought the rain. I do not know how much carrion there could have been for them in such a residential area, but supposedly there is a lot of death in the tropics. We sometimes saw a nervous *jutía* scurry across Primera Avenida into one of the weedy lots we faced. My father got happily excited on those occasions, because he was seeing a country animal in the city, a transplanted country animal, like himself. The two common species of *jutía,* members of the genus *Capromys,* are Cuba's largest native land mammals. These rodents can attain a length of two feet and a weight of twenty pounds. Our only other native land mammal is the tiny, slender-nosed, and even shyer *almiquí (Solenodon cubanus),* a nocturnal insectivore never seen by me. The *jutías* make a more satisfyingly sized, though still modest, meal for birds of carrion or prey.

The full number of our apartment had other predatory associations—something to do with Batista's police. My mother and aunt joked about it with one hand over one side of the mouth, as they were in the habit of doing with jokes that could get one into trouble.

For the move of summer 1989, I barely had the energy to accomplish the task of packing Kurt's and my disparate belongings into transportable bundles. I went through the process with a dazed body and a racing mind. My friend Laura, who lifted weights for fun, helped us load and unload a truck one day. But there were two days of hauling. Kurt shouldered most of the burden, and he did so cheerfully. I felt this was only right since it was he who had insisted on our finding a new apartment because we had been cramped for space and because he had reacted to the ceaseless moves of his early age by assimilating the strategy. Thus we had given notice, just before the telephone call from my mother.

In the week between our return from Miami and the start of my job we found a new apartment. I remembered from my first marriage that there were nice apartment complexes in Greenbelt, where rents were more reasonable than in Silver Spring and I could be near the university. We drove up Greenbelt Road. I spotted a nearly completely obscured sign to a complex. We liked their floor plans. We could rent more space for less money. We put down a deposit.

As I scrubbed clean the empty Silver Spring kitchen the day after Bastille Day, I collapsed on the floor, unable to move. I began repeating feverishly—in Spanish, I think: *Hail, Holy Queen, Mother of Mercy, our life, our sweetness, and our hope. To thee do we cry, poor banished children of Eve. To thee do we send up our sighs, moaning and weeping in this vale of tears. Turn then, o most gracious advocate, thine eyes of mercy toward us, and after this our exile show unto us the blessed fruit of thy womb.* Sometimes as I intoned it over the next few hours, I got stuck on "and after this our exile," which was the whole point.

This was the first time I had said a formulaic prayer since I stopped being Roman Catholic. But back when I had had prayers, the *Salve Regina* had been my favorite—because it spoke of exile, of course, and therefore felt mine. And in my prayerless fourth year of college, as I studied *The Golden Ass,* I had come to admire the *Salve* doubly because in its beauty and the pain of its voice it so resembles Apuleius' exaltatory invocation to the Queen of Heaven. On the floor of the kitchen that we were fast abandoning, I was as desperate as Lucius had been when he said his prayer from within a bewitched ass's body. Only I lacked an outward signal to warn others to treat me differently or to call a halt to the responsibilities of normal time. Wearing mourning had not worked. I was so haggard I had begun to look in the mirror and see my mother. In feebleness, I started feeling my parents' old age. I was a half-orphan, as they each had been when I was born. The world still expected me to function.

On 1 July I had danced on the Mall with Oshún, one of the queens of heaven, flanked by the Capitol and the Lincoln Monument. For the Smithsonian Folklife Festival the members of a *cabildo santero* had been brought from Cuba. They erected on the Mall of U.S. monuments a pink precinct for their Cuban-Yoruba gods. The *cabildo* was dedicated to Santa Teresita, the goddess Oyá, so they hung a banner with the picture of the lovely mystic Carmelite, St. Thérèse of Lisieux, her syncretic *santa*. They hung also an apron with patchwork, Oyá's own cloth. However, the ceremony to be witnessed would honor Oshún, goddess of the rivers and sweetness and fertility. As Nuestra Señora de la Caridad del Cobre, she was Cuba's patroness. It was her picture alone among saints' that my father carried for a time in his wallet. It was in the waters outside her exile precinct in Miami, impossibly far from her original shrine in the town of El Cobre, that my father's ashes had been tossed.

Cubans gathered on the Mall from what I assumed to be various, far-flung destinations. We drove in behind a group that was hanging out the back of a packed station wagon. Many of the U.S. Cubans present were *mulatos* or blacks, an unusual occurrence in an exile audience. Many of all colors had been initiated. At the time of greeting the elders of the *cabildo,* they rendered the initiate's obeisance.

The women in the troupe were dressed in gingham in the colors of their *santos.* The daughter of Oshún, of course, wore yellow. She was beautiful and her skin was cinnamon; she fitted, I would have said too perfectly, the Oshún type. I do not know how the *cabildo* could be so sure that the goddess would indeed descend to possess her devotee, but it was expected. The women danced with equal energy to the irresistible drumming, doing the steps of the different *santos,* some so masculine that they grabbed their groins in macho braggadocio, some very feminine and flowing. But only Oshún's daughter among them was said to have become possessed. As the drums beat a rapid tatoo, she ran into the precinct.

She reappeared later dressed in a beautiful golden gown and turban, looking like a queen. While the drums continued to play, those who wished to be blessed by the goddess were encouraged by the *yanqui* interpreter to line up before the platform where she stood. He explained that it was customary to place a monetary bill in her turban as an offering. Everyone else carried ones. I had already spent my one; all I had was a ten. It made my heart rise into my throat to think of dispensing with a ten when our circumstances were so bad, but I needed to be blessed. I stood in line with it in hand. Oshún rubbed those who came before her about the shoulders with a yard of velvet. Strangely, it was blue; I thought that was the color of Yemayá, the goddess of the ocean. Oshún rubbed a girl on a wheelchair all over her body, recognizing in her a greater need for healing. When my turn came, I was very nervous. I struggled to introduce the ten-dollar bill under the hem of the golden turban. Perhaps she gathered from the denomination of the bill that my troubles were acute or perhaps my grief screamed from my face or perhaps a divinity truly was present and knew my story. Golden Oshún, goddess of the river, began to rub me vigorously with her blue cloth of cleansing and as she did so she danced, so that she drew me into a dance inside the circle of her arms, and I danced too, raising my arms to hold onto her lightly whether I was supposed to or not (I do not know). We danced, in her beatific wave, Oshún, the pleasure-loving, trying to ease this sad daughter of Oyá in her watch at the cemetery gate.

I left ravenous for sweets. And all the way home I craved yellow foods: papayas preserved in syrup, dried apricots. I made rice pudding with sweet dried fruits and cinnamon, coriander, and nutmeg. I was so scattered for several days that I could not write, but I was not disturbed by it. For the first time in a long time I felt calm and refreshed. It did not last long, but neither do vacations. "You danced with Oshún!" Kurt marveled and marvels still.

The previous weekend, after an unsuccessful trip to the Folklife Festival in scorching heat and humidity, Kurt had accused me of bringing sadness into our household. I had then gone walking along a shoulderless, curving stretch of East-West Highway, tempting the furious traffic to kill me, as if suicide were my only inheritance.

## III

*We have to remember that we can't remember. My fear really is that memory is in exile.*

—Elie Wiesel in *Parabola* magazine

In 1989 the planet in its violent shifts and storms seemed to echo my own turmoil. An earthquake interrupted the third game of the World Series between two teams from neighboring cities. A devastating hurricane tore up Caribbean islands and Charleston, South Carolina; Cuba and Florida, however, were left unscathed.

Washington, D.C., on the other hand, steadfastly denies that it has weather and so it is paralyzed by snowstorms and crippled by summer lightning. Storm advisories and the first snowflake send suburbanites scurrying, for a one-hour trip can turn into a six-hour odyssey. On 14 June, Washington was struck by a freak storm whose onslaught coincided with the start of rush hour. Kurt was working in the city at Idle Time Books. He picked me up in my big, old burgundy LeMans after I got out of work. In Foggy Bottom and Adams-Morgan we had gotten only a hard rain and a lot of darkness. But on his way to retrieve me, Kurt heard on the radio that the storm, possibly (but not actually) accompanied by tornadoes, had caused extensive damage in other parts of Northwest D.C. and was tying up traffic on 16th Street, our route home. We headed for the Rock Creek Parkway through 22nd Street. But then, just in time, a radio bulletin warned us that parts of the parkway were impassable. In a quick maneuver away from the turnoff to Rock Creek, Kurt opted to take the Connecticut Avenue route to Military Road.

From the zoo on, we crawled along Connecticut. The farther uptown we went, the greater the flooding and apparent property damage on all sides. Intersections were creeks, trees were split, restaurants and bookstores dark. Prevalent among drivers was the unusual spirit of camaraderie that arises during the first hours of emergencies from our evolutionary encoding as a species that must cooperate to survive. As cars, unable to accomplish an amphibious transformation, succumbed to tide and current on Connecticut Avenue, blocking the lane, drivers in the other uptown lane let mobile lane-changers get in. I was thankful for my 1979 Pontiac boat.

Having reached the Nebraska Avenue corridor to Military, we decided to park and wait out the rush hour. From the zoo, a fifteen-minute trip had taken us one and a half hours. We parked a block or two away from Connecticut next to a tree with the thick trunk of many years' growth split asunder. Branches, once sources of shade, now littered the street, as did power lines. We stepped into the rushing water of the street with great care.

Connecticut, with its darkened restaurants and shops, resembled a set for a day-after-the-nuclear-war movie. It was quiet but for some somber and dazed survivors—and, of course, the line of cars heading out of town. Asian men in black and white waiter outfits stood outside their places of employment. We could not go in for a drink. "No electricity," they explained. Little candles shone inside some darkened restaurants. Some lucky customers who had been enjoying cocktails before the deluge stuck fast to their chairs, unwilling to give up comfort for an arduous journey that might end in bad news. Our mouths were dry. My reserves of $H_2O$ had collected in my bladder.

Sixteen blocks down from where we had parked the car, we found more signs of normal functioning. A Pier 1 was open, with electricity. We went in not to shop but to enjoy the possibility of shopping. Since downtown seemed to be the direction of light, we decided to take the metro from UDC to Cleveland Park, where we might eat Indonesian. The lights were on not only in the Ivy's Place dining room but also in its women's bathroom. We ate *gado-gado*. We drank Thai beer. We turned the emergency into a celebration, holding hands, now and then putting our arms around each other, joking. We were in a fine Sunday festival mood as we made our way back uptown to the car. Some lines from a poem by Edna St. Vincent Millay in one of my Catholic high school freshman English anthologies kept running through my head: "We were very tired, we were very merry/We had gone back and forth all night on the ferry."

The ride home was frightening. There was no light to guide us save our headlights. People moved like shadows, unpredictably, from our right and our left. They carried their own glowworms but their manner could not be discerned. Were they residents surveying damage, or were they looters or murderers on a violence-bent prowl? Trees lay in mortal swoons at haphazard angles on and off the street. A torn branch strewn in the path of the car might not be seen until we were almost on top of it. Standing water might conceal danger. Power lines hung off their moorings, swinging above us like snakes slithering from vines. We felt in our slow crawl that we were noncombatants trying to escape from a strife-torn city and that we would not breathe freely until we had passed all the checkpoints, all the contrary militias—Druze, Phalangist, Shi'ite.

For the property owners of upper Northwest the evening was a calamity. For Kurt and me it was a gemstone memory, a making-do in adversity, a party in a bomb shelter. But Kurt and I were together and we were both writers, and that is what we writers, ultimate pragmatists, do. We find the meat in the rot. We digest the dead. We are Old World vultures cleaning bones in towers of silence at the edge of cities so that the citizens may build. We are the turkey buzzards—the *auras tiñosas*—circling in the distance in every Cuban landscape, Saturday mornings with my father in our VW, my mother saying "*¡ay!* so ugly," I loving them because they were beautiful when they flew without moving their wings and brave when they dug their beaks into worm-filled corpses and took the smell of rot away.

The semester before my father shot himself I had written for a workshop in mixed fiction and non-fiction narrative styles a thirty-page account of the Cuban exile experience of what in the United States is referred to as the Bay of Pigs invasion. I told my family's story of those dreadful days, but I fictionalized it by calling my father Casimiro. I kept Miró's name intact because he was in the historical record.

Typically for a Cuban endeavor, the fragment was born of anger. Some months before, I had gone to hear a lecture given by a leftist literary critic on the novelist Don DeLillo. As the critic spoke of the bitter Bay of Pigs veterans who enter into a conspiracy to kill John F. Kennedy in the novel *Libra*—a work of fiction, I emphasize—I felt the critic's derision for our pain. Here was another gringo dismissing us as crazies. And at the time I was not familiar with Don DeLillo's work, but he could not know, not the way a Cuban could—especially not the way I could. When the opportunity came for the narrative to be written, the subject spoke itself.

But though the 1961 invasion did much to blight my father's life, it was not the blight's only cause. As I worked on my thirty pages with a May 1989 deadline, I realized that they were part of a much longer book, one that I would get to someday after I finished the one I was then working on, but not for several years. In the meantime, because my father's memory grew increasingly uneven, I would force myself to go to Miami that summer and I would interview my father, though I would not let my parents know that I was coming until I had absolutely resolved upon my trip and had chosen the dates.

The interviews were important to me. Through them I would try to put into some kind of chronological order the many stories that my father had told me about himself, narratives that for me, since I knew little about Cuban history except a fraction of what I had lived, were part of a fluid set of disconnected events without markers in the larger history of Cuba. I would save up to buy a tape recorder to help the interviews flow more naturally. I would be vague about what I would use the information for. For my own knowledge mostly, I would say, and it would be true that for a long time I had craved that knowledge for my peace of mind. Whatever book I managed to write, whenever I put my hand to it, I wanted it to tell truth—even if it was truth in fiction. My greatest certainty about my proposed book was that I would not be able to publish it until after the death of my father.

My father did not give me time to interview him. I was shattered not only because he went from us in a blaze of anger, but also because I feared that in destroying his brain he had destroyed my past, annihilated the reservoir of our family memory and my link to my history. He had aimed the gun there—though badly—at the head, at the repository of what I most had wanted from him.

In truth, my father's ability to remember had been long on the wane. I noticed early mild symptoms of this degeneration in my adolescence, but they reached a frightening peak when, in my early thirties, I asked my father for further details about a sister of his, named Julia, who had died very young. At least, he had once told me that there had been this Julia, besides the siblings that I knew of, María and Antonio. He treated my question as preposterous, as an invention. Julia? There never had been a sister Julia, leaving me to wonder which of his memories had been an invention.

A baker, the father of a high school classmate of mine, seeing on Calle Ocho in the mid-1980s a man he thought might be my father, asked him, "Are you María's father?" My father answered with indignation, "Father? María is my sister!" leaving the poor man in a state of open-mouthed perplexity. Afterwards, when my father saw his mistake, he laughed at himself. I failed to find the humor in his story—Peter denied Jesus, he didn't forget him—but I am willing to consider as a defense, though not a strong one, that no one in my family calls me María.

I was very dependent on my father's faculty to recall past experience because my mother's was frighteningly unreliable. To assay it was to walk on quicksand. Most often, my mother simply does not remember. My questions are answered with a shut door. On the other hand, occasionally my mother does remember. In a way, this is more unsettling than her lack of recall—because of the third possibility: the many times she thinks she remembers but, in fact, is creating a patchwork out of different events and her own fantasies.

I felt betrayed—desperate—when my parents failed to remember, as if they were keeping from me something that was rightfully mine. Without their memories, I feared, I could not be myself. I once suggested to my father that he engage in a systematic enterprise of remembering: that he write his memoirs, that he place within an orderly framework the tales that he had spilled as an old tree shaking off golden fruit in a breeze. He laughed. He thought I could not be serious. He laughed because he did not want me to be serious. No one would be interested in his life. He had tried other book projects, and they had come to nought. He did not say all of this. He just laughed.

From my sad trip to Miami, I returned to the chapter I had set aside a few very different days before. The most painful part of the task was changing from present to past tense all references to my father. "His hands were," not "his hands are."

I soon abandoned the fictional disguise. I could not bear to assign to other characters with alien first and family names our own experience. We had gone into exile with no possessions but our selves. Our lives should remain our own. If in keeping our identities I could not escape our pain through devices of distance—well, I could not escape our pain anyway. When I made the decision—and it did not take me long—I breathed a sigh of relief and plunged ahead into the great bone crusher, as my father would have called the task, *trituradora de huesos.*

From the moment my father killed himself, I did not have any choice about devoting my attention and resources to the task of writing about us. I became possessed sitting next to his casket. I did not take notes then, but I set out upon a mission of remembering. I had finally found my daughterly duty. My father had often said to me, "The only inheritance I can leave you is an education." I had been educated and had not known what to do with it. He taught me language and my profit on it had been to curse him from the distance.

Responsibility in Cuban culture is passed from father to son. It is up to the first son—who probably has been named after his father—to succeed in the world at least as well as his father. It is up to the son to fight his father's wars. The three top men of the Consejo sent their sons to fight in the invasion of Girón. José Miró Cardona, Tony Varona, Antonio Maceo, all three sent their young sons to be men. My father had a nine-year-old female child. There was no glory in raising a child to carry out the dispersive duties of a Cuban daughter: to marry, to bear children, to care for her household, and to set an example of virtue for the world (while contributing to the family's finances through a job that pays a decent wage). My father's vision for my future was monocular. I was expected exclusively and absolutely (remaining an undistracted and therefore unpolluted pillar of marble virtue) to exceed his success in the world—a goal I should be able to achieve without difficulty because I had been given the advantage of education. I prepared myself to be a writer, but to write what?

Proper disposal of the dead is also a female responsibility. Clytemnestra sent Electra to pour libations over Agamemnon to banish his haunting of her dreams. Antigone gave up her life to bury Polyneices. My mother and her sisters cleaned their mother's fresh corpse and pinned her into a lavender cocoon.

Now I allowed my father's obsessions to become mine. For all of my adult life I had hated his obsessiveness. I had seen him as an old man raging in a desert, an ancient maddened anchorite who railed at a world that did not hear. I feared that if I let his words reach me, I would become like him. I ran away. I longed to have a normal life, but I could not: I was his daughter. After the end, I decided to be his daughter.

"Alfredito is like a son to me," my father would say to people who called to pick over the latest grains of information about conditions in Cuban prisons. Alfredito's mother, Rosa Riva, called every Saturday; she would have called more often if my father had been home. Her obsession fed my father's. Alfredo Izaguirre Riva ranked second only to Cuba itself in the catalogue of my father's obsessions.

In January 1959 when he was only twenty, Alfredito Izaguirre was named director of *El Crisol* by his father and was put under the tutelage and care of my father, the subdirector. Together they struggled to produce an honorable newspaper while the government intensified its control over it, as it did over the rest of the Cuban press. On 4 June 1960 *El Crisol* was forced to close. My father left the country two weeks later. Alfredito remained.

On 19 July 1961 he was arrested at his apartment in the Edificio FOCSA for being party to an audacious and well-equipped plan. If the plan had succeeded, an attempt would have been made on Fidel Castro's brother Raúl's life, a supposed retaliatory attack by the Cuban government on the U.S. Naval Base in Guantánamo would have been faked, and the United States would have been armed with a justification for invading the island. He was tried on 2 February 1962 and given a death sentence, which was commuted to thirty years as a result of efforts by the Inter American Press Association to save their youngest member.

He was shunted around the government's principal political prisons: La Cabaña, the Isle of Pines, Guanajay, Castillo del Príncipe, La Cabaña again, and finally to Combinado del Este. He suffered torture, beatings, solitary confinement. Throughout he remained the most obdurate of the *plantados,* refusing—as a *political* prisoner—to participate in the so-called Political Rehabilitation Plan and to engage in forced labor. He knew he would one day be made to pay dearly. That day came at the Isle of Pines when, challenged by guards to perform labor for only a few seconds, he refused. As Armando Valladares recounts in *Against All Hope,* Alfredito was beaten into a coma.

This was the son my father wanted, this man of preternatural courage and principle. I gave up dessert for him during Lent; I said fervent prayers for him. But I could not be Alfredito. I had no courage for physical pain. My father sometimes spoke of what Alfredito and the other prisoners endured: compulsory nakedness, exposure to heat and cold, filth, vermin, bayonet thrusts, rifle-butt blows, and narrow cells barely large enough for a human. I could not survive that prison. I would not have remained in Cuba to commit brave acts of *clandestinidad.* I would have gone into exile before danger got too near. Exactly as my father had.

Sometimes I resented Alfredito because no one around me seemed to remember how youthfully reckless his clandestine activity had been; at other times, because I could do nothing that would equal his feats in my father's eyes. I felt intense guilt about my resentment because Alfredito's testament to truth and his fortitude in suffering had, in my eyes, made him a holy being.

Alfredito was released from prison in November 1978, and he left for Miami a few days later. I was long gone from there. My last image of him is from Cuba, one school day while I was home for lunch. Alfredito stood tall in the frame of the door to our Río Mar apartment and discreetly asked my aunt Nena for some pajamas for my father who, drunk, had crashed himself into a house and into the hospital.

In August 1988, after my summer of work and just before my first semester at the University of Maryland began, Kurt and I drove the Pontiac on a few days' journey to and through his native New Hampshire. It was not a good trip. It rained one night when we camped. I reached inside my purse and got stung by a wasp, a yellow jacket, for the first time in my life. Attacks on fingers hurt like hell. The rest of the time, Kurt and I argued. We tend to disintegrate on home ground, leaving the other in a loneliness not of his or her own making. Still, one cannot say these things to outsiders. The face I put on it was that we had had a pleasurable trip to the mountains and lakes of New Hampshire.

I knew I was taking a risk. There was a never-stated convention between my parents and me that I would use all my vacation time to see them. Only being in love could have emboldened me to break with this tradition. My previous method of circumventing it had been to spend leave time in my apartment so that I would not have to tell my parents I had time off—or not to take vacations at all. When I left Refugee Policy Group in August 1987 I took with me a hefty check for unused leave that had accumulated only partly because there was seldom a time when I did not have something due. I traveled a lot, but that was for work, and that was acceptable to my parents and my employers.

Because I got so little of it, I prized my rest time. I resented having to spend it with parents who did not seem interested once I was there. In November 1985, I took a week off from work to see them. They were living in wretched, isolating Mundy Street, in a low-income, multiracial building to which they had been assigned according to their place in line for HUD housing. The severe, fortresslike building stood in the midst of a neighborhood of poor U.S.er blacks so hostile to a light-skinned presence that when, ignoring my parents' earnest admonitions, I stepped outside the iron-fenced grounds, a passing young woman yelled at me, "Honky bitch!" and raised her arm as if to throw something more solid than words.

Acknowledging that I was on vacation, my father asked me if I had any special desire to do anything. I said that I wanted to see the beach. My parents put on some peculiar clothes for visiting the beach. My father wore dress slacks and lace-up shoes. My mother put on her little black chunky-heeled pumps and some stockings, which I hoped were only a reflection of her owning nothing like trousers or sneakers.

We headed for Key Biscayne. There are strips of beach along the Rickenbacker Causeway. "There is the beach," my father said with a wave of his hand. He seemed to think that was sufficient. He was talking of turning around and heading for home.

I said, "But aren't you going to stop? I'd like to walk on the sand a bit."

My father corrected me, "You said you wanted to *see* the beach." He was not joking.

But he capitulated and parked the car in one of the lots in Crandon Park. And looking very put out and angry, he walked the long stretch from the parking lot and over the mounds of sand on the beach. My mother negotiated the same in her little black pumps with chunky heels and her stockings.

"Well, here is the beach," my father said when we had gotten near the water's edge.

"I'd like to walk along the water a bit, if that's okay," I said.

My father did not look as if it were okay, but he resigned himself. My parents sat down on the sand, my father in his dress slacks, my mother in her black skirt. I walked a bit along the lovely water. I missed the ocean. I lived too far from the ocean. Even with the knowledge that two people looking like stray, deflated puffins sat waiting for me to return, I found peace in the water, into which I waded just enough to have my feet blessed by ocean. I was polite. I took no more than fifteen minutes. We returned to my parents' apartment.

We made another attempt at an outing. This excursion, to a shopping mall dedicated to conspicuous consumption, was my parents' idea. It was near them, in Coconut Grove—but in the trendy, rich side, not the dangerous, poor side. The interior of the mall was so blue that I felt almost as if we had dived underwater upon entering. We were a strange trio: two old people, silent,

bent, halting, uncomfortable, and utterly uninterested in any-
thing that was happening but angry about something; and their
apparent granddaughter who seemed to want to dissociate herself
from their monumental awkwardness by walking yards apart. We
made our forced march as fast as my parents could move, with-
out stopping to see anything, without walking into a store. There
was nothing for us to buy there. The merchandise seemed
designed for denizens of alien worlds, drug kingpins and rich
blonde women. It was embarrassing to be there.

Even as we walked, my mouth and mind grew sluggish and
my eyes closed involuntarily to hide the world. My emotions
retreated so completely that I felt cold. I was slipping inexorably
into depression. I know to be frightened of my depressions. They
throw me into a pain so deep and a pit so dark that suicide seems
a prospect as bright as a brass Christmas tree ornament.

In visiting my parents I had come into a dreadful silence, a
silence that brooked no interruptions—no casual comment,
question, or reaction. The cold, lonely silence that can kill an
infant mammal. While we sat in the apartment, while we rode in
the car, while we looked at the beach, my parents said nothing.
At first I thought we might attempt conversation at dinner, but
my father forestalled that. He always brought a radio to the table.
It was tuned to a Miami Cuban radio station. Throughout din-
ner we listened to a voluble man lead lively conversations on his
talk show.

The last night that I would be there, my mother talked to me
after my father had gone to bed. She told me that she felt very
isolated. They were so far from her friends in that apartment
building. And she could not leave my father to go see them; that
was out of the question. She could not leave him alone. After he
died she would see her friends, she told me.

At the airport my father said, "Come anytime you like." I
looked at him in astonishment.

During my visit I had clipped articles from the *Miami
Herald* to pass away the time. "I'm doing this for work," I told

my father. He asked me what articles I was looking for. I told him at work we were interested in anything having to do with refugees from any country, questions of asylum, social service issues that might affect refugees. The *Miami Herald* was a particularly rich source, I said. My father offered to clip articles for me. I was surprised but delighted. Shortly after my departure, I received a trickle of clippings from my father. One was an op-ed piece about the sad plight of old people living off Social Security, as my parents were doing. Another, from 14 November, was headlined "Abortion Distorts Title X Debate." The other was about a proposal in New York State to require AIDS tests of applicants for marriage licenses. I wondered how many hours my father spent obsessing about the possibility that I might contract AIDS and about what I would do to get it.

I understood little about the visit. My depression and my deep guilt about not being able to take my parents out of an unacceptable living situation distorted my view of the scene before me. But also I just plain did not see. Instead of seeing my father as mad—and therefore in urgent need of psychiatric attention—I applied Dr. N.'s analysis to his behavior. I treated him as a sane but neurotic man who had so much anger toward me, who wanted so intensely to punish me, that he would bring a radio talk show to the table rather than speak with me, a present, flesh-and-blood daughter who had come a long way to see him. I interpreted all of his behavior as rejecting statements directed at me, not as symptoms of a greater, deeper breakdown in reason.

In the same manner, I would take his death personally, as a message to me, a bullet to me. In this view, by shooting himself, he had rejected my mother and me with violence and finality. I railed violently therefore at his absent shade. It would take a more reasonable psychotherapist, Dr. Sch., to point out to me that perhaps my father's suicide had very little to do with me, that my father, from all appearances, had suffered a personality breakdown a long time before.

After my 1985 visit to my parents, I decided not to spend my precious vacation time on them. I did not know how long I would or should stay true to this resolution. Forever? Dr. N. encouraged me to stay away from my parents. "Why do you want to visit them?" he asked. He would only scoff at notions of duty. I knew that he wanted me to say that I wanted the pain.

My next visit was for free. I did not have to take vacation time, pay for my ticket, or listen to Dr. N.'s derision. Refugee Policy Group undertook a project to examine the special circumstances of elderly refugees. Old Cubans were a logical target population; there were so many. I was sent to investigate. I was to arrange three days of interviews with refugees and service providers. We scheduled my trip for Tuesday, 17 February through 19 February 1987. I could have taken leave that Friday and stayed on through the weekend, but I did not want to. I asked my father if I could borrow his car to go to my interviews. He said no, citing vague insurance reasons. RPG paid for a rented car as was its custom. It was one of the better visits. I had my own activity and mobility. I did not stay longer than I could bear.

I had lined up interviews to begin a couple of hours after my arrival. My last one of the afternoon was with Manolo Fleitas, the head of the Miami branch of the federal Office of Refugee Resettlement. For decades he had run the Cuban refugee program.

Manolo Fleitas sat, lord of his own office, filling his chair, filling the whole space. He took out a cigar and told me, "You don't mind if I smoke." Cigar smoke causes my windpipe to constrict most unpleasantly, but I did not argue. Fleitas asked me which exiled Boza I was related to. I told him.

"*¿Tu padre sigue tan rabioso?*" he asked me. Was my father still as prone to raging?

"He's worse," I said, feeling grateful to have this unasked-for confirmation of my experience from an outsider.

Fleitas swept his cigar through the air and said, "Your father is the only honest man in Miami." He said this with a smile that acknowledged that he was exaggerating but perhaps not by much.

For my refugee interviews, my father arranged a meeting at the Colegio with the aged or aging journalists who made up the executive board. Present were Laurentino Rodríguez, the *decano,* the youngest of the group; Roberto Pérez, the *vice-decano;* Willy del Pino, the executive secretary and the eldest among them; and Gustavo Gómez, the treasurer, a Mason who would die only a few months after my father. They sat in a semicircle, my father and the other men, in that office that was a temple to history, under the pictures of the journalist heroes José Martí and Pepín Rivero. I had interview guidelines on a piece of paper, but mostly I just let them talk. They spoke of the difficulty of acquiring a new tongue, of the financial problems associated with re-establishing themselves. They longed for the past, of course, and Willy del Pino, who had been a sports writer, brought out photographs of Kid Chocolate, a boxer he had managed long ago. But the journalists talked more of the work they had done in establishing a healthy Colegio, a well-functioning, expansive network. These were men who prided themselves in their effectiveness.

The previous evening I had interviewed my parents with the questionnaire in my hand. Without assuming the role of researcher, I might never have dared ask them about their lives. Perhaps, if I were not doing a job, they would not have answered so directly. They told me that the worst part of growing old away from one's native land was the loss of influence, the lack of contacts who might help, the absence of relatives and friends who might provide support. Having to start over in middle age, when their energies were diminishing, had been immensely difficult. Living in a strange country, with strange institutions in which they had not become invested from youth, rendered them weak. They felt powerless.

The cordial, animated men of the Colegio told me similar things, but most seemed to have retained their optimism. With one exception, they seemed to face their lot with a positive attitude. I noticed the contrast so sharply because my father was seated next to Roberto Pérez, who was a warm, cheerful man.

Among the men, my father was the bitterest and the coldest. Looking at my father next to his peers, I saw how odd he was.

After my interview at the Colegio, my father took me nearby to El Capiro shopping center where Gabriel de Orozco worked for a press. Orozco was an old journalist friend from the glory days of *El Crisol,* when he and his wife and two sons would sometimes join my parents and me and the family of another *Crisol* reporter, Rosalina García, our *comadre,* on our frequent Saturday outings. Orozco had been a strong, vital man then. But he had been thrown into prison twice in Cuba and spent ten years behind bars. His first conviction had been supported in part by the evidence of a photograph taken during one of our family outings.

We had been visiting Soroa, a center of orchid culture and the site of a beautiful waterfall. We had made a tortuous climb down slippery stone steps along one side of the fall. Then it had occurred to the men to wade out to some rocks in the middle of the pool fed by the falling water. My father had first attempted this feat with shoes and socks on. Later his long, pale, veiny, skinny, hammer-toed feet would have to wait a long time while his nylon socks dried on the wooden railing of the thatched-roofed restaurant. But while they were capturing the rock, the men were all full of bravado. Once they had landed, like marines capturing a very small island, Orozco, to add to the victory whoops, pulled out a gun and waved it in the air. What he was doing with a gun I do not know. The women certainly, but even my father and the other men must have found the presence of a gun at a family outing preposterous. Someone committed the imprudence of snapping a photograph of Orozco gun in hand. Holiday snaps may be used against you in a court of law.

The Orozco at El Capiro was a small, ovate-headed old man. Wrinkled like other old men. My father had told him we were coming. As soon as he saw me, he rushed to embrace me. And he wept. He just wept. We had not seen each other since those old days of weekends and antics. I had been a little girl. He had been virile, in charge, he had thought, of his life. Then he had spent—

did he say twenty?—years without seeing his sons, who had been sent into the safety of exile. His sons had grown up without him, but like him they liked to hunt. Naturally, he wept. And then, my presence a catalyst, he went into a fit of reminiscing about the times that had been important to him but which seemed, perhaps only on the surface, to have nothing to do with my father and me. With astonishing fluidity he swept before us the lively organized dances of his youth, the fine orchestras, the first sight of his wife, and his joy at being accepted. My father had little patience with the personal. But as we stood there in the reception area of an office, Orozco continued to let the protagonists of his youth and his regret glide before us like ghostly dancers in a line. Finally, my father's impatience would tolerate no more and we left. Of course, I had not asked the questions on my form.

That evening and what I spent with him of the next day, my father told everyone who called that Orozco had wept upon seeing me. It was a great marvel to him. My father never wept, not even on Saturday, 18 June 1960, when he left us standing at Rancho Boyeros Airport in La Habana, weeping after him, so that he could settle himself—he thought, in San Juan, Puerto Rico—before calling us out of the country. He did not shed a tear even when he hugged me good-bye, me who adored him, me who had always trusted him to protect me, and he could not have known the separation would only last two months. But of all the times when he might have wept, he came closest to it then. He said later that he had felt an impulse to cry, but how could he allow himself, he was a man.

The day after the Colegio meeting, I had set up an interview with a psychiatrist connected with the University of Miami who had done work with elderly Cubans. He was in late middle age himself. His parents were either very old or dead. We talked for some time about the intergenerational conflicts that are so acute in exile communities. The younger generations are not just different because they grow up at a different time; they are doubly different because they grow up in a different country. And if I thought things were bad between parents and children, I should think about the differences between grandparents and grandchildren. Sometimes the grandchildren did not even want to speak Spanish. But there were troubles enough between elderly parents and their sons and daughters who must work so hard and bring up their own families and perhaps did not have enough time for their old parents. He told me about one woman patient of his who had tried to commit suicide by swallowing pills. She said her son did not care about her anymore.

"I tried to explain to her that her son may not pay as much attention to her as she wants him to but that he has his own life with its own requirements. For example, your own parents." he said to me. "They probably don't like the fact that you are so far away, up in Washington. But if your parents complained to me that you live far away and they cannot see you, I would explain to them that you are doing what you think you need to do to pursue a career. But they may not understand."

I thought he was trying to make me feel guilty. I thought he was criticizing my lack of regard for Cuban duty to parents. I hoped my parents would not talk to him because they knew, as I did, that I was not up north to follow a career. My career had been sidetracked by a need for income-producing employment, and one can find such employment in most places, especially at my rates. I had my reasons, but perhaps they would not be sufficient for this Cuban psychiatrist.

That evening at 7:30 I took a plane back to the task (building a life) that so commanded my attention—and which I had also managed to botch.

I do not know what my research of February 1987 came to. A meeting was organized with other Washington organizations to discuss elderly refugees, but by then I was going or gone from Refugee Policy Group. Some sort of group report was planned into which my notes would be incorporated. I had interviewed old people and administrators at a project for the blind and the director of an old people's center. They hoped I would be able to do something for them. Some assumed that because I was from Washington I must be working for the federal government. They did not know the futile workings of Washington think tanks, the useless production of reports to be distributed by the hundred, the taming of lost youth and lost hope into guidelines for service bureaucrats. I am glad I kept Orozco to myself. But I still feel a little sick otherwise.

My past history of visits played no small part in my reaction when my mother said to me in September 1988, "Your father is very depressed. He would feel so encouraged if you came." She did not insist. She should have. But my mother is never forceful in her serious requests.

My first semester of graduate school was just then getting under way, I pointed out to her.

"Whatever you can. Even if it's a short time," my mother said.

I could see Dr. N.'s reaction. He would laugh, "You're going to cure your father's depression!" I knew I could not. I knew that he might barely take notice of my presence. I knew that being with him when he was so depressed might do damage to me. Going to graduate school had required me to abandon my cobbled financial security and now required of me all of my attention. I had been out of school for fourteen years. I had Middle English to tackle.

"I don't know when I'll be able to," I said to my mother.

She did not insist. But her words stayed on my mind. When winter break came, I was newly married. I could hardly leave my new husband or go stay with him in my parents' apartment, especially with my father like that. The idea of going to Miami to interview my father in the summer seemed the least unsavory of the choices.

I did not go before summer, and in summer I was too late. As long as I live, this will be the memory of the last time I saw my father.

In May 1987, when I was sent by Refugee Policy Group to Costa Rica to inquire into possible self-sufficiency projects for refugee women, I made a one-day stopover in Miami, where I must change anyway. Because my parents had little familiarity with airline regulations, I knew that I could make the one-day-only stop seem to be an airline-imposed limit. And after all, I had just seen them in February.

I arrived in Miami the afternoon of 20 May. During the first couple of hours the visit went well because I was full of stories about how wonderful Costa Rica was—how adamant its citizens were about democracy, how beautiful, varied, and protected were its natural resources. My father became animated, for a change. He liked stories of other lands. The sum total of spots on the planet that had been trod upon by my father were located in the western part of Cuba, a few cities and suburbs of the eastern United States, Puerto Rico, and the Dominican Republic. He told telephone callers what I was saying about Costa Rica with great relish.

Then I committed a terrible error. The fact that I could commit it is testimony to how I had lived the previous seventeen years, distancing myself as much as possible from the exile community, its strict orthodoxies, and its internecine controversies. I knew nothing about the consuming arguments that raged. I thought, foolishly, that as long as I opposed Fidel I was on the side of the angels.

However, at the same time that I attempted to maintain my distance from Miami, I burned with curiosity about Cuba—not the political system, with which I was all too familiar, but with the nitid sunlight of its days and the flowered fragrance of its nights. I wanted to remember what the breezes felt like, but I could only occasionally, when the right familiar wind got stirred up in Washington and transported me back. My parents could remember vividly the fruits they had eaten for over forty years, but my exposure was much briefer. What was it exactly that we all longed for? Therefore, when a scholar with whom RPG occasionally worked, someone who from the safety of a northern college town studied Cuban migrations, asked me if I wanted to go along on a group visit to Cuba, I said yes. He had begun organizing the group trip when moderate scholars at the Universidad de La Habana showed receptivity to the idea. He asked me to make certain that this was a good thing for me to do. Would it create problems for me with my father? He was not Cuban but he knew my exile community much better than I did.

I told him, "No problem. Cousins of mine have gone back for visits."

My father's cousin Onelia and his nephew Fernando had both visited relatives on the island, as had many other exiles. I did not see the significant difference either in the nature of the visit or in my condition as Ramiro Boza's daughter.

Therefore, the afternoon of my last visit to my father, I casually said to him, "I may have an opportunity to visit Cuba."

"What?" he said.

"Someone I work with is organizing a trip to Cuba."

My father sat up in his chair and shook his head as I had seen him shake it so many times when he disapproved of something that I, at the age of twelve, was doing. He shook his head and he covered his eyes with his left hand. I hated to see that. He made frying egg sounds. I hated that too.

"How can you go to Cuba?" he said.

My mother who had been in the kitchen peeked in. "What is she saying?" my mother asked with curiosity.

"She says she is going to Cuba!" my father answered derisively. We all three withdrew into our own individual silences and remained safely there through the evening.

The next morning, as I sat eating my breakfast, my father walked up to the table in an agitated state. "I wanted to say a few things to you," he said with labored breathing, with that catch that his emphysema or whatever gave him. "You cannot go to Cuba," he told me. "You cannot go. You cannot do this to me. Do you know what it will do to me here when people say that Ramiro Boza's daughter has gone to Cuba? Ramiro Boza's daughter, inconceivable! My heart! You are going to give me a heart attack!" he said, placing his hands on his heart.

And that I would not tolerate. "Your heart!" I said. "For years you've threatened me with a heart attack. That is blackmail and I'm not going to pay attention to it anymore."

My father jerked back, struck, and then he smiled ironically for a moment. His bluff had been called. But the tortured night he had spent with his excruciating imaginings—his daughter shaking Fidel Castro's hand? his own name vilified on the Miami airwaves?—remained on the table.

"Don't worry. I will not go to Cuba," I said. There was nothing else for anyone to say.

Therefore we were all silent that afternoon at the airport. As usual we were early. This was not a comfortable day for sitting around waiting in airport lounges till the time drew reasonably nearer for my 1:50 flight. I decided to go on to the terminal. We all stood up. My mother held her arms out to me and we gave each other a hug. I went up to my father. He stood rigid. His arms remained down, pressed tightly to his sides. I forced my father to embrace me. I went up to him and put my arms around him. He seemed startled at first. Without really wanting to, he let his forearms go up to meet mine. *Pro forma.* He growled something like *adiós.* I left for my long walk down the airport concourse. "When my father dies, I'll go to Cuba," I thought to myself.

The next Monday at RPG, I received a phone call from my colleague. "Why did you leave? We're going to Cuba in a couple of days," he said. "Because you weren't around we had to plan the trip without you."

He told me that a former (and, as it turned out, future) high official of the Immigration and Naturalization Service was one of the members of the travel party. Well, she could go and still not be a Communist, but I could not go; that was how things were.

"It's too bad you're not coming," my colleague said. "I would have asked you to give a talk about Cuban writers in exile."

I knew nothing about Cuban writers in exile; Irish writers of the early twentieth century I could have done; Argentineans in and out of libraries maybe. I told my colleague none of my problems. With enormous thankfulness at not joining him, I wished him a good trip. "When my father dies, I'll go to Cuba. Only then will I be free," I thought to myself.

Dr. N. thought it a sign of my father's paranoia that he feared that people in Miami would know that his daughter had visited Cuba. On the contrary, my agreement with Dr. N. that my father's thinking was distorted was a sign of how distant I had become from the way things operated in Miami and in Cuba. My trip would have been known. Cuba would have publicized it—not because of me, but because of my father. Miami would have heard it. My name would have been written in the exile book of the damned and my father would have been pilloried, my father who had lived a life of political purity with only private stains. So much was at stake in a one-week trip to see Cuban sky and maybe even my aunt. I understand this now—but not then.

I have not gone to Cuba and I will not go to Cuba, not even now that my father is dead—not until the government changes. It is possible that my heart-clutching father did not believe me when I said I would not go. He believed firmly in his honor but not in mine. I thought that he might sometimes torture himself with fears of my sneaking off to Cuba in between our Saturday phone calls. Already in his mind I was a traitor, a daughter one does not embrace.

# The Realm of
# the Hungry
# Ghosts

For the first six months after my father's death I was afraid I would be visited by his ghost. Terror gripped me as I sat in my parents' bathroom at night a few days after his suicide. My mother kept a night light on all the time, but I also turned on the lamp above the bathroom mirror. The rusty brown traces of my father's blood where the small tiles joined were there, light or no, beheld or not. When one afternoon my husband touched me in the shower, I stared at him wide-eyed with disbelief. My father might be on the other side of the curtain. I said to Kurt, "Please, no."

My mother was firm in her desire to remain in the blood-stained apartment. She would banish memories. She did not entertain the possibility of ghosts, the supernatural having very little relevance to her life. Yet when suicide occurs, some expect that ghosts will come.

My freshman year in Barnard's Reid Hall dormitory, we roomed by twos, and when a boyfriend from out of town came to visit, the girl's roommate politely searched for another empty bed. Several months into the school year, I was told by my Chinese Jamaican floormate Beverly that she never had and never would spend the night in my room because a previous tenant had committed suicide. I had never before encountered this fear of revenant suicides, but afterwards, on some nights, I thought about the girl who had jumped off a campus building—or so Beverly said.

You would think that suicides, of all people, would rejoice upon entering the death they took such pains to secure and would steadfastly remain within its kingdom. Yet many will not buy a house if it has a connection with an old, bad death. We assume that suicides will not leave us alone. They leave us with blood to mop up and threads to weave back into the cloth of lives. They leave us with unfinished business in sleepless nights.

"And again, for fugitive, to life condemned," posited José Martí mercilessly in one of the more conventional pieces of his generous, revolutionary existence—revolutionary in poetry as well as politics. Some scholars mark the publication in 1882 of his collection *Ismaelillo* as the beginning of Modernismo, a movement that would infuse new life into the Spanish language and would, for the first time, create a truly Latin American literature.

Professor José Olivio Jiménez, who taught us Spanish American literature one fortunate semester at Barnard, was the first to introduce to me the notion—"some critics have the view," he said—that perhaps José Martí's death was a kind of suicide. It was as stunning a revelation about a national, quasi-mystical hero as his other one, that Martí, *el Apóstol,* fathered a daughter by the wife of an invalid.

Did Martí admit to himself the nature of the death that he sought? He had written that self-killing would doom a soul to return "like uprooted oak from high Erebus." Perhaps he wanted to return—as strong as a tree, to see the job through to the end.

Soon after my father's death, I found the ragged poem in a volume that my father had given me years before of José Martí's complete poems, edited by Zamora in Buenos Aires. The poem was part of Martí's collection *Flores del destierro,* or *Flowers of Exile,* left as a manuscript until 1933. Its title, "To a Classicist Who Spoke of Suicide," suggests to me that Martí went to his room and attempted to get a troubling meeting out of his system, then painfully dedicated his efforts "To a battered old man."

> *Let the good Christian awaken*
> *the slumbering kiss,*
> *take in hand the deadly iron,*

*but not toward his temple, insane,*
*but toward earth, converted into plow.*

*Look at yourself, by the floor*
*the vast skull broken,*
*dyed in your blood the modest veil*
*of your daughters, and to the thicket*
*the body thrown, and to heaven, the opaque soul.*

*And I look at the shining*
*lord, dressed in ire*
*and the flash of lightning, his brow*
*cloud with burning gold*
*and down from heaven hurl the impatient one.*

*And like uprooted*
*oak from high Erebus*
*look at yourself by the winds dragged*
*and torn apart and again,*
*for fugitive, to life condemned.*

*For how in the delicious*
*still waters of death*
*can equal right to peaceful rest*
*be claimed by the strong soul*
*and the cowardly, the reprobate and the meek?*

Like many other men of action, my father paid too little attention to poetry.

For Martí, "night is the propitious friend of verses," for then "serpents, by day entwined round thought, sleep." His days were spent in journalism; his evenings, in patriotic meetings. Only at night was he free to abandon himself to the great, high madness of connections and the frustration of words. He so welcomed this liberation of a caged self that he wrote, *"Dos patrias tengo yo:*

*Cuba y la noche."* Beyond Cuba and night, I have a third country; I sometimes fear that to have so many is to have none.

Did Martí sleep, I wonder. How could he have enough time to allow the stimulation of work to flatten and let sleep in before his many duties tugged him to start his day? When great matters press, sleep flees from us.

Even under the best of circumstances, I have a tendency toward nocturnal insomnia. My brain waits for the quiet of night to give me its occasional gift of exaltation or, at the very least, the pleasures of a book. If my brain is troubled, it is at night that it sings to me its shrillest songs, the ones that cause me to pace inwardly. After my father's death, I became the enemy of fickle, slighting sleep. I was loath to enter a state in which my control would be minimal and anything might visit me. Sometimes two shots of dark *ron* Bacardí, even three, mixed with Sominex had no effect on me. I just had to ride the wave of anxiety and take notes. Sometimes the wave was rage.

I became a creature of night who was afraid of the dark. The first months after his death, I expected to find my father waiting in the rooms of our apartment. I did not, as had been my wont, enter the bathroom in the dark. I stood at the threshold and reached inside to flip the light switch to "on." I expected a cold hand to grab mine as I did so. I envisaged bloodstains in front of my sink in Maryland. I turned on the light and my bathroom was a normal bathroom with toilet paper and soaps and contact lens solutions, and nothing outré was within. In the light, my kitchen contained a cherry dining table and a white bookcase that held a clay tea set given to me by my husband on my birthday, cheerful bowls, varied cookbooks, a tiny willow basket Kurt and I had bought on our wedding night. To walk into my study at night required me to draw on my reserves of courage, for it was in the study that I wrote most intensely about him. I feared he would be there to tell me what he thought of what I was saying. Yet, when illuminated, my study was comfortably messy with the papers that I had strewn about and the books I had piled up and the yellow notes I had stuck onto the frame of my computer screen. I was forced by reason to assume that the dark contained the same as the light. Nothing unusual lurked in my rooms. I was the one who was haunted.

My mother too could not sleep. Perhaps she feared dreams she could not remember. Her regular doctor sent her to a psychiatrist who, because she was on Medicare, would only see her once every three months. He prescribed several expensive pills that, of course, were not paid for by Medicare. My mother decided that there was nothing wrong with her. "It is what I went through, " she told me. She stopped seeing the shrink, did not buy more pills, and just waited out the bad time.

Three weeks after my father's death, toward early morning, I dreamed that I was walking down a long path and that other people were walking it too. It was important that I keep going until I had reached the object of my journey, although I was not certain what that was.

Suddenly, from far behind me, I heard my father's voice. "Come get me," he commanded.

I turned in the direction of his voice and saw him. He was a bent old man standing in mist in an offshoot path that looped endlessly from a place I had passed long ago.

I knew that if I went to him I could be trapped, but I was moved by his pathos and pulled by my guilt. Then I remembered something important. Without leaving my place, I said firmly to my father, "You're dead."

With a look of resignation, he vanished. I continued my journey.

One day in September, after the university semester had started, I slept in the afternoon and I dreamed that I was lying awake on my bed. Outside my bedroom window, my father floated like a tethered balloon. The blinds were drawn over part of the window, so I could only see arms and a sky-blue short-sleeved shirt. They were his arms and his shirt, and even after I had truly awakened I found it difficult to shake the feeling that my father's ghost floated outside my window.

The Tibetan *Bardo Thötröl* seeks to guide you, child of noble family, in your transition through the choice-replete threshold from this life to the next. It warns you that a dim yellow light will glow, calling to the desire within you, speaking to your unspoken needs. If you go to it, you will be cast into the realm of hungry ghosts, where you will suffer with constant hunger, endless thirst, without possibility of satisfaction.

In Singapore the hungry ghosts are given their own festival. For thirty days each year, ghosts roam the world. They visit their relatives, smell the joss sticks, admire the candles, look at the food.

In *santería,* the ghosts of ancestors get hungry from time to time. They must be given drinks of water, coffee, and rum. Cuban dishes are prepared for them, but without salt. The ghosts like candles and flowers with the offerings. They demand a good cigar.

Living people with backyards can leave food for the dead in the bowls formed by the roots of trees. The only place inside a dwelling where the dead will eat is the bathroom. Until recently, elimination was performed in detached structures, at a more proper distance for crotchety relatives and souls that should be departed.

The dead, however honored and missed, disrupt the living with their demands. In Cuba, through *santeros,* they asked for Masses, Gregorian ones, no less. The request may not seem onerous, compared, say, with Hamlet's father's, but it was difficult if all you had was a menial job. The dead take no account of the vicissitudes of living.

It must be said that the dead do not chew with teeth, a distinction recorded by their ethnographer Lydia Cabrera. They eat the spirit of the food.

I was afraid that my father was hungry. I was afraid that if we stood before each other, by the force of his need he would suck from me my plasma, my life, and I too would become a hungry ghost. In nights of my sharpest panic, I did not imagine he would do that. What I feared then was that he would approach me meekly in his form of a bent old man and say, "I will tell you the truth."

In my twenties, I wrote this:

> *Dracula counted himself*
> *a man of breeding*
> *a sensitive man*
> *a lonely man*
> *who asked only*
> *for a few moments' company,*
> *a tender neck, and a quick*
> *puncture.*
> *Yet superhuman effort was required*
> *to catch a live one*
> *who would not produce*
> *in the dark some phrase*
> *or gesture or superstitious artifact*
> *revealing*
> *to the detriment of his desire*
> *a loathsome antique prejudice*

*against empty veins*
*and fear of dawn.*
*In unconsummated death he pierced*
*flesh with*
*(for a lover)*
*strange exponential passion*
*not to make of two one*
*but of one*
*thousands,*
*thinking immortality of sorts*
*a thing to be passed on*
*and indeed having no choice*
*in his chemistry's needs*
*he spread through blood*
*like a disease*
*his doom to failure*
*the thirst of his insatiable desire*
*—such a need, such a desire*
*that must through centuries*
*drink and drink again*
*and lead a living race to thirst.*

My Hungarian psychiatrist of that era, Dr. G., had a special liking for me because I was an exile from Communism. In her home office decorated with woods and quiet rugs in a bucolic New Jersey suburb, I told her, "I am afraid I have inherited my father's taint." I did not know what the taint was. I showed her the poem. I told her that a phrase kept recurring to me: "I would drink my own veins' blood and coagulate my selves together for this lifetime." It had a lonely feeling. The words "when the friend is a whole universe away" kept playing in my mind. I felt doomed. I told her that I wanted to add: "and merely memory wrests from the night air his voice, distorted, the echo of my betrayed desire."

Several months after my father's death I had vampire dreams. A gigantic Dracula walked the street, and I shouted out to some women not to go down an alley where he waited.

"Beware!" I yelled, even beyond sleep, for my husband stirred and asked, "What?"

"It was a bad dream," I said, but I had difficulty convincing myself of it, for I lay in bed with an aching bladder and I dared not get up to empty it.

A later night, I dreamed that I was walking in a city and the sun was shining. It was a hilly city, for the sidewalks sloped. All around me, lovers were turning on lovers with new vampire fangs. In the eyes of new victims there was anger for the treason against them and self-hatred for what they had become. Strewn all over the street were new vampires dripping blood from their faces, leaning on their elbows, showing their teeth, looking betrayed and betraying.

*"El pez muere por la boca,"* my father sometimes reminded me. Fish die through the mouth. In spite of his delicate digestion, I saw him dive joyously for abundant hooks—in his younger years, anyway. Nothing too exotic, mostly Scotch whisky and good Cuban food, but in quantity. He rolled up his sleeves and dug into the *masitas de puerco* (big cubes of pork, to me) or the chicken with his hands. He got greasy up to his elbows. His face got covered with grease too. His hair hung over his forehead. *"Yo soy guajiro,"* he crowed the essence of his being. He was a peasant born—and proud of it. His origin was his strength.

A couple of years after our arrival in Miami, a Cuban fisherman cooked up a special fish soup and invited my father and some other men to lunch. When my father returned home, he went straight to bed, where he quickly entered a too-deep, snory sleep. It was not his habit to go to bed after a meal, since he considered it a dangerous practice: embolisms, he was certain, were more likely to occur. As he lay there, the smell of fish filled the bedroom. In fact, after a while the bedroom smelled like the point on Southwest First Street where a fish-processing plant and the Miami River coincided underneath a bridge.

When I said to my mother, "Papi certainly must have eaten a lot of fish soup," she said, "That's all the alcohol he drank."

She was right that he had also been drinking, for an alcoholic smell was mixed in with the fish odor. I was getting sick without having partaken of either substance. When my father recovered, he boasted that he had eaten *como un monstruo.* He usually said, *"Comí como un bárbaro."* The graduation from barbarian to monster was significant.

I had a different kind of bravado about food. I enjoyed the adventure of the undiscovered. As an adolescent, I was the one who asked for escargots as my father detailed for me, with a grimace, a snail's slimy trajectory over soil and rot. As a young child, I had spent hours watching snails in the garden and sidewalk in front of my grandmother's house, and I had come to the conclusion that they were cleaner than humans, for they even washed where they walked.

I was not put off by internal organs either. *"Ris de veau,"* I would order with confidence that a tasty meal would ensue. But I do not think that I could order *ris de veau* now that my mother's thymus has been surgically removed, hardened but whole like something to marinate and then roast with vegetables on a skewer.

On occasions when I asked for the most foreign item on the menu, my mother followed my lead with a girlish excitement at embarking on adventure. She worshipped progress and The New. She was an advertiser's dream customer. If a new detergent came into the Food Fair, its bright packaging proclaiming a great advance in science, she bought it. We went through many strange mixtures of ice cream, the most severely bizarre of which was aqua blue with butterscotch-colored (and perhaps flavored) swirls.

My father had suffered real hunger as a child. He told stories of an entire family of cousins in Las Cañas sitting around a pot of bean soup waiting for the spoon to come around because there was only one. The cousins fed him out of charity. The floors in the houses were bare earth. When my parents and I rode out into the country and I saw the *bohíos,* the thatched-roof huts of Cuban peasants, bordered by palms and circled by vultures in the air and by roosters on the ground, I felt a direct connection. This was mine, my origin. The hills, mine. Red earth, mine. For others, they were mere symbols to be manipulated to represent patriotism and Cubanness. To me the poverty of peasants was not abstract, but a knife that had carved my father's body. If I felt these curses and glories of Cuba as mine, how much more my father. A peasant is lost without his land.

Because he had suffered hunger, my father wanted me fed. The family activity from my childhood to adulthood consisted mostly of going to restaurants. My father "took us" to restaurants; that is how we viewed it, even though the bank account declared the money to be jointly held by both of my parents. He seemed to derive deep satisfaction from being our host. As he saw it, these were his principal responsibilities toward me: food, roof, and education. His mother had tried to provide these to him as best she could while she lived, but his father had been remiss with all.

One of my favorite ways to spend a Saturday was to go to restaurants in the countryside near La Habana where horses were available for riding and whole pigs were roasted on spits in outdoor fireplaces lined with fragrant leaves. There were two such restaurants that we knew of. I had a favorite; I preferred the sedate mare I was always given to ride there. The adults went for the food. The juice of bitter oranges and garlic, *el mojito,* was poured on the pigs as they turned. While I rode the gentle mare in the company of our *comadre* Rosalina's children, I thought of how the thick flesh of the pork would cook so that its surface would be brown and crackly like caramel while underneath it juices flowed. The pork *chicharrón* was the only part of the meal I liked.

After dinner, my father stood at the bar with Rosalina and her husband Miguel and any other men who may have accompanied us and he ordered a drink that was served in a cordial glass. It was dark in the bottom and was topped by a creamy beige layer and a maraschino cherry. He stirred it together. He let me eat the cherry and take a sip of the drink. It was sweet and still tasted of the cherry I had eaten.

In Cuba I was picky about food because I was a child and this is the way of children. My parents, however, somehow did not know of this characteristic in children, and therefore they saw in my behavior a particular curse. Every night I was fed the same thing: *palomilla* beefsteak (thinner and tougher than the U.S. version), fried potatoes, and fried sweet potatoes. The adults knew I would eat it and I knew I could tolerate it. The adults did not feel their efforts at varying my diet had paid off. My father spoke of trying to get me to eat ground meat by buying expensive cuts, though by the age of seven, I did not remember this incident and wondered how many years had passed since its occurrence. If I rejected a food once, it was never tried again. If something succeeded and was easy, it was resorted to all the time.

My parents and other relatives worried because I was skinny (by their standards). My uncle Rafael González de Mendoza, my mother's sister Cuca's husband, often said that I was going to stretch like elastic: the taller I got, the skinnier I would get. To forestall this possibility, I was prescribed by my pediatrician many supplements, including vitamin B complex, all to be administered by injection. The last such lovely series was described to me by my mother as containing peanut oil. At the age of eight, I was already showing signs of an early onset of puberty, and my Cuban mother and my Cuban pediatrician agreed that I must not face such bodily changes while thin.

I was terrified of all sharp metal objects designed to puncture the human skin. I fainted at blood tests; I still faint at blood tests. The administrat of my many series of injections was poor Tía

Nena, who must have cursed the day she took basic first-aid training and learned how to use a syringe. As I considered that any one injection could prove to be lethal and as, at any rate, I knew how to postpone the unpleasant moment, I insisted on kissing every loved one good-bye before each shot. Because the injections were usually administered at my grandmother's house, there were frequently a lot of people to bid fond farewells. Then, of course, I had to say my prayers—and I knew a lot of prayers. Finally, when my patient Tía Nena could stand it no more, I lay down on the bed she shared with my grandmother, exposed my buttocks, clenched my teeth, and got set to scream, for, in truth, the injections hurt.

I might have been less skinny if only I could have eaten of my then favorite cuisine, Chinese, every day, but unfortunately it was reserved for occasional treats, when my father took us to El Mandarín, a restaurant across the street from the Havana Hilton, whose sign I could see from our usual table. I once wondered aloud why a misspelling of Habana had been put up in large letters on a building. My father told me that our city's name was written differently in English. I thought that we ought to know best how to write the name, in our language, in our city. The hotel disturbed me.

The interior of El Mandarín was pink and elegant and serene, cushioned from the convulsions of the world, as establishments catering to well-to-do tourists usually are. Male customers' success in the rough world was attested to by well-tailored suits and silk ties. Sometimes we saw groups of Chinese men eating out of bowls that they held close to their faces. I was fascinated with the chopsticks, which to me seemed to be made of ivory; my parents told me they were ivory. Among dishes, my principal choice was the wontons; they must be ordered every time. I also liked the duck with almonds. But to me the food only delayed, almost unbearably, the best part of the meal: the ritual at the end. For then in a black box with a scrollwork ivory-colored top, the waiters brought us each a hot, steaming towel fragrant with a scent that was at once clean and flowery. I covered my face with the towel and breathed in the hot perfume. One day, at the end of our meal, two of the restaurant men in suits—owners or managers—brought me a set of chopsticks and one of the black and ivory scrollwork boxes in which they carried the towels. They bowed and smiled with the enjoyment that adults take in children.

"For you," they said.

They were giving me a gift. I was very excited, and as usual, when someone was showing generosity to me, I was also confused.

"They're giving me these things!" I said to my parents, hoping for clarification.

These were precious objects to me. The only thing the restaurant men had not given me was the scent.

With a sentence, my father banished generosity from the room. He said, "They'll be getting it out of my bill, one way or the other." *Praise God from whom all blessings flow. Praise Him all creatures here below. Praise Him above ye heav'nly host. Praise Father—*

On Broadway a few blocks from Barnard was a Cuban Chinese restaurant where I ate often during my freshman year. A bright green awning welcomed patrons in, but the food was greasy and the formica-table decor unappetizing. A couple of the waiters said they had worked at El Mandarín. After I stopped needing to cling to every connection with home, I did not return to the restaurant, for I found the downward trajectory of one of my prized memories too depressing.

Food should be either nutritious or cheering. I had a good appetite for sweets. During recess at Colegio Baldor—my first school, my Cuban school, my Ur-school—I ate jaw breakers, Life Savers, and candies hard outside but inside filled with liquid honey that poured out over my tongue. At home I devoured Vick's cough drops, a box at a clip. But my favorite sweets were chocolate bars. I ate a prodigious number of flat, striated Nestle's bars with an imprint of the manufacturer's name that could be bitten off one letter at a time. I ate Nestle's bars, never Hershey's. The ultimate treats, though, were the long Toblerone milk chocolate pyramids that my father sometimes bought for me at the concession stands of hotels. I ate them slowly, staring at their components: the pockets of honey nougat, the almonds. Milk and honey. I thought of Canaan.

My mother and aunt permitted my sugary gluttony, because, as they saw it, food was food and at least I was eating something. My many cavities did not concern them; everyone in their family—and, in fact, on my father's side too—had rotten teeth. For several months when I was eight, I was given chocolate ice cream every day for breakfast. From an early age, I hated milk in its undisguised form, but I loved ice cream. My mother reasoned that ice cream was a good way for me to get calcium. It was a difficult time. My father was leaving the country and my maternal grandmother was dying. Before, I had eaten awful gruels for breakfast but only because he sat with me as I tried to force them down. He came home from closing the day's edition at three or four in the morning, but when I got up at 6:30, he opened his eyes and tried to amuse me into eating as I sat with my bowl at the edge of his bed.

In a way the most special of ice creams was the plain chocolate or vanilla in a waxed paper cup that my grandmother bought for me from the ice cream vendor who pushed a cart and rang chimes down her isolated street. Sometimes, unpredictably, when she heard his chimes, the idea would strike her that it might be fun to get me a frozen treat and she would walk laboriously to the porch on her swollen legs and wave him over. She made sure to get from him the strange flat wooden spoons wrapped in white paper that ice cream vendors dispensed in Cuba. I ate the ice cream near my grandmother so that her smell—a mixture of soap, talcum powder, and warm wrinkled skin—would waft over me and blend with the smell of the ice cream and the wet wood of the flat spoon.

My favorite ice cream for flavor was the caramel ice cream that could sometimes be bought at Howard Johnson's stores. After the revolution, it became very difficult to get. Even in the best of times, it only came to me as an occasional treat, its value being somewhat increased by its rarity—but not entirely: I do still prefer caramel ice cream and I take it as a sign of irony running amok in the universe that though I have been exiled to the land that marketed that unforgettable caramel ice cream of my childhood, I am unable to find any.

Next to Howard Johnson's caramel ice cream, I liked the vanilla-with-chocolate-swirl that one could buy from the ice cream truck that broadcast a jingle in front of Río Mar. The chocolate of the chocolate swirl seemed almost solid. Another ice cream novelty to which I was partial was coconut ice cream that came packed inside a piece of coconut husk. A lot of fruit ice cream was made in Cuba, especially by the Chinese. My mother moaned with nostalgia after the ice creams from the *puestos de chinos,* or Chinese stands. Well, I do not know if she was sneaking in some ice cream without my knowing it or if all of those memories are from before my birth, but I do not remember having been taken to eat fruit ice cream at a Chinese stand.

My indifference toward everyday, Cuban, non-sweet food created problems between my mother and me. My mother thought that I refused to eat in order to persecute her. She did not do the cooking—the maid did—but she took my pickiness personally. One lunchtime, I stabbed at the fried egg before me and inflated my cheeks as I did when I did not want to eat—*hacer globito,* my father called it, "to make a little balloon." Eggs tend to be a problematic food for children. But to my mother, my attitude was an affront. My mother's rage was like a windstorm suddenly stirred up. She pulled me off my chair and slapped and slapped my body while screaming at me, and I was terrified that she might not stop until she had killed me. When she did stop, I realized I had nothing left to lose. I did not eat the egg. And I felt all the more powerful for it.

When we went into exile and my father impressed upon me the direness of our financial situation, I willingly ate almost anything placed before me. I felt guilt for my past sins of pickiness. My mother had never cooked before exile. She found herself in Miami with no one to guide her. She felt deeply motherless. For once I understood her. Within the limits of my youth, I was cooperative. Finally, I made one exception. I announced that I did not want to eat chicken anymore. I said I did not like chicken. I could not explain it at the time, but on these chickens that my mother was preparing the blood and vessels were still visible. I gagged as I ate them. They were nothing like the fried chickens from El Caporal that we sometimes bought on long rides on the Carretera de Rancho Boyeros toward the airport. I had especially loved the breaded, fried livers. True to my predilection for internal organs, my favorite part of the chicken was its hard, muscular heart.

Many Cuban children had trouble adjusting to the U.S.-style food served up by the Riverside Elementary School cafeteria. I took to it right away. School fare at least had more cookery experience behind it than my mother's experiments, although some of the school's results, especially the spinach that dripped with the water it had been overboiled in, remained dubious. To me the school lunch was worth every penny of the twenty-five cents it cost. I was at first apprehensive about not returning home at midday, but my father told me that was the way things were done in the United States.

In Cuba, at Colegio Baldor, it had been otherwise. In kindergarten we had only had half days; my parents signed me up for the morning session. Although this may have been an early attempt at shoe-horning me into the mold of a day person, it nevertheless felt good to come home at lunchtime and have the rest of the day free to go on interesting excursions with my father or to stay at home with my aunt Nena, who was my paid baby-sitter every workday from midday till my mother returned in the late afternoon. In *preprimario* (which followed kindergarten) and in first grade, the school's white Number 11 bus picked me up in the morning and brought me back early enough for me not only to have lunch but, before that, to be bathed by Nena. After I had eaten, she took me downstairs to the Río Mar's entrance to wait for the afternoon pick-up. On the Number 11, the driver (man) and the peace-keeper (woman)—I cannot think of the given title of her post—were demonstratively warm-hearted. I thought the driver handsome enough to be in movies.

When we moved to El Nuevo Vedado, near my grandmoth-er, school conditions turned more unpleasant. The driver and peace-keeper of the Number 29 bus were indifferent. What was worse, I was the penultimate child to be dropped off at lunchtime. The bus meandered over hilly territory, and by the time I got to our apartment I was nauseated. The bus attempted to pick me up again not long after I had stumbled out of it, reeling.

I say the bus *attempted* to collect me because very often I refused to return to school, dramatizing for the adults present how sick I felt. Once when my father was home at midday, he threatened that if I did not get on the bus and he and my aunt took my temperature and I did not have a fever, I would be pun-ished. I was in fact pale, as humans invariably get when they are suffering from motion sickness. The thermometer went duly under my armpit. *Axila*—I loved the genteel name for armpit. Thirty-seven degrees, read the answer—that is, 98.6 Fahrenheit, exactly normal.

"Well, 37 is a slight fever in children," my father stated with blessed inaccuracy.

I was sent in for another round of doctor visits, the obvious in my case, that some people are prone to vertigo, being too simple an answer. My parents, who attended school only while they were very young and were still trying to be good children, would not on my behalf go up against the authority of school administrators and complain about even something so minor as a long ride for a little girl, much less about what was more profoundly the matter. My parents were not sophisticated enough in the ways of children to read in my extreme reluctance to return to school for afternoon session some hidden, powerful reason that had nothing to do with bodily disease and everything with emotional discomfort.

After my journey through *preprimario,* class days at Baldor had been restructured to devote the entire afternoon session to the study of every subject, save religion and physical education, in English. The restructured curriculum was an amazing feat of prescience on the part of the school administration, for the first term thus affected, my first grade, began September 1958, three months before the triumph of the revolution. Each half day—Spanish-language morning session and English-language afternoon session—was taught by a different teacher. My Spanish-language teachers in both first and second grades were intelligent women with normal psychology. Quirks came with the knowledge of English and the ability to guide us through foreign textbooks to the world that our northern neighbors' eyes saw, a world of chaotic orthography and alien customs of snow.

My first-grade English teacher was a warm, pretty woman who wore her dark hair up in a roll and doted on me—a little too much. She used me to keep order in the class. She made the other members of the class begin each day by putting their heads down and me by standing at the blackboard writing down the names of all who did not comply. She thus put me in an unbearable position vis-à-vis my fellows. When I reached my limit, I felt that I did not have the authority to say, "I do not want to do this anymore." Therefore, trembling, I said, "My *mamá* does not want me to do this anymore." The teacher wrote a letter of apology and explanation to my surprised and embarrassed mother. My mother gave me an angry talking-to, but she did not betray me.

In second grade, the year of the meandering 29 bus, I fell into the clutches of an English-speaking teacher I would fear and hate. She was originally Cuban (either by birth or heritage) and had recently returned to Cuba from a long stay in the United States. I do not know if she had been keeping away because of Batista; I wish she had stayed away because of Fidel. She had a daughter, who was next door in the other second-grade girls' class—taught by our teacher's sister. The grass on the other side never looked greener.

The sister we had been so unfortunate as to draw as our lot had hair that was frosted some sort of fake grayish beige. Her most natural expression was a sneer. She was divorced or divorc-ing. In my kinder moments I attributed some of her obvious bitterness to that process, but then I went through it myself and I noticed that I remained a decent person. In second grade I did not know that all over the world children are placed at the mercy of adults with serious emotional problems; I only knew that she became mine.

A girl called Elaine (though she was Cuban) sat next to me. She was quite talkative. One day early in the school year, she was saying something to me when she was not supposed to. Students at Baldor were permitted to speak only when called upon by the teacher or at recess; even on the bus we must keep our speech to a monkish minimum of flow and volume. The English-session teacher caught Elaine and me talking and scolded us. I was very ashamed, because I had been brought up never to give anyone outside the family cause to censure me.

Suddenly the teacher said with scorn in her voice, "Look at that one. She's still laughing."

When I glanced up, I saw with horror that she was looking and pointing at me.

"Go stand in the corner. Let's see if that wipes the smirk off your face," she said to me.

A loud gasp went up from the class, for I had a reputation for saintliness. I went and stood in the corner behind a full-length, folding window shutter so that I was completely hidden from the rest of the class.

"All the way behind it," ordered my torturer, "so no one can see you."

By looking up from my louvered prison, I could see the lovely fanlight that topped the window. It was a feature of colonial decoration throughout Cuba. My mind held an image as if my life depended on it. It was of a photograph I had seen of a very thin seventeen-year-old José Martí wearing prison chains that had been applied to him by the Spanish for writing a letter. Our *Apóstol,* skinny, with huge eyes. I knew that students had been martyred by tyranny. Every 27 November we commemorated in a national day of mourning—*día de luto,* a day for hanging black crèpe—the killing by firing squad of eight students of medicine falsely accused of defacing a Spaniard's tomb. I knew that it had happened when Cuba was still a colony of Spain, the nation that left us, her descendants, little choice but to feel a fascinated, wounded ambivalence. The year had been 1871, but I did not know that; past time had no shape for me, and I felt that I did well enough to remember the date of my parents' birth and marriage. But there they had been, eight students, falsely accused, executed.

After a while—it seemed like a long time—a girl asked if I could please be allowed to sit down. It was Elaine. I do not remember if her intercession was heeded. When I was finally released from my imprisonment, I returned to my desk with a weight of shame and rage that left me with no power to concentrate on the trivia of the classroom. I thought only of what words I would say to the teacher at recess. I must clear my name. I knew I would have to maintain control over my anger. I would have to seem reasonable and respectful, though my sense of injustice was a rising wave inside me. I knew that in the contest between us she had all the cruel power. I rehearsed my words frantically, over and over. *"Señorita,"* I would say. *"Señorita,* I do not deny that I was talking, but I did not laugh."

At recess, I rehearsed and rehearsed some more. Finally, I could wait no longer. I approached her. *"Señorita,* I do not deny that I was talking . . ."

At that moment her sister approached from the other direction, and the bitch simply turned her back to me and began speaking to the sister, as if I had not been there at all, as if I were not a human being, as if I were a fly buzzing above the hard courtyard in front of Baldor's financial office. *Blessed are those who hunger and thirst for righteousness, for they shall be satisfied.*

When our first-grade English teacher, who had since left Baldor, returned one day for a visit to our classroom, she said, "Oh, I wish I could kiss you all. Especially you, María del Carmen. She's such a good student, isn't she?" she said to the second-grade English teacher.

I studied our crazed despot carefully. "Oh, yes," said her scowling face. I had noticed that teachers never contradicted each other. I hoped the yes had tasted bitter in her mouth.

One day during a spelling lesson she announced that she would give an award to anyone who could decipher what a man who delivered letters was called in English. *Postman,* I thought, but I dared say nothing.

"Come on. Can't anyone figure it out? A man who fights fires is a fireman, a man who works for the police is a policeman," she said derisively.

As she waited impatiently, she got more sarcastic. *"Mailman,"* she finally said. The way she said it was peculiar. I wrote in my book *mail-o-man.* Maybe her English was really not that good.

*Postman* still sounded right to me as well. I raged against myself for my silence when I learned at home from a dictionary that my instinct was, after all, correct. For thirty years I kicked myself for not giving my answer, as if I could have thus shown her that I was not someone to trifle with. On the other hand, sometimes I have thought that perhaps she would not have recognized *postman* as correct and I would only have provided her another opportunity to jeer at me.

It is odd perhaps that this teacher whose name I do not remember should inspire venom in me so enduringly and play this part of stubborn old ghost clanging her chains, disturbing my more desirable guests. It is not odd that I do not remember her name, since we called all teachers only *señorita,* regardless of marital status, as if they were not human beings but rather the respect that we must give them and the position that they held (sometimes in spite of clinical paranoia). Of the many *señoritas* and named U.S.er teachers, she alone remains for me a symbol of complete, capricious, abusive power. I learned important lessons at her hands. I never forgive the abuse of power. When I come across it, I vow revenge in the name of the child who dared not even wish, because she had been told in school such thoughts were sinful, that the pain in her tormentor's life would only be exceeded by the agony of her death.

In the eighth grade at Saints Peter and Paul School, I was assigned to the class presided over by Sister Phillip Marie, like all U.S. teachers, a teacher with a name, but, as with most nuns, a strange one. The brides of Christ carry odd married names and, at least among the Sisters of St. Joseph, sometimes the names of men. Of the nuns who have crossed my path, the one with the oddest, most sternly beautiful name was Sister Theophane: Sister Derived from or Pertaining to or Having the Nature of a Manifestation of God. The abstraction of her name suited her. She did not want to be in the world, but thinking about the world. Her thirst for study had driven her to accumulate many academic degrees. In her laboratory in the science building of Immaculata–La Salle High School, Sister Theophane, our antique, deeply wrinkled eleventh-grade chemistry teacher, bent her incongruously solid body over her retorts as lost in catalysts and vapors as a medieval alchemist.

Sister Phillip Marie was another matter. My older friend and neighbor Nely had idolized her when she had spent a year under her tutelage. I wondered about Nely. I could not hold a high opinion of any adult who stood firmly by the idea that the hated Henry VIII of England was called Henry VIII because he had eight wives. But never mind; I was accustomed to being more intelligent than my teachers.

On the occasion of 20 May, Saints Peter and Paul School planned to celebrate Cuban Independence Day in an evening program at the auditorium. At least half of the students were Cuban. We had put on a show for parents and parishioners on St. Patrick's Day also, and it was a strange experience indeed to hear the chorus of "When Irish Eyes Are Smiling" being sung with a Cuban accent. Perhaps even sillier was our pretended nostalgia for Galway Bay, wherever that was.

When I was in the eighth grade, Ireland was to me a green, shamrocky, distant land that kept the United States supplied with priests and nuns. Cuba, on the other hand, was ever present and most important. I considered myself to be something of an expert on Cuban matters. If I had any doubts, at home I had an authority. One of the non-nun teachers was Cuban. She was an unhappy-looking woman. Her husband was in prison in Cuba, or some such thing. She taught the other girls' eighth-grade class. It was her job to get us ready for the 20 May presentation. Away from Sister Phillip Marie and the U.S.-born kids, she rehearsed the Cubans among us in the Cuban national anthem. It was in this that the trouble lay. She did not know it properly. I did. My Cuban school had been thorough in its teaching.

One Friday afternoon at Baldor, after the weekly patriotic exercise of the *acto cívico,* to which I looked forward because I enjoyed the songs, poetry, grandiloquent dramaturgy, and historical patriotism, our eponymous founder had gotten on the public address system and justifiably berated us for mangling the words of our national anthem. It was not, he said, *"en cadenas vivir es morir / en afrenta y oprobio sumidos. . . ."* There was enjambment between one line and the other. The words really went: *"en cadenas vivir es vivir . . ."* In other words, to live in chains is to live submerged in affront and opprobrium, not, as some would have it, *to die* sunk in said shit. The much respected Dr. Aurelio Baldor did not phrase it that way, outraged though he was that Cubans, especially students at his institution, would not know their national anthem. It would have helped us to know what the hell *afrenta y oprobio* were; perhaps some of us later learned their meaning all too well.

Citizens of the United States are not surprised when people stumble over the words of their national anthem. Who picks these awkward, bombastic martial songs as embodiments of a people's spirit? My mother now insists that it was her sister Nena who frequently referred to the Cuban national anthem as carousel music. Well, while it is true that I sometimes confuse the two women since both filled the role of mother in my early years, I know that I have heard my biological mother make the comparison as if it were hers. As a child, I thought her/them disrespectful.

Anyway, the sad-looking eighth-grade teacher obviously had not gone to Baldor; she wanted us to die in affront, not live in it. I took things very seriously in those days. I found her version to be an affront to the intended sense. Moreover, I thought it disrespectful to mangle our national anthem in front of a roomful of people. I was extremely patriotic. Besides, I did not want to look like an idiot. I was very upset. When we returned to our own classroom after rehearsal, away from the Cuban teacher, I decided that I had to do something. Sister Phillip Marie had told us that if we wanted to correct a teacher, we should phrase it with respect and uncertainty, this way: "Sister, I think there is a mistake. . . ." (As opposed to, "You blathering imbecile, kings are not numbered according to the women they espouse. Have you lived all your forty years of life with your head in a hole in the ground?")

I raised my hand. I stood up as we had been instructed to do. "Sister, I think Mrs. ———— is making a mistake with the national anthem."

"How dare you suggest that a teacher is wrong! Sit down!" the nun screamed back at me.

Later in the afternoon, I did her some sort of favor for which I had been asked, and she said to me, "I scream at you, and then you do this for me," which I took as a kind of apology.

When I got home I cried. I felt the hand of injustice and tyranny again upon me. I fantasized about overthrowing the nun. My father too was angry: we were going to sing our most important patriotic song incorrectly and a *yanqui* nun—*una estúpida*—who did not know what was what had screamed at me for trying to prevent it. It was a family crisis. That evening at the radio station my father searched until he found a copy of the anthem I could take to school as proof, as I had asked. I put it in my bag, but I did not have energy for the fight. I tried to give my correct version of the anthem with utmost diplomacy to the Cuban teacher.

"My father found this copy of the anthem," I said. "Would you like to have it?"

She said she did not need it. I did not tell her that she did. The copy of the anthem rode back and forth to school with me for a few days. The evening of the program, we lived and died in our chains on the auditorium stage.

After my experience with Sister Phillip Marie, I learned not to correct teachers when they were out of earshot, but rather to do it to their faces. I took a special pleasure in this. Our tenth-grade purported religion teacher, who spent considerable time giving us lessons on how to sit, provided many opportunities. No, Miss Puello, Solomon was not David's grandfather, and, no, the Acts of the Apostles are not attributed to Saint Paul; the multiple-choice exam you wrote up is wrong.

Our senior year at Immaculata-La Salle, we had a nun for our first-ever boy-girl mixed religion class. The nun had the most equine head that I have ever seen on a human. She liked playing basketball with boys and the more masculine girls. At the start of the first grading period, she told us that the direction of the class was entirely up to us. We could choose the discussion subjects. We were mostly repressed Catholic adolescents—I myself was already a repressed ex-Catholic adolescent. The boys dominated the class, a dynamic that was proof of the need for single-sex educational institutions. The boys steered us toward a continuing discussion of what sexual arrangements we should adopt if we were stranded on a priestless desert island. According to many of the boys, anything should go. An Irish-descended boy with many siblings even defended incest.

When the report cards came out, nobody got an A. The highest grade was B. We were all angry, but during our first class session after report cards, students began their complaints to the nun by using tangential, groveling arguments, such as the need to maintain high grade-point averages for college admission. When the nun said, "I didn't think the class was discussing what you should have been discussing," I stood up.

I said, "Sister, if you had a specific idea of what you wanted us to discuss, you should have told us. Instead, you left it up to us to choose the topic. We shouldn't be penalized for choosing our discussions, as we were instructed to do."

Silence fell over the room. When they had recovered, my classmates began at first softly and then loudly to express support for my position. After class, they thanked me for having said what I had said. The grades remained as they had appeared on our report card, but we never again saw the nun at Immaculata–La Salle High School. Later we heard that she had suffered a nervous breakdown. I know it is not reasonable, but I took full credit. *Aux armes, citoyens, formez vos bataillons. . . .*

The public generosity of Riverside's twenty-five-cent lunch disappeared with my entrance into private schools. Therefore, I took my own lunch. My mother packed for my lunch every single school morning cold hot dogs with ketchup inside white bread, until I protested. She greeted my protests with surprise, "But I thought you liked it." Before the cold hot dogs, the lunch of every day had been cold omelet that started hot, oozing the egg-and-onion smell onto everything in my purse. The hot dogs were succeeded by bologna, I believe. At the school cafeteria I bought several ice cream bars a day, which came supplied in a phallic shape. I explained to the other girls at my table that I was sexually frustrated, a common explanation for things going awry in our Catholic high school.

I became a plump adolescent because my taste buds were starving. My mother reserved her innovation for the purchase of junk food, not only blue ice cream, but also daily cellophane-wrapped cakelike snacks from such nutritional nihilists as Hostess and Tastycake. Some of these specimens, especially the ones topped with shredded coconut or filled with jelly, were so sickeningly sweet as to be nearly inedible, but when I came home from school I forced them into my mouth and followed them with a dish of ice cream and several tumblers of Coca-Cola.

What awaited me for dinner was an awful thing to contemplate. The news broadcast for which my father worked in the evening at a Spanish-language radio station got advertising from catering firms, or *cantinas,* which flourished in Miami like weeds in response to the new needs of families whose women could not prepare dinner because they worked outside the home, a frequent economic necessity in exile. As part of their payment for air time, the companies gave one member of the newscast staff free service. My father, who did not eat dinner at home, accepted this premium on behalf of my mother and me. I am certain he must have used my mother as an excuse—so the *vieja* won't have to cook. There was clearly an economic saving to be derived from having dinners provided by strangers five days a week. And my father would not have to worry about his delicate digestion since he ate dinner with us only on Sundays.

Every week the *cantinas* delivered to customers a list of possible offerings for the following week from which we were supposed to select one dish in each of four categories, the last one being dessert. It was mostly a wish list. What one got was likely to be very different. At least, our dinners were always a surprise. Perhaps the company felt free to substitute in our metal containers whatever its owners wanted, since we were not paying for the contents. Often we got two starches; they had a tendency to look bluish gray; they were usually hard. Although we never ordered salad because it consisted of sadly wilted iceberg lettuce and little else, salad frequently arrived—steamed.

The food was packed in four stacked aluminum tins with loops through which a handle was passed to keep them all together. An aluminum cover topped the top tin and the stack. The containers were washed each night by the consumer and put outside the apartment door; in the afternoon they were replaced by a new, filled set. The caterers' preparation in quantity was bad to begin with. The cooks were not careful or skilled with spices or cooking times. Blandness was their usual standard, though occasionally weirdness prevailed. But the worst damage came, I think, from having the food sit for hours getting oversteamed during delivery in those metal containers. The food was a punishment for hunger.

Mercifully, there was no *cantina* delivery on weekends. For our Saturday dinners alone together, while my father worked at the radio station, my mother often bought frozen pizzas that were abundantly topped with green peppers, onions, sausages, and cheese. They were made by an obscure, probably local, establishment and still in memory taste better to me than most I have had later in restaurants. My mother heated up the pizza, and we sat together to watch our favorite program, *Secret Agent*. Patrick McGoohan, at least in his role as the stern principal character, was thought very handsome and masculine by my mother. The secret agent had an ice sliver in his heart, gave short shrift to women, saved his efforts for more important matters of Western security and anti-Soviet politics, dressed unostentatiously, and occasionally smoked a cigar. I too was attracted to McGoohan, while girls my age squealed over young singers with ready smiles, but I knew exactly the reason for my preference. I always imagined him wearing the dry sting of Eau Impériale, like a true man, like my father. Even his wrists resembled my father's. My mother, I think, has never suspected that some traitorous turn in her brain's gray matter would have forced her to choose my father, the completely wrong man, over and over again.

After several years of *cantina* dinners, finally one day I swallowed my guilt over the work that edible meals would make for my mother and the expense it would bring to my family. I told my mother I could not stand the catering anymore.

She looked at me with surprise. "But you had never said anything!"

Most evenings she and I together had disparaged the quality of the food in front of us. What I had failed to do, and did not realize I needed to do, was to say explicitly, "I do not want this." "I do not like this" was not sufficient.

We ate better after that. Even when we ate out of Chef Boyardee or Franco-American or Campbell's cans we were eating better than before. When I tell my catering story, I am sometimes asked what my mother did at home all day. The question has often struck me as strange. She cleaned the one-bedroom apartment. Once or twice a week she hauled laundry to the laundromat on Eighth Street. She did some sewing. Over and above that, my mother has appointments with the universe that we can never hope to understand.

"Cooking is an art," my mother said to me recently. When I was very little, she hired a housekeeper who could cook anything that was asked of her and give it her own touch.

"Her *mariquitas* were like no other *mariquitas* I have ever tasted. They were perfect," my mother said. *Mariquitas* are fried plantain chips that must be crispy yet retain their flavor. "Everything she made was delicious. She knew she was a good cook."

I asked her what had happened to the housekeeper. "I don't remember if she quit or I had to let her go. I don't remember. But she had the art. I don't."

I have known women so angry about being called upon to care for others that they have slung the products of their kitchens like insults on the plate, daring families and guests to partake of their ugly poisons. However, when my mother did turn to cooking—after the period of trial and error and under-cooked chicken—she produced some memorable dishes: lamb ragout full of turnips, carrots, and potatoes; *arroz con calamares,* with soft, meaty cuttlefish; Basque omelette bursting with shrimp and Spanish sausage. She insisted on obeying recipes, not trusting her ability to follow her nose, the culinary path of instinct. But to her credit, she found sources that respected the work of condiments. Many of the meals I remember were served at midday on Sundays, the only meal of the week when all three of us sat down together. Apparently, my mother did not consider just the two of us to be worth such effort; I was much easier to please than my father.

If we had dinner guests, it was almost always Sundays at midday. My clearest memory of those occasions is of my mother standing before the range stirring a pot of *masitas de puerco,* sweating, and looking miserable and worried. The smell of the pork impregnated everything in the apartment for a day. In my early adolescence, my father went through a stretch of such frequent dinner invitations that I developed nausea at the first whiff of pork. It was hence understood that I would eat something else.

The guests were usually my father's, never my mother's. (I got to invite a high school friend on a couple of occasions.) Often Papá's friend Lázaro came with his wife Lidia and their daughter Lidia Clorinda and niece Marta. The girls were supposed to be company for me, but I recall once hiding from the party even though they were there and I liked them. My excruciating menstrual cramps gave me the excuse to shut the door of the bedroom on the jokes and the liquor. The commotion was just outside the door, on the other side of a thin wall, but I was separate, in a pocket of calm. I could retreat to my cramps and *Wuthering Heights*. I learned that day to appreciate the strangely luxuriant feminine cave of withdrawal—comfort above all—and a good book. Because of later habit, however, it is Jane Austen whose image reigns in my mind as presiding deity of such occasions. I will miss my periods when they're gone.

My father palliated his guilt about making my mother work to produce Cuban Chinese fried rice or traditional *arroz con mariscos* at a hot stove in hot weather by announcing each and every time, apropos of nothing that had gone before, "Because, you know, *la vieja* likes the kitchen. Most cooks don't like to eat what they cook. But, listen, how she lives what she's eating. You can see it. She lives it."

What I had seen was my mother's sweaty look of anxiety during the preparation, so I once asked her, "Is this true?"

"No, it's just one of his inventions," she said.

Ever since then, whenever my father went into his "she loves to eat what she cooks" routine, my mother and I looked at each other and then shook our heads slightly.

What I hated even more than the smell of pork was the smell of the liquor that was consumed in alarming quantities at my father's dinners. My father always kept J&B Scotch in stock, sometimes Chivas Regal. Often he made delicious lime daiquirís. He made them very icy and very strong. He was resolutely unwilling to make a drink that was not a test of the recipient's abilities to handle alcohol—a test of machismo for men and women. If I had some, I usually stopped with one. I hated the liquor's effect on the adults, but most of all on my father. He got very loud and outrageous. He had to be the center of every party. He weaved a bit. What upset me most was the flaunting of his sexuality. Once when he was pouring a daiquirí into a woman's glass from the blender pitcher, some of the mixture started spilling over.

Another woman, the beautiful wife of a younger coworker, shouted, "Look, it's coming out!"

My father immediately looked down at his fly. "What a scare!" he joked. "I was afraid something else was coming out."

I was thirteen, fourteen, or fifteen. It was the sort of thing he allowed himself to say in front of me and to which I was supposed to react by not absorbing it.

"Oh, I can say anything in front of her," he responded if anyone pointed out my presence as an obstacle.

I was supposed to hear of sex and remain sexless. I was supposed to assimilate one standard for him, one for most of humanity, and another for me. He could say anything in front of me because I possessed no feelings.

My mother did not have many visitors. One Saturday afternoon, her former boss Águeda, a woman for whom my mother had great respect, paid her a visit. They had not seen each other since Cuba, maybe four years. My father was getting ready to leave for the radio station.

Águeda said to both of my parents, "I can't get over how much Carmencita resembles the daughter of a friend of mine. The other girl is older, but they look so alike."

My father asked, "Where is she from?"

"Santa Cruz del Norte," Águeda said.

"I passed a lot through Santa Cruz del Norte," my father said, and he laughed.

Águeda looked reprovingly at him. My mother was very embarrassed.

For me the joke was devastating. My father had indeed passed a lot through Santa Cruz del Norte. Not only was the Hershey mill there, but he also had cousins there. He had taken my mother and me to visit them on a day when the sky was as gray as cold metal and a great wind blew, filling me with excitement. The thought had never occurred to me that my father with his tomcat ruttings might have created half-siblings for me here and there as he wandered. I had looked up the word *bastard*.

I knew, mostly through the Old Testament, that men produced children who were illegitimate. Abraham lay with his servant Hagar because his wife Sarah was barren. But the Lord performed a miracle and Sarah conceived a child, although she was old. Because Isaac was born, Hagar and her son Ishmael were cast out. Therefore Hagar and Ishmael became eternal exiles.

I did not want to share my father. Either I was an only child, I felt, or I would be dead. I would banish the Ishmaels under my roof, force exiles into exile. Yet I was both Ishmael and Isaac. To Ishmael went my braver dreams of freedom. My Isaac had the angrier part: kneeling on piled stones and wood for sacrifice, looking back at my father's hand to see what weapon it held over me.

After Águeda's visit, I asked my mother if my father was serious about the girl from Santa Cruz del Norte.

"I think it was supposed to be a joke," my mother said, frowning. "It's an obnoxious joke, isn't it? And to say such things in front of Águeda!" Or me. We both hated the way he was in company.

We visited Lázaro's house frequently on Sundays. Although I was a teenager, I was expected to tag along with my father on his round of visits. It would not have occurred to my parents that my age gave me a right to a life of my own. After all, my mother accompanied my father on the visits to his friends.

Lázaro's family was all right. I did not regret having chosen his wife to be my confirmation sponsor. Their daughter Lidia Clorinda was interesting to talk to, older, severe, and imbued with a desire to get out of Miami. Marta was a bit more cheerful and flighty. It was she that my father grabbed one day when music was playing and he felt like dancing.

My father was not a great dancer. In dance his principal virtue—and his partners' downfall—was his energy. Even as he enthusiastically pulled a woman to and fro, his feet did a version of the *zapateo,* the traditional Cuban *guajiro* dance that, like so many other folk dances of European origin, emphasizes energetic flat-stepping with first one foot one-two and then the other, in a repeating pattern. My father's feet were long and his partners did well to beware. No matter what the dance may have been meant to be—to him all dances were alike—he employed a signature movement with the right foot: he frequently lifted it so that the calf formed a stiff, right angle to his thigh. This movement was particularly useful for swinging the partner around with great brio.

After her dancing encounter with my father, Marta asked, almost out of breath. "Is your father like this at home?"

I told my mother what I had been asked. "How can he be like that at home?" my mother said.

For us he saved his depression and his silence. With us he was stone.

At his wake the poetess told us, "But I can't believe it. He seemed well. He was always so merry, so ebullient."

"That was a mask," my mother told her angrily. "A mask he put on outside, in front of other people."

I hated the way he was with other people, not just his pose as wild man of the festival, the orisha Changó drumming on the *tumbadora* till the animal skin tears. I hated his obsequiousness toward his friends and toward bosses and U.S.er coworkers, all of whom outranked him.

He became celebrated for mixing a drink many found irresistible. It was a concoction of—as far as I can recall—rum, condensed milk, evaporated milk, eggs, and cinnamon. He did not add sugar syrup because he used condensed milk, though some people did add it and Cuba was the Sugarbowl of the World (according to Roget's thesaurus) and he was her loyal son. He did, however, add Scotch whisky even though it was not called for. He asked my mother to taste the mixture. When she said it had enough alcohol, he added some more. The potion had a French name: *crème de vie.* It lived up to the suggestion that it might kick life into those who were failing. It went down sweet, but, oh, was it strong. He made big batches of it and once took some to his *yanqui* coworkers at the Associated Press. The trouble was that his coworkers liked it and thirsted for more, and now and then he would feel obliged finally to give in and buy the liquor and make another batch, this time resentfully.

Because it was a sweet drink, he himself did not drink much of it. He wanted to please outsiders.

When I was ten or eleven, we were invited to a real U.S. Thanksgiving dinner by Ted Ediger, my father's boss at the Associated Press, and his wife Rae. They had invited as well some U.S.er friends, a couple. When we sat down at the table, Rae, trying to be a gracious hostess, asked me if there was a Cuban prayer of thanks that I wished to say before the meal. If there were Cuban prayers of thanks, I did not know them. No Cuban I had ever shared a meal with said grace. And even now that I am looser-tongued in front of strangers, I would not presume to have the right to dictate a conversation between others and God.

"No," I said softly, shook my head, and looked down.

When I raised my eyes, I saw that my father was glaring at me; I was being uncooperative with his boss's wife; I was passing up a chance to say beautiful words. Well, if he had been asked to say grace, he would have left them all with their jaws hanging, wondering, after so many gracious statements about generous hosts and distinguished guests, what had happened to the Lord. The U.S.er woman who was a guest said grace for us; she crossed herself, so I deduced that she was Roman Catholic.

I have no idea of what we ate, only that my father kept laughing at everything that was said by any of the U.S.ers, whether it was funny or not. At one point Rae began a sentence with "I recently had surgery," and my father's guffaw had already started when he realized, finally, that he had better step hard on the brake. He did not laugh softly. His laugh erupted from his chest, drowning out all other sound. I kept fantasizing about a hole to hide in. My mother had found her psychic hiding place and was eating placidly, paying attention to nothing.

After dinner we sat down in the living room. Ted Ediger and his other male guest were having a discussion I had not heard the first part of, but suddenly the man said, "That's like that book *Fields of Diamonds*," when my father let out such a hearty laugh that his eyes shut and he seemed ready to weep. He was still shaking with gasps of laughter and kept repeating, "Fields of diamonds!" as his U.S.er companions explained to him that they had been referring to an inspirational book. I realized even then that my father must be very uncomfortable finding himself in an environment in which he did not master the language or the culture and which was presided over by his boss, but I wished he would shut the fuck up; I wished he did not feel that he had to be the life of any gathering in order to earn his meal.

There were no further invitations from the Ediger household until Ted was killed out of state in a highway accident in his Volkswagen. A few days after his death, Rae organized a gathering at their house for his friends, a kind of memorial. My father felt honored by the invitation and he took seriously his position as guest at such a solemn occasion. No doubt even as he drove there he rehearsed the winged words whose eloquence would bring Rae to tears, for he could not say things simply. It would not occur to him to say, "I am so sorry. How do you feel?"

My father returned home disgusted. The people had chatted as if at a cocktail party. Even the widow was serene, talking with her guests, asking my father if she could get him a drink. I suspect he feared the same atmosphere would predominate at his own funerary observance. There never was a chance that it would.

## II

In Miami my father was nostalgic about the feasts of his Cuban past, nothing in the present equaling the succulence of memory. Lamb in this country was not good, he said. It was not served young enough. He suspected it was really mutton. He remembered eating baby lamb at its most delicious tenderness at his hangout in La Habana, El Uncle Sam. As he spoke of the *corderito,* my father rubbed his index and middle fingertips against the fleshy belly of his thumb. Although he knew a moderate amount of English even in Cuba, he pronounced the name of the bar-restaurant as if it were composed of Spanish words, with mourning-dove *u,* fully sounded *e,* and brief consonants. My mother sometimes pronounced it in English for the hell of it. But he hardly ever took her there, and then only with me. The glorious feasts of my father's intense memory were eaten away from us. They were political dinners, he said. El Uncle Sam was a watering hole for journalists and politicians. My mother usually had a sandwich for her weekday evening meal.

My father took me around to El Uncle Sam sometimes if he had to stop off at the newspaper on Saturday mornings, our time together. Everyone at the bar said how cute, and then my father was lost in a political discussion; its substance was beyond my ken, but not my father's forceful certainty.

He did take my mother and me to eat a meal at the tables of El Uncle Sam once. Many forks and spoons flanked the plate. I had heard of such places, and I realized with alarm that I was at one. My father said he would guide me, but the thin, middle-aged waiter, well-known to my father, of course, noticed my distress. He told me to choose from outside in. He had the severe look of someone who will not tolerate eccentric behavior in his domain. It was my habit to put those parts of the meal that were not edible, bones and grizzle, for example, up against my plate, on the tablecloth. The waiter saw me put a discard next to my plate. He would have none of it.

"The place for what you don't want to eat is inside the plate, at the far edge," he told me.

My parents agreed with him, and they repeated his instructions. I was incensed at them. In all our years together, my behavior had been given tacit approval through daily acceptance by those in authority. They never told me there was another way. I had to be told by a stranger. I was very embarrassed, and I never wanted to return to El Uncle Sam.

Like my father, I have carried around with me my vivid memories of food not experienced since Cuba. When I learned that I would go to Costa Rica in May 1987, I told everyone who would listen that it was the fruit to which I looked forward. My two favorite fruits in the world, I said, were the *anón* and the *mamey,* and I had not eaten either since leaving my country. The *anón,* known as sweetsop or sugar apple in English, is made up of many bundles of pulp the color and taste of cream. It has a yellowish green skin and many seeds. The *mamey* is shaped like a U.S.-style football, I said, with a leathery brown skin and carmine-red, velvety flesh, like a mild, firm custard. At its center, it has a large, glossy black pit shaped also like a football. As a child, I loved to draw the cut fruit with my Prismacolors—Carmine Red #926 with Vermilion Red #921 for the overtones was perfect for it.

What I did not know, because my parents and I were all native to the western part of our island, was that it was necessary elsewhere to specify for my much-missed drupe *(Pouteria sapota)* the name of *mamey colorado,* for elsewhere the simple name *mamey* referred to *Mammea americana,* a whole other fruit, which my father called *sapote,* while many other people throughout Latin America applied this latter name to my great favorite, the *mamey colorado.* An appellation much used in Cuba for *Mammea americana* was *mamey de Santo Domingo,* for the sake of differentiation and clarity.

I remember only the vague contours of a conversation between my father and mother one Saturday afternoon in our apartment in Río Mar in which my father provided a précis of the points under contention in the *mamey/sapote* controversy— but I could not follow the specifics and did not retain them. I was willing to call fruit by whatever name my father chose for it. I more clearly remember a much later statement made by my father in Miami on the subject of the *mamey colorado.* He claimed that its importation was forbidden because U.S. authorities believed that its stone was abortifacient. Not yet questioning the truth value of my father's statements about *mameyes,* I despaired of ever eating them on U.S. soil.

Our first Saturday morning in San José, my boss Susan and I went to a large indoor market in a busy part of the city. I knew that the names of fruits were likely to be different—since I became a foreigner, the fruits of my childhood have proved difficult to translate—but from *anón* to *anona* is a short hop, and I spotted it right away. I found nothing I could call a *mamey* by my Habana reckoning. A stall had a pile of fruit under a hand-lettered sign proclaiming *"Mamey."* One of the specimens was displayed, as had been the custom in Cuba, with a wedge cut out of it to show the quality that, by not always realistic extension, was expected of all its fellows. The drupe was not football-shaped but rounder. The pit was kidney shaped. The meat was orangey yellow. I wondered if my memory could possibly have deceived me about the uniformity of the football shape. But I could not be wrong about Prismacolor's Carmine Red. I assumed that what I had before me was a local variant, for I did not then recall my father's conversational survey of regionalism in *mameyes* and *sapotes.* Not knowing that I was tangled in a verbal jungle from which only the knife of taxonomy, Latinate and scientific, could extricate me, I purchased the fruit.

Back at the Holiday Inn, we set up our luncheon on Susan's table. We dived into the fruits of which I had so long spoken. The *mamey* was overwhelming in its ripeness, which reached almost the point of putrefaction. Even worse, its insides, like that of the market specimen, were yellowish. The *anón* was easier to take, but not the stuff of dreams. It was too sweet, too ripe. I had failed.

"Maybe your taste has changed," Susan said when I expressed my disappointment.

At the time I wondered if I had really squirmed out of the lock of my own memory, or if I simply did not know how to choose tropical fruit. I do not know how to choose tropical fruit; it is one of the prices of living in a stable, northern land. But in memory I can taste the subtly sweet, creamy meat of my *mamey* decades after last dipping into it with a spoon or licking at its transformation into carmine-colored ice cream. Who would have told me the last time I took a bite off a *paleta de helado de mamey,* ice cream on a stick, perhaps purchased by my grandmother from a wandering vendor on the street of San Juan Bautista, that it would be the last—who would have had the heart?

The market place in San José where my boss and I bought the fruit reminded me of the *plaza* in La Habana where as a family we often shopped. The *plaza* was a covered market where purveyors of different foods had their stalls. In some resurgent U.S. cities, this old arrangement is being tried as a novel draw for affluent customers; they leave out the smells.

We always walked in through the poultry room, where our nostrils were assailed and then comforted by the smell of feathers, blood, and fowl droppings. The large chamber was lined with cages full of chickens, some crested roosters. We paused for my father to ponder. Because my father was born in the countryside, my mother gave him absolute power to choose fish, fowl, flesh, and fruit—this in spite of his having left his red-earthed land for La Habana by the age of eleven, and in spite, also, of my mother's being a meat broker's daughter. After my father died, she held out a cantaloupe melon to me and asked me if it was ripe enough to eat; I felt panic for her.

With method or without, my father decided what chicken he liked the looks of best for slaughter. When we went into the poultry room, the chicken was alive. It had feathers. It clucked. It jerked its neck as it walked. When we were finished with the rest of our shopping, and walked back out through the poultry room, a plucked, dead chicken wrapped in paper awaited our payment. We put it into our straw shopping bag with the rest of our purchases. We walked out into the cement lot toward our car, stepping over chicken shit and blood stains and feathers and rotting vegetables. "Chickens crap when their necks are broken," my mother explained to me.

My father struck up conversational relationships with the vendors. He always called the poultry seller and the fishmonger by their names, and he joked with them and asked after their health. He treated them with *tú*, the informal second person singular, but they called him *usted*. He established tacit mutual contracts: he would be a faithful customer if they consistently steered him toward the freshest products. Without them, he would have been lost, his lack of peasant craft revealed. Fortunately for him and for us, the system usually worked.

I loved lingering at the fishmonger's glass counter full of ice where pink and gray translucent shapes nested. I love the cool, subtle smell of fresh seafood, and it was particularly welcome then, after the chicken abattoir. My father might look at me and ask me if I wanted shrimp. "I have to get her what she wants," he might say to the man. "She's the one who gives the orders in the house."

In the odoriferous parking lot of the *plaza,* my father traded for me Heroes of the Revolution cards with the enterprising urchin who waited about to carry packages for customers or perform other odd jobs. It is a strange memory, for my father hated the revolution. But I was interested in collecting the baseball-like cards that came out after its triumph. A lot of the children had them, so my father offered a young boy money for pictures of the bearded, gun-carrying men who were ruining his life.

Picture cards were not all we collected in the months after January 1959. It was fashionable to collect as souvenirs bullets carried by the victorious *rebeldes*. It mattered little that the actual bullet had not made it into battle. To ensure that these minor missiles were not turned against their donors or other human life, they were emptied of gunpowder before transfer into civilian hands. My twenty-two-year-old cousin Elsa showed me proudly the bullet she had obtained with her charm. It was large with a long nose that ended in a sharp point. My mother occasionally brought me surprises from work, usually some candy or pastry. After Elsa got her bullet, my mother brought me one instead of the usual sweets. The bullet that my mother got from one of the rebels at Agricultura, a nice young man by her report, was smaller than Elsa's. It had a rounded nose and a nice scar in the barrel where the bullet had been pried open to remove the gunpowder. The nose was more reddish, more coppery than Elsa's, and so I knew that it possessed interesting qualities that Elsa's lacked. However, I never showed it to my cousin, because it was not as large and imposing as hers.

When I was very little, my father sometimes took me to the big *plaza* at Avenida Carlos III. He was friendly with one of the vendors there and stopped for long chats. He sometimes sat me on the counter. Once, the friend offered me a Coca-Cola. He brought it to me in a bottle with a drinking straw peeping over the rim. I was about three years old, and I had never drunk anything through a straw.

I asked my father, "Papi, what do I do?"

"You blow!" he said.

I blew. The gassy brown liquid went spurting all over my father's clean, starched, white *guayabera,* his best shirt. Years after I had reached adulthood, he still told the story, and each time when he got to the *"¡Sopla!"* part, he partly covered his shut eyes with his right hand and laughed and laughed. He enjoyed and admired practical jokes. At the age of three, unwittingly, I had played on him one of the best.

In Cuba, about a week before Christmas, we put up in our apartment both a Christmas tree and an elaborate *nacimiento,* or crèche.

I was involved with every second of the tree trimming. I would not now decorate a tree as we did when I was six years old and drawn to shiny objects, but then it was an activity worth a year's wait. On the tree we hung: strings of colored lights vaguely the shape of small Italian peppers; a string of lights that contained a colored liquid that bubbled (even the shape of these lights was interesting to me, each consisting of a bulbous, brightly colored base supporting the clear glass tube through which the crucial ebullition was observed); glass balls, some round and some in other shapes, in colors that had been applied to them in a thin, paper-like layer that I liked to study when—the way of all glass— the balls came crashing down due to human, or other, more inexplicably caused, accident; metallic spirals in icicle shapes; tinsel; wreaths made out of gold tinsel; angel hair. We topped the tree with one of those glass ornaments that sort of resemble an onion dome on a Russian church but end in a long, dangerous-looking spike. I liked to hold it on its side when we took it out of the box because to me it looked like the head and beak of a fantastic bird. Then we sprayed tree, balls, lights, all, with fake snow. *El arbolito.* I once asked why we put up a pine tree covered with artificial snow. I was told that it snows in the North in winter.

"*Arbolito, arbolito,*" went the Christmastime song. I enjoyed the tree decorating—I did not want it to stop—but its connection to Christmas remained tenuous for me. It was something one did for fun, like throwing confetti and blowing whistles at carnival time. But I did not think of it as authentic. After all, not only did it never snow in Cuba at Christmas, I thought that probably it had not snowed on the original Christmas in the

Holy Land. All the pictures I had seen of Christ's birth were snowless and full of palm trees, not unlike Cuba, except for the aridity. Whatever clime I inhabit, I dream of a warm, snowless Christmas, just like the ones I used to know.

We had a record by the very popular Olga Guillot that on one side contained "Noche de Paz" ("Silent Night") and on the other "Blanca Navidad," in a Spanish version that cleverly avoided, as far as I remember, any mention of snow *("O, blanca Navidad, eres una sublime inspiración . . .").* To make sense of the song, I interpreted the whiteness to which it alluded as a radiance that emanated from the Christ Child's halo.

We could trim the tree without my aunt Nena, but we could not have had a *nacimiento* without her. The *nacimiento* was of a completely different order. It was the best of Christmas. Yet not until recently did I realize what a gift the *nacimiento* had been, a gift from my aunt to us, and most of all to me. For my aunt did not live with us. She spent several hours of each weekday in our apartment, but it was her place of work, not territory that was hers. Sadly, she had no space but our apartment for her assemblage. In the late afternoon she shut the door on what her creative rage had wrought, and she left us for the room she shared with her mother in the house of Rafael, her older sister's husband, with whom she had not exchanged friendly words for years.

One day in mid-December I would find, upon returning home from school, that my tall bookcase had been moved to a corner of the living room, laid shelf-belly down and back up, and that already my aunt had covered the flat surface with a brownish paper on which were glued green bits like grass. Into the middle of the papered expanse, she had cut a hole, revealing the mirror that she had hidden there to form a lake. She had most likely also finished molding mountains against the wall. To make them, she bought a green and brown paper sold specifically for mockups of such terrain.

Within a frame of mountains, at the left front edge of the stage, we placed a modest open stable and we peopled it with a beautiful, tranquil Holy Family. I loved unwrapping each figure of Mary or shepherd or Magus, old friends I had not seen for a year. They were hand painted, imported from Europe—from Spain, I think, judging from the crèche sets I've seen in shops near Washington. They were beautifully crafted, with a care that made of the features on each face an individual and in such a scale that each participant in the Birth and Epiphany fitted realistically into our landscape. Looking at a tape measure, I guess that perhaps the clay adults were about twelve centimeters tall, but my judgment about scale is one of the features I most distrust about my memory.

For hours I watched that world created out of my family's fantasy and rediscovered each piece and saw how it fitted with the others and how together they made up a landscape of country and town and celebrated a crucial moment of history (I thought). We had an ox and an ass for the manger, sheep for the shepherds, both at the manger and in the mountains. In the mountains too angels sang to the lonely shepherds. A lion roared on an angelless mountain. On the outskirts of the town was a well. A village woman carried pails of water suspended from a brace across her shoulders. Ducks and geese swam on the mirror lake. Date palms thrived at this oasis. The landscape through which important news must travel seemed vast.

The Magi had just completed their long journey. Melchor, Gaspar, and Baltazar they were called, *los Tres Reyes Magos,* although the account in the gospel neither numbers nor names them nor calls them kings. Baltazar, by tradition, was the black man; he was always mentioned last. I assigned the name Gaspar to my favorite; I thought he looked the wisest, but maybe he was just the oldest and most ethereal. Such wisdom as these travelers possessed weighed down upon them as they bowed in adoration of the Babe. It had creased their skin. They had carried their precious balms so long that their clothing smelled of incense. Their robes were decorated with gold. They knelt before the shape of a star that had been cut into the wooden stable. My aunt had placed a light bulb behind the hole to replicate the brilliance of the star that had guided the learned men from their distant world to see a foreign, miraculous Child King. I was disturbed by the metaphor of monarchy: it diminished the one who had come. Two Cuban palms flanked the stable.

Much of the year I would have said that with good reason Christmas Eve was called Nochebuena, Goodnight. Yet at the very end of that night, as we strove to get our packages together, I thought it should instead be called Shortnight. Nochebuena at my grandmother's house was a time of such intense anticipation that once the awaited event was over, I felt deflated, my Christmas Eve gone at the pop of a balloon, and another year to wait.

The part that seemed eternal was the food. My father certified and celebrated the traditional authenticity of each item at the table. Each one had to be there, like offerings at a ritual. He catalogued them: roast pork, guinea fowl, *moros y cristianos, yuca,* salad with radishes—there must be radishes. It being his house, my uncle Rafael was host, but the one who ran things was my father. Ever the loud guest, he pretended to quarrel with my mother's family until each dish made its appearance. "Where is that roast pork? You have me here waiting for that *lechoncito.*" "And does the salad have radishes? You have to give me radishes." I never observed him eating radishes the rest of the year.

It was the Cuban custom to end the meal with *buñuelos,* figure eights made with *yuca* starch and sweet potatoes, kneaded, shaped, deep-fried, and covered with molasses. I always associate *buñuelos* with my grandmother. It was one of the few dishes she made in her old age, and only for Nochebuena. My mother does not know how to make *buñuelos,* which require a lot of training, dexterity, and grace under pressure. Some women make them their specialty. As the youngest daughter, my mother was not brought up to be a repository of the family's culinary tradition. I recall a faint taste of anise.

Much more easily dispensed were the *turrones* imported from Spain, varieties of nougat made of almonds processed in disparate ways until they achieved varying consistencies and extremes of sweetness. My favorite was the kind named after the town of Alicante, both because it contained almost-whole almonds in a white substance that was similar to something in my adored Toblerones, albeit harder, and because it was covered with wafer material identical to that used for communion hosts. At an early age I was told of the quasi-Eucharistic quality of the wafers by adults who had not received communion much past their first time. (My paganic father, of all people, was, I think, the only one for whom first was not the only communion.) I took the wafer reverently into my mouth, training, I thought, to do something holy. Dishes full of dates were set out, dates from palms like those in the pictures of the Holy Land that had so influenced my view of proper holiday tradition.

As Christmas approached the radio played, *"Allá en la Siria hay una mora que tiene los ojos mas lindos que un lucero encantador."** I knew what a Moor was; my parents had a porcelain bust of a dark turbaned woman. But I did not see what she and Syria had to do with a Cuban Christmas. I must constantly seek interpretation of what I saw and heard, for it was a time altogether different, in which the exotic was let loose by tradition. It was the time of the guinea fowl.

The guinea fowl lived with us for a while before Nochebuena. At least one wire crate arrived each December. According to Cuban taste, the fowl must be slaughtered just before they are consumed. They must be absolutely fresh. They were amazing to me, these awkwardly gaited birds covered in silky dark gray feathers with a purplish suggestion and small white dots resembling the kind of exquisite fabric I dream of finding already made into a dress someday. We kept them on the balcony of our fancy condominium until it was time to take them to the butcher's or my grandmother's—I am not sure which. My mother has no idea where they were taken after our apartment. They somehow ended up at my grandmother's table, cooked. It was then, and still is,

*"There in Syria is a Moorish woman who has eyes lovelier than a bewitching star."

easy enough for me to imagine my severe aunt Cuca* snapping the guinea fowl's neck just below the white, leathery cap of the head. One year we were sent a live pig by a politician who did not consider sufficiently the fact that pigs are difficult to keep in apartments. The pig did not stay.

Once on a drive back toward the Washington, D.C., suburbs from the Eastern Shore of Delaware and Maryland, I saw guinea fowl cross the road. "Guinea fowl! Guinea fowl! Stop the car!" I shouted to Kurt, who slammed down the brake, afraid I might have seen a collision coming. We got out of the car, and I could not believe it, there, running across somebody's long, sparse front yard, as if crazed by cosmic humming imperceptible to us, were five guinea fowl, an apparition.

Eventually—but at length—after the adults were done eating and I was done picking at the many foods, my favorite part of the evening was permitted to take place: the gift exchange. On the night of 5 to 6 January, the wondrous Magi, my dear Melchor, Gaspar, and Baltazar, traveled throughout the world leaving toys for all children. On the other hand, Nochebuena gifts, which could include clothing and other practical outfittings, were either for or from the adults and children present before us. We carried the gifts in large shopping bags. *Las jabas*— I even got excited about the bags. We each reached into our particular bag and handed out presents in whatever order they had fallen—each of us a giver and a receiver. I got to give out presents I may have helped pick but had not paid for. When I asked my mother in exile what she missed the most about working at a job, she said sorrowfully, "Oh, having my own money to buy Nochebuena presents!" There was power behind each *jaba de Nochebuena*. That one evening of the year ended with a room full of people, adults included, ripping through gift paper.

I was an acquisitive child. Even if I did not get quite what I wanted, I approached each gift exchange full of hope. The last Nochebuena I fully celebrated as a child, when I was a mere six

---

*Cuca was her nickname. Her legal name was María Luisa.

years old and a few days away from the fall of Batista, I got a large box from my uncle Rafael.

"It's what you said you wanted most in the world," he told me.

This sounded very good to me, but I wondered what I could possibly have labeled that way, and when. It was with dumfounded surprise that I reached into my box and discovered that the item I most wanted in the world was—a thermal pitcher! Rafael and Cuca and their daughter Elsa kept similar ones in their rooms. Theirs were filled every night and some afternoons with spring water and ice. I had indeed been fascinated by the plastic-lined stopper, which formed such a tight seal with the opening to the pitcher that a pleasant sound, like a toad's, was made by removing or replacing the stopper. My new pitcher, that obscure object of my desire one hot day, was cream-colored and came with two glasses and a tray. Its plump substantiality was balanced by a graceful polished metal handle. On the one hand, I knew that it was remarkable that Rafael had paid such close attention and had remembered my—doubtlessly passionate— declaration. On the other hand, I went home with a new nervousness about the destiny of careless statements.

I remember a few individual Nochesbuenas. There was the time my uncle Rafael invited so many people that tables had to be rented and set up, end to end, in the garage and out the driveway. At any time, at will, I can exactly recall the smell of Rafael's garage. It was a combination of exhaust, gasoline, and Sherwin-Williams paints, not the sort of ambient air that stimulates the appetite. Somehow I managed to be fed inside the house, away from the multitudes. I have never felt at home in crowds.

One Christmas—it may have been 1958—my father and Elsa got into an exceedingly jolly mood, apparently with the help of liquor, and they decided that the neighborhood ought to be serenaded. I was invited to come along and I went, although the thought of making noise within earshot of strangers mortified me. I think I went because I did not want the beautiful Elsa to have my father to herself. I went because I adored them both, and because I thought I might somehow be able to calm them down and avert disaster. My father's sleeves were still rolled up from the pork dinner. He took his fun as serious business. He and Elsa took off on their rumba around the block, shouting out rather than singing seasonal songs, of which they did not know very many. My father attempted to sound as off-key and ridiculous as it was possible to sound. Those who heard what my father did to the first *i* in *Siria* as he yowled out *"Allá en la Siria . . ."* could not have had thoughts of peace on earth. Mercifully, the rumba only went around the block, but by the end of the escapade I was being called a grouch and a *guajira*—"peasant" in this context being synonymous with "shy."

Twenty-eight December was *el Día de los Inocentes,* in which we commemorated, by trying to trick one another, the slaughter of innocent male infants by order of jealous King Herod. On that day one had to tread carefully in my household. My father was neither subtle nor gentle. "Look, what's that stain on your shirt?" he might say, pointing to the middle of my chest, or perhaps, "Look, a cockroach!" When I looked down, he would hit my nose. *"¡Inocente! ¡Inocente!"* he ridiculed his victims with the finger-pointing ungraciousness of a ten-year-old boy. I learned early in life the dangers of naiveté, the deadliness of innocence. I have always awakened on 28 December—or the first of April, when the Trickster extracts his due in the United States—with the mission of getting others before they get me.

Horror stained the happiest of seasons. Injustice disturbed the peace of my search for reason. All the Nativity stories were Christological midrash, but never so called. The Christ was born six years before the birth of Christ; no one took notes. I was left to reconcile inconsistencies. The wise men foolishly told Herod of the arrival of his rival. Ambitious Herod, who valued power above all, did not send one of his agents to follow the wise men to the vulnerable cradle of the infant threat. The angel warned only Joseph of danger; let the other infants in Bethlehem be slaughtered; God cared only for his own.

Go into exile, go, only that can save you. Blood stains the streets. Do not look back. At Colegio Baldor we saw the image: Mary, with Jesus in her arms, rode a donkey, while Joseph, their protector, walked beside them, eyes intent on the road that would lead them to the safety of a strange land. Later I would read what John Donne wrote: *Kisse him, and with him into Egypt goe, With thy kinde mother, who partakes thy woe.*

December 1959, I was still in Cuba, but I did not celebrate Christmas. A few days before, I was stricken with measles. My fever rose so high that one night I saw a crescent of stars near the ceiling of the right corner of my father's bedroom where I lay. I was sure it must be the star crescent on which rode Our Lady of Charity, the patroness of Cuba. I had longed to be visited by the Virgin. I was puzzled that she should come to me as Our Lady of Charity because I had been pledged by name to Our Lady of Mt. Carmel (same Virgin ultimately but different aspect). I thanked the Virgin over and over for the blessing of her visit, and whenever I drifted off to sleep, I would catch myself and open my eyes and look to see if she were still there, and she was, that whole night. I was especially grateful because one day at recess some girls from another class had started screaming that they had seen the Virgin and then the next afternoon some girls from my class had sworn that they had seen her too. But I had not seen her, and I had held close to my chest this sign of my unworthiness, of the sickness of my soul.

I still had a fever on Christmas Eve, so I was not allowed to go to my grandmother's house. My father went to dinner while my mother stayed with me. I wish I had a clearer memory of this final Christmas we spent in the same country, but I was angry to have had to miss my favorite day of the year and resentful that my relatives had gone ahead and enjoyed it anyway. I was woozy with fever, and I did not know that there would not be another chance. Earlier in 1959 we had moved to an apartment in El Nuevo Vedado only a few meters away from the block my father and cousin had serenaded. Since they were so close, several of my maternal relatives accompanied my father home after the meal. I cannot remember who came—probably Nena, Rafael, and Elsa. I think that even my grandmother, who very rarely stirred from her home except to keep doctors' appointments, came to see us. It was her last Christmas. She would die nine days before my mother and I left Cuba.

At first, in Miami, my parents mumbled excuses. I understood in part the deep loss my mother had suffered. I had suffered loss too. "Your grandmother is dead. It would not be the same," my mother explained. "We are all separated. It would not be the same."

Because anything we did in Miami would have been different from our custom, my parents celebrated next to nothing of the holiday from the Christmas of my eighth year ever after. Christmas Eve and Christmas dinners could hardly be distinguished from dinners on other nights. Sometimes we were invited by acquaintances of my father's for a meal, and on those occasions we had some of the traditional dishes, my father remarking upon their appropriateness but in lowered spirits.

We spent our first Christmas in Miami with the family of a man who had had a numbers *(bolita)* business near the Uncle Sam. My father renewed his acquaintance with him one day when we were walking through our new neighborhood a short time after our arrival in Miami and suddenly on Second Street we heard someone shouting, "Ramiro! Ramiro!" The man, who was easily overcome by laughter, could hardly believe that he had looked out of his screened porch and seen a person he imagined in La Habana.

That first Christmas in Miami, I was struck by the hope that since Santa Claus visited children in the United States, he would visit me.

"I think Santa Claus is going to leave me something," I said to my parents fervently.

"Poor children don't receive as much," my father warned me.

I had never understood this injustice. Every Christmastide in Cuba there was a big drive to collect toys for poor children for *el*

*Día de Reyes*. It had seemed absurd to me. Why would such kind spirits leave less for poor children rather than more? Why would humans need to augment the gifts of the Kings who had visited Jesus? I asked my father about this once when I spotted an advertisement for a charity as we drove through an exclusive residential development to visit a member of the Cuban senate. My father made an answer, but I did not commit it to memory, since I found it unsatisfactory.

Because I had left all my dolls in Cuba, my obstinate faith in goodness told me that Santa Claus would bring me a doll. I also wanted a bag for baby bottles such as I had seen in use by real mothers. When Christmas morning came, I was excited to find on the old red sofa a doll in the shape of a pretty honey-blonde girl about four years old whose blue eyes could be made to open and close. It was the very one I had pointed out in the toy aisle of the five-and-dime store as being my favorite because her hair color was similar to mine. As I looked at her in our living room, I noticed for the first time that she wore two left shoes made of plastic. Next to her was a 5-by-3-inch vinyl plastic bag with blue piping and a snap closure that revealed, when opened, a small plastic imitation baby bottle. I was deeply pleased that the two things I had asked for had materialized. To my mind the toys proved something beyond themselves.

"You see, he came!" I said joyfully.

To curb any future desire, my father sat down on the red sofa, before which I still stood admiring my presents, and he said, "The Three Magi Kings and Santa Claus are lovely stories told to maintain children's illusions, children's beliefs. In reality they do not exist. Parents sacrifice to give their children presents, and we sacrificed to give these things to you even though we are poor. You must remember that you are now a poor girl." He got up and left the room. He got up and left me there after striking me with lightning.

*Sacrificio*—that was the first time my father had used the word to describe an action he had taken on my behalf. I would do anything to avoid his performing a sacrifice ever again—yet sacrifice would henceforth characterize all his gifts, all his discharges of responsibility to me. I had been betrayed with a lie. I had only asked for gifts because I believed a spirit could give them to me through spirit means, not expenditure. The moment I realized that I had believed in magic, I knew the world to be devoid of it. It was unfair, really, it seemed to me, not to be offered a warning rather than being allowed to incur the burden of guilt. When I felt guilt, which was most of the time, I usually found enough for twenty people. Where others might carry a pebble, I found a boulder and strapped it onto my back and walked everywhere with it, and you might have thought that was beyond the endurance of such a wispy girl. I felt guilt for all my past Kings' Day avarice, for the letters I had written under adult guidance and had placed in my shoes on the night of the fifth of January, for the mountains of toys that relatives and my father's friends and mere acquaintances sent to me saying that *los Reyes* had left them for me at their house. Most of all, I felt guilt for the recent desire of mine that had compelled my parents to spend money they barely possessed. I never, ever again asked for another Christmas present—or birthday present, for that matter. I think I was always given something by my parents at Christmas, most frequently a shirt. After I left for college, they gave me money.

Through all the years in Miami, my parents taped onto walls the Christmas cards we received. That was our sole Christmas decoration, unless you count the strange little manger scene made of plastic that my mother purchased at a Woolworth's or Kress and placed on top of the television set. Most of the effort was directed outward. My parents joylessly bought presents for my father's friends who during the season visited or were visited. We got presents from them in turn. It was a burden on all. Men exchanged liquor. My father suggested that for women my mother and I buy a perfume called Réplique. It was not a fragrance my mother had ever used. We did not know precisely how he had come upon this obscure scent, but we could guess.

Every Christmas since I graduated from college, I have stayed away from Miami during the holidays, even the year I knew I would be alone on Christmas Eve. My father himself had taught me that it was better to be alone than in bad company. However, that year when I was loneliest on Christmas Eve, I was not alone the next day. For Christmas dinner I invited a Jewish coworker, the only person I knew who was remaining in Washington. "So, do you celebrate a different event at Christmas than at Easter?" he asked me.

And still I did not regret my decision to remain. If anyone asked, "Aren't you going to Miami for the holidays?" I answered angrily, "My parents never celebrate Christmas." Celebration is forbidden by our culture to those who are grieving. My father every day commemorated his loss, his country's loss, the reasons why our lives could not be normal.

When I left my first husband, I left behind, through forgetfulness and urgency, the first set of Christmas decorations I had acquired in the United States. Since he was Jewish, I do not imagine that he was inclined to use them. I had purchased the bulk of the ornaments in the late 1970s on a day-after-Christmas sale at a large department store that, fortunately for me, had not managed to sell much of its good stock. During that holiday season I had decided that I did not want to go through another December without festivity. I did not call the holiday Christmas; that would have been too Christian for me. I claimed to be celebrating the winter solstice—paganism being more acceptable—even though I am Cuban and late December in Cuba is not frightening, as it must have been before the invention of electric lights in more northerly latitudes where the nights were so much longer and the cold so pronounced that the curse of the season, the death of the sun, had to be overcome with fire and loud sound with which to coax him back to life. In Cuba for Nochebuena and Navidad we sometimes had to wear a sweater or a jacket, which was fun, since it represented change.

For several years after leaving my first husband, I did not bother with decorations; I had more pressing concerns. But with time my mind turned to Christmas again, and then it did so with a vengeance for all the years of deprivation. In Kurt I found someone who like me could not resist the lure of a store full of tree trimmings in wood, fabric, or glass, miniature toys, charms for children. The first Christmas, we looked at each other stunned when the checker at Behnke's Nurseries' Santa Claus Shop told us the total dollars due for our purchase. We were much poorer in money than in imagination—or desire.

Kurt, whose native land and conifers are covered with snow at the Nativity and remain that way till April, learned some very old, beautiful carols in his childhood. Like me, he loves to sing. He taught me the haunting plainsong *O, come, o, come, Emanuel, And ransom captive Israel, That mourns in lonely exile here, Until the Son of God appear. Rejoice!* He introduced me to "Fum, Fum, Fum," a carol from Spain. The Spanish word *villancicos* had existed for me in Cuba without much reality to support it. If there were Spanish carols, why had Cubans sung so few of them? Since coming to the United States, the songs of Christmas have been my principal consolation for the lost Nochesbuenas. They leave too soon, these musical butterflies, and even if they return in eleven and a half months, January will again come (Christmas beginning and ending too early in the United States), and I will not have sung enough of them, will not even have thought of every one I know, before I lose my license to sing them.

I was taught, as a child, that it was all right to catch and kill butterflies because their lives were so brief anyway. I caught them sometimes on walks along Primera Avenida from the swimming club to the Río Mar. I pressed them between the pages of one of the animal books that had helped me to identify them. I had a monarch, of course, and a specimen of *Heliconius charitonius ramsdeni,* the zebra, with broad black and yellow stripes. The butterflies' corpses left a golden dust on the pages and on my fingers. I was told not to touch the dust to my eyes, for it would make me blind. Despite the danger, I liked to be able to study from so close the remains of these beautiful insects.

Then, our last year in Cuba, something occurred to change my perspective. One day I noticed that amusing caterpillars banded with yellow, black, and white crawled on all the surfaces of all the leaves of an ornamental shrub in front of our apartment building in El Nuevo Vedado. The display lasted long enough to give me something to look forward to as I waited for my dreaded 29 bus. Suddenly the caterpillars disappeared. One day some weeks later I discovered that the shrub was covered with fluttering pieces of orange glass, darkly veined like church windows. Monarch butterflies! I was so excited about the transformation that I felt ashamed of my past and never killed another colorful flyer (not yet extending my mercy to moths).

I assumed that monarchs were very common, for I saw them and their relatives everywhere in Cuba. Then we went to live in a section of Southwest Miami, near the Miami River, that was mostly pavement, and I did not see butterflies. Yet as difficult as it is for me to accept it, it is likely that the monarch butterflies continued their cycle of annual migration from the North to Cuba, unimpeded by politics, free to travel, eating in the midst of want the leaves of plants unsuitable as human nourishment, long after sight of our country had become for us impossible.

The first Christmas Kurt and I spent together was the last one my father spent alive. At Behnke's, Kurt and I found a miniature artificial Christmas tree with pliable branches and tiny decorations, all of which fitted into a mailing tube. We, newly wedded, in our happiness sent it to my parents. When a suitable time had passed, I asked my mother during our weekly phone call, "Did you receive the little tree we sent you?"

"Yes," my mother said, showing no enthusiasm, "I put the decorations on it. I don't know if I put it up correctly."

My father did not mention it.

The following Christmas, seven months after his suicide, my mother volunteered, "I don't think I'll put up the little tree this year. I'll wait till next year."

I had set up my tall tree—I insisted on the beauty of my Christmas, and I could get away with it, for I lived among U.S.ers who would not see my celebration as disrespect—but I was surprised that my mother had given a thought to holiday observance, for my parents had endured their exile Christmases in numbness, not noticing the living child before them, not daring to look back in memory toward the land of the dead. They had spent their Decembers since 1960 trying not to see what was lost, while I had spent them cataloguing what I was not given. One by one, those with whom we feasted long ago have died in the distance. They have slipped off the earth. Only a few of us, mostly women, separate, remain—but Cuca is gone, and how much longer can Nena survive?

Two weeks before Christmas 1990 my mother set out the little artificial tree. *"Ya puse el arbolito,"* she told me, as if it were a foregone conclusion. Already on their way to her were tiny decorations that Kurt and I had chosen with my mother's tastes in mind: several animals, a sewing basket filled with minuscule scissors and bolts of cloth. During the next two phone calls my mother spoke with wonder about how much detail the makers had gotten into objects so small. She declared herself content to spend Christmas alone with her television.

"It is a day like any other," she said, "but people charge it with so much."

It is a celebration of fire that Christians have tried to subdue into a dream of peace.

## III

My father was very particular about coffee. He liked my mother's best. In a saucepan she boiled the grounds with sugar and water. When the moment seemed right, she passed it all through a sock-like filter attached to a circular metal rim that rested on a stand with long, skinny legs. She must have had to wash the fuzzy strainer every day. The coffee came out thick and sweet. It tasted solid. For years my father poured out a bit onto his demitasse saucer for me to drink; *el buchito,* my parents said. My mother told me that as a child she frequently asked her father for some coffee in a saucer too, because that little swallow tasted better to her than any other. She was the penultimate child. This was the only sign of notice she ever mentioned.

My father was very rude about coffee that was not prepared to his taste. I grew nervous when he accepted offers of coffee when we visited his friends. I wanted to stop him. I knew the foolishness of his assent and wondered why he had not learned from past experience. When he took that first swallow, he thought nothing of making an obvious, leonine grimace, as if gall had touched his tongue, when the coffee failed to meet his standards. He continued to grimace as—out of a twisted politeness—he took a few more sips.

He could be very rude about food in general. He had a favorite phrase that he thought was very witty, though no one else found it so. "Better I have eaten," he would say, "worse, never." He used it one time when we went to a Japanese restaurant. I was then in my twenties and was paying my parents a visit. I offered to treat them to a dinner of Japanese food, which I very much favored and they had never tried. My father said he knew where there was a Japanese restaurant, in an area he did not frequent. I suggested we look for it on a map. He reminded me that *guajiros* do not use maps, that they can steer by recognizing objects that they pass. My father, the aging *guajiro* journalist, drove for more than an hour around the same territory, certain that the restaurant must be around there somewhere. In his distraction with trying to find his goal, he twice narrowly missed crashing into other cars. We did finally spot the place, and we had dinners of sukiyaki and teriyaki—nothing too remarkable but quite pleasant. At the end my father insisted on picking up the check.

He said, "Better I have eaten, worse, never."

My mother told him, "You say that to people and you think you're being funny, but you're really being obnoxious."

The morning after my father's wake, Kurt, whose one year of Spanish at the University of Maryland had not been a smashing success, lunged into the foreign culture of Southwest First Street, stopped at the first *cafetería* that he found, and requested, *"Por favor, un cafecito para dos."*

The woman behind the counter was nonplused. She looked at him as if trying to decipher why even a bearded U.S.er would want to divide the minuscule portion of a *cafecito* into two. Ah, he didn't want her to divide but to multiply. She nodded. She gave him a double portion of *café*. Kurt came back with a *cafecito* for himself and one for my mother, plus a story.

Each day he looked forward to his Cuban coffee adventure. The day that he decided to try something new, a *cortadito*, which is a small version of the *café con leche*, my mother and I were glad that he told us of his intentions first. He was going to use a quite perplexing word for it—*cafetaza*, I think. I am sure the women at the coffee stalls looked forward to his coming.

"You're developing some very bad habits," my mother said to him one morning when he came back with *café*. I was stunned at her use of such easy, idiomatic English. I stared at her mouth as if that would confirm the words' source. "Where are you going to find *cafecitos* where you're going?" she asked him.

My father had a predilection for H. Upmann cigars. I liked the smell of the unlit cylinders of leaf lying as straight as tin soldiers in the rectangular wooden box, as vegetal as royal palms without their fronds. The boxes themselves held happy discoveries in their covers of raised, colorful, old-fashioned pictures and gold lettering and borders.

As far as I was concerned, cigars were superior in their potential rather than their activated state. I was always uneasy when my father brought match into contact with cigar end, for I knew that as the smoke built I would start to choke. He never noticed that; he enjoyed them. He came, after all, from Pinar del Río, Vuelta Abajo, where the world's finest tobacco was grown.

On 1 January 1959, my father made this prediction and this vow: "This new government is not going to last long. I won't smoke another cigar until Fidel Castro's government has been overthrown, and remember, gentlemen, that I like cigars." He never smoked another. A few days later he made another prediction, "This will be the most sanguinary dictatorship that has ever been seen in our América."

My father claimed that his brother Antonio Boza (my father frequently referred to his siblings by first and last name) was the second-best *torcedor,* or cigar roller, in Cuba. My father's mind had a tendency toward competition and categories. However he may have come up with the ranking, he could also provide the name of the first-best. It was partly physiologically determined, he said: the palms of one's hands must neither be too dry nor too moist. My father had dry, smooth hands. Tobacco leaves would not catch in them enough to be shaped, and thus he had been rejected as *torcedor.* He explained to me that cigar makers received a good education on the job. That was probably why he thought it an enviable profession. A man was paid to read to the *tabaqueros* as they labored. He read them newspapers and books—novels, philosophy, poetry. Only men with good voices were chosen for the honored position of reader. I thought of the monastic custom of taking meals while a lector read from the Scriptures, but I said nothing. It was certainly an odd religion my uncle picked up in the cigar factory. He was a Communist long before the revolution, or so my father said.

Cuco was one of my father's nicknames. At the wake, El Negro from Artemisa turned to Juan Pérez, our cousin Onelia's husband, and asked, "Cuco was Cañita's brother?"

"Yes," Juan answered without hesitation.

I held my breath, wondering what I was hearing. I could not take another shock. I did not want my family to have some deep, dark secret—that my father was not who he had said he was, or that his siblings were not as previously reported. Juan and El Negro must have seen the quizzical distress on my face, for they explained to me, "We called Antonio Boza 'Cañita.'" Las Cañas, Cañita. I sat back with relief.

*El pez muere por la boca.* My father's passionate eating was reserved for special occasions. And for memories of youthful days when he "ate like a barbarian." During most of my life he was a fastidious eater at home. Either he treated food as a poison or he indulged in it to such an extent that he got sick, confirming food's harmfulness. With my father there was no middle way about anything.

Some foods inspired in him a particularly deep suspicion. He never ordered *zarzuela de mariscos,* the Spanish seafood stew, because it usually included among its cast of ingredients a large clam. My father believed that clams were either small or they were toxic. When I ordered the dish, which I liked very much, he contracted the muscles of his chin in disgust and said disapprovingly, "Those big clams." I never got sick from them. My parents are among the few Cubans ever to have eschewed *paella*. My father disapproved of the mixture of seafood with chicken and pork, as if it were under strange rabbinical prohibition. He liked *arroz con mariscos,* which kept the presentation of seafood pure.

My father's protectiveness toward his digestive system was not altogether unreasonable, for it could easily be sent into paroxysms. His emotions went directly to his gut.

On a Saturday in my adolescence a call came for my father telling him that Alfredo Izaguirre Riva was dead. Anyone who had witnessed the savage beating meted out to Alfredito at the Isle of Pines would have assumed that it was his corpse that had been driven away to the hospital. As soon as my father hung up the call, he ran to the bathroom. My mother and I could hear the noises of his diarrhea. Actually, she ran into the bathroom with a bout of her own after my father was through; it is the only time I remember such a thing happening with her emotions.

One Sunday afternoon during one of my visits from college, my parents went to see my father's friend Alberto Pavía, who had been hospitalized. As soon as they returned home, my father sat down in an easy chair and said to my mother, "Bring me water."

Slowly during my adolescence I had come to resent my father's treating my mother as a servant. She brought him the coffee that she made for him. It was she who brought to the table his red gelatin with canned peach slices. But that evening I knew that my father had spoken to my mother as if she were a servant and he a pasha. When my father said, "Bring me water," I shot back, although he had not addressed me, "Why don't you get it yourself?" He looked angry but he said nothing. He closed his eyes, as he did at times when I said something he did not like, and he shook his head while framing his face with his hand, his thumb under his chin and his index finger to his temple. Our hands had big reaches.

Later my mother, the person from whom he had ordered the water, said to me, "How could you say that to him? It hurt him a lot." I was surprised to hear that. "He left the hospital with nausea. It made him sick to see Pavía dying."

I had not known that Pavía was dying, and I was immediately sorry I had said angry words to my father at a time like that. It was just like me to choose the wrong moment to fight my hopeless battles. But even if I had known, I am not certain that I would have had sufficient empathy for a person who had watched a friend wither from the memory of youthful robustness into death.

One *Día de Reyes* Alberto Pavía had given me my fraternal twin dolls Alberto and Albertina. He was a stocky man with a big, bald, square head. My father had a lot of stories about working with him at *El Crisol,* which he always told while shaking his head in wonder. Papá approached the editing of any Pavía article with extreme caution, for Pavía, able crime reporter though he was in his own way, could commit mayhem upon logic and the language. There were the times he wrote, "Into our offices came a man and a Chinaman . . . ," and, "The victim had a gold tooth, apparently prosthetic."

Because he had a good working relationship with the police, Pavía often got special tips from its officers. One evening, nearly exploding with excitement, he called my father, who was in charge of the next edition, with a fantastic scoop. "A flying saucer has landed in La Habana! It's blocking the street. The police have arrived."

"Are you sure?" my father said.

"Sure. The captain of police is here himself," Pavía answered.

"I'll hold the edition till you can give me more details." It was the scoop of the century, my father thought.

He told the compositor to prepare a large headline reading "FLYING SAUCER LANDS IN HABANA." But putting out a headline like that was too great a leap into the unknown for my father. He sent someone else to check. This emissary found the flying saucer to be of earthly manufacture. Out of it popped the reigning blonde star of Cuban entertainment, a woman who had modeled her looks on Marilyn Monroe. As it happened, she was starring in a soon-to-be-released film with an outer space motif, and the alien landing was meant to garner publicity. Joining her as her guard in a motorcade away from the non-flying, now-identified object was Pavía's contact, the captain of police, who had been part of the hoax all along.

"I would have been ruined as a journalist!" my father would exclaim whenever he told the story, and his eyes, near tears, would shut with his laughter.

I remember Pavía as a very good-natured, simple man who liked children and had a devoted wife who in exile had to take jobs cleaning hotels. There had been a darker side to him. Once during one of his frequent drinking bouts, Pavía walked into the *taller,* where *El Crisol* was physically put together, and fired a couple of gunshots into the air, a few yards from where several craftsmen and journalists, now very startled and nervous, had been working. Among the journalists were my father and François Baguer, a white-haired man of elegance and dignity, from his manners to his impeccable suits.

"I want to kill somebody! I want to kill somebody!" Pavía was shouting.

Some of the men managed to subdue Pavía and to wrest the gun from his hands. Then my father looked out the window and saw François Baguer, who had been talking with him when Pavía appeared, now standing on the sidewalk at the corner, a safe distance away from the mêlée. To get there, this dignified man would have had to scramble over the window railing and drop a considerable distance to the sidewalk.

"François, how did you get there?" my father shouted to him.

"I don't know," said François.

Pavía got into awful, infernal drunks, my father said, but then swore off liquor completely after his son was killed in a car crash.

I am my father's daughter. Now my head has taken over as detector of stress, sending me migraine headaches when my choices become untenable or the barometric pressure changes, but until my mid-thirties, that function of exquisite gauge was carried out by my digestive system. For much of my life, I thought of my father whenever the pressures of life and heredity doubled me over with abdominal spasms.

In high school I was forced by my excellent scholarship—and my pride—to take trigonometry and pre-calculus my freshman and sophomore years respectively. My high school offered successful students advanced courses in no field other than mathematics. I had—have—no aptitude for mathematics. Language to me is the drawing of a breath. I had no intuitive feel for math, and I knew it. I found real-world sciences accessible. But mathematics seemed to me to have nothing to do with human life.

Algebra, which I had taken in eighth grade, was all right; it was logical. But the next course on the menu was geometry. I feared that I would not properly be able to assimilate the study of space; I knew that I had trouble not only with imagining space, but simply with moving around in it. To avoid the shame of doing badly—that is, getting a grade lower than an A—in a regular full-year course, I took a quickie summer course with some of my friends before I began high school. Naturally, it was a disaster. Our teacher, one Brother Cyriac, would open the book to a new chapter, say, "But you know this already," and go on to the next. It was with this insecure foundation in geometry that I attempted trigonometry and pre-calculus. I memorized the material for each exam and quickly forgot it afterwards. Studying for finals was a nightmare.

Every morning of my first two years of high school followed the same disgusting routine. In the darkness of six o'clock, my mother came into my room and handed me a glass of milk with dissolved chocolate powder—or, egad, strawberry. I drank it while she laced up my saddle oxfords. After she was finished, she handed me a cherry Lifesaver; it was supposed to overwhelm the taste of milk in my mouth. I got up, went to the bathroom, and once there, usually while I was brushing my teeth, I vomited. My parents yelled at me. They said it was my tooth-brushing that caused me to vomit. But I refused to stop brushing my teeth in the morning, and anyway I knew that my nausea each day preceded my attempts at dental hygiene.

My sophomore year ended. My friends signed up to take calculus the following year. I refused. Brother James, the advanced math teacher, called me a coward. But I knew what I needed. As soon as I stopped taking math, I stopped vomiting in the morning, although I continued to brush my teeth. Even my periods got regular. I took a course in Spanish for the Spanish-speaking; its lessons have been useful all my life.

Barnard asked of me no math; its science requirement could be satisfied with psychology. However, the college offered other, serious pressures: for the first time in my life, I was swamped with competition. My digestive system became erratic in new, mostly diarrheic ways. Coincidentally, Barnard had a very liberal health plan. While under Barnard health insurance, I underwent a barium enema, an upper gastrointestinal tract barium x-ray, and a proctosigmoidoscopy. For the proctosigmoidoscopy, I was sent to a St. Luke's Hospital proctologist I had never met. I had been warned at the Barnard health service that the doctor would have to turn the probe when it got to the sigmoid and that I could feel discomfort then. I am not sure when the turning took place; the procedure was very painful from the first moment. As I lay on my stomach, squirming, a big red-cheeked, blond-haired Valkyrie of a nurse—she looked as if prison wardening might be her ideal profession—barked at me insistently, "Stop moving! You have a glass tube up your rectum!"

The results of the tests were all negative. I could have told them. The professionals were acting as if there were a medical cure for heredity. The tests gave me something to talk about with my father during our weekly phone call. He had been through them all—repeatedly. We could talk about the awful texture of the barium shake, the difficulty of holding the barium enema, the unspeakable horror of sigmoidoscopies. We were family, one blood.

The walls at *El Crisol* were covered with large, colorful caricatures of its journalists. My father's office was graced by a very good, wicked likeness of him. Thick straight hair hung over his forehead and a thick lower lip jutted out. He was a cool bohemian. In his hand was something that looked like the sort of round flotation tube with a hole in the middle that I used for the beach—the kind that Lifesavers candy was designed to resemble. When I was very young, I assumed my father was carrying a *salvavida* and was heading for the beach in the picture. But there came one day when that no longer made sense and I asked. "It's a cushion one sits on when one has a hemorrhoid operation," he explained. "People here thought it was funny."

My father underwent his first hemorrhoid surgery in Cuba. In the United States, a few years after our arrival, he had to be operated on again. The U.S.er surgeon at the time claimed that the Cuban surgeon had botched the first operation, but the fact is that my father had to be cut by the U.S.er proctologist's knife again and again. It was strange to hear my father calmly tell stories of his proctologist's alcoholism. "They say that he goes into a bar and drinks shot after shot of whiskey until he consumes a whole bottle. Then he has his driver take him home. But he's always sober when he operates, they tell me." He trusted desperately in the doctor, even though nothing could prevent recurrences of the swelling and even though the man subjected him to some indignities, for example, performing a proctoscopy on him while a large group of medical students looked on.

Food could be a poison to my father because he had diverticulosis and he had never developed the prescience to tell what might catch in the sacks that his own intestines had produced against him. He was put on many diets, most of them bland, contrary to current thinking that fiber is what is needed. But that is the sort of abstemious life one leads only reluctantly. He might allow himself to eat beans one day. The next day he would have diarrhea so violent that he would start bleeding from the rectum. Nothing else scared him as much as blood in the stools, even with a history of painful but nonlethal malfunctioning.

When I was eleven or twelve and he was recovering from surgery, I would find his briefs in the bathroom stained with blood.

My mother jokingly asked a man who had come to visit my recovering father, "Have you come to see the menstruating girl?"

I was embarrassed. My father, for his part, closed his eyes and shook his head to suggest, through his disgust, that my mother had lost the infinitesimal amount of judgment he had thought she still possessed.

As he got older, he feared much worse than comparisons with the gender he misprized. He thought the blood in his stools spelled death, even if the blood was bright red and obviously fresh.

During his last year, my father worried obsessively about his bowel movements. When he made his weekly phone call to me, that was what he talked about. He might feed himself large amounts of fiber upon a doctor's advice and when that brought about a purging and he did not have a bowel movement the day after he had shat himself empty, he became convinced that he had intestinal blockage, certainly malign. The son of an older colleague of my father's had to undergo a colostomy because of such blockage. My mother told me after my father's suicide that he had become obsessed that he would have to undergo the same fate, to carry his waste matter in a bag. He thought this in spite of frequent diarrhea and despite tests, conducted a few months before his death, that showed his intestines to be free of cancer or other obstruction. He was certain that his torturing digestive tract would extract from him the ultimate payment.

My father's dentures pinched, or they slipped and let food get caught in the space between them and the gums. His mouth hurt all the time, the pain eclipsing other thoughts, perhaps even those of Cuba at times. The simple act of mastication was torture. If my father did not tell me about his bowel movements when he called, he was likely to tell me about his dentures.

My father's dental substitutes had not always been a source of pain. In Cuba he was comfortable with his partial dentures—and I was fascinated. At will my father could take out some of his teeth, smile great gaps at me, reinsert the teeth, and smile again at me with apparently perfect dentition. He could put his removable teeth in a glass. Through the glass, I could look carefully at the pink fake gum stretched like a membrane between pearly, real-looking teeth. One easy day when I was only two or three, I announced to the little girl in the next balcony, a girl with whom I often chatted, *"Mi papá tiene los dientes postizos,"* "my dad has false teeth." For some reason, even after I had reached adolescence, my father could laugh about this till his eyes threatened to water.

In exile my father believed in patronizing only illegal dentists, men who had been dentists in their home country but who were not certified to practice in the United States. My father's dentists were all Cuban, but for a while I was taken by my mother to a Dominican man in our building who practiced with a portable drill from the living room of his apartment overlooking Southwest Fifth Avenue.

The Dominican dentist was a friendly man who seemed perennially, and therefore excessively, relaxed. I do not remember his name, but his wife, in her permanent deshabille, bore the exotic name of Semíramis. They attempted to rename me. In the

Dominican Republic they had known a María del Carmen who had been called Maité, they said. My mother did not approve; to her, quite rightly, Maité was for María Teresa. But on the dentist's living room chair, with the black drill's extension in my mouth, I was Maité.

Many of my milk teeth that did not fall out quickly on their own had to be pulled out because they were badly decayed. My permanent first molars, which grew out during this period of apparently depraved dental hygiene, also developed caries. This upset me particularly because I had meant to be a film actress and I had never seen anything but perfection in a movie star's mouth; I must find another profession.

Novocain was, I suppose, too expensive or too difficult to obtain for ordinary use. Most of my dental work, by the Dominican and subsequently by a Cuban, was performed without any anesthetic. I know how hot a drill can get and how you can come to feel that searing heat on your nerve, how the dentist then has to stop to let the bit cool down before continuing to grind until the drill becomes too hot again. I did get injected with an anesthetic—whose needle, naturally, caused me to start to black out and then to vomit on the Dominican dentist's living room rug—when I was ten years old and the core of my lower right first molar began throbbing and the dentist realized that he would have to drill out the filling and go deeper. He put in an experimental cement—a "Swedish paste," he said—to work on the dentin.

When I was in college, the molar began throbbing again. I had a root canal in the office of my first in-laws' fancy East Side dentist who was reputed to have worked on Ava Gardner's mouth. His son, newly installed in his profession, specialized in root canals. The father was mild-tempered; the son, on the other hand, kept complaining, as he painfully introduced little rods into the pulp of my teeth, that I salivated too much. The root canal was perfection of a kind, but the Dominican dentist and Semíramis took my vomit on their rug with better grace.

My last year of high school I learned that—paying more, certainly—some Cuban parents in Miami sent their children to pleasantly antiseptic offices of board-certified dentists who put up colorful posters with Mr. Tooth and Mr. Brush and diagnosed their patients through x-rays. My father had been so resolutely loyal to illegal dentists, on my behalf and for himself, that I had never considered another way.

My father patronized an old acquaintance, a nervous man his age whose fingers smelled strangely comfortingly of cigarettes and soap. The hands, however, also shook alarmingly. He filled a cavity or two of mine. He did much more extensive work on my father's mouth.

My father decided that his old, rotten teeth were not worth rescuing. One day in the living room of our apartment at 440, with the sun streaming in through the three tall windows, the nervous dentist pulled out most of the teeth that remained in my father's mouth, leaving only two on which to anchor future dentures. He gave my father several shots of anesthetic. Then he pulled out tooth after tooth and, as he pulled, he threw these discarded pieces of my father into my mother's plastic cleaning bucket, awash in my father's spat-out blood.

No subsequent dentures fitted. Perhaps too much nature had to be substituted for. My father blamed the botching of one set on the already-nervous dentist's intensified fears of a crackdown by whatever authorities enforced dental practices. Another set my father blamed on a technician's rush. Maybe when my father decided so masculinely to pull out his teeth, he did not expect to live out two decades without them.

"It had to happen," my mother had said absolutely. "No one can stand that constant torment that he poured on himself." Afterwards, I wondered about the constant torment poured on my mother by a man who pondered the advisability of each bite of food, worried about its course through his digestive system, and made it a matter of life or death that it come expeditiously out of his large intestine.

When I arrived for his wake, I found the refrigerator full of cans of a strawberry-flavored liquid food supplement and little else. Some semi-medical person whose brother-in-law distributed it had recommended it to my father. Medicare paid for it, so the distributors brought cases and more cases to stack in the closet. My mother helped consume it. During our visit, Kurt and I bought groceries several times hoping to feed ourselves and to persuade my mother to eat a more varied diet.

"I don't plan to cook for a long time," my mother announced. "There's a lunchroom near here where two women cook. They're simple meals but pretty good, and it's not expensive. I think I'll go there most days. Other days, I don't know, I'll have sandwiches."

In Cuba, my mother had felt free to hold down a half-day job because she had my aunt Nena to look after me. In exile there was no one else to keep an eye on me, so my mother did not take a job, even though there was greater need for a second income. My father held down two jobs. Even after I became an adolescent, my parents insisted I needed looking after. When I left their vigilance for college in New York City, my father came up with another reason for my mother not to work: she had to be home to prepare his lunches.

I do not know if my mother really wanted to work, but I know that she found cooking a burden. Supposedly what she disliked most about it was deciding what to make for the next day. It seemed to me that her repeated requests for instructions were her weapon against us, a payment extracted from a family that persisted in expecting nurturance from her day after day without reprieve. "What do you think you would like to eat tomorrow?" she asked me each evening as I sat at dinner. "I would like to know what you would like to eat while you're here," she asks me the first morning of my visit if she has not already asked me a week before my arrival. Then she expects a day-by-day menu, which she writes down in orderly fashion. On Wednesday, I want *arroz con calamares.* Well, then, what vegetable do I want with that? Sometimes her mind gives my requests eccentric twists. If I say I want cucumber and tomato salad, she might serve cucumbers one day and tomatoes the next, because her imagination does not allow for the possibility of mixing the two. Her preference tends toward one-vegetable salads. My mother also wants to know at the beginning of each day at what time dinner should be on the table. It is always exactly and inflexibly on time. Every day of their lives together, she asked my father what to eat the next day and when to eat it. Usually she asked at meals, when he was too full to think about what form of satisfaction his next day's hunger would find most pleasing. "Why do you ask me now that I'm full?" I heard him fume several of what must have been many times during his twenty-nine years of exile—and, in fact, nearly forty-seven years of marriage, for in Cuba it was my mother who gave the housekeeper instructions. She complained to me that my father was cruel and querulous about her questions. She has never seen the reasons for his objections.

She said she would not cook, but she does. She makes herself thin vegetable soups that follow the dullness guidelines that doctors have set for the elderly. Yet when we visit her, she cooks complicated dishes. She separates the cucumbers from the tomatoes, but she gives us unexpected treats. Without my asking for them, because they are a lot of trouble, she makes *croquetas de jamón,* a dish that in restaurants can be mostly tasteless filler but that she forms between her small hands into thumb shapes that are fat and meaty and swollen and larger than life, and she fries them until they are redolent with their onions and parsley and your hunger has one object and knows no bounds.

Years before my mother suffered a transient ischemic attack, her doctor wanted her to cut down on her consumption of fats. Her red corpuscle count was admirably high, her heart was healthy, but her triglyceride count was unacceptable. He asked her if she ate a lot of meat. She did not and does not. She makes her thin soups and puts onion and green pepper into foods without first sautéing them. She eats ice cream, however, at least one large bowl a day. *"¡Ay, sí!"* she says. "What else is left to me?" And I imagine her in her loose, pink and orange sleeveless housedress, bending with intense concentration over bowls of ice cream, saying like Yeats, not that she knows Yeats, "They were not such a plague when I was young; what else have I to spur me into song?"

I am still my father's daughter. The day after his wake, I had to run to the bathroom soon after my mother's bustling in the kitchen had roused Kurt and me from our sleep on the sofa-bed. As I sat on the toilet doubled over with intestinal spasms, I noticed that my joints also ached. When I came out, I told my mother, "I have diarrhea."

She said, "I know. I heard." I was sure she could not be grateful for this lingering replication of her husband.

Because I felt terrible, I stretched out on what had now been closed up to be a normal sitting sofa. Kurt sat at the end where my feet were. I was facing the windows. My mother sat in a rocking chair in front of us. She had on her lap a big manila envelope. She said, "I want to go through all of these old cards and post cards from you. Do you mind if I throw some of them away?" She had spoken to me earlier of going through "all those papers" that my father had collected and kept. "Because your father kept every single piece of paper in case he would need to prove something to the housing people or to somebody else, and yet they tell us downstairs, 'You don't need to keep papers.'"

I did not want to think about what my father might have wanted to document by keeping my correspondence through the years. Now that he was gone, I assumed from my mother's behavior, she saw no need for such proofs.

She did not merely look through the cards silently to make her choices. She read them aloud. "You used to write so childishly. You sent this card right after you went off to Barnard. It says, 'I hope this little squirrel will keep company with my squirrel parents so they will not feel lonely.'"

I had to run to the bathroom with another bout of diarrhea. My entire body ached, especially my eyes. Although I had put on a sweater on this hot day, I started to tremble after I returned to the sofa. I asked for a thermometer. My mother had been doing all her talking and reading in Spanish. When my mother left the room, Kurt asked me, "What's she doing?"

"She's insisting on reading all these cards from my past, as if I needed to hear them now. I don't want to hear them."

My mother brought me an axillary centigrade thermometer, like the ones I used in childhood and adolescence. She continued to subject us to my correspondence. "You used to write as if you had honey in your mouth," she said with a regret that did not equal mine for all the other, many years when I commemorated birthdays and other days of obligation, punctually, dutifully, searching for enough words to write in the small space of a card that would not violate me, phrases that might show concern without capitulation, would curb the howl of rage while avoiding pretense at an intimacy whose absence wounded me. On the television still stood the frame that held, in one half, my father's picture and, in the other, the card bordered in blue, I-Can't-Thank-You-Enough-for-Being-Such-A-Wonderful-Father.

My mother pulled out post cards from my travels during my previous marriage, old cards that said embarrassing things, cards, the later ones, that bore only polite wishes for continued health. Even after we had ascertained that I, who rarely developed fever, had that day a real fever of 38.6 degrees Celsius, my mother continued her excavation into the envelope that held the documentary evidence of the long years of what must have seemed willful alienation from my father and her.

I finally said, "I cannot stand to hear any more."

She silently gathered up the cards as complacently as she had stopped the meals from the *cantina.* Kurt noticed that she did not, after all, throw any of my cards away.

The light from the windows hurt my eyes. I changed my position on the sofa so that my head was where my feet had been. I discussed with Kurt the fact that I would not be able to eat later that night or the next day any of the little bit of food that was in the refrigerator. I asked him to get me some foods recommended for those suffering from diarrhea.

"They say to eat a B-R-A-T diet," I told him.

I had read that in the health section of the *Washington Post* once, but I always have to think about what the initials stand for, and the fever was not making it any easier; the *a* in particular gives me trouble. "Bananas—I don't want rice—applesauce, and toast," I finally deciphered.

As soon as Kurt had set out cheerfully for the Winn-Dixie a block away, my mother came up to me and, touching me on the chest and peering at my face like a cat, she said, "Don't you think you are a little spoiled?"

Along with my convalescent food, Kurt brought back some strawberry ice cream. As soon as the carton had been taken out of the shopping bag, my mother scooped out a big bowlful. On it she poured some of her highly caloric, strawberry-flavored liquid food supplement. After the snack, she returned to her place in the rocking chair.

"I want to hear a story," I said. Whenever I was ill as a child I asked for stories. My mother and my aunt told family tales. I did not care if I had heard them many times before. Like the one about the time when my grandmother Luisa, when she was still a young girl, went to the amusement park wearing her brand-new wide-brimmed straw hat. The name of such a hat in Spanish is *pamela;* that was one of the best parts of the story as far as I was concerned. My grandmother got on the roller coaster. As soon as the cars started moving, her *pamela* flew off. All during the ride, she was disconsolate. She wept because she had lost her new *pamela.* When the ride was over, she got up from her seat and happened to look back. There in the car behind her lay my grandmother's *pamela.*

When I asked my mother for a story, she was not surprised. I figured that since she already thought me spoiled I might as well go for broke. She could not think of a story, so I prompted her with questions. Yes, Canela the dog had been hit by a car, she told us. She was an affectionate animal who followed my mother and her siblings to school. While faithfully pursuing them one day, the dog was hit. Óscar and José Luis, the youngest sibling, found her and carried her home but nothing could be done. Yes, she was the color of cinnamon, more or less.

I asked my mother to tell us how her family manufactured kites at home in order to make some money during the Depression. I had grilled her for information years before when I was writing a fictionalized account of the family enterprise. ("You baptized everybody," my mother complained because I changed the names.) But I wanted to hear the story again, this time for pleasure, and I wanted Kurt also to hear first-hand about this family of mine that survived the worst times by making paper dreams.

To the Salas family, the correlation between kites and food on the table was direct. There were nine mouths to feed. My grandfather was a meat broker, a middleman, hardly a good business to be in during a period when people considered a dish of cornmeal a meal—and lucky to have that, thank you. Óscar thought up the idea of making kites. There were always boys and men willing to buy them. One detail I missed when writing about the kite manufacture was that in the early days the family worried that although their kites' composition showed a lot of imagination and care, the paper did not look as taut as that of more experienced kite makers.

"The kites lacked the professional touch," my mother said.

One day Óscar visited a man who had been in the craft for a long time, and he noticed that the man sprayed his kites with alcohol. As the alcohol dried, the paper stretched perfectly. Óscar devised a rack for airing the newly sprayed kites, with a compartment for each, and he made a special sprayer.

"Óscar was very inventive. It's a pity that circumstances didn't enable him to make something more of his life," my mother said. "The kites were entirely Óscar's idea," she said, leaning forward in the rocking chair, toward Kurt.

She sometimes stumbled over the English words with which to describe to Kurt the materials they had used, and I had to translate. My mother turned her hands, palms in, palms out, as she described how she and her siblings had folded the paper, how they had arranged the kite spars. Her hands were tiny, foreign to me, reminders of her mother's hands. Months later, my husband still thought of how my mother had turned her little hands, palms in, palms out.

*El pez muere por la boca.* Dr. N. told me, "The surest way for somebody to kill himself with a gun is to put the gun in his mouth. If he doesn't do that, he can miss and become a vegetable." My father only held the gun to the right side of his skull. He didn't eat the bullet. And so he lived another fifteen hours. He lay on the bathroom floor making a sound between gasp and groan. My mother imitated the sound for me, and I thought immediately of the fish I caught in the Everglades on my first honeymoon. My first husband told me that fish must not be killed at the moment of capture; they do not stay fresh that way. We strung the living fish through its mouth to the back of the canoe. It bellowed so deeply during our trip back through a mangrove-lined channel that the canoe vibrated. As I paddled, I kept thinking of the images of the Sorrowful Mysteries in the colorfully illustrated guide to the rosary I had brought with me from Cuba: Christ being whipped while chained to a pillar, Christ crowned with thorns that cut into his forehead. But I was docile to my first husband in matters about which, I was unceremoniously informed, I knew less than he. When we reached land, he cracked the fish's head and stilled its voice. At our rented cabin, we baked the fish with a little butter. With a dash of fresh lemon, it made a delicious dinner.

In the film *Lethal Weapon* the cop character Martin Riggs, played by Mel Gibson, considers suicide while a Bugs Bunny Christmas special rattles on the television. He takes his Baretta in his hands, wipes off the handle—in case someone else's fingerprints are on it, I assume from experience; suicides can be very exculpatory of the living. He points the gun toward himself. The camera closes in on the gunpoint. We see the gun from a suicide's angle. Riggs drives the gunpoint into the center of his forehead. Changing tactics, he moves the barrel of the gun into his mouth. His teeth clench around it. A finger touches the trigger. He seems almost to be gagging on the gun. He does not shoot. He explains later that he has a special bullet for the occasion: one with a hollow point. This, he says, will guarantee that he will blow the back of his head off. He claims that putting the gun under the chin is just as good as putting it inside the mouth. Suicides owe it to themselves and everyone else to be careful.

Kurt and I had never seen the film. On 12 July, a few weeks after my father's suicide, we rented the video because we were packing for a move only two days away and we thought a good action film might relax us. That I broke down when I saw this scene, that we clung to each other shaking and yet unable to look away is not surprising. The next morning I watched the scene again.

A month later I bought a copy of the videotape. As I watched it, I wondered how my father had learned to load a gun. It is not something I would know how to do. He had told me once that he had practiced firing a gun, with a male cousin, I think, or a friend. He was young, and in my image of the day the sun had always shone.

Several times I have replayed the tape. I keep trying to understand the degree of detachment from life that a human being must attain before he can look down the open end of a gun barrel and pull the trigger. I keep trying to measure the flailing rage that must precede this disposing of a life as if in a dream.

Then God said, "Let us make humans in our image, after our likeness, and let them have dominion over the earth." So God created humans in God's own image, in the image of God, God created them, male and female.

"Call us yours and yourselves ours," God said to them. "Love us in yourselves."

And God saw everything that had been made, and behold, it was necessary. Thus it continued for millennia of unmeasured time.

However, within creation was a being who called himself Lord-God. His disposition would not allow him to be satisfied within what was. To him the unmeasured seconds seemed immeasurable eternities wasted, when he ought to be building an empire. Instead, God had left little to do.

One day Lord-God decided that there may not be much to do, but there was much to redo. He began his work by recreating a sky and an earth beneath the sky. On the day of this endeavor a mist rose from the earth and covered the ground, obscuring but moistening.

From among all of God's creation, Lord-God was most impatient with humans because they were most like God and thus happy with their place in creation. Therefore he trapped a male human and he took wet red soil and formed a man like the man that had already been created but who, being made of the clay of the new earth, was also unlike him and therefore unlike God. Lord-God breathed the man into the clay's nostrils and the man became a living being upon the new world.

Lord-God led the man into a garden where Lord-God had planted some of the beauty that God had created. Among palms there were royal, corojo, thatch, petticoat, and big-bellied, and, whether Lord-God meant them to or not, they lent grace to the man's days and to his nights they brought a sweet, haunting susurration. Trees there were for shade and support: mahogany, ceiba, sabicu, strangler fig, copey, gumbo limbo, lignum vitae. For fragrance, Lord-God planted frangipani, sweet acacia, and night-blooming jessamine; for color, hibiscus, jacaranda, queen's wreath, fancy-leaved caladium, heliconia, and cassia. Orchids and bromeliads stirred the man's wonder—that such beauty should find sustenance in air! To feed the man, Lord-God selected plantings that would yield good fruit: mamey colorado, sweetsop, soursop, custard apple, star apple, satinleaf, mamoncillo, canistel.

But Lord-God did not want the man to fall into his old God-given complacency. He thus commanded the man, saying, "Look around you. Look at the garden I have planted for you. You may freely eat of every tree of the garden; but of the tree of the knowledge of good and evil you shall not eat, for in the day that you eat of it you shall die."

Lord-God pointed an argillaceous finger to specify a tree with large, broad, many-lobed leaves that looked as if they could be waved over the body to bring air into the moisture of hot days. A taxonomic puzzle—the leaves seemed to belong more to a philodendron, the trunk to a palm. From the thin trunk hung clusters of big, fat fruit. The fruit was green.

"Otherwise, my man," Lord-God said, "this is Paradise."

The man wandered among the plants in an ecstasy of naming. In his native tongue he named them. He repeated the names for Lord-God.

"It is not good that the man should be alone," Lord-God thought.

So he brought animals into the garden, animals that flew or slithered or swam or walked. The man named them too. Excited, he recited their names to Lord-God. He recounted their habits and their structural relationships.

Lord-God grew impatient with this loquacity. He put the man into a deep sleep in the garden. Then he drew out one of the man's ribs, closed up the chest opening, and formed a woman from the rib bone. She too was different from her former self, this new bone of clay, this woman.

Now the serpent's shape determined its skill at subtle infiltrations. It had no venom but lots of information. It saw the woman one day when she lay, languorous, on a bed of ferns, where the noonday heat had rocked her into the edge of a dream. The serpent whispered close to the woman's ear, "Psst. Has the lord of this place told you not to eat of any tree in the garden?"

The woman was a light sleeper. Startled, she answered, "Lord-God spoke to my husband, not to me. But my husband told me that Lord-God said that if we eat of the fruit of the tree of knowledge of good and evil, we shall die."

"Lord-God lies," said the serpent. "You will survive the eating of the fruit, and your eyes will be opened, and you will be like God, knowing good and evil, whatever those may be."

As it happened, Lord-God had neglected to take all of the woman's memory when he remade her. She had often looked at the tree of knowledge, a delight to the eyes, and her memory had made her hungry for its heavy fruit. For days the spheres had been turning from green to yellow. Their rotundity reminded her of her full breasts and of her happy belly. After her conversation with the serpent, she could not clear her mind of the vision of the plant.

Finally one day, the star apples and canistels and soursops would not satisfy. The forbidden fruit drew her. They hung from the tree like suns. She tore one down. She split it with a sharp stone. The split revealed meat like the sun at its long daily farewell and perfectly round black seeds like the spots in her eyes when she looked at the sun when it was high in the sky. She tore the fruit halves apart and she bit into the sunset meat. Juice ran down her chin and three tears ran down her cheeks. The fruit was sweet and musky and strange, but she was unchanged—and she had wanted to be like God. For the first time, she knew deep, unassuageable pain. Then she remembered.

She searched for her husband, her only companion. She put a slice of the delicate fruit into his hands. "Eat, beloved, and refresh yourself before hearing what I have to say," she spoke to him from her love and her sorrow. They sat against the trunk of a ceiba and she cradled him in her arms. She said, "This is wisdom: Death defines us. What we are else will elude us. The liquor of our happiness will always have within it a mixture of our sorrows. Ambition will triumph over goodness and sense. And though we are not yet cast out from this fair and fragrant place, we are exiles."

# Girón

The woman who lived across from us in apartment 4 burst out of her screen door as soon as she heard the creak of ours, as if she had been waiting for my mother and me to get back from our grocery shopping.

"They're on television. They're on television. Come!" she said, as her solid silhouette beckoned agitatedly with its hand.

It was always dark in the hallway of the old apartment building and our eyes were still dazzled from the unrelenting brightness of sparsely vegetated Miami streets. Holding open our black screen door, my mother unlocked the inner, solid wood door, shoved her errands cart in, and took the few steps across the hall to our neighbor's apartment. I felt cold from the thought of crossing her threshold. A few weeks before, the neighbor had found a scorpion lurking in the darkness before her door. Since then, I had been afraid of my steps in that hallway.

The animal I hate the most is the scorpion. In the countryside, when my father was a child, he once pushed his foot into a boot and felt something twisting inside it, tickling him. He drew his foot out immediately. He turned the boot over, and out crawled a big, dark brown scorpion.

Somehow I went inside the neighbor's apartment, for I stood there with my mother and the neighbor. Her apartment was the mirror image of ours in layout, but it had apparently been blessed with more caring previous tenants than ours.

When we moved into apartment 3 seven months before, my mother had scraped off layers of brown dirt from the bathroom and the kitchen, and the place still showed signs of past abuse. It was difficult for us to imagine how anyone could have lived that way. The Anglo owner did not think it his duty to clean apartments for new tenants. He was Roman Catholic and had many children; when my mother and I went to Mass at Saints Peter and Paul, we sometimes saw him there with his unhappy, unkempt brood. My father claimed that, before the Cuban influx, the building had been destined for demolition.

In a couple of years we would move into the more favorably historied apartment 4, by way of improving our existence, and we would put our television set in the same corner where our neighbor now had hers, to the right of the three tall windows. Perhaps it was the only logical place for it in that apartment.

Our neighbor's television flashed us fuzzy, grayish images of uniformed men. "Brigada 2506," read a patch shown by the television. I inferred from what the neighbor and my mother were saying that on that day, 17 April 1961, these men had gone on an invasion of Cuba.

"How can they be showing film of something that is happening right now?" I asked. I was nine years old.

"It's just a film of their training in Central America," the neighbor explained.

Obviously she could understand the English narration better than my mother and I could. She told us that she was Puerto Rican, but that her husband, a merchant seaman, was Cuban. I had wondered why he was away from home so much. I wonder now—did not know to wonder then—if he was on one of the merchant ships that participated in the invasion, if that was the source of our neighbor's agitated interest.

The newscast then showed a scene of men full of resolve signing up to go to Cuba and fight. They were registering at a table set up by the Cuban Revolutionary Council.

"Ah, the Consejo!" I turned to my mother, truly excited now. The Consejo were our people.

It might have been the next day, in our apartment: my mother became enraged. We had been listening to the Spanish-language radio. They were saying how many were in the invasion force and what route they had taken. Or at least some version thereof, true or not. We may in fact have been listening to the CIA's disinformation campaign, maybe just to speculation.

"Men!" my mother said, livid. "Men are such gossips! They want to show everybody that they know what's happening, so they tell everything."

My father was not the least of these men. He was director of the department of press and information of the Consejo Revolucionario Cubano, the coalition of disparate groups and clashing personalities that had come together because the U.S. government had insisted that heated disagreement be put aside under one leadership. The White House wanted one organization, so that a victorious invasion force would have a government to install. The squabbling groups warily and grudgingly agreed to form the artificial alliance of the Consejo a mere few weeks before the invasion. From his post my father could act as close advisor and press secretary to his good friend José Miró Cardona, the man who had emerged as the Consejo's president.

For days my father, the information chief, without being specific about the nature of the event, had confided to just about everybody who called him at home that something big was going to happen; he could not have told them when because he did not know when. Yet he made frying-egg sounds with his tongue and ran his hands over his hair when he spoke of what had been said on the radio. "They might as well have sent Fidel a copy of the plans," he said angrily.

My parents' anger of those first hours was, as it turned out, misplaced. The news broadcast by exiles carried nothing that was news to Fidel Castro. He had known for some time that a major action against him, possibly an invasion, was imminent. No, a vast anger belonged, but it belonged elsewhere.

*Nos embarcaron,* as we Cubans said in our slang to mean "we were fooled" long before we were sent sailing with little more than U.S. promises on the invasion to Girón, and now with so much more reason. We were embarked, *compadre,* and we were disembarked too.

Since early in 1959, clandestine groups had carried out sabotage in Cuba, some conducting strictly Cuban operations but many maintaining ties to supply lines from the North. Some members of this underground had been trained and infiltrated by the CIA. Two important acts of sabotage were carried out days before the invasion.

On 6 April in Santa Cruz del Norte, El Central Hershey, the refinery whose security Corporal Chávez had defended by condemning my father's head and whose productivity was aided by the effort of my father's young body bending under the weight of sugar sacks, was destroyed by a blaze so terrible and beautiful that anyone who had glanced from the darkness of ocean toward that stretch of coast would have marvelled at the sight of a town made of fire.

On 14 April, a group led by a Cuban man who had been infiltrated by the CIA into his native country poured white phosphorus into the air-conditioning system of El Encanto, the most elegant department store in La Habana, where the lace, and everything else, was of the best quality. As if bewitched, that great emporium of luxury split and spilled its blazing top story onto Galiano, the street where *habaneros* shopped back when there were things to shop for, where I walked briskly many times with my father or mother, sometimes to reach bus stops under covered portals, where I longed for the spell-binding wares of the gardenia seller, who carried in her wicker basket flowers to pin. The single creamy blooms on glossy leaves allured me with a fragrance whose piercing, green beauty penetrated my chest and would not grant me permission to depart even after my mother had unreasonably refused to buy one for me because their white color said to her that they were flowers for mother-orphaned women, like my grandmother, to wear on Mother's Day.

They were all put at risk, the saboteurs, even those who were CIA-infiltrated. For the CIA would not warn any Cuban that the invasion was imminent. "I don't trust any goddamn Cuban!" shouted Marine Corps Colonel Jack Hawkins, the CIA's military commander. Even the men that the United States had sent with invasion-related missions to Cuba were left to learn of its occurrence from Cuban radio. Therefore, they did not have time to do their jobs. One man was supposed to have been given a signal to blow up a bridge leading to Girón. He was given nothing; Fidel Castro's convoys of militia-filled trucks rolled in safety over the intact bridge to destroy the Brigade. Five Cuban infiltrators were executed and seven drew long prison sentences.

Not wanting to leave it all to Fidel Castro, the CIA, which did not trust any goddamn Cuban, imprisoned Fidel Castro's opposition. On 16 April, Miró Cardona and the other leaders of the Consejo Revolucionario were spirited away by the CIA from a hotel in New York to an air field in Opa-Locka, Florida, where they were forced into barracks and kept under lock, *incomunicados,* as if they were dissidents made to disappear by the repressive government they opposed. When they had been picked up by CIA men in New York, they had thought that they were being taken to join the invasion force. In effect, they had been kidnapped.

Inside the barracks, the Consejo leaders heard on the radio a statement supposedly issued by Miró in which "Miró" declared that fighting had begun in the cities and in the hills of Cuba. It was Miró's first awareness of the statement, which had been issued by a *yanqui* ad agency upon dictation by the CIA's own E. Howard Hunt.

Upon learning of the kidnapping, Arthur Schlesinger, Jr., the historian then on President John F. Kennedy's staff, flew to Opa-Locka. As he walked inside the gray barracks, a wave of desperate, angry men washed upon him. Weeping from frustration, rage, humiliation, the proud and dignified Miró begged to be permitted to die on the beaches with the young men of the Brigade, among them his son—the sons of all, all were their sons. It was with the nation's sons—not alone upon a beachhead already stained by their blood—that the Consejo had agreed to set up a government that the United States would soon recognize, a republic of coral, mosquitoes, and crabs.

The United States ordered six, and only six, of Brigade 2506's World-War-II-issue airplanes to fly a raid two days in advance of the main amphibious landing, restricting their targets to Castro's three principal airfields. The use of napalm was forbidden. With strict limits on planes, targets, ordnance, and amount of flight time over the island, the Brigade could not accomplish the once-established, now seemingly abandoned, goal of destroying Castro's entire air force. However, the air raids were highly effective in at least one respect: they sent a loud warning to the Cuban government that an important hostile action had begun. The CIA military command, in effect, shouted its secret, and you can trust any goddamn Cuban to hear and understand.

Arise, people of Cuba, Miami radio and the CIA's Radio Swan exhorted. The CIA planners of the invasion had counted on popular support to duplicate the Brigade's efforts. In fact, they had devised an invasion strategy in which spontaneous popular support was an absolute requirement for success of the entire mission. When the Brigade got there, popular support was in jail.

After the warning air strike, the Castro government started rounding up the opposition and anyone who conceivably might be in the opposition and anyone who was related, however distantly, to someone who might consider being in the opposition perhaps. At least one hundred thousand people were arrested in sweeps throughout the island. The devilish efficiency of this round-up was made possible by the joint action of the militia; the army; the block-watch committees who could identify those who might possibly hold unorthodox beliefs; and the dreaded secret police, the G-2, which was headed by an ugly man whose similarities in name and origin to my father (Ramiro Valdés, poor Artemisa family) vexed me.

Much of the underground was arrested, as were people given to speaking their minds. The bishops were confined. Husbands and wives were detained, their children scattered to relatives. Anyone who had ever fallen foul of a watch committee was deemed a possible threat to internal security.

Tensions ran so high on the island that my uncle Óscar, who disliked the government but had never been politically active, suffered a heart attack that kept him in the hospital for a month. My aunt Nena informed my mother of their brother's brush with death only after he had recovered and had been sent home; whether she did not want to worry my mother or simply could not communicate with us due to the hostilities is not clear.

The arrested were herded into schools and stadiums and stables, wherever a door could be locked against escape. Because it was the largest theater in La Habana, the Teatro Blanquita, two buildings down from the Río Mar, was considered suitable to hold a multitude.

On 20 June 1960, the Blanquita had been confiscated from ex-senator Alfredo Hornedo Suárez, the uncle of my father's long-time boss at *El Crisol,* Alfredo Izaguirre Hornedo, who in turn was the father of Alfredo Izaguirre Riva, who would lose his youth and almost his life in prison. They were a wealthy family, the Hornedos. They also owned, among other things and besides the newspaper, the Hotel Blanquita, which stood on Primera Avenida in Miramar between the Río Mar and the theater. My father sometimes said that the Hornedos had so much money that they could sit on their doorstep and throw out five-peso bill after five-peso bill and not make a dent in their fortune.

For me the Teatro Blanquita had once been a kind of prison. I was caught in its lobby in claustrophobic panic when a performance by Sarita Montiel, the Spanish singer, let out during a downpour and adult bodies blocked all the exits and pressed around me and did not let my mother and me near freedom and fresh air, and in that heat they remained, the rows and rows of tall humans who stood as walls against my breath, until the rain had diminished. It seemed like an eternity till my mother and I walked in the oxygen and the mild rain.

The program had started with a showing of Montiel's film *El último cuplé*. When the production number for the sunny song "Valencia" came on, the film was stopped and the curtains were opened to reveal dancers positioned on steps and costumed as Valencian orange harvesters, exactly as they had been in the film. Sarita Montiel then came out onto the stage singing "Valencia" and was greeted with excited applause. After she sang and said charming things and received flowers from the audience, the curtain closed and the film continued to the end. This was tactically questionable, since the melodramatic film deteriorates rapidly from that point up to the last moment, when the heroine dies after singing the first song of her come-back appearance at a big theater (bad heart). I suppose there was some benefit to be derived from the real audience's sense of gratitude at not having witnessed a similarly fatal performance on the stage of the Blanquita.

For several weeks my mother and I had structured our entertainment around the songs from the film. We had the record, and my cousin Elsa at a previous performance had obtained a lyric-filled program that helped us learn the songs more completely. As if any Cuban could miss the perhaps fortuitous connection, the makers of Edén cigarettes had placed a prominent ad on a page of the lyrics to a strangely decadent song that interwove the arguably disparate pleasures of lovemaking and smoking—with the accent on the latter—and featured the crucial line "Smoking is an Eden *(un Edén),* genial, sensual. . . ."

As I think over the lyrics now, I realize that its real subject is the singer-narrator's erotic dependence on a man's blowing smoke from his mouth into hers, an act she wants him to perform right now: "Hurry, because that way you drive me crazy; run, I want to go crazy with pleasure, with pleasure." Although most of the psychosexual implications of the song were lost on me at the time, the connection of smoking with a languid kind of glamour was not. My mother smoked cigarettes occasionally when she was relaxing in the early evening. She sat in a rocking chair, not a chaise longue, and she did not welcome a "solicitous and gallant lover" like the woman in the song, but she did put on a face like that of an actress playing an exotic role. I thought I would smoke on a chaise longue when I grew up (but that was before the U.S. Surgeon General's report on lung cancer). I begged my mother to teach me how she sucked in smoke through her mouth and blew it out her nose, and one of those evenings on the balcony, she succeeded in getting me to do it correctly. She succeeded so well, in fact, that on the rare occasions when I do smoke—usually one escapade a year is all I can tolerate, and not every year—I must blow the smoke out my nose. Observers assume that I am performing parlor tricks, and the smoke coats my nostrils with a brown film that nauseates me in the morning.

Even if they interfered with my future enjoyment of vice, I would not have given up any of the many lessons of the soundtrack of *El último cuplé* and another Montiel showcase film, *La violetera* ("The Violet Seller"). Some of the keenest pleasures were linguistic and narrative. There were new words to learn, like *garbo,* which was just like an actress's name, and *zalamera,* which made me think of the south of Spain, even without my knowing its derivation from the Arabic. There were nonsense words like *catacatapún* to enjoy for the sheer silliness of them. There was a phrase, *mi moza,* at a particularly tender moment in a lovely song for which *mi Boza* could conveniently be substituted. And there was the combining of interesting words with extravagant story, a complete entertainment package. My favorite song was the sad (of course) tale of a woman who is asked by a bullfighter to step on his cape with *garbo* (meaning gracefulness, not an actress) because he is going to make from the piece of cape on which such a pretty foot has trod *un relicario*—a reliquary! Unfortunately, one Monday in April, the bullfighter is gored. But he sees her standing in the crowd, and as he lies dying, he withdraws from his chest a reliquary—and he sings to her some more. For a child like me—admittedly, a small universe of people—a song just could not get any better than that.

They were *café-concert* sorts of songs, and my mother was familiar with many of them prior to the advent of the film *El último cuplé.* Following the example of a famous *cupletista,* in her youth she had sung *cuplés* as if striding from table to table of captivated clubgoers. She knew a longer, more heart-breaking version of the lovely "Nena," which was to prove, even in the abbreviated version, deadly to the Montiel heroine in the film. This song expressed more genuine feeling than most of the other songs on the album, chronicling at first the fear and then the actuality of losing through death a man loved for many years. I cannot say that I understood the depth of such emotions at the time. I also could not connect, no matter how I tried, the song to the Nena I knew, my accommodating aunt who had not married and who spent her days taking care of my grandmother and me; I did not know that her physiognomy was that of a Greek tragic heroine. *Nena, me decía ciego de pasión.* My mother made some fine distinctions ignored by Montiel. In my mother's version the man was "mad with passion" in the earlier episodes, but "blind with passion" as he lay dying. His kiss in early stanzas was a "divine flame," but in the final stanza, a "last flame."

I did not want to be entirely dependent on my mother for coaching on these songs, since she possessed a powerful soprano voice attracted to theatrical heights I could not reach at the age of (approximately) six and she was exceedingly particular about performance. Therefore, I asked my grandmother if she would copy out for me the song lyrics that appeared in Elsa's much coveted program. My grandmother agreed, and she had been at the task of copying out the songs in her strange, old-fashioned hand with fancy squared-off loops when my aunt Nena came upon us and began to berate me for asking my grandmother to perform such a difficult task. My *abuela's* eyes were not good (she used reading glasses with black frames and thick lenses), my *abuela's* hands hurt with *artritis*—I forget what else Nena threw in my face. "No, no, I'm all right," my grandmother said, but Nena held on to her arm and badgered her into stopping. My grandmother must do nothing. I felt so guilty about having asked my grandmother to do something taxing that, although she gave me the songs she had copied out, I could hardly bear to look at them, and then I felt guilty about not using them.

But still I sang. The expectant time leading up to our attendance at *El último cuplé* was my mother's and my festival of song. Sarita Montiel's performance itself was eclipsed. I saw my mother's desperate fear that we would die from asphyxiation in the crowded lobby, and, standing closer to the ground and having less access to air, I feared it too. At my insistence, my mother tried holding me up so that my face could rise above the crowd, but her arms were weak and she was so full of her own panic that she soon had to put me down. A friendly man standing near us held me up, but this position generated a new dread, that of being separated from my mother. I imagined the coolness on Sarita Montiel's face as, without hindrance, she walked out of the performers' exit elsewhere in the building and stepped into a long black car. Recently when I asked my mother if she remembered the program we saw with Sarita Montiel at the Blanquita, she said, "No, no, I don't remember what was in the program, and I don't remember a film, but do you remember at the end all the people crowding into the lobby?"

On 17 April 1961, about 5,000 women and men suspected of possessing a potential for counterrevolution were bused in waves to the Blanquita, where they remained incarcerated for six days. The lines at the grossly inadequate sanitary facilities were interminable. There was only one lavatory for the women. The discomfort this created was most acutely felt by those who were pregnant or menstruating. The theater, which had been designed to employ air-conditioning, was ventilated during those terrible days only through a few windows on the top story. The heat was oppressive and pervasive. People covered every available inch of space; they sat on the dust of the stage, in the aisles. They sweated but could not obtain water except in the unreachable lavatories. The militia distributed very little food, most or all of it provided by relatives on the outside. All the time there was noise, from weeping, from screaming, from the anxiety that clawed. Two people died from heart failure and one from a stray bullet from a *miliciano's* gun. A young woman, screaming, lost her fetus amidst the crowd at the Blanquita.

Six thousand people were herded into the Palacio de Deportes in the Vedado section of La Habana. The militiamen created their own sport at this sports palace. One night they turned out the lights, shot at random into the crowd, and then turned on the light to see how many people they had hit with their bullets.

One hazard at all the temporary detention centers was harassment by militia members who considered their captives the enemy by virtue of having been detained. Soon the captured men of the brigade would also be detained at the Sports Palace.

My father was not home most of 17 April, of course. He was never home for natural or international disasters. During the invasion, he was attending to Consejo business—answering press calls and trying to learn something for himself. But he always left me, even when he was not involved in events. He left me so that he could inform the other families, the normal families, who huddled together in times of crisis, around a radio, together—at least, that was how I pictured them. I like to think that there is loose in the world an army of children of journalists whose mother or father was never home during the scariest times, during hurricanes, floods, coups, and wars—an army of adults who as children learned to thrill at the sound of wind and water battering the windows of their shaky habitations, because a crisis was under way, survival danced on a razor's edge, and a parent, elsewhere, knew all the latest developments.

There was talk of sending journalists as correspondents to the front; the fighting was expected to last longer than an instant.

I asked my mother, "Is Papi going to go be war correspondent?"

"I should think he's too old," she snapped. I could tell she hoped she was right.

He was fifty-two. He did not go. And there was nothing but debris on a beach and mosquitoes in a swamp to go to anyway. But two or three days after his death, my mother unearthed pictures of my father signing up for military service. The day she showed us the photographs, she thought that we were looking at images of his registering for the Brigade reserves in April 1961. On the brown paper bag that must have held the pictures for a long time my father had written: "Photos of my enlistment to serve in the army of the United States to fight against Castro." For some reason he had seen fit to sign the bag "R. Boza."

Almost certainly, the photographs were taken late September or early October 1962 during the course of yet another U.S. government hoodwinking of the Consejo. My father and his journalistic colleagues from the Colegio Nacional de Periodistas were offering themselves up to a special Cuban corps of the U.S. Army that would, he thought—they all thought, again—help

*Ramiro Boza with other journalists signing up for military service.*

liberate Cuba. His shock of thick, black straight hair was brushed back. Black still, and he had just turned fifty-four. He was always trying to tame that hair, but some strands stubbornly rebelled and, as he worked, they frequently fell forward onto his forehead. He was a lion born with Asian hair.

"He looks fierce," my husband said. "But then, in all of his pictures he looks fierce."

Recently, as another Girón anniversary was approaching, my mother said in response to something completely unrelated, "That's how these *americanos* are. They tell everybody different things, trying to keep all their options open, and in the end they do what is most convenient for themselves. Just like the time around Girón. They told your father he was favored to be war minister if a provisional government was established. Your father was unhappy and I was scandalized. Your father knew nothing about war. He didn't even like the military. They told people whatever came into their heads."

I had long stored out of reach that Saturday when my father came home and said, "They talked to me about being war minister," and I said, incredulous, "Not information minister?" and he answered, "No."

It could be argued, of course, that there was a certain advanced but improbable logic in putting into a position of power over the military in a country prone to militarism a man who distrusted the military and had, in fact, been persecuted by it. In a just world, he would be ideal. But justice did not frequently enter into the machinations of the CIA. Maybe he was their flavor of the day; maybe they thought they could win my recalcitrant father with war.

"It was all a game," my mother says. "It was all a game to them, a game they were playing with us. There were different factions in the Consejo, and the CIA was telling them different things, testing which one would be most convenient for the United States. Because that is all that the United States cares about. They do this. They manipulate. They formulate their strategies. They are cynical. It's all a game of strategy to them. They promised so much, and in the end they sent Cubans to die."

U.S. people call this disaster Bay of Pigs. Cubans call it Girón. We honor the men's ordeal, and our tragedy, and so we prefer a name without taint of insult, free of the reference to a derided animal. I admire pigs, their gruntings and bristle and deceptively naked pink and especially their strong smell of fertile earth, but in Spanish the word *cochino* is used to refer not only to the animal but also to a dirty person, and in English also *pig* is used as an insult to humans, an insult particularly employed by the rebellious young in the 1960s and 1970s to refer to despised figures of authority. I have sometimes heard U.S.ers produced by that era pronounce the name of the Bay of Pigs as if it characterized those who participated in it.

There were battles on two beaches, Playa Girón and Playa Larga, both on Bahía de Cochinos. They were bordered by the Ciénaga de Zapata, a vast, redoubtable swamp whose difficult name called up for me in my childhood images of a place utterly hostile to humans and presided over by crocodiles and mosquitoes. I asked if anyone ever ventured there, into that Zapata Swamp, into the troubling *ciénaga*.

I call this disaster in a place of desolation Girón. U.S.ers think that the "Bay of Pigs Invasion" was an event that took place in April 1961. Yet it is in the nature of disasters to endure in their effects. For Cubans, Girón continues. About this I am all Cuban; I am a wronged party. Forgiveness, taken to mean simply the decision no longer to feel resentment, is logical; it releases us from a knot of gall. Willful forgetfulness is not. It makes no sense to disregard the lessons of experience. We remember who has wronged us so that we will not allow him again into a position from which to repeat it.

They came to us with blandishments, the whispering men, with susurrations (for only *our* ear) of mighty assistance. They said whatever they wanted since the ear is a cup without a bottom. They represented the U.S. government this time, we had to assume, for they had before. They had been our contacts, the various men all speaking as if from the same source of authority. A colonel at the training base in Guatemala told Miró and Tony Varona of the Consejo not to worry about the small size of the brigade. They would have thirty thousand more men. He did not say specifically from where. But it was understood. From where else but the U.S. armed forces could the United States deploy thirty thousand men?

It was with surprise and disappointment that Miró received the figure of fifteen thousand men from Adolf Berle of the State Department. So said Miró in his testimony before the Taylor Commission, whose proceedings remained locked up tight for decades, the silence making us look like raving lunatics while U.S.ers believed our fertile imaginations had fabricated their promises and the public endeavored to canonize the blue-eyed presidential brothers.

The brigade members were told that they did not have to worry about being so few, or about their ratty ships and outdated planes, because during the invasion they would have an umbrella, an umbrella provided by the United States in planes flown by U.S. pilots. On the second day of slaughter, to the end, the CIA was still telling the brigade that air cover was coming to protect them, they would not be let down, air cover was coming. But this was the umbrella they received: in response to much begging, John Kennedy finally permitted U.S. Navy planes to provide "escort" to the brigade's rickety B-26s for one hour (i.e., U.S. planes would fly between brigade and Castro planes). The U.S. Navy pilots had no permission to fire unless they themselves were fired upon, which no Castro pilot was stupid enough to do. The brigade got not the umbrella, but the rain.

The CIA pushed the Cubans to the hilt and to the assault. What did I, a child, learn from the flimsiness of U.S. promises? No one but Cubans cared if Cubans died on the beaches. Giants are cynical. They know that even when they nap there may be casualties when they roll over.

However, not only Cubans died at Girón. The Kennedy administration did not want to acknowledge it and the CIA, of course, would not verify it, but four U.S. pilots with Anglo-Saxon names from real towns, USA, were killed over Cuba. They were supposed to be trainers, but at the hour of battle they flew for the brigade. No one would acknowledge their deaths, much less their bravery, to their bewildered families until Everett Dirksen, Senate minority leader, unearthed their past in 1963.

My father heard that navy men from the United States wept as they stood, ordered into immobility on the decks of their powerful ships just outside firing range from Girón. They were almost close enough to see Cuban faces. They were not panelled securely in distant Washington meeting rooms. In *Bay of Pigs: The Untold Story,* Peter Wyden confirms that they could see us and they were filled with shame.

In 1973, I became a U.S. citizen. I mistakenly took it as a sign that I had forgiven a little. *(Gentlemen may cry peace, peace, but there is no peace.)* My father also became a U.S. citizen, but he never forgave. There were times in my childhood and adolescence when I thought it a toss-up whom he hated more: the Communists or *los yanquis.* Fidel he at least understood because they shared a nationality.

The name Kennedy seemed to drip from my father's lips with acid. It was a sign of my father's deep involvement in the matters of the Consejo that he mentioned Robert Kennedy's name as often as John Kennedy's. It was with Bobby Kennedy that Miró met in early April 1962, receiving from him assurances that the policy of the president toward Cuba had not changed; perhaps unwisely, Miró took this as hopeful. And it was through Bobby that Miró obtained an audience with the president a few days later on 10 April. For Bobby was the doorkeeper.

Years after the catastrophe, my father repeated to visitors and the visited, "I would say to Miró, 'Pepe, do not trust him. Do not trust either one or the other brother.'"

My father was faithful in his hatreds. He was firm and merciless. He would not barter the adamantine purity of his enmity for Christians' bullshit, variable pity. And he was discriminating. He would not, like many other Cuban exiles, generalize a distrust of the Kennedys into a distrust of their party. He would register as a Democrat. His hatred for the Kennedys was personal.

The day President Kennedy was killed, I walked dry-eyed part of the way from Riverside Elementary with a friend who was more of the U.S. than of Cuba and would not stop crying. I was attempting philosophy on her.

"Life is like this," I told her.

When I arrived at our apartment, my father was on the telephone. He was saying, "The tragedy is that it did not happen sooner."

I thought that was the way I was supposed to view it. My mother and I watched the burial on television. I was resisting the tug to tears in the commentators' voices. But then they panned to the widow's quietly mourning, stunned face, and my mother began weeping, and having seen my mother, I could not stop my tears. My father stood above us showing us contempt through his glare, but we finally wept.

Perhaps my father hated the Kennedys all the more intensely because not many other names and faces were available to receive his anger. There were other guilty men, men who hid their true faces and true names behind masks of friendliness, professional liars and manipulators, thieves of truth, employees of the Central Intelligence Agency. The guiltiest was Richard M. Bissell, Jr., graduate of Yale, master weaver of plots, whose hubris blinded him to the fact that webs can only be woven by spiders—and plots, by writers of fiction. He thought not only that he could control the tendency of events to evade prediction, but that he could tempt destiny by equipping an invasion army with junk, by sending them to a swamp, by launching them even after every condition for success had been violated. But Bissell was not the only one. There were all the other adventurers and spooks; men like E. Howard Hunt who vaunted behind-doors knowledge and made promises, anything to anyone, just to get us to do what they wanted; the scurrying soldier-ant men of whose statements the Kennedys could disavow knowledge and wash their hands.

My father wrote a book recounting the perfidy of the Kennedy brothers, showing, to his lights, how the United States, chief among Western democracies, was handing its power over to the dark claw of Communism. In fact he did not think highly of democracies. He thought that their weakness for allowing all points of view contained the seeds of their undoing. He prophesied that we would all fall under the domination of Communism unless the United States quickly took heed. *"¡Se están entregando al comunismo!"* he shouted often. "They are giving themselves over to Communism!" Very frequently he used the word *entreguismo* to describe a pervasive attitude of capitulation. Usually, the context was *el entreguismo de los Estados Unidos.*

For a time my father was obsessed with his book about capitulation and betrayal. He was no more obsessed with his work in progress than any other writer, but I had had no prior experience of the phenomenon. Because my father invested so much attention and hope in it, I did too. First there was the writing. Then he would have to look to its publication. In those days of exile there was no way to get a book published unless one paid the printer oneself. My father inquired into the cost. He went so far as to get a commercial artist to draw up a cover for it; the young man came to the apartment to discuss his ideas.

My father did not dissemble that the book was written in anger, and in fact considered the intensity of the book's rage to be its chief virtue. He was proud of giving the U.S.ers hell.

Because of my youth, my father did not expect me to understand his book completely, he said. But when he had finished writing it, he proudly gave it to me to read. It was not very long. He had bound it inside black embossed report covers. He had left wide margins that alleviated somewhat the impact of the multitude of corrections made necessary by the digital dyslexia that overcame him on typewriters. (This obviously hereditary condition would years later precipitate my alacritous embrace of the personal computer.)

I looked at the table of contents. One of the chapters was "The Myth of Nazism." I thought that there was little doubt that Nazism had existed and that it had been a bad thing. My mother had told me of horrible deeds as she read *The Rise and Fall of the Third Reich.* Therefore, I asked my father about the odd chapter title. He explained to me that he believed that Communists used the bugbear of Nazism to scare people toward the left, to keep them concentrating on a danger that was past while Communism crept ever closer. My father thought the Nazism chapter might upset some people but said things that needed to be said. I was not so sure of that need. The chapter certainly upset and embarrassed me.

I do not remember many other things about the book, just that it was angry and rhetorically anti-Communist—but at the time I liked that. When I finished reading the book, I said some encouraging things about it—that it was hard-hitting, for instance. My reaction may not have been equal to what my father expected: I did not call it the best book I had ever read. But, then, I was a child. He could attempt to dismiss my muted response with, "Of course, you are still too young to understand it all." My mother's reaction was reserved. I only remember her eyes looking down at her sewing, her face impassive, as the subject of the book hung between my father and me.

In December 1973, the Jewish parents of my first husband visited Miami for our wedding. My parents invited them to their apartment for dinner.

"Which do you think is worse," my father asked my then-future now-former father-in-law, "Nazism or Communism?"

"They're both bad," said my ex-father-in-law diplomatically.

"Communism is much worse," my father said, and I wished the floor would swallow me.

From the time of my middle adolescence, I could not think about my father's political book without relief that he had never published it. He was all set to gather up the funds for self-publication when he sent it off to Miró in Puerto Rico for comment. Miró advised him not to publish it. "Take care, Ramiro," he said.

My father never spoke of the book again. He stored the manuscript away in a closet. However, it is one thing to abort a book and quite another to expel the tortured thoughts and the fury that conceived it, and these remained, creating monsters in my father's head. Now and then I heard the book buzzing within its cramped storage. Sometime it got thrown out, no doubt at the prompting of my mother who, once when I questioned her about its whereabouts, referred to the manuscript disparagingly as "*¡Eso!*"—"That!" Now she cannot even remember it once existed.

For several years of my childhood, I blamed the long tongues of Cubans for the failure of the invasion—our long tongues collectively, my own included, as if I had said anything about a subject I knew nothing about. "If only we had kept quiet," I thought repeatedly, thinking of my father's impassioned complaint to visitors, "Fidel had everything but a map of the invasion." Yet it was the Guatemalan newspaper *La Hora* that on 30 October 1960 broke the news that an invasion of Cuba was being prepared on Guatemalan soil with the backing of the United States. The *Hispanic American Report* transmitted the news to the United States, where it was first noticed by *The Nation,* which suggested that journalists might do well to beat those bushes for news. The *New York Times* followed with several stories. On 10 January the *New York Times* printed on page one an article describing the location and purposes of the Guatemalan camp.

We were not as indiscreet as the U.S. press, but still it must be admitted that Cubans have an unusual relationship to secrets. Much of Miami knew an invasion—a something—would soon take place. Cuban exile leaders gave assurances of the certainty of the event. Exiles live on hope, no? What better opportunity to raise it? The U.S.ers of the CIA, whose *métier* was secrets, were out of their element. If they were surprised by our openness, it was only because once again they had failed to understand us. We Cubans attempt to dispose of secrets as soon as we have acquired them. They burn holes in us. We like to think that the world keeps no secrets from us, and to prove it we tell those secrets that we have been told.

In Miami the only valuable thing that Cuban men could share was official secrets. When we visited them, the men would begin to say, "There is going to be an action . . ." then they would break off, looking significantly at my mother and me, hesitating to tell my father in front of us of their latest CIA-backed nuisance-run against Fidel—or their current wishful thinking.

And my father, not wanting to be left out, would wave toward my mother and me and say, "You can say anything in front of them."

On such occasions I felt that I had receded and become one with the sofa on which I sat. My mother would dispose of the signs of life on her face and resemble stone. Sometimes I was ashamed, because she looked like an idiot. Official secrets were a male coin that would buy us nothing. My mother and I spoke with no one who would be interested.

When, in Watergate's aftermath, revelations were made of the CIA's covert actions against Fidel Castro—the memorable plan to make his beard fall off, for example—I was surprised at the U.S. public's thunderstruck amazement. It was not just the naïveté but the ignorance that surprised me. "You mean you didn't know?" I asked acquaintances who spoke of governments and morality. "But I heard all of this as a child." I shook my head in wonder. We could have told them their secrets, we the Cubans of Miami.

The exile newspaper *El Mundo,* for which my father had worked part-time during our early months of exile, had headlines at the time of the invasion that, my mother says, made her hair stand on end.

When she told me in 1991 that she still thought about those headlines with horror, I said to her, "If it's any consolation to you, the invasion did not fail because of anything revealed by exiles."

"Oh, I know," she said with surprising certainty, as if she had known it all along. "In spite of the lies they told us, the *americanos* didn't want to do anything, just as they sent their young people to Vietnam to die, in the end, not to accomplish anything."

"But this can't be published," my mother said to me after one of my many questions about Girón.

"A lot has been declassified," I said. "Books have been published. For example, the imprisonment of the Consejo in Opa-Locka. That's how I knew they were in Opa-Locka."

My mother had thought it was New York, so I told her the story. Like a reverse fortuneteller, I could read my mother her past.

But what mattered to my mother and me at that moment, two weeks before the thirtieth anniversary of the invasion, was my mother's rage finally coming to the surface. I had never suspected that she held this particular reservoir of anger. She had gone through the awful events of April 1961 as she did every other crisis with my father: silent, presenting an inhumanly calm face. My mother's now spoken rage was a sweet blessing. "They locked them up. They didn't want them to speak for themselves. They wanted to control everything and to use them. They wanted to manipulate them to do only what *they* wanted. Expedience, that's what this country cares about."

"But this can't be published," my mother said. My father tried to free himself of his silence. Miró died before his pain had been declassified. The members of the Consejo and the soldiers of the brigade kept a crushing trust of secrets forced upon them by men who betrayed them. Why keep them then; why behave so honorably? My guess is that they were afraid not to.

The scorpion, whose life is secrets, waits in darkness for us to expose our vulnerable places. In my grandmother's house I heard of a man who was killed when he dozed off in a rocking chair and a scorpion fell from the ceiling onto his bare throat.

My mother benefited from one once, however. Before she forgot the incident, she sometimes told about it with the most matter-of-fact voice. She looked up from my crib and saw a scorpion on the wall above it. She bet on its corresponding number, 43, in the lottery—and won. Each time I heard the story I felt panic. There had been a scorpion right above where I lay as a baby. She seemed not to have considered this aspect of it. When I asked her what had happened to the scorpion, she was rather vague. "I guess it must have been killed. I don't know."

Black tile covered the floors in my grandmother's house. One evening, as I was walking into her bedroom from the dining room, I saw just before the doorway something dark but differently dark from the tile. I saw it only out of the corner of my eye, but by the time I reached my aunt Nena in the well-lit bathroom that connected with my grandmother's bedroom, I was hysterical. I made a conscious decision to become hysterical. I could have been calmer, gotten the words out correctly, instead of the gibberish that panicked Nena. But if I had said calmly, "There's some strange vermin in the dining room," Nena might have gone about her business and given little thought to this *bicho raro* I spoke of. "It's probably just a big cockroach," she might have said, instead of rushing out to tell the others.

It was my sour aunt Cuca, the true mistress of the house, who found the animal.

"It's a scorpion!" she cried. "It's gone into the kitchen."

I envisioned it hiding from us all under the refrigerator, so that there would be no conclusion, so that we would never know, when we were in that house, when it might strike at us.

But my uncle Óscar was visiting too. I heard him moving things in the kitchen. He found the scorpion and beat it hard with a broomstick—whack! whack!—against the kitchen floor.

Then he carried the arachnid on the broom to the quiet street, threw lighter fluid on it, and set it on fire. I finally came out when Nena told me it was on fire. I walked out to the curb while it still smoked. For hours I checked on its remains. There it lay, retaining its body of braided bread ending in a half-moon stinger—a black, charred rope, and immobile.

When I read *1984* in high school, I knew what punishment Big Brother's government would reserve for me. If a box of rats was Winston Smith's destiny, then a box of scorpions was mine. Perhaps this gives you power over me. But I have just freed myself from the burden of a secret.

I despise secrets wilfully kept, information designated for hoarding. And I am no less unsettled by involuntary secrets. I fear my brain will keep secrets from me. I have tried to pull my memories from their holes in the earth and preserve them in amber resin. But, against my will, some of them slink out of my reach; I do not know if away, forever gone, or into some deeper, more secure hole to await my inattention. I hear things slither in the darkness; I know some of them have stingers.

I say that the U.S.ers never knew how to deal with us. I do not suppose they were really trying to consider our sense of dignity. Sometime after Girón, a bomb was set off in a car used by Miró. Fortunately, everyone slept. The FBI decided to subject those closest to him to polygraph tests. As if doubting those who loved him made sense from a logical point of view, considering how many Cubans heatedly disagreed with Miró and how many spies Castro had infiltrated into Miami. The bomb went off in the middle of the night, when no one would be likely to use the car. It was intended to scare, perhaps.

When the FBI asked my father to take a lie detector test, he was deeply offended, ashamed. To save face he felt he had to tell us all, "Miró told me, 'Humor them, humor them, Ramiro. They do things this way.' "

Yet if my father had not told us in the first place, we would never have known that he had been asked to subject his integrity and the sincerity of his friendship to a test by machine. Nor would anyone else have known, certainly not all the telephone callers who were told the same story. Having been privately shamed, my father felt compelled to make a public confession.

It was not our last contact with the FBI. One afternoon after I returned from school, two gray-suited agents as indistinguishable as models for shirt ads showed up at our door. My father was not home. My mother asked them in. She motioned them to the patched red sofa, but they would not sit until she had sat. This was a stellar moment in my mother's life. No one had ever shown her this particular courtesy. She smiled, and that moment she reminded me of a pleased, petted cat.

The men only asked where my father was. "I don't know," my mother said, slowly shrugging her shoulders and willing her lower lip to protrude. This was her standard answer for bureaucrats. The FBI men left.

They did eventually find my father. It is possible that they had known all along he would not be home, their visit having been meant to leave an impression.

The FBI was curious about my father's ability to predict when Orlando Bosch, the eccentric, obsessed anti-Castro superactivist, the physician turned saboteur, was next going to strike, what Polish ship at anchor in Miami he was going to subject to a bazooka attack, which stretch of Cuban coastline he was going to riddle with mischief. His exploits included sneaking badly needed arms to insurgents in the Escambray Mountains. To many exiles, he was heroic.

Not having learned the lesson of Playa Girón, the FBI was still giving ponderous weight to a Cuban's access to secrets. The solution to the puzzle of my father's mantic ability was simple. When Bosch was preparing to attack, he telephoned my father. Papá would get the scoop. Bosch would get the publicity. Thanks a lot, Orlando, my father told him the next time, but from now on call my *americano* boss Ted Ediger at the Associated Press, why don't you? Henceforth, Bosch called Ediger and the two men became friends.

The FBI's interest in Bosch derived from what my father called with derision *el pacto Kennedy-Khrushchev,* which, as he saw it, had sold the future of the West to the Russians out of cowardice. It would make no sense to exiled Cubans, but it was the case that after the October 1962 missile crisis, the United States would stop any acts of aggression against Cuba, its enemy, the very country against which it pressed a trade embargo. This is not to say that laws had not previously been enacted against using U.S. territory as the departure point for an attempt to cause civil strife in another country. But such laws had been enforced only sporadically. After October 1962, local discretion was curtailed. The federal government conscientiously enforced its new agreement with Khrushchev. Even if Cubans thought it worthwhile to risk their own lives on a bombing raid against a military installation or a sugar mill in Cuba, if caught on U.S. land or water, they would be arrested by the same U.S. government that had once outfitted them for an invasion. For Cubans a similar about-face was impossible. It would have required us to surrender our national identity for the great, gray cloud of ambiguity on which the U.S. government floats. Men like Orlando Bosch refused to admit helplessness before the gaping loss of Cuba, no matter what the consequences. Destructiveness, most frequently bizarre, is the last refuge of the frustrated.

You can see Miró's picture in *Life* magazine's 19 January 1959 celebration of the Cuban Revolution. For *Life* the image is uncharacteristically out of focus. Light splashes back to us from Miró's glasses. He appears as a spirit who has not quite accepted the call to materialize. He is probably reading. The caption on page 31 states: "PREMIER is José Miró Cardona, former dean of Havana bar whom Batista drove into exile because he protested court takeover by the dictator."

Miró looks more concrete in Peter Wyden's book. His jaw slants with the fervor of his phrase. He makes an emphatic point with his right fist. His left hand holds a cigarette whose burning end has almost reached his fingers. The same hand holds a piece of paper. He is pictured in the author's gallery of Cuban politicians. The copy at the center of the page begins: "The CIA found the fiery Cuban exile politicians hard to handle, especially . . ." Miró is described as "president of the exile government which the CIA expected to establish once the brigade had gained a foothold on Cuban soil." And so it might have been. Elsewhere in the book Wyden describes Miró's glasses as "owlish." They were that and more. Their heavy rectangular frames emphasized the squareness of the head that they bisected, making the weight of such a knowledge-filled brainpan all the more evident.

The pictures do not tell you that Miró was a lover of the opera doomed to live in a climate of popular song, though you can detect in them the sadness that his layers of civility and culture were trying to filter and soften. As he held me on his lap, I felt my hand would sink into his chest until I pulled it out, bathed in that sadness.

I knew that my time spent with Miró had a value beyond ourselves. Therefore, even waiting with him or for him seemed important. For me the strangest thing about Miró was that he did not drive. Before learning about this peculiarity, I had thought that all men knew how, but no, Miró had to rely on Nena Pérez or my father or someone else close to him to take him where he would go. I turned this over in my mind because I was struck by the contrast between Miró's power—perhaps only imagined, but certainly believed in—and this weakness.

One day my father, mother, and I took Miró to the airport when he was making a trip to Washington that was burdened with so much importance that one would have thought the airplane would have been unable to overcome gravity. He was to have meetings, perhaps with the president of the United States.

Miami International Airport was a quiet place in the early 1960s. One could sit undisturbed in the plentiful vinyl-covered chairs of the waiting areas. A U.S. reporter, however, interrupted the quiet conversation between Miró and my father. The reporter was wearing a short-sleeved shirt with bright stripes on a white background—what outsiders view as Florida wear—and he had light brown, slightly disheveled hair. He did not write for the Miami press. He worked for one of the national news magazines.

"Could I ask you a few questions?" the reporter asked in the English in which he conducted the interview.

"A few questions," Miró said firmly but graciously.

"If Cuba is liberated . . . If the United States assists the Cubans . . . ," the man jabbed with his questions.

After several of these, Miró protested, "If, if—these *ifs* are terrible. Can't you phrase your questions any other way?"

The reporter was stumped. I concluded that he had not been one of the brighter students in his class. A couple of times he seemed to be ready to make a start, but each time he shook his head. "I don't know what to say," he admitted.

"Suppose," Miró suggested, pronouncing the word slowly so that the *o* was very satisfyingly round.

The reporter smiled gratefully. "I see your English is better than mine," he said amicably, and he continued the interview, beginning each question with *suppose.*

Law and the need for humans to take a stand before the lawlessness of governments brought José Miró Cardona and Fidel Castro together. Miró was a professor of law at the University of La Habana, where he taught a restive younger generation of citizens to defend the rule of law—the civilization that a desire for freedom and honor had built and which he carried in his nature, like his decency, as foundation for the rest. Among his students was Fidel Castro. The student, in this case, changed his master's life completely.

"Miró told me that Fidel was a brilliant student," my father confided. "Don't tell anyone." As if intelligence could be news about the devil.

In April 1956 Miró defended Major Ramón Barquín, whose planned coup of young officers against Batista was betrayed. Later, as head of the Bar of La Habana, Miró signed the 15 March 1958 proclamation of the Joint Committee of Cuban Institutions calling upon Batista to resign. Because he was suspected of having been the author of the document, Miró had to go into hiding. He took refuge in a church and donned a priest's cassock. He did not shave off his mustache, which might have given him away. But I cannot think of anyone who would look more convincing as a priest than Miró, with a mixture of rectitude and benevolence suitable for the listening side of the confessional. I could not look into his broad thoughtful face and not trust him.

From the church refuge he made his way to the Uruguayan embassy, and from that sanctuary he wrote a letter to the bar in which he reasserted the illegality of the Batista government and the right of humans to resist oppression. Miró thus began his first, brief exile. In his letter from the Uruguayan embassy he had quoted Martí, of course: "Dangerous dignity will always be preferable to useless life."

José Miró Cardona could not resist the times' call to the moral man. Clarions sound louder to the sons of heroes. And he was the son of José Miró Argenter, the Catalan, chief of staff to General Antonio Maceo, the Bronze Titan, hero of the War of Independence. Similarly, I suppose, Miró's own son, also a lawyer and also José—José Antonio Miró Torra, in this case, and nicknamed Pepito—could not do otherwise but enlist in Brigade 2506 although he had several children, all still young. He was only a private; upon his capture the Cuban government had difficulty believing his low rank.

Miró felt much affection for my father. I am not sure what drew men to my father. Perhaps it was his singularity, his way of flaunting his extremes so much that you believed he would always be honest with you. Women may have been attracted to the same thing. But for them there was only pain in it. The limits of male friendship offered a much safer haven.

My father was in awe of Miró. I never saw him have this attitude toward anyone else. Not to that extent. My father did idealize some men, his buddies—only, finally, to disparage them when they disappointed him. But to hear him speak of being in Miró's presence, you knew that he felt he had attained a high privilege.

"He sits there at the table in his pajamas on Saturday morning, while Ernestina makes him his coffee. And she is in her bathrobe. And he asks me, 'Ramiro, what do you think we should do?'"

I hated to hear my father talk this way. It made him look weak. I could not tolerate weakness in the only parent who had a track record of strength. My mother too spoke of Miró respectfully—even my mother, I should emphasize—with the tones she generally reserved for the women she particularly admired. She expressed no resentment that my father's work for Miró kept him away such long hours. But then my mother was not like me. She never expressed resentment of anything that kept my father away.

My father made only one criticism of Miró, albeit with more admiration than censure. "I tell him, 'Pepe, you're surrounded by hyenas. You need claws.' But his hands are soft. He has no claws." And then my father would transform his own hand, which was an exaggeration of my hand, into a vulture claw.

So many times my father sought to keep me safe with his death-defying grip. I have a small piece of a photo taken at a meeting in the intense year of 1959 at the offices of Rufo López Fresquet, the finance minister. All participants, myself included, received a pen to commemorate *el Día del Periodista.* The picture had to be severely cropped before we dared take it out of the country because in a search *milicianos* might recognize someone who had parted ways with the government (for example, the finance minister) or U.S. authorities might spot a *fidelista.* All that remains in the narrow fragment is a stack of pen boxes, the dark hands of a man next to me holding a cigarette, myself looking very serious and discomfited, and my father's right hand, draped like a gigantic paternal tarantula over my chest, pulling me close.

I never felt so much a part of his flesh as when I looked at his hands, which were arch-hands, artists' studies in hands, statements on the length of bones and the utility of tendons—his hands, which were bigger than mine, not attenuated by femininity and bent by arthritis beyond the alarming obliquity he passed on to my right middle finger. My right palm bears a mole in copy of his. Flesh and bone, I and my father. And now his hands are ashes.

*Myself, pen boxes, and my father's hand.*

## II

On the first day of 1959, a month before my seventh birthday, I woke up to the startling news that the government of Batista had fallen. There was confusion and there was television. Statements were being issued from Oriente Province by a group known as the 26 July Movement. They were declaring Santiago de Cuba to be the new capital. That alarmed me; part of my identity was to be a child of the capital. A new man's name seemed to be important: Fidel Castro.

Just the previous evening life had been quite different. My parents and I had gone to a theater to watch the film *Perri,* a Walt Disney quasi-documentary of a squirrel's life. My mother and I were mad for squirrels, which to us were exotic animals. The only squirrels in Cuba were the ones scrambling about the trees in the zoo. After the movie we had eaten sandwiches at a sidewalk café—the best *mediasnoches* in La Habana, my father had said.

Over the next few days I learned what a *revolución* was. As usual, classes were not scheduled to resume until after 6 January. Each morning I arose and joined my mother, and we watched on the television the approach of tanks and jeeps toward La Habana, the westward march of victorious bearded men who were detained in every town along the route by jubilant crowds.

One of those mornings my father happened to be standing behind us when an announcement was read: the prime minister of the new rebel government would be Dr. José Miró Cardona.

My mother turned to my father and asked, *"Él?"*

My father nodded and scowled; he seemed to know already. My father had just showered and was pushing the tongue of his black belt through the buckle and under the leather keeper. He had probably only come home to freshen up after spending most of the night at the newspaper trying to track the shape of the change.

What had we neglected to do that New Year's Eve, that passing from 1958 to 1959? Like the Spanish we eat twelve grapes at midnight. But we Cubans do not stop there. From our doorways we throw out buckets of water to get rid of the old year's *salación*, or curse. My own formula is to shout, *"¡Llévatelo, viento de agua!"* First I throw the water, and then I tell of the time when, engaged in an identical ritual, my mother sailed over a small wall, bucket in hand, propelled by the momentum of her throw, following the trajectory of the water. I let people think my mother's aerodynamic feat occurred on a New Year's Eve. I throw the water and Kurt says, "Didn't your mother have an adventure doing that?" as invitation and opportunity for me to tell my tale again.

There was one tradition that my family did not take seriously but was of grave importance to the *santeros*. Each New Year's Day the *babalawos,* the prophetic priests of Orunla, divine the character of the coming year. I remember my father joking in 1959 about the prophecies that were published in a newspaper. The *babalawos* had fallen short of predicting the momentousness of events that would alter our nation forever. Had the coconuts or the god kept silent? Had we not eaten quickly enough the twelve midnight grapes? Was there such a long-accumulated curse in our Cuban house that an entire nation hurling water off balconies and rooftops could not wash it away? No one then saw the many eves to be spent toasting the year's turning with "Next year in La Habana," as the Jews for centuries had said, "Next year in Jerusalem," until to say it seemed a cruel joke on ourselves and we stopped.

Naturally, before January 1959 I had heard that things had been stirred up, *revueltas,* for some time. As my uncle Rafael, aunt Cuca, and cousin Elsa prepared to leave in their going-out splendor for the movies on Saturday evenings, many sardonic comments were exchanged about maybe somebody planting a *bombita* in the theater. Because of this levity, the explosion of a bomb midfilm did not seem very threatening to me, though my mother told me that at least one young woman had lost a leg in such an *atentado*.

Once I recited a rhyme I had learned from the adults around me, and I was instructed severely not to repeat it. It went: *"Sierra Maestra, Sierra Cristal, cierra la boca que te la voy a cortar."* The rhyme and the rhythm were imperfect, but it contained a good pun between *sierra* (mountain range) and *cierra* (close). I was disturbed, however, by the nonsense of the command to "close your mouth or I'm going to cut it out," because a mouth, which is already a hole, cannot easily be cut out. I also learned the word *clandestino*.

I heard careful mentions of a radio journalist called José Pardo Llada, an acquaintance of my father's who was supposed to be in the distant, forbidden place called the Sierra. Pardo Llada's subsequent brief, puzzling career as publicist and apologist for the early Castro government was of great interest to my father. Throughout his copies of the various installments of *Diario de una traición* by Leovigildo Ruiz, my father marked the margins PARDO whenever reference to his former colleague appeared. Pardo Llada sought asylum in Mexico City on 25 March 1961. He settled and thrived in Colombia, away from the once-extolled revolution.

On 13 March 1957, I was taken to the Hospital Infantil by my mother to get inoculated against polio. The only comfort in getting a dreaded needle stuck into a soft fleshy part of my body was that I got to roll the word *poliomielitis* around on my tongue. My mother drew a sufficiently grotesque portrait of children mangled by disease to render me willing to allow strangers to puncture my flesh. Anyway, on the occasion of injections I was usually less dilatory and histrionic with strangers than with long-suffering relatives. Mamá must have switched her half day of work from the afternoon to the morning so that she could pick me up after my own half workday—my morning of kindergarten.

Once the ordeal of the injection was over for the two of us, we went to Woolworth's, or as Cubans called it, El Ten-Cén, and did some shopping. At El Ten-Cén I particularly liked to have very foreign strawberry ice cream sodas, which one ate at a counter that wound its way around part of the store and had fixed stools. Or, better yet, I might choose the more familiar chocolate shakes with bits of crushed ice in them, which were mixed upon request at a small counter in the center of the store and then were served in paper cones inside cold, metal bases. After our treat and shopping, my mother and I caught the bus home. It was only then that we heard that some men had attacked the Presidential Palace.

The Ataque a Palacio was carried out by members of the Directorio Revolucionario, an anti-Batista organization founded by university student leaders who had substantial disagreements with Castro's 26 July Movement. A plan that drew on eighty men armed with sub-machine guns, carbines, and pistols could not be kept secret, though that was the intention. Batista knew several days before the fact that an assault on his residence was planned. Though he did not know exactly when, he prepared. The attack on the Palacio was supposed to result in Batista's death. Instead, most of those who entered the perimeter of the Palacio—the first assault wave—were killed. While the attack was under way, one set of Directorio members took over radio station Radio Reloj and announced that Batista had been killed. (It is little wonder that four years later Cubans did not believe the propaganda from Radio Swan: the victorious invasion, hell.) Batista was safely holed up in the upper story of his palace. In the meantime, Batista's army and tanks—tanks inside one of the busiest sections of the city—were headed his way to quell the rebellion. For hours soldiers fired indiscriminately—even out over Parque Zayas, where people took innocent leisure. Several bystanders were wounded; even a tourist from the United States was killed.

My father, the journalist, getting a constant account of unfolding events, frantically tried to locate my mother and me. He called the hospital to tell us to go straight home, but we had already left the security of poinciana-shaded, residential El Vedado, where the children's hospital was located, for El Ten-Cén, on busy Galiano between San Rafael and San Miguel, ten blocks away from the Presidential Palace. If he had known where we were, the anxiety would have threatened to burst his chest, while we moved about normally, unaware that blood coursed through nearby streets.

I had no special feeling about Batista, but he was the only president I had known. His tenure thus seemed eternal. His coup had ousted the elected president, Carlos Prío, a month and three days after my birth. My mother's family made humorous remarks about the March Coup, informing me indirectly that there had been something sleazy about Batista's coming to power.

For most of my life in La Habana my father was the editor of the political page of the newspaper *El Crisol,* The Crucible. With someone's departure, he was later promoted to the post of sub-director (in U.S. terms, the managing editor—and in this case a powerful one, for his director was twenty-one years old). But children are conservative—at least I was—and I continued to think of him as *el jefe de la plana política.* No matter how I tried, I could not picture him as this new, vague thing, the sub-director. *La política,* at least, was a territory. He walked me through the palmy courtyard and then through the ornate doors into the Ayuntamiento, the city hall whose tall, columned spaces seemed to require of us hushed voices. He shouted loud greetings to all men, seemed to know all men. If he and another man had confidences to share, they could whisper to each other out of my hearing, their heads towering over me like the bending tops of coconut palms.

The strange thing about my father's post as political editor is that I had—and have—no idea of what his politics were in the 1950s. His activism was over before I knew him. All my father told me of his politics was that he refused to take bribes. He made much of this. "They know they cannot buy me." From this I learned that some people were for sale. Because they could not pay him direct bribes, my father explained, politicians gave me presents. My father took his right hand to his chest, then glided it smoothly away from him at a slight angle. "They know that for me my daughter is everything." I wondered if it was okay for me to have those presents, since they were given in lieu of bribes. I hoped my father did not secretly blame me for being his one weakness, for enjoying the would-be bribers' largesse—and I did enjoy the largesse. As we made the circuit, my father and I, of the haunts of politicians, I wondered which had been my benefactors; anonymous and indistinguishable they all were to me even if names were uttered. I left the business of gratitude to my father, for whom the gifts had been intended, even if they were toy kitchen ranges with oven doors that opened or dolls that said *"mamá"* when you tipped them forward and then back.

It was in our exile that I first heard my mother call Batista derogatory names. My father would say to guests, "If it hadn't been for Batista, there would have been no Fidel." And they would go on to talk about all the money that Batista stole from Cuba. *"¡Miserable!"* my mother would say with venom. "Wretch!"

If my parents made such comments to each other in Cuba, they did so out of my hearing. Or perhaps this was one of the things about which they spoke to each other in English. That my parents should have employed their then halting English to conceal their meanings from me during my early life is one of those many ironies that make me occasionally suspect that whatever God is, It has a perverse sense of humor. Anyway, by second grade in Cuba I understood enough English to discourage their no-longer-secretive device. In high school in Miami, I concealed my adolescent confidences to girlfriends by using private

English-language codes with vengeful pleasure. I had hated my parents' English exclusion.

Whereas my parents were unwilling to give me any kind of political guidance in Cuba, my cousin Elsa, fifteen years older than I and my idol, was eager to fill the void. From the time of its triumph, she was an enthusiast of the revolution; she was enthusiastic about me too, and affection is a most effective teacher. She liked the revolutionary slogans: *"Patria o muerte," "Cuba sí, yanquis no,"* and *"Fidel, ésta es tu casa"* (an invitation Fidel took quite literally in many cases).

Elsa took me to pick up an official collection can at a perfunctorily official office of the revolution so that she could go asking door to door for money for the families of those killed or otherwise injured on 3 March 1960 by the explosion of the ship *La Coubre,* a French vessel loaded with armaments and ammunition purchased in Belgium by the Cuban Ministry of Defense.

The entrances to churches in La Habana were full of beggars of various disadvantaged or religious sorts. Why someone not in need would volunteer to beg for money was beyond me. Later in life when Miami nuns annually ordered us to peddle deceptively named World's Finest chocolate bars for our school, my father each time forked over the money for a box so that I would not have to humiliate myself by attempting to extract the kindness of strangers.

Elsa and I stood in line for several hours with others who were itching for the privilege to turn mendicant. The revolutionaries in the office did not seem particularly grateful, or worse, the least bit efficient. They didn't seem to know which end was up or how to distribute cans. The line stood frozen under the warm sun. I was thankful to God that by the time Elsa got the slotted tin she was too tired to drag me begging.

Of course Elsa bought the official line that the *Coubre's* conflagration was an act of *yanqui* sabotage. The double explosions, the first at 3:15 P.M. and the second at 3:45, cost eighty-one lives. Fidel Castro was able to make much bellicose political hay out of it, as the United States had done with the *Maine* in 1898. In fact, in his speech the next day, Castro mentioned the *Maine* and the celerity with which the United States had come to view the explosion of that ship as an act of war. He acknowledged no responsibility for the foolish unloading of such explosive cargo, contrary to international law, in a regular commercial city dock, the Pan American Docks. It was Fidel's chance to turn to the East for armaments. It was my cousin Elsa's chance to become involved in something outside herself and the walls of the paternal house that held her. It would take her thirty years to change her mind—but at least she had the courage to admit her mistakes.

As soon as we arrived in Miami, I made the easy transition to anti-Castroism. I did it in a wink, the day we arrived. Someone in the apartment where we had been brought from the airport turned on the television. On it appeared film of U.S. properties being expropriated in Cuba.

"You're not going back," my father said to my mother and me.

Immediately I understood what my political position should be. I understood also the breadth of the tensions that had existed between my parents and those members of their families who were pro-revolution, hints of which I had begun to notice after my father left the country the others considered a newborn social paradise.

My father's relatives were no great loss to me because I had never felt close to any of them—except for my cousin Rodolfo, that is, who had gotten willy-nilly whatever enthusiastic admiration I might have given to a one-year-older beautiful brother. (His cheeks were like apples.) But my mother's revolutionary relatives, my companions—Nena, Elsa, and Rafael: I was at once ashamed to have followed them in their enthusiasm and inconsolable at their loss.

For years I was ashamed of my revolutionary complicity at the ages of seven and eight. As if I should have known better. As if I could have. My father's friends had held high positions in the new government. In exile, every time I heard my father tell the story of his having said soon after the 1 January victory, "This will be the most sanguinary dictatorship that our América has ever known," part of me was proud of his clear vision while part of me bristled. I had not been told; I had not been given guidance. I had repeated many revolutionary slogans and parroted a stream of stupid, slogan-based opinions, and never did my parents stop me. They had made a fool of me. I had my integrity to preserve.

Only my parents could have guided me toward reason and away from revolutionary fervor. Information from other sources was pro-revolution. The electronic media were Fidel's. Colegio Baldor, my school, was shut down by the director on 5 February 1959 because of a dispute with some of the elementary school teachers. When the school reopened in April, it was under "intervention," the revolutionary euphemism for government control; newspapers too, like *El Crisol,* were "intervened." Aurelio Baldor would seek exile like us, but his intervened school taught us the new anthem of the revolution for a Friday patriotic pageant. *"Adelante, cubanos . . ."* began the catchy ditty, difficult to forget. I wonder how whoever wrote it fared; was the person killed or jailed? By second grade, our Cuban history books had been updated to include in the back pages the triumph of the revolution and brief biographies of its leaders. As usual with school textbooks, we did not reach the end. In fact, I do not remember getting beyond the War of Independence. It was a good compromise with the new government perhaps: have the material in the books but do not teach it.

One day early in the revolution, as the bus was returning us to school after lunch, we passed a man in olive green talking to a group in the street. "Fidel! Fidel!" one child screamed. All the children save one rushed to the windows on the left to shout out greetings to the man in olive green who may or may not have been Fidel. I did not move from my seat because talking and leaving one's seat on the bus were against the rules. The bus minder angrily ordered the children—those out-of-control others— to sit down and be quiet. When we arrived at school, we were not allowed to go on to our classrooms but were made to wait for someone from the administration while I nursed bitter thoughts about the injustice of blanket punishments and the desirability of a world devoid of other children. The vice-director was usually in charge of discipline, but in my mind's eye it was the director himself who spoke to us. He was stern but not unkind. He said that certain enthusiasms were understandable but that discipline and order must be maintained. The extremely strict rules of the school made it possible for us to be reprimanded for cheering Fidel.

One night a short time after the revolution, while we were still living in Río Mar, our housekeeper and the housekeeper of someone else in the building took me for a walk along Primera Avenida with a member of the rebel army. He was just a soldier displaced by his army's triumph to La Habana from Oriente, the province of the Sierra. I do not know quite what he was guarding on Primera Avenida—whether he was protecting us, the residents, from counterrevolutionary invasion or, more likely, protecting the rest of the capital from us. Many foreigners and wealthy Cubans lived in the luxury buildings on our seafront avenue of the Miramar suburb. Rolando Masferrer, a senator who had his own army of thugs in Santiago and longed to establish a more authoritarian dictatorship than Batista's, had lived half a block away.

At night a rifle-armed *rebelde* kept watch at the entrance to the Río Mar. My father had to remain at the newspaper till three in the morning to close the edition. One night my mother looked through the Venetian blinds of a bedroom window to see if he might be coming home. Instead she saw a few feet below her on the drive-up ramp a rebel with a rifle. Instantly my mother stepped back from the window. What if the rebel had mistaken her movement and fired, she wondered, as her heart beat like a tympanum.

Perhaps the rebel who scared my mother was the very one with whom the maids and I struck up an acquaintance. He too carried a rifle. We walked only next door to the Hotel Blanquita, whose penthouse old man Alfredo Hornedo occupied. I always felt antsy to get going somewhere in such circumstances, but the adults stopped at a reflector-lit planter in front of the hotel. The conversation between the women and the shaggy man in olive was full of silences and ellipses, not what I was used to, and that made me all the more nervous. Finally the *barbudo* brought me close to him. He pulled me onto his lap and kissed my cheek through his dark beard. I had never been so close to a beard. I reached up and touched it.

"I have children at home like you. I haven't seen them for a long time," he said, and his eyes were very sad.

After going into exile in August 1960, I remembered that evening as a horrible transgression. I chastised myself for having allowed myself to be kissed by a bearded *rebelde* nostalgic for his children in the far mountains. I never told my parents.

On 20 July 1958 a meeting of most of the Cuban opposition groups was held in Caracas. The organizations established the Frente Cívico Revolucionario Democrático. Miró became its coordinator. The Frente named Fidel Castro commander-in-chief of the armed forces and Manuel Urrutia, a judge, president of the abstract government-in-exile, the fate that would someday be Miró's in another exile. The difference was that in January 1959 Urrutia's phantom presidency would get translated into an actual post, even if his power remained abstract. It was perhaps because of Miró's position in the Frente, as well as his past civic advocacy, that Fidel Castro chose his former professor to be the first prime minister. Miró also had the sort of social democratic credentials that lessen the stress levels of U.S. presidents. The sage Lao-tzu warned: "Favor is inferior. If you get it—be alarmed! If you lose it—be alarmed!"

Despite his activism, Miró, like any academic, was accustomed to weighing matters from various angles, to seeing shades of meaning, possibilities of outcomes. But in 1959 the youthful enthusiasm and excited faith of many of the victorious promoted only one perspective for all eyes. Miró's most heated opposition against Batista had focused on the dictator's abrogation of judicial processes. Now, days after the rebel government had been installed, the constitution was being revised by decree. The death penalty, prohibited by the constitution, was applied to *batistianos* and others who labored against the revolution. A constitutional article forbidding the retroactive application of a penal law except in cases where it favored the accused was amended to permit punitive retroactive application to those who had collaborated with Batista.

Miró, who saw the totalitarian course these steps signaled, attempted to resign in protest; his shoulder was but weak resistance against an unstoppable wheel. What was coming was the reign of Robespierre, not the Constitutional Convention. Like President Urrutia, the other liberal, Miró lasted in the job, which was never real, a little over a month. On the morning of 13 February, Miró Cardona presented his resignation, which this time was accepted. Fidel Castro became prime minister on 16 February to popular acclaim. On 15 May, Miró was named ambassador to Spain.

Soon after the revolutionaries' triumphant march from the east of the island to the capital, the shouts of *"¡Paredón! ¡Paredón! ¡Paredón!"* were routinely echoed by the blast of firing squads. The *paredón* in its own way was a euphemistic abstraction: it referred to all the walls against which men and women were executed. They were executed by means of *fusilamientos,* that is, rifle shootings. The times brought me many new words.

In a way it is understandable that public rage would burst with such menace. In January 1959 photographs began appearing in magazines like *Carteles* and *Bohemia* and in newspapers bearing graphic witness to a past slaughter of which I had had no notion. Piles of skulls and bones. Scars of torture. Bloody photographs all. I wondered where these secrets had hidden, where these bones were buried, these scars concealed. These photographs, were they all new, or had some been stored somewhere waiting for a safe day? It all seemed to have happened in another country. On another planet. Acts performed by alien beings. Yet the public rage did not have to do only with Batista's atrocities. There were many things to be angry about besides: poverty, misery, the unfairness of life.

We watched the *fusilamientos* on television. I was seven and then eight, and I watched the jerk of bodies when the bullets hit, then the slumping of the corpse. Once the bullets had done their work on them, these people were considered *fusilados*. I noticed that some of the condemned were tied to posts while others stood their ground as they waited before the firing squad for their death. What bothered me most about the procedure was that some of the people went through their last moments wearing blindfolds. Several ex-military men insisted on looking as their executioners leveled their rifles at them, but the eyes of most of the condemned were covered. I asked my aunts and uncles why. "It's done out of mercy, so they won't see the guns firing at them," one of them answered me. I could not understand that at all. I thought it greater cruelty not to see what was happening.

Standing in my parents' bathroom, hours after my father's death in my thirty-seventh year, I wondered if my father had looked into the mirror as he pointed the gun at his head. But my mother was careful to tell me in detail how she had found his gasping, profusely bleeding body. After the shot, my father had slumped back and curled toward his right side. She pointed out how the fall of his body had dislodged the right-hand sink support. He had given his back to sight at the end.

I think it may have been he who taught me this poem by Martí from *Versos sencillos*. As a child, I declaimed it before him:

*I want to leave this world*
*through the natural door:*
*in a cart of green leaves*
*to die they shall take me.*

*Do not put me in the dark*
*To die like a traitor:*
*I am good, and as a good man,*
*I shall die facing the Sun!*

In 1960 it became clear to some that the firing squads would not stop with the *batistianos.* Just before my father left Cuba that 18 June, he asked Miró and his secretary, Nena Pérez, to keep a protective eye on my mother and me. For three weeks Nena Pérez called us from their law office, a dark woodsy place as I remembered it, referred to as a *bufete,* as law offices were called in Cuba—*el bufete de Miró* with woods. Were we all right? I wondered if my mother was communicating with sufficient urgency how desperate we were at our failure to get a visa and how needy we were for action on our behalf by those who might have some influence. I feared I would never see my father again.

Finally in August, when the right string had been pulled, the correct word uttered, my mother and I left for Miami. The calls from Miró's office had ceased for some time. On 2 July, Miró had resigned his post as professor of law at the Universidad de La Habana, and in a forthright letter to Osvaldo Dorticós, the replacement president of Cuba, he resigned also from his ambassadorship (which had not been much of an appointment anyway since he was recalled in January after a public spat between Fidel and the Spanish ambassador to Cuba, Juan Pablo de Lojendio, suspended relations between the two countries). Miró's letter spoke of conscience and loyalty. On 4 July, Miró sought asylum at the Argentinean embassy. Thus began his second exile, and mercifully, eventually, our first.

Dr. Humberto Sorí Marín's credentials as an *antibatistiano* were impeccable. The idealistic lawyer began his life of danger by taking part in civil resistance in La Habana but later joined the olive green army. At the Sierra Maestra he acted as advocate-general. One of his duties was to draft, upon orders from Fidel, a law that permitted summary courts-martial and punishments, including execution, for those who committed acts of violence in Batista's name. This law was signed in the Sierra Maestra, 11 February 1958, when the *rebeldes'* authority to enforce national laws was a mere hope in young men's hairy heads.

After the rebels' victory, the new government claimed that its right to hold trials of *batistiano* war criminals derived from the 1958 rebel law. The rush to judgment fairly took one's breath away. The 1958 law was applied retroactively to crimes allegedly committed before its proclamation. Rules of evidence were not followed. And especially in Oriente, where most of the fighting had taken place, trials were sometimes dispensed with altogether.

Because he received international criticism for summary executions, Fidel Castro decided to hold a televised war crimes trial, a show trial, on 22 January. Television had been very good to Fidel Castro. He had won control of the country first in the mountains and then on television. Three weeks into his rule, he had already made better use of the medium than any other national leader before him. Cuba had a greater number of television sets per capita than any other country in Latin America. Before rapt audiences he had paraded his telegenic young *barbudos,* who received kisses and rosaries from mobs of ecstatic maenads in prim dresses. He was master of the electronic podium. People sat in comfortable chairs and sipped cool beverages as he held forth hour after hour, never seeming to tire of his speech-making, which was full of quotable, snappy lines—the first sound bites. The camera drank him in, sweat and all. A miracle that might have been missed by the standing crowd of forty thousand was captured for television viewers numbered in the

hundreds of thousands. During the major speech at Camp
Columbia on the evening of his triumphant entry into La
Habana, a white pigeon flew onto his shoulder and perched
there. To many it seemed a sign of divine anointment. Well, any-
way, anointment, the more sardonic said.

Fidel Castro selected Humberto Sorí Marín, his advocate-
general from the Sierra, to participate in the televised three-
member, all-rebel courts-martial tribunal. Major Jesús Sosa
Blanco of Batista's army was the principal accused. The trial was
held in the 17,000-seat Sports Palace. I watched Sorí in his beard
and his olive green uniform intently because my father spoke of
him with familiarity.

Witnesses from remote villages in Oriente stepped up to the
microphone. Peasants with their strangely simple language and
their bashfulness told of atrocities, often only after persistent
prompting, sometimes contradicting themselves or one another.
There were eyewitness accounts, but little hard evidence was pre-
sented, although Sosa Blanco had probably committed at least
some of the killings of civilians for which he stood accused. The
partisan audience howled, interrupted, cried insults and
*¡paredón!* It was obvious that the man was hated. Throughout,
Sosa Blanco remained ironic. I remember most clearly a detail
that is not mentioned by the chroniclers. Sosa Blanco was bald-
ing. He seemed naked.

Then public opinion turned against the trial. When Jesús
Sosa Blanco described himself as a Christian thrown to the lions,
he struck a nerve. Yes, people thought, the trial had resembled a
Roman circus. Sorí Marín threw out the conviction. A new, more
private trial was held, this time with limited press coverage. Sosa
Blanco was found guilty and executed by firing squad. I remem-
ber the execution; I watched film of it on television. He declined
the blindfold. It was the first time I observed the killing of some-
one I had seen talking and smiling, even if he had been an *esbirro*,
as rebels called *batistiano* officials, and not flesh but an image on
the television.

Despite his participation in the war crimes trial, Sorí Marín's official post was neither minister of justice nor judge; he had been named minister of agriculture. However, on 17 May 1959, in the small town of La Plata in the Sierra Maestra, Fidel Castro and his entire Council of Ministers—but one—signed the Law of Agrarian Reform. Absent was Humberto Sorí Marín, the minister of agriculture, a fact, of course, that Cubans noticed.

When my father read in *Cuba: The Pursuit of Freedom,* by Hugh Thomas, that the law ordering the redistribution of land through the break-up of latifundia had been presented to the cabinet already drafted without previously having been seen by Sorí Marín, my father had one of those painful fits that I have inherited from him and that occur when we encounter a published statement that is at odds with a significant fact as we see it.

"Thomas has an error there," he said. "The reform law was known as the Sorí Marín Agrarian Reform Law!" And he repeated it with rising vehemence, "The reform law was known as the Sorí Marín Agrarian Reform Law!"

My father was remembering only one corner of the circumstance. He was really facing an enigma that shut its mouth as tightly against intrusion as a starfish. There was the agrarian reform law drafted in the Sierra Maestra and publicized by clandestine radio as that which a successful revolution would establish. Hugh Thomas notwithstanding, Sorí was probably the principal author, or one of the principal authors, of this draft law. However, *caveat emptor,* once power had been achieved, the previously advertised agrarian reform law was not what Fidel Castro wanted to apply. A new agrarian reform law must be worked on. The versions are many and varied about what happened next. Others with more radical or Communist Party connections were set to work on one draft while, depending on the account, Sorí Marín either was left out of the process or did further work on the moderate Sierra law or simply stuck by the Sierra law. What is certain is that the law that was finally promulgated did not meet with Sorí Marín's approval. He thought it extreme, and he refused to go to La Plata for the signing. My father wrote in big block letters on the margin of one of the pages of Carlos Franqui's *Family Portrait with Fidel,* which he gave me, "LEY AGRARIA SORÍ," where Franqui discusses the several-simulta-neous-drafts theory.

On 11 June 1959 Humberto Sorí Marín was fired from his post as minister. He left the country, but he returned to join the new underground—rebellion in Cuba being a revolving door. In preparation for the coming invasion of Girón, the CIA sent Sorí Marín back to Cuba to coordinate the six underground groups working independently throughout the country. The CIA thought the groups needed coordination in spite of the fact that they had been carrying out acts of sabotage successfully without it. With many precautions, a meeting was arranged between Sorí, Rogelio González Corzo (who had attained renown under the code name "Francisco"), and other leaders of the underground in a house in Miramar the evening of 18 March 1961. González Corzo was a former associate of Sorí's. Sorí, as minister of agriculture, had appointed González Corzo to be director of agricultural programs. (Sorí had also appoint-ed to an important post Manuel Artime, who would later work underground with González Corzo and, upon leaving Cuba, would become the Consejo's civilian representative within Brigade 2506.) The Miramar meeting proved to be a great reck-oning in a little room. The men who entered the house were betrayed, and in one sweep Fidel Castro decapitated the under-ground.

On 19 April, even as the Cuban government dealt the Girón invasion its last blows, many who had been accused of counter-revolutionary activity were tried. Twenty people received thirty-year prison sentences. Seven were condemned to death. On 20 April seven men were executed in the Fortress of La Cabaña. Among them, Humberto Sorí Marín was executed—*fusilado.*

I have lived in a flyweight place and time, where the effect of individual action is indiscernible. I have not listened to Radio

Habana recount the execution of my friend Sorí while I, Ramiro Boza, a man of action, sat with my hand before my shut eyes in my exile—impotent and uprooted, but safe.

In the copy of *Diario de una traición, 1961* that I inherited from my father's library, my father had marked with a vertical line down the left margin the entry for 19 April that lists those brought before the revolutionary tribunal in the Cabaña fortress. Above the paragraph, he wrote in block capitals, "SORI, EUFEMIO." He marked with square brackets both in the right and left margin the paragraph that lists those condemned to death. He enclosed within parentheses and marked on top with an arrow the paragraph under 20 April that lists those executed in the dawn. Above the paragraph he wrote again, "SORI, EUFEMIO."

My father had spoken many times of his admired friend Sorí Marín, but through his marginal notes he introduced me to someone else, someone whose death he had marked with a first name. This executed man's full name was Eufemio Fernández Ortega. I wondered if my father's use of the first name denoted intimacy, though I realized that in this case it might simply be shorthand, for the first name was much more unusual than the surname. I asked my mother if my father and Eufemio Fernández were friends.

"No," she said emphatically. "Fernández was a *pistolero*," that is, a gunslinger. "He was not of your father's circle."

I told her the man was a gangster for Prío.

"You see," she said. "Your father was probably just taking note of the man because his name might come up in discussions or in his writing."

This did not assuage me. Writers' notes usually reveal either assignment or passion.

Eufemio Fernández had been head of the secret police under President Carlos Prío, who was deposed by Batista in 1952. But he had had a longer history of political gangsterism. He had been trained as a lawyer and practiced occasional journalism. In 1957 Fernández's path at least once tangentially but concretely touched mine, for he was apparently one of the material supporters of the attack on the Presidential Palace that brought an army into the streets near where I was having a chocolate shake or a strawberry ice cream soda after receiving a polio shot.

I wondered if my father, through his marginal notes in *Diario de una traición,* may have been drawing attention to the strange company people keep at their execution: Sorí and Eufemio, two men who were unlike one another, facing one firing squad. Then I noticed a more meaningful connection. Under the *Diario* entry reporting on Sorí Marín's trial, my father had underlined the name of one of the defense lawyers, Manuel Mariñas.

I asked my mother if this was the Manolo Mariñas, my father's good friend, who had insisted on paying my father due honors at the wake.

"*Sí,*" she answered, lengthening the *í* as if this was a fact with which I ought to be familiar, "he defended Sorí."

I asked if my father and Mariñas had been friends in Cuba. My mother said yes. Mariñas was a good friend of Miró's, she said; they may have met at Miró's *bufete.*

Mariñas had taken my father seafood dinners during his last, tortured years in Miami, and their talks and the meals were, according to my mother, one of my father's few pleasures. After my father's death, Mariñas continued to bring my mother seafood, although she did not know what to do with so much of a perishable item, and the first time Mariñas brought her seafood in her widowhood she had wept from the weight of memory. One day after a year had passed, he brought fish, but as usual he had not called ahead, and she was out. He had to take the fish home, I suppose, for it would not keep. She thinks he may have been annoyed with her for not being there.

The next time he saw her, he pressed money into her hand and said, "You should get the fish yourself."

"You do not have to do this. Why do you create this obligation for yourself?" she asked him.

"It's because of Ramiro's memory," he answered.

He continued to give my mother an envelope containing $20 every few weeks because of my fauther's memory, until finally she firmly asked him to stop, to stop taking money away from himself.

In response to my questions, my mother volunteered to call Manolo Mariñas and ask about the Sorí Marín–Eufemio Fernández connection. It was Mariñas's wife, Isabel, who answered the telephone, but she was conversant with the details—and my mother feels more comfortable talking with women. Señora de Mariñas told my mother that, no, Eufemio Fernández had not been caught in the raid at the clandestine meeting place, that he just happened to have his trial the same day as Sorí. She said that Fidel Castro hated Eufemio Fernández because Fernández had once slapped him. She said that when guards came to take Sorí Marín away to be executed, Eufemio Fernández hurled himself upon them, though this action could not avail.

For several years before the revolution, my mother had worked four hours a day, the schedule under which government offices operated, in the archives section of the improbably named Caja de Retiro de Obreros y Jornaleros del Estado, las Provincias, los Municipios, y las Corporaciones Autónomas (Retirement Fund of Workers and Day Laborers of the State, the Provinces, the Municipalities, and the Autonomous Corporations). To the credit of all who worked in that office, it was usually referred to as La Caja in casual conversation. As a child, I made a game of saying the full name, however.

Soon after the revolution there was a mass firing at La Caja, and my mother was one of the casualties. My father spoke to Sorí Marín, who gave her a job in the archives of the Ministry of Agriculture. She far outlasted Sorí Marín in the job, keeping it till just before our departure from the country.

One day while Sorí was still minister, he toured the archives. Upon being presented to my mother, he said to her, "Ramiro is an institution." She liked that very much.

She liked her job as well. She especially enjoyed going through old files full of letters that had been hand written by past presidents and others of renown. The history in her care appealed to her despite prodigious dust, to which she is allergic, and nonsense, which could be found everywhere in those days. A short time after her arrival, all employees were forced to take a literacy test. I suppose this was part of the campaign to weed out *botelleros,* those who lived off sinecures from past administrations. When the results came out, my mother's supervisor could not believe that she had only finished the sixth grade, for she got 98 percent on the test.

Mass firings followed. During the test, a woman had asked my mother where they were supposed to work out the problems. "On the back of the paper, I guess," my mother said. Another woman scolded them fiercely for talking during the test, as if she were the teacher, and they, a couple of first graders. Not long after, my mother passed the scolding woman in the corridor. She was weeping; she had been fired. In telling me the story three decades later, my mother still relished her triumph.

In post-revolutionary Agriculture, office politics remained the same as in offices everywhere, even after agrarian reform and purges and changes in minister. My mother wanted to index the files so that anyone could use them. Her supervisor did not approve of it.

"Why do that," he asked, "when I know where they are?"

My mother was appalled that documents circulated in and out of files without being stamped with date of receipt or transmittal. She proposed that a consistent practice of stamping be adopted.

"Are you sure you only studied to the sixth grade?" her supervisor asked with suspicion.

Before 1959, revolution in Cuba was a revolving door. Sorí Marín got caught in it. Fidel Castro bolted the door in place by claiming sole proprietorship. But revolution is part of the Cuban national psyche. Therefore, those who opposed the established state that Castro had become called themselves revolutionary.

The name Consejo Revolucionario de Cuba followed a respected naming tradition among Cuban political groups. Our War of Independence, which began a mere sixty-six years before 1961, was led politically by Martí's Partido Revolucionario Cubano and waged by an army of patriotic insurgents. The battle whoops of these *mambises* still echoed in our collective consciousness. The men of the Consejo truly saw themselves as revolutionary. Miró insisted on it in his speeches. In his statement of resignation from the Consejo he would refer to the "revolutionary organizations represented in the council." All the people closest to Miró were *antibatistianos,* liberal in social ideals (even my father). To their U.S. supporters, the Consejo's revolutionary rhetoric must have seemed convenient from a public relations point of view. The United States could say that a new government under these men would return to the revolution's ideals as they had been expressed before the revolution veered from its reformist course and became bloody. To some extent, the Consejo believed this.

But agrarian reform was on the minds of few in the exile community. Fantasies of revenge were more frequently present. At any beauty parlor on Eighth Street you could hear women's wishful plans to get even with the militiamen who had made humiliating comments about the underwear in their suitcases when they were leaving the country or had sniffed covetously around their house, eager to move in.

"Blood is going to stream through the streets of Cuba," the hairdresser might declare, holding her pointy scissors perilously close to your ear, while your mother nodded at the women but had no tales of revenge to tell.

One time my mother made the mistake of disagreeing with the salon owner. Cuba, no, Cuba was not paradise, my mother said; she had worked for years, since she was an adolescent, at

Farmacia Sarrá for nearly nothing—and even then she was still better off than a lot of people; oh, it was very nice for the hairdresser that her husband had owned property and a business in Cuba and had been able to buy her her own beauty parlor; she had one here too, didn't she? The hairdresser's response was to cut my mother's short, black waves so unevenly that it took nearly a year for the damage to grow out. With irony my mother described how the salon owner welcomed her back like a long-lost friend.

My father certainly had no desire for revolution. He wanted to make war against the Fiend, Communism, but he brooked no rebellion. In the late 1960s he spoke about the youth movement with allusions to Sodom and Gomorrah, and he raged at me about my intransigent rebellion.

"He's forgotten that he was a rebel," my mother said with such sadness that I knew that the part of him that had most beckoned her had died.

And Miró was driven by morality, not revolution. He was willing to allow the Roman Catholic Church final authority over his person. My father told with wonder of Miró's scrupulous adherence to Lenten proscriptions. Miró had been given a can of turtle soup. Was it fish or meat, Miró pondered, and would not eat of it lest it be meat. My father turned for advice to the Miró household when, though only ten years old, I resolved to observe the rules of Lent, much against my family's secular tradition.

"At Miró's house they say that children under twelve are exempt," my father told me.

But he could not persuade me toward moderation. I felt responsible, unlike a child, having learned of the obligation. I attended Mass with neighbors and listened to calls to martyrdom and penance. I had put on my hairshirt and was singing Confiteors in the desert. I knew that somewhere I had something to atone for.

Pepe Miró loved the opera. He had studied in Italy. How marvelous that sounded to me, to have studied in Italy. And the only reason for his going so far away seemed to be that he had wanted the knowledge it would bring, the experience. Miró was very unlike my family; we had produced no intellectuals. But I did not then apply the word "intellectual" to him. When I thought of him in Italy, I merely held in my mind the image of a string quartet dressed in white playing in a mosaicked courtyard by a fountain and a potted feather palm.

When I got ready to apply to colleges, my mother wanted to know what my plans were for my education. "One can no longer afford these days to have an education just for the pleasure of it," she said, meaning that it must have practical application.

I majored in philosophy.

I learned just how much Miró loved opera long after the Council disbanded, when we stayed in his house in Río Piedras near the University of Puerto Rico, where he was a law professor. I was fifteen. My father asked for vacation time from the Associated Press without checking with Miró first, and thus he planned our family's trip to Puerto Rico for the time when Miró would be touring the United States. The plan, once made, remained made; my father would not have gone to his Associated Press supervisors to ask for a change of leave. We stayed in Miró's empty house and visited Nena Pérez in San Juan and Miró's son in Ponce.

During the day, large, fat toads (enormous, I thought) plopped about the edges of the back entrance of Miró's surprisingly rural house. At night, tiny frogs called *coquís* kept up a racket that was not as infernal as advertised, but I could not sleep anyway. I sat in Miró's study. I did not turn on a light. As the sun came up, the photograph on the wall beside his desk grew better defined, first in shades of light and dark and then in color. Gradually I was able to see Miró standing next to Jacqueline Kennedy in the playing field of the Orange Bowl stadium on the day when Miami celebrated the return of Brigade 2506. Miró had let his sadness rise up and coat his being into the rigid pose of the defeated leader. The First Lady wore pink. She asked us to cleanse ourselves in her preternatural serenity. That day Miró saw his son again. But for my father the day had a sound like a death knell. Since the missile crisis of October he had been a man without hope, for had not he and all the world heard John Kennedy declare Fidel Castro inviolable?

The United States' preoccupation with Cuba was on the wane. Cuba had for a brief time been a national obsession. By the time the cheering Cubans gathered at the Orange Bowl, a new obsession was gestating. Eyes were turning east. In Southeast Asia the United States saw an opportunity to display its strength and determination, its ability to influence the course of events. U.S. advisors in Laos were ordered into their official uniforms—were permitted to become overt—three days after the invasion of Girón. But Laos, so prominent once, like Cuba, on front-page headlines from 1960 through 1963, would soon be eclipsed in U.S. life by its neighbor, Vietnam. In 1961 the South Vietnamese army had been deteriorating rapidly, but the United States had sent military aid, and the situation was said to be vastly improved. The United States could forget the Bay of Pigs. The United States could stop Communism in Southeast Asia.

My father saw the shift happening, and he suspected that the United States would forget about Cuba. He knew it positively when the Gulf of Tonkin Resolution was passed. Some Cubans were enthusiastic at first because the United States was being tough on Communism. My father told an excited caller that it meant that we were doomed. It was inconceivable to Cubans that the United States could forget about Cuba, but it did.

"Johnson called us a showcase of Communism in the Americas—a showcase," my father pointed out forcefully to caller after caller. "You know what you do with objects in a showcase. You look at them. You dust them off once in a while. But mostly you don't touch them."

*Nos mandaron pa' la Cochinchina,* as we say—said even before our displacement. Among us slang is prophetic. Cuban exiles' anti-Communism forced them to support verbally the U.S. government in its new war, but they were unable to understand why the United States would consecrate so much blood and war matériel, so much of the psyche of the nation, to such a distant war in the name of stopping Communism when Communism was only ninety miles away. Fidel Castro too was amazed. I heard young Cuban men in Miami ask why they should fight in Vietnam when their fight should be in Cuba. It was an unreasonable request the United States made: to expect us to die for their interests on a foreign shore when they had deserted us on ours.

Pepe Pérez San Román, commander of Brigade 2506, after his release from Castro's prison could find happiness in no ordinary employment, so he enlisted in the U.S. Army. When he got orders to go to Vietnam, he resigned. Alexander Haig, then a colonel, contemptibly accused him of cowardice and greed and threatened to try him by court-martial. President Lyndon Johnson got him an honorable discharge, and he did not go far away to die.

The welcoming celebration for our heroes at the stadium the afternoon of 29 December 1962 was one of the last public acts of the Consejo before Miró resigned and walked away from a public life full of shape-changers and men in shadows. Much of Miami's attention was focused on the event. The 1,179 surviving captives from Brigade 2506 had been ransomed for $53 million in medicines and baby food donated by U.S. corporations. They were 1,179 men who had not been as lucky as the very few who had been rescued at sea or who had been on vessels that did not make it to the beach. But they were 1,179 men who were luckier than those who were killed in the battle or getting to the battle or were captured on the beach and asphyxiated in the back of an unventilated truck. Ten had been murdered that way, prisoners of war asphyxiated in the back of a trailer truck designed for freight but holding in the punishing sun of midday 149 humans who desperately cut with belt buckles small holes in the aluminum sides and took turns breathing and banging against the metal sides, demanding what outside was free, air. Those who had survived the first few hours of capture had endured indignities to body and mind in prison at the wistfully named, dank, drafty old fortress, Castillo del Príncipe, the Castle of the Prince, and at the dreaded Isle of Pines where life as pain could be minutely studied: the slow starvation, the diseases of starvation. One man died untreated for hepatitis. They had been called mercenaries. At the time of the trial they were accused of being traitors and war criminals. Cameras were set up for the occasion. But the trial would not be televised, because the men would acknowledge nothing, because the men kept their dignity. They lived for twenty months, as our national anthem says, sunk in affronts and opprobrium, uncertain that they would escape being shot. They were 1,179 men who could be viewed as lucky only by applying the same angle of relativity that could render the bee hummingbird large when compared to an amoeba. They were luckier than the political prisoners who remained.

In May 1961 Fidel Castro had offered to exchange the brigade prisoners for an "indemnification" of 500 bulldozers from the United States. He called it "indemnification"; he insisted that the United States owed him reparation for what had been done to Cuba by the invasion. Early efforts to arrive at ransom fell through because of the implied capitulation in the exchange. Neither Fidel nor my father forgot the demand for indemnification. When the barter came in December 1962—$53 million worth of necessary goods for Castro—my father was enraged. The United States should never have agreed to the exchange, he insisted. We must never give an inch to Castro, who would wave it all in our faces as proof that the U.S. was admitting that reparations were justified. Fidel Castro was mocking the exile community and the United States. The men of the brigade became soldiers for a principle; they should resign themselves to suffer prison for that principle. My mother sometimes told me that it was fortunate that my father had no sons. Of course, what my father really wanted was for the United States to invade Cuba to rescue the prisoners, all the prisoners, all of Cuba.

My father went to the Orange Bowl, full though he was of anger; he had to. My mother and I both wanted to go, but she felt that it was my father's place to invite us. She made our desire explicit only after the event, later that evening.

"You two wanted to go?" my father asked with surprise.

"Of course," my mother said.

"Why didn't you tell me?" he asked.

Because we had not spoken up in time, my mother and I watched the ceremony only on television, with its selective close-ups. We saw the happy tears of the mothers and wives who had their men back. The First Lady spoke in Spanish. She was gracious and her dress was sleeveless. The president said empty words about returning the Brigade 2506 flag to a free Cuba—someday. Miró got back his son.

Because it was the Christmas season, toys were given out to children at the stadium. My father came home with a doll for me. The doll, in the shape of a baby, had a vaguely masculine air, perhaps because he wore blue. I named him Johnny because he had come to me from the president's show; my sympathies and antipathies sometimes ran a few steps behind my father's. Johnny could be a companion to Carmencita, the doll that had come to me so bitterly my first exiled Christmas.

When the light moved further into Miró's study, I saw his boxed sets of opera recordings. At home the only operatic records I had were a couple of aria selections sung by Alfredo Kraus, whom I admired as much as my classmates admired the Beatles. I knew that *Don Giovanni* was the last opera Miró had played before departure because he had left it on the floor, leaning against the record shelf. Or maybe he just listened to it more than to any other. I read the libretto, checking back and forth to the English translation. It seemed to me that the words should have been translated into Spanish, which was closer and the original of the original. I thought with pleasure of how Miró could understand the Italian with ease.

I knew the story well from Holy Week presentations on Cuban television of José Zorrilla's *Don Juan Tenorio*. I loved the play, and every year I looked forward to seeing my favorite actor, Otto Sirgo, in the part. It was pure pleasure, like so much else that was associated with the holy. At the same time, sin lay in the smallest things, and I did not need reminders to beware when a stone ghost offers his hand.

One afternoon in the summer of 1959, I was taken by a white school bus to confess my transgressions at the sunny but unfamiliar Church of San Juan de Letrán in preparation for my first communion. I knew that I must be absolutely truthful and thorough, for God knew all, saw all, heard all. Surprisingly, the priest behind the carved wooden screen, the dreadful unseen authority, benignly presumed, without knowledge or even sight of me, that my soul had remained in a state of innocence only venially removed from postbaptismal grace. The terror that pervaded me as I knelt on the other side of the free-standing confessional arose from my contrary assumption: that I was guilty of terrible things. I answered yes to every sin the priest asked me about.

"Have you told lies?"

"Yes."

"Have you been disrespectful toward your parents?"

"Yes."

I even said yes to a question I did not understand. From talking to the other girls afterwards, it became obvious that the priest had questioned us all about the same menu of sins. I asked a classmate what the last question had been.

She said, "Have you fought with your brothers and sisters?"

"Oh."

I then worried obsessively about having accused myself before God of an impossibility, about having botched my first confession. Lying in confession was a sacrilege, which was a very serious sin. I tried to reassure myself: all other children were my brothers and sisters—I could reason even then like a Jesuit—and in that sense my response was true.

When the Río Piedras morning finally awoke my father, I showed him Miró's records and he said, "Play what you want."

But we could not master the intricacies of the stereo system. The needle made a strange sound as it touched down on the first record of *Don Giovanni*. I still hope we didn't scratch it.

## III

*And the ransomed of the Lord shall return,*
*and come to Zion with singing;*
*everlasting joy shall be upon their heads;*
*they shall obtain joy and gladness*
*and sorrow and sighing shall flee away.*

Miami was hardly Zion. Pepe Pérez San Román's gladness was small, a thing of moments in his family's embrace. Perhaps the cheering of the crowds at the Orange Bowl resounded in his ears with strange, accusatory sarcasm. It is in the nature of people of conscience to blame themselves too much. During twenty months of imprisonment, Pérez San Román's constant companion was the thought that he had led 1,543 men into a tragedy. He had asked his men to trust him in his trust of those who, at the crucial event, betrayed them all. In the beginning, at El Príncipe, he could see it in the men. They looked at him as if he had betrayed them or, at the very least, abandoned them. He did not try to defend himself against an accusation he half believed. Later, through the hunger, dysentery, and the daily vexations that all suffered in the Isle of Pines, the others learned to look farther away for blame. He did not learn.

If Pepe Pérez San Román had not had absolute faith that help would come from the United States, he would have been mad to lead men into the assault, and Brigade 2506 would have been mad to follow him. There may have been some within their ranks who would willingly participate in a suicidal mission because their need to act overrode their need to preserve their lives—but there were not 1,543 such men. And it is an act of insanity to go forth with only 1,543 soldiers to capture an island that extends 780 miles from west to east (from Cabo San Antonio to Punta de Maisí, as Cubans intone), especially if the territory is defended by thirty-two thousand regular soldiers and between two and three hundred thousand militia intent on keeping control of it.

The CIA told the brigade that Castro's soldiers would not fight but, rather, would defect and join the liberators. The brigade wanted to believe this. In a televised interrogation, brigade member Felipe Rivero was asked by Carlos Rafael Rodríguez, Old Communist hierarchist, if he, Rivero, like his companions, expected an uprising. Rivero answered that he and the other men had not intended to commit suicide.

Suicide was expected. When Pepe Pérez San Román was moved from Girón to the Sports Palace in La Habana, militiamen searched him for the suicide pills they were certain he would use. Pepe Pérez San Román told Haynes Johnson, who interviewed him for *The Bay of Pigs: The Leaders' Story of Brigade 2506,* that he was not that kind of man.

Cuba is ringed by twenty-five hundred miles of crenelated, reefy coastline. It is a hell of a place to send an invasion force of 1,543 men without first admitting the truth of aerial reconnaissance photos, without believing Cubans who had fished the waters. A coral reef lay in wait in the approach to Girón. As Wyden tells it, the CIA dismissed its own evidence and its own operation commander's suspicions. Of course, it brushed aside informed Cuban protestations. CIA experts knew better. And so, as the Brigade approached the beach, boat bottoms were ripped and some men drowned. In islands, the Englishman wrote, nature builds a fortress for herself against infection and the hand of war.

Cubans committed a fundamental philosophical error in agreeing to become invaders of Cuba. The body fights against invasion from anything that it perceives as foreign to itself. We consented to become foreign to ourselves when we agreed to approach with weapons of war the containing walls of our island. The people of Cuba reacted as should have been expected. We exiles were blind drunk with the need to go home.

There had been another way. Anti-Castro insurgents would have welcomed reinforcements, though not U.S. orders. A thousand *alzados*—from peasant, working class, and professional backgrounds—fought a guerrilla war in the Escambray Mountains in the central province of Las Villas. Among the Escambray group were some who had gained experience in the arts of this sort of war when they had fought alongside Fidel. This new guerrilla force, like its predecessor, had taken up arms spontaneously. They waged their war mostly without assistance from the United States, except for an occasional drop of supplies. These drops were frequently botched; now and then someone narrowly escaped being killed by a falling sack of beans.

From the earliest stages of its planning for the Cuba Project until the autumn of 1960, the CIA envisioned preparing men for guerrilla warfare. At first the training given to brigade members concentrated on guerrilla tactics. Then the plan changed. An amphibious assault, which had originally been proposed as supplemental to the clandestine infiltration, became the main show. It was the way to ensure U.S. control.

The U.S. planners did not even keep open the possibility that the landing force would blend into the insurgency in the mountains if it met with too great a resistance. For most of the life of the project, the landing was planned for the port of Casilda, next to the city of Trinidad, at the foot of the Escambray Mountains, allowing reasonable access to guerrilla territory. This plan, however, worried the Kennedy brothers when they were told of it. Would not a landing near a principal city be too visible? Would there be civilian casualties?

To please the president, because secrecy, even of an invasion by 1,543 men armed with loud and lethal (if insufficient) ordnance, must be maintained, the men of the CIA chose a new site a hundred miles and an impassable swamp away from the Escambray Mountains: Playa Girón and Playa Larga, two beaches on Cochinos Bay.

Afterwards the president and some of his principal advisors would say that they had not realized that by landing at the Bay of Pigs the men would be unable to retreat to the Escambray Mountains. Yet surely a map must have been brought out to illustrate the landing options. Hatch marks would have indicated the Ciénaga de Zapata, six hundred square miles of swamp, the eastern end of it sitting between Girón, the primary landing site, and the Escambray. The map would also have clearly shown that the distance between Girón and the foothills of the Escambray was forty miles, too long an expanse for any brigade to traverse without risk of capture, even without the natural barrier of the swamp. Intractable swamps, like Zapata, usually harbor only a very small human population. Yet no one asked how a mass uprising, an absolute requisite for the success of this invasion, could be touched off in the Ciénaga de Zapata?

On Tuesday, 18 April, Erneido Oliva, deputy commander of Brigade 2506, hero of the Battle for the Rotunda at Playa Larga—a man so brave that he stood alone without cover in the middle of the open road and pointed a cannon at an approaching tank—wanted the remnants of the brigade to make an attempt to reach the Escambray Mountains, in spite of the distance and the swamp, so that something might be salvaged from their costly effort. But Pepe Pérez San Román, his commander, disagreed. Surely there would be *castrista* troops between them and the mountains, he argued. And, for certain, U.S. ships would come that day with ammunition so that they could continue the fight. They must stay where the ships would find them, the U.S. ships that would certainly come. Then it got to be too late to head for the Escambray Mountains, as no U.S. ships, but Fidel Castro's army, surrounded them.

Pepe Pérez San Román had been appointed commander by the arrogant, deeply disliked U.S. trainers at Base Trax in Guatemala. Cubans possess an innate hatred of orders, but some hate them more or less than others. Pepe Pérez San Román, a soldier's son, was himself a career military man, first for Batista and then against him. As an officer in the Cuban army, he had been trained not only at the military academy in Cuba but, probably more impressive to his *yanqui* overlords, also at Fort Benning and

Fort Belvoir in the United States. He had many factors in his favor: he could follow orders, he had the capacity to believe in the United States, and he had proven to be a capable soldier.

No doubt in his post-Girón hell Pepe Pérez San Román agonized over the reasons why he had been cursed with selection. In fact, a small rebellion had followed his appointment. Some of the members of the brigade thought that Cubans should choose their own leader. Because he did not have the full confidence of the brigade, and because he was a man of honor, Pérez San Román resigned his command and asked to be allowed to be an ordinary soldier. But the *yanquis* said that *they* were the power and that Pepe Pérez San Román was the commander.

Still trying to do the honorable thing—and still trusting that the United States favored honor—Pepe Pérez San Román asked those who supported him as commander to step to the right from their formation under the hot sun. Most did so, but one hundred men stood steadfast in their protest. Among these, twenty were singled out by the *yanquis* as the instigators of the revolt. They were interrogated and spirited away to inaccessible Guatemalan mountains where they were kept under guard and shod with thin slippers against escape until two weeks after the invasion. They were kept *incomunicados*.

The long, insect-infested prison nights offered Pepe Pérez San Román many opportunities to wish that he had dug his heels deep into the ground and stood immovable with the rebellious one hundred. He had thought, with the United States behind us, how can we lose? The United States had never lost a war. The United States was a powerful boss to have, but that power failed Pepe Pérez San Román.

Pepe Pérez San Román's calls from the beach for U.S. help were numerous and increasingly desperate. The man at the other end of the radio was "Gray"; "Gray" was all the Cubans knew of him. Grayston Lynch, as his parents named him before he became classified, was the brigade's link with U.S. power, their commander on the scene. Grayston Lynch was a brave man but he was CIA. In the end, all he had to give was false hope. Never trust the support of anyone who has been ordered not to give you his full name. "We will never abandon you," Gray said. He lied. Perhaps he himself could not bear to believe it was a lie.

No help came. Men in jeeps sat with chests opened by bullets. Men exploded in the sea. Men were eaten in the sea. They died slowly in boats. In a fertile island, they went mad in a swamp without water. Some wandered for two weeks before capture, surrounded by thorns and quicksand, drinking urine and the blood of snakes. The snakes of Cuba are all harmless to humans. The mangrove cuts, the rock cuts, the coral cuts, the sun—too much sun—kills.

> *For waters shall break forth in the wilderness,*
>     *and streams in the desert;*
> *the burning sand shall become a pool,*
>     *and the thirsty ground springs of water;*
> *the haunt of jackals shall become a swamp,*
> *the grass shall become reeds and rushes.*

From the UPI photograph of Comandante José Pérez San Román, leader of the defeated Brigade 2506, a thin, defiant, haunted man stares at us from behind two vertical prison bars and two diagonals. A twenty-nine-year-old commander. The muscles of his angular face are clenched. The greatest defiance in life is possible only to those who do not care if they die. He developed tuberculosis in jail and was cured of it in exile; I cannot think that the cure was a blessing to him.

If I ever met Pepe Pérez San Román, I do not remember it. He may have been one of the stream of political men to whom I was introduced in childhood without my understanding their significance. On 17 October 1989 an article by Myra MacPherson in the *Washington Post*—the style section—held painful news. Pepe Pérez San Román had killed himself. It was five months after my father's death; my grief was still fresh. Pérez San Román's death seemed too much sorrow. Another Girón casualty.

As I read and wept through the *Washington Post* article, a strange feeling came to me. It was envy. I envied Pérez San Román's family his way of suicide. Here was a man who thought of others even in his despair. He called his sister to tell her he loved her. He visited his grandchildren. He spoke with his brother. He left a letter addressed to all his family, each person specified. In his apartment he arranged in plain view some of the items he wanted family members to have. In my poverty, I saw the noble generosity of his preparations.

Sometime on the night of 9 to 10 September, he took an overdose of medicine. His passing was peaceful. He had been a military man. In the past he had raised his gun on behalf of his family; he chose not to use it against them. Instead he took the lethal pills that the enemy in the Sports Palace had read as his future.

Pepe Pérez San Román's last request was like my father's: he asked to be cremated and to have his ashes scattered over a body of water. But he did not request the Atlantic. He asked that the ashes of his body be enfolded by the Brazos River in Texas, where he had lived for a while. I would like to think that pleasant memories of days spent at the river influenced his choice of the Brazos, but I will not call it his resting place. Some people allow themselves no rest. The river's waters empty into the Gulf of Mexico whence Pepe Pérez San Roman's remains might haphazardly be borne toward the same treacherous coasts of Cuba where he experienced guilt, betrayal, and defeat. Cuba's children long to return in life or in death.

*Strengthen the weak hands,*
  *and make firm the feeble knees.*
*Say to those who are of a fearful heart,*
  *"Be strong, and fear not!*
*Behold, your God will come with vengeance,*

> *with the recompense of God.*
> *He will come and save you."*

Flames leaped from my father's tongue as they had from Isaiah's. Both men wanted to ignite other men—men always—into action. What my father and the other heart-broken political men in Miami who passionately foretold the imminence of victory did not consider was that prophecy, as the creature of time, operates in the duration of time, in its generations, in its centuries. If the God of the Jews exists, he has tried their patience most profoundly. *No hay mal que dure cien años ni cuerpo que lo resista,* my father said, Cubans say: there is no evil that can last one hundred years, nor body that can take it. To my father and to other desperate Cuban men this was of little comfort. They wanted change, which is constant in the universe, to go their way, and immediately. They did not want to live in exile, where each year would seem a hundred of pain. To them Cuba was everything.

My father, Pepe Pérez San Román, my mother, all the other exiled men and women, and I have had decades for analysis. We have had decades to turn the facts over and over in our hands as if they were skull charms dangling from an iron necklace. They are maddening facts that can drive one to a bullet or to pills as they scrape skin and constrict breath, and one says, "I might as well." The importance of these facts resides in their meaning, which is discernible in the pattern of their linking. We may forget details, but the anguish of facts' meaning, the iron chain, remains, never fully out of mind, making us incapable of normal living. We were sacrificed.

All plans for the invasion assumed the prior destruction through air strikes of *all* Castro planes on the ground, a lot of the damage to be achieved during a strong D-Day effort. However, the State Department wanted both the brigade planes and the number of attacks to be kept to a minimum so that the air strikes would appear (heaven knows to whom) to come from self-supplied Castro opponents inside Cuba.

The brigade had been given seventeen World-War-II-issue B-26 bombers. The CIA and others in the U.S. government thought that shoddy equipment would certify the "Cubanness" of the operation. Castro's own small but not-as-shoddy Cuban air force contained Sea Furies, which were British prop fighters, and T-33 training jets armed with 20-mm cannons. The B-26s were no match for Castro's planes.

The CIA had established the brigade's air base in Nicaragua, from which pilots had to fly six hundred miles to have the mere forty-five minutes over Cuba that their fuel tanks would allow. Air bases on U.S. territory, of course, were out of the question: that would too openly violate international agreements, not to mention deniability going up in smoke.

Air superiority was considered essential to the mission, yet the air strikes' potential was nullified by Washington bunglers to whom effectiveness in a Cuban-staffed operation was an overt sign of U.S. involvement. The elements of surprise and military effectiveness were discarded in order to satisfy Kennedy's principal condition: that the badly written fiction of U.S. non-involvement be advanced, that secret plots remain concealed. Thus was it that an air strike employing only six of the seventeen brigade planes was ordered to be carried out two days prior to the invasion—six planes that could only knock out part of Castro's air force.

Recklessness on such a scale must have terrible repercussions. The air strike not only gave Castro advance warning of the invasion and allowed him both to mobilize his armed forces and imprison the opposition; it also gave his representative the opportunity to complain before the United Nations. The U.S. ambassador to the United Nations, Adlai Stevenson, enraged at having been deceived by the Kennedy administration and embarrassed about the foolish part he had been made to play before the other diplomats, furiously insisted that future air strikes be called off. The president of the United States acceded to his employee's demand: he called off the crucial D-Day raid on planes remaining on Castro's air strip. The already slim chances of the brigade were destroyed. Pentagon men who reviewed the plans could only whisper, with mouths that must previously have shouted thousands of commands, their opinion that the machinations of the CIA were militarily impracticable: the invasion would fail if even one Castro plane was left whole. Yet the men of the ill-equipped, undertrained brigade, making their way in old boats to Cuba, were told to expect not only air cover but an easy victory.

One reason why the invasion was thought to be incapable of surviving even one Castro airplane was that every piece of equipment requisitioned for the brigade was shabby, not just the aircraft, but the transports, everything. The CIA did not even bother supplying with machine guns the five merchant ships from the Spanish García Line that it contracted for the mission. Machine guns would not be needed, said the intoxicated CIA; no one would fire upon the boats. Eduardo García, the owner, had to insist on machine guns. These were installed, but the CIA neglected to teach the crews on some ships how to fire them.

The greatest danger in case of an air-to-sea attack was not the equipment that was lacking but rather the cargo that was present. The CIA loaded the hulls of the ships with the exceedingly dangerous combination of ammunition and highly flammable high-octane gasoline. Ships' crews might be incinerated. The brigade doctors had been promised a hospital ship. They did not get one.

To protect secrecy, the invasion force was ordered to disembark at night, contrary to accepted procedure for amphibious landings. The CIA did not make provisions for evacuation by sea. Those U.S. ships that were sent to the area were ordered to stay too far off shore to conduct rescues. They were within sight but out of reach.

The facts of the invasion exhibit a pattern that is as discernible as it is painful: in all matters dealing with the preservation of exile Cuban lives, the United States failed us, treated us as expendable. By contrast, in October 1962, during the missile crisis, the Kennedy administration drew up plans for a possible invasion by sea that would land in Cuba 180,000 U.S. troops under a first-day umbrella of 1,080 attack sorties from the air. But U.S. lives would be involved then, you see—U.S. lives going up against Cuban lives.

Because in the wretched spring of 1961 Kennedy wanted a silent victory for an invisible hand, he insisted that no official U.S. forces be used, and yet at every turn he weakened the potential of ours. Kennedy asked the impossible of Richard Bissell and his CIA colleagues, and they did not tell him that what he asked for was impossible, and they scrambled to give him the impossible, jettisoning essential parts of their plan where the principal disadvantage of the cut was the further endangerment of the brigade. Kennedy thought he could preserve a secret that anyone with access to the *New York Times* knew about. We were sacrificed for nothing.

Yet the government that wanted total deniability wanted also total control. Power over everything connected with the invasion—training, operations, equipment—was in U.S. hands. They chose our commanders. They mixed together *batistianos* and *antibatistianos* although the two groups could not bear the sight of each other, let alone fight cohesively on the same side. They decided where, when, and whom we would fight. When the U.S. canceled the brigade's second air strike, some of the Cuban pilots wanted to fly their missions anyway, but they knew they would not get past the rifles of the *yanquis,* their keepers, their friends, who were guarding their planes against them.

The men on the ship *La Playa* were told that they were going to arm and join a guerrilla force in the province of Oriente, where many among them had been born, but they were really only being used as a diversion. When they learned that they were entering a trap of rocks and breakers and Castro vehicles only to draw attention away from another invasion to the west, they refused to proceed as ordered. They took their CIA agent prisoner. They refused to be part of a sacrifice of pawns.

Would that we all had mutinied, in Miami, on ships, in the air. All of Girón was a trap. Decades later we are still stuck, shipwrecked in the mouths of Playa Larga and Playa Girón, scraping ourselves on the facts.

A short time after the death of John Kennedy, my father brought home from work two copies of a book of photographs taken by Associated Press photographers of the assassination and the funeral, bound inside dark covers and distributed by the AP as a memorial.

"Take one to the library at your school," my father said to me, thinking that this would be easy.

I knew it would cause confusion. But the next morning I dutifully took the book to Miss Wilson, the nice librarian at Riverside Elementary.

She seemed puzzled. "It's for us?"

"Yes," I said, "my father works for the Associated Press."

She looked at the book as if she would not know what to do with it. She took it to the office where she processed books. I suspected that there were channels that books had to go through. Approvals. Acquisitions procedures that this book was not part of. Besides, it was a book for adults, about death and funerals.

I sometimes worked as an assistant to Miss Wilson before school, and when my class had library time I checked the other children's books out. When Miss Wilson's mother died, I worked up the courage to do the right thing according to the rules of Cuban society. Her first day back, I went to see her after school. I made sure we were alone in the library. All day I had rehearsed what I would say.

I walked up to her and I said solemnly, "Miss Wilson, I'm very sorry about your mother's death."

Her cheeks tensed as if she were going to cry, but she stifled the impulse. I did not know that weeping was a necessity for people who grieve. I thought I had caused nice Miss Wilson pain.

And here I was with the Kennedy book, bringing up death again. And this time one that was difficult to classify according to our school's Dewey decimal system. I feared moreover that the book would somehow get marked "Gift of the Boza Family," and that we would go down in the tradition of the school as people who had admired John F. Kennedy and who wished to give this tribute to the school where I had first heard the news of his death.

On the afternoon of the assassination, we of Mrs. Evelyn Lee Thompson's sixth-grade class had been at recess when we were called inside. Over the intercom, Miss Chase, the principal, told the whole school that the president was dead. She did not say much else. Just that we were being released for the afternoon and we should talk about the death with our families. It was a wise but loaded order. My family's reaction was perhaps more vehement but not substantially different from many other Cuban families'.

It was persistently irritating, Kennedy's swift subsequent canonization by a citizenry who found it difficult to accept that a young, vital man had died and his fresh flesh had perforce been consigned to the worms of earth. We all felt compassion for his children, for his beautiful and—we did not know it then—betrayed wife. But for my father and for other Cuban exiles, the decades of Kennedy hagiolatry brought constant pain. They clung to him in hatred even as he shifted shape in their grasp. For each facet of his personality there was a canceling opposite. Who was John F. Kennedy? It may be too simplistic a summation of his being to say that he was a politician, yet he was that principally and consummately.

Who was John F. Kennedy? On Wednesday, 19 April 1961, the members of the Consejo, after they had been released from their CIA imprisonment in Opa-Locka, arrived at the White House full of rage and grief. Kennedy soothed these desperate men with his concern for their sons and with his assertions that the United States would not abandon its commitment to Cuban liberty.

In a speech before the American Society of Newspaper Editors the next day, Kennedy vowed again not to abandon Cuba. He painted for the editors a pretty though untrue picture in which the brigade commander had gone "to join in the mountains countless other guerrilla fighters, who are equally determined that those who gave their lives shall not be forgotten and that Cuba must not be abandoned to the Communists. And we do not intend to abandon it either." But they did. Earlier in the speech Kennedy had said, "Nor would we expect or accept the same outcome which this small band of gallant Cuban refugees must have known that they were chancing, determined as they were against heavy odds to pursue their courageous attempts to regain their island's freedom." And yet, no, they had not known what they were chancing.

When the men of Brigade 2506 were ransomed in December 1962, Kennedy got the potentially hostile Cuban public that filled the Orange Bowl stadium to cheer his speech wildly. Upon being given the brigade's flag by Erneido Oliva, he turned to José Pérez San Román and to José Miró Cardona and he said, "Commander, Doctor, I want to express my great appreciation to the brigade for making the United States the custodian of this flag." Kennedy paused before his next sentence once more rolled the Cuban crowd into the vast sea of U.S. promise and power, "I can assure you that this flag will be returned to this brigade in a free Havana."

*"Ich bin ein Berliner!"* he had once said, although he was clearly and demonstrably not one.

What most Cubans know of *doctrina martiana,* of which they profess to be adherents regardless of political tendency, is what they have seen on park marble and schoolroom walls or heard declaimed in speeches and as patriotic mottoes. In his larger work, José Martí embedded aphorisms that the generations of later Cubans have extracted. And so every child hears, "Children are the ones who know how to love. Children are the hope of the world," and she feels unequal to what is expected of her. Martí's gnomic statements are so well-turned and so imbued with noble wishfulness that people like me feel like cads for analyzing their truth value while people like my father fly on the wings of his lofty words. Martí wrote some very unlofty, frightened things about women. Therefore I am inclined to be skeptical.

About politics Martí did his best thinking. A thorough reading of unexcerpted Martí might have warned Cubans not to place their trust in the United States. In his last letter, meant for his Mexican friend Manuel Mercado, and dated 18 May 1895, the day before he died in Dos Ríos, Martí wrote: ". . . every day I am in danger of giving my life for my country and for my duty—since I understand it and have the energy with which to carry it out—of preventing in time, with the independence of Cuba, the United States from extending itself through the Antilles and falling, with its greater force, upon our lands of América." He feared annexation to that "restless and brutal North that despises" us, the countries of *"nuestra América."* "I lived in the monster," he wrote, "and I know its innermost recesses—and my sling is David's."

In a letter of 25 March to Federico Henríquez y Carvajal, he expressed his hopes not just for Cuba but for the world: "The free Antilles will save the independence of our América and the honor, already injured and in doubt, of English América, and will perhaps accelerate and ensure the balance of the world. See what we do, you with your youthful gray hairs and I, dragging, with my heart broken."

If souls of the departed can observe earthly events and feel torment for us, then Martí's very heaven must be a painful hell. We went from colonization by Spain to intervention by the United States. The U.S. expansionism that Martí had so intensely feared fell upon us. During its intervention, from 1899 till 1902, the United States government tried to impose upon Cuba a system modeled on the U.S. example. The concerns and wishes of Cubans were swept away. General Leonard Wood, the U.S. proconsul in Cuba, ruled like a tyrant and brought to our country all his northern vices. For example, when Cubans, including General José Miró Argenter, wished for universal suffrage, he disregarded it, insisting upon property requirements. The U.S.ers, our protectors, showed us the contempt they felt. In his civil report for 1902, Wood expressed despair of building a republic based on the shining U.S. model "in one of the most unhealthy countries."

We finally got independence on 20 May 1902 because Wood tired of us while we did not tire of our desire for independence, and because the United States' own Teller Amendment (U.S. Congress in this one instance be praised) expressly forbade annexation. The United States, however, did not relinquish its imperial tie. In the spring of 1901, the United States Congress formulated the Platt Amendment, which our U.S. overseers forced us to include in our constitution. Through this amendment, which alternately or even simultaneously would be hated and appealed to by the Cuban populace throughout the twentieth century, the United States reserved the right to interfere in Cuba whenever, in the opinion of the U.S. government, things were not proceeding properly in our country.

This state of affairs must have presented itself in 1906, for the United States took over our government, appointing a U.S. man named Charles Magoon to be our governor. He was not a tyrant like Wood, though, like Wood, he had been imposed upon us by a foreign power. Because my father never bothered to teach me Cuban history, I did not know in his lifetime what he meant when he said scornfully whenever corruption was mentioned, "Cubans learned politics from the *americanos*."

On 28 January 1909, the governance of Cuba returned to Cuban hands, more precisely, to the Liberal president José

Miguel Gómez y Gómez who had fought in all three of our wars of independence, including the appropriately named Guerra Chiquita. In 1910 Senator Martín Morúa Delgado, a man of African ancestry and Liberal Party affiliation who had been elected president of the Senate, proposed an amendment to the electoral reform law that in its final wording denied recognition to political parties whose membership was drawn entirely from one "color race" and which pursued "racist ends." Morúa had perceived in the rise of the Partido Independiente de Color a threat to the Liberal Party's popularity with black voters. Minor uprisings, initiated by the PIC, followed in Oriente and Las Villas. President Gómez, who did not favor the amendment, was quite capable of re-establishing the peace.

However, U.S. businessmen were scared out of their wits by the improbable specter of a widespread black uprising, and they turned to Washington for rescue. On 25 May the warnings from the United States began. If the Cuban government could not or would not protect U.S. citizens and property, U.S. forces would be sent to provide that protection. President Gómez sent a letter to President William Howard Taft asking him politely not to rush toward an unnecessary intervention. Just in case, that day the United States sent three destroyers toward Guantánamo. On 31 May U.S. armed forces landed in Daiquirí—the eponymous town in Oriente, not the frosty lime-and-rum drink. On 5 June four companies of U.S. Marines landed near Guantánamo. There was little danger to U.S. businesses in general, but Taft's Secretary of State Philander C. Knox (a man whose name had accustomed him to expect distrust?) expanded the application of the Platt Amendment to include "preventive" action. Since January the United States had been itching to intervene in Cuba. Agitation by veterans of the Army of Liberation who were angry that some government posts had gone to veterans of Spain's enemy army had made the United States nervous. On 8 June, Gómez sent a delegation to Washington to ask Taft please, please, please not to intervene further militarily in Cuba, not to get so nervous, it was bad for one's health, and, besides, so much nervousness might move him to shut down the Cuban government and install a *yanqui* proconsul, as indeed the law of both our countries said he had a right to do, but it was too severe a step. Don't intervene us, Mr. Taft, pretty please with all our sugar on it.

Although it would not be openly diagnosed until 1914, during the first Menocal administration, in the summer of 1912, bubonic plague arrived in Cuba. Like the U.S. Marines, it came by sea.

In 1916 the Conservative General Mario García Menocal y Deop, youngest major general in the Army of Liberation, stole by extravagant fraud his presidential re-election from the Liberals. The Liberals responded with armed revolt. However, stolen election or no, Menocal had been educated in the United States and had managed a very large U.S.-owned sugar mill. This Conservative was altogether the kind of man that the United States liked to deal with. The United States, still in possession of its full Plattist powers, did nothing about Menocal's illegal re-election, although even our Supreme Tribunal spoke up about irregularities. So cocky was Menocal that he repeated his outrageously obvious multiplication of Conservative votes in the election held to rectify the previous one's fraud. In April of 1917, while the war over the election still raged, President Woodrow Wilson committed the United States to a wider war, World War I. Wilson could not afford for Cuba to remain neutral because Cuba supplied the allies' sugar. General Menocal obligingly declared war on Germany. On 15 May 1917, the U.S. government warned that, since the Cuban government was its ally in the war against Germany, those Cuban insurgents who persisted in fighting the Cuban government could be considered enemies of the United States and so treated. On 14 June 1917, U.S. troops were sent to Cuba under cover of a reason that no one believed: that they needed to be trained in a warm climate. Their presence was probably requested by Menocal. Sixteen hundred Marines were dispatched to Oriente and a thousand to Camagüey, where they stayed until 1923 while Menocal stole pesos and dollars and anything else that came his way.

In 1933 Cuba had a revolution. Some call it *la revolución del '30* because it was in that year that violent struggle began. But it was in 1933 that the efforts of students and workers, culminating in an August general strike, succeeded in ousting the repressive president, General Gerardo Machado. Rebellion was so widespread that the United States, seeking the stability that U.S. business interests desired above all, let it be known to Machado that the United States too thought it was time for him to go. The proconsular U.S. ambassador, Sumner Welles, who had been dispatched to Cuba by his friend, President Franklin D. Roosevelt, just for this crisis, chose Carlos Manuel de Céspedes y de Quesada to succeed Machado.

Céspedes had been the Cuban ambassador to Mexico. He was a vague man without a constituency. His salient qualification for the post was that he was the son of the original Carlos Manuel de Céspedes, the shouter of the Grito de Yara, which began our Ten Years' War of Independence in 1868. The most interesting fact about the younger man was his mythic conception and birth. He was conceived upon his mother Ana de Quesada by her husband, the Father of Our Country, *en plena manigua,* in the thicket of battle, where Céspedes was President of the Republic at Arms. Finding herself pregnant, Ana de Quesada traveled to New York, where she gave birth to the twins Carlos Manuel and Gloria; alas not Castor and Pollux, not Romulus and Remus, not the divine Ibeyi, for this is where myth stops and nineteenth-century reality empties on us a chamber pot. The twins were educated in the United States. In Sumner Welles's eyes, this must have shone as the younger male Céspedes's chief virtue. On the other hand, Cubans saw little virtue. He lasted one month in office.

A sergeants' revolt led by the sergeant-stenographer Fulgencio Batista, in concert with worker and student activists, overthrew

Céspedes's government. A pentarchy was installed with popular support. The power of rulership was divided among five people—and a radical idea of governance was sprung upon the world. The pentarchy represented some of the various groups that had struggled against Machado. They were Ramón Grau San Martín, professor and medical doctor, who had links with the Directorio Estudiantil; Sergio Carbó, a radical newspaper owner and journalist (his son, Ulises Carbó, also a journalist, would join Brigade 2506 and would be captured); José Miguel Irisarri, lawyer; Guillermo Portela, professor of criminal law; and Porfirio Franca, a banker.

Eventually the pentarchy took a more conventional approach and elected to the single presidency of the republic Ramón Grau San Martín. Grau eschewed the procedure of taking the oath of office before the Supreme Tribunal. He did not want to swear to uphold the Constitution of 1902, as it contained the Platt Amendment—which he immediately, unilaterally abrogated. Instead he stepped out onto the balcony of the Presidential Palace and announced before the crowd that he derived his power from them, the Cuban people, that he had assumed office in the name of an authentically revolutionary government. He advanced the motto: "Cuba for the Cubans." He nominated a cabinet full of progressive men, while still maintaining around him the students who had been his original constituency. Laws were passed that would have exerted a deep influence for reform in the country. Many of them had been proposed by Antonio Guiteras, a progressive Liberal member of the cabinet.

But the country—which moreover was suffering, like the United States, through an economic depression—was riddled with instability. And Sumner Welles did not like Grau and he did not like the students. How could he, how could the United States like a Cuban president who rejected the Platt Amendment? The United States refused to recognize Grau's government. And, through its proconsul Sumner Welles, the United States carried its disapproval further. Sumner Welles, who walked through the discursive halls of La Habana broom-straight in a black suit in the middle of a heat wave, played faction against faction. What Welles whispered in the ears of one band and then another, all with quarrels against the revolutionary government, seemed to signal the support of the United States for the very pair of ears listening, in exclusion of all others. In seeking the stability he promised U.S. businessmen in Cuba, he spread the seeds of instability and discord among Cubans.

In the meantime, U.S. destroyers ringed the island. Sumner Welles finally settled on his man, one on whom he smelled such ambition (he had risen quickly to colonel) that he knew that the United States could count on him. In him at last Welles had the strong military man so necessary to keep in check the heat of Latin blood. The man was the former sergeant-stenographer Fulgencio Batista. When Jefferson Caffery arrived on 8 December as Welles's replacement, he came well versed in Welles's version of the situation, and the harm, anyway, had already been done.

In January 1934 the army under Batista deserted Grau. Most parties, including members of the pentarchy, agreed on a compromise candidate for the presidency, the engineer Carlos Hevia, who took his oath of office on 17 January. (In 1961 he would be a member of the Consejo Revolucionario Cubano and one of the men held captive in Opa-Locka during the invasion.) Hevia's full name had the resonance and improbability of legend: Carlos Hevia y de los Reyes Gavilán, or Charles Hevia and of the Kings a Hawk. Still, he was soon deposed.

Antonio Guiteras, the minister of governance under Grau, insisted that Hevia appoint a new head of the army, but Hevia kept Batista at the post. In protest, Guiteras called for a general strike. This tactic backfired. Using the disorder of the threatened strike as an excuse to Caffery, Batista declared his original choice, the pliable Colonel Carlos Mendieta, president. (He also had his army shoot down Guiteras and other members of the organization Joven Cuba as they were trying to leave the country in May

1935.) The Mendieta government was recognized by the United States only five days after his appointment by Batista. Militarism had won. ("I have never been a militarist," my mother says. "There are those who are attracted by the gleam of helmets, but not I.") Thus began Batista's career as puppeteer behind a string of puppet presidents. He was so driven by his carnivore hunger that he willingly accepted the extranational string tied to his own back. Thanks in large part to the United States, Batista would haunt our politics till 1959, with the already known disastrous results. A window of opportunity was shuttered with the defeat of the revolution of 1933.

There was such chaos and such hope those hundred days in 1933. The chaos was in the crowds that grew wild and blood-thirsty, running in the streets searching for old Machado supporters and *porristas,* members of his army of goons. They killed several *porristas,* and they sacked a lot of houses. My mother was very much against Machado and very much for the government of Grau (the 1933 one anyway). Although she was only sixteen years old, for some time she had read everything she could get her hands on by Sergio Carbó and another *anti-machadista* journalist, Pizzi de Porras, whose fifteen-year-old son would commit suicide when cornered by the army in a factional revolt of November 1933. My mother's brother-in-law Rafael was a pro-Machado Liberal but quietly so. However, his two brothers were actively and openly pro-Machado. During the *machadato,* they were able to get my mother's brother Mario out of jail when he was arrested for passing out leaflets announcing a revolutionary meeting. The ex-wife of one of the brothers, in turn, was able to save their hide and their valuables when Machado fell and the crowd she had joined rampaged its way to their house seeking something to destroy; she was able to per-suade her cohorts to move on to another target. The crowds were out of control, frenzied with vengeance, unwilling to tell friend from foe. Although one of my mother's cousins, Rubén Ortiz Lamadrid, had broadcast an anti-Machado clandestine radio program, he prudently climbed onto the roof of his house when he saw the crowd come by.

My father's position in 1933 was complicated. He was a twenty-five-year-old Liberal, a member of the "big tent" party—in this sense, not unlike the U.S. Democratic Party—that could accommodate within its ample, multicolored folds such colliding entities as Machado, Batista, and Guiteras. My father spoke fondly only of *viejos liberales,* such as the subject of a favorite story, a stirring Old Liberal speaker who, when a gunshot went off at a gathering, stopped mid-oration and exhorted with fervor, "Run, Liberals of El Perico!" Still, a Liberal he was—and one that needed to work for a living. Although my father often told with pride the tale of the March 1935 strike, he did not like to discuss his activities during the *machadato.* He was a member of an anti-Machado underground cellular organization, the OCRR (or Organización Celular Radical Revolucionaria). However, he was embarrassed because at the same time he was employed at the Ministerio de Hacienda, or Treasury. Other members of the cellular organizations worked in government posts, but Ramiro Boza always had to be perfect, beyond reproach. Some of my father's obituaries suggest that he was long a reporter for the Treasury Ministry. Therefore, the Central Hershey job he held in 1935, when Corporal Chávez read him his fate, was simultaneous with his work at Treasury. (This Hershey job was an improvement over the one he had held as a youth, of carrying sugar sacks.) All along he was also involved in labor agitation. My father's practice, in Cuba and in exile, of holding down multiple jobs—a practice dictated to him by necessity, both economic and psychological—complicates the task of chronicling his life for daughter or obituary-writing friend. The chronology of my father's life is not a canal but an Amazon: simultaneous, noncontiguous events occurring in vast water—tributaries meandering through thick forests.

Whether conflicted or not, Cubans felt that they could not remain neutral in the first half decade of the 1930s. There were elements of disorder and a generalized anxiety, but many Cubans were willing to go through a time of rapid changes if in the end they could possess some tangible form of liberty. Order, or the United States' idea of order, won over freedom and progress; it was an imposed, imported version of order that could not stand.

In 1934, under the Mendieta-foreground/Batista-background administration, Cuba and the United States, through the signing of a new permanent treaty, mutually abrogated the hated Platt Amendment. The Platt Amendment for a long time had refused to die. When it was finally expunged, it became a ghost so stubborn that all the craft of all the *babalawos* and all the *santeros* could not keep it from haunting Cuban crossroads in the night.

Even without a Platt Amendment to execute, the United States had intervened in other countries of the hemisphere, particularly in those ringing the alluring Caribbean. The United States dispatched to Nicaragua an occupation force that remained from 1909 to 1933. In 1916 the United States sent into the Dominican Republic a contingent of marines, which stayed till 1934. From 1915 to 1934, Haiti came under the direct rule of the United States. In 1954 the U.S. Central Intelligence Agency, through dirty tricks and a supposedly secret hand, engineered the ouster of Guatemala's leftist president Jacobo Arbenz. I say "supposedly secret" because afterwards the true agents of events were no secret from Guatemalans or other Latin Americans. Still, the CIA and the Eisenhower administration were pleased with their nearly effortless success. A few years later, they thought that they could replicate it in Cuba, and with equal ease—Cuba and Guatemala being, to their minds, very similar.

The men who raised their parched faces hopefully to the sky from the undrinkable swamp of Zapata and the men who, not yet despairing, held on to blasted-out pieces of boat in the shark-infested Caribbean waters off Playa Girón did not have to be students of history to know what our history had been. Secure in that history they waited, still believing in the undying ghost of the Platt Amendment, while a hallucinated Sumner Welles, still dressed in black, paid a visit. In the deadly light and water the Cuban men waited for the United States to intervene militarily to change the government it and they hated, waited for the United States to act toward Cuba as it had always done. Before 1961 the United States had recognized no limits to its actions toward Cuba. On 20 September 1960, John Kennedy had said in a campaign speech, without irony and with implied criticism only of the change in affairs: "Three years ago, when I was in Havana, the American ambassador was the second most influential man in Cuba. Today the Soviet ambassador is." The United States chose a most unfortunate time to trace boundaries, with men waiting, exposed in the water.

Imagine with what amazement Cuban exiles watched as Lyndon Johnson, undisturbed in 1964 by whatever had been Kennedy's scruples, sent U.S. Marines to the Dominican Republic to settle the political atmosphere. In December 1989, U.S. President George Bush decided to invade Panama in order to oust Manuel Antonio Noriega, his obsession. He cited as his reasons an outstanding U.S. warrant for Noriega's arrest on drug running, the shooting of one U.S. soldier, and offensive behavior toward the wife of another.

Our own difficulty in defining our country's relationship with the United States has colored all our public discourse and has, in turn, interfered with our adequately defining ourselves as a nation. As with anything Cuban, opinion has varied extremely, loudly, and often violently. There have been many who much of the time have not found the relationship acceptable and many who have wanted Cuba to seek its own solutions. But since the 1840s, when annexationist Cuban landowners conspired to free us from Spain in order that our island might be swallowed by the Union of States, there have been many who have always looked to the North for salvation, whether economic or political. One part of the Cuban nightmare inheres in the Plattist dream.

In October 1962 Cubans on both sides of the Florida Straits watched impotently as a few men in the governments of the United States and the Soviet Union decided our fate and humanity's survival. We were at the bull's-eye of a target that spanned the Northern Hemisphere. We had been placed there by the bullet hunger of powerful men. We can measure the power of men by the potential radius of destruction of their suicides.

Nikita Khrushchev wanted to increase the lethal power of his nuclear arsenal. He could destroy the United States only by means of his intercontinental ballistic missiles and his bombs stashed in submarines. His intermediate- and medium-range missiles were useless against the United States; with them he could only attack Europe. A missile gap yawned at his feet, and thus a power gap. The U.S. Jupiter missiles in Turkey were a constant reminder of the inequality of his situation. The Jupiters were old, but they were too near his Black Sea dacha.

However, there was Cuba, Key to the Gulf, Gateway to the New World, strategic Pearl of the Antilles, friendly government, neighbor to the common enemy. Obliging, tropical Cuba. Vulnerable, comradely little Cuba. The United States had attempted and botched one invasion. It might not bungle a second. No superpower could be that stupid?

Nikita Khrushchev appointed his KGB station chief in Cuba to be ambassador. The trader in secrets presented a most secret proposal to Fidel Castro. The Soviet Union would like to install medium- and intermediate-range missiles on the soil of Cuba, the man said softly.

Fidel Castro, crazed for power against his supremely powerful neighbor, agreed to bring in the contagion of nuclear weapons into Cuba. No one—not even the *yanqui* imperialists—had ever exercised so much power over Cuba; no one had ever brought it so close to destruction.

Fidel Castro wanted the United States to know his new power (his "basic power of the universe," he might swagger, ironic, to Harry Truman's words). He wanted Nikita Sergeyevich, his ally, to emplace the missiles openly in Cuba. He would erect against invasion by the United States a lance-railed fence, bristling and lethal. Nikita Sergeyevich, however, was not interested in deterrence, but in power. He insisted on keeping his missiles secret. He insisted on complete Soviet control over his thirty-six active missiles and thirty-six one-megaton nuclear warheads, eighty Hiroshima effects in each one. Complete superpower secrecy and control—Cubans, as always when faced with these unfavorable conditions, acquiesced.

The Soviet military told Khrushchev that missiles in Cuba could be disguised as palms. Cubans know palms. Residents of my father's native province of Pinar del Río began noticing long tractor trailers from which protruded even longer cylinders. Soon exiles in Miami knew that there were missiles in Cuba, but the U.S. government would not listen to beneath-contempt exile rumor. CIA director John A. McCone returned from his honeymoon to find that U-2 reconnaissance planes were avoiding the western part of Cuba, where the missiles might be. He ordered flights over Pinar del Río. On 14 October photographs of a missile site under construction in San Cristóbal brought back proof of something that could only lead to crisis.

On 16 October, in the first meeting of the Executive Committee of the National Security Council, Secretary of State Dean Rusk presented this analysis: "We ourselves are not moved to general war. We are simply doing what we said we would do if they took certain action. Or we're going to decide that this is the time to eliminate the Cuban problem by actually eliminating the island."

José Miró Cardona appeared on Miami television with soon-to-be-familiar U-2 photographs. He pointed. He answered questions about meaning. But no one, on any side, knew the meaning. He spoke emphatically of the threat that Cuba represented to the United States and to the world so long as Castro was in power. He was hopeful that the United States was going to do something definitive about changing the government of Cuba; he did not know to fear how radically this might be done.

Miró was hopeful because on 10 April 1962 he had met with Kennedy, and things said there by the U.S. president about "six divisions" being what was needed led Miró to believe that military action against Castro soon would come, this time with the open participation of Cuban exiles and U.S. forces. "Six divisions" had a reassuringly conventional sound. Even in his resignation statement of April 1963 Miró would insist that the Soviet Union would not have entered into a war over Cuba because Cuba was not in its normal sphere of influence.

Cuban exiles were certain that the United States would cite the Monroe Doctrine, which had been a principle of U.S. foreign policy, variously interpreted and applied, since its formulation in 1823 by President James Monroe and his secretary of state, John Quincy Adams. In its pure form, the doctrine declared that the Western Hemisphere was no longer a place for European political activity and interference. It had been of great importance to the history of Latin America, both in its positive use, as recognition of the definitive independence of Western Hemisphere nations from their former colonizers, and in its misuse, as justification for overlordship by the United States in the hemisphere. In 1962 Cuban exiles wanted—and expected—the doctrine to be applied anew to the situation in Cuba, for we viewed the island as having become a misplaced Soviet satellite, tied increasingly to the Eurasian superpower economically, militarily, and ideologically and sharing its aim of exporting and supporting Communist initiatives throughout the world, especially in Latin America. The missiles were tangible proof of the overreach of Soviet ambition in the New World.

The hour of liberation was near, we thought in Miami. It was an electric October. My favorite corner of the Riverside Elementary School library, the biography section, housed a book on the life of the (so-termed) "Firebrand of the American Revolution," Patrick Henry. In this book I found a speech to present to my father, who loved oratory, and I repeated it as I walked rapidly and incessantly, like a zoo wolf, around the apartment. "Gentlemen may cry peace, peace, but there is no peace," I declared, aiming to follow the example of Demosthenes, who had been shown roaring at the ocean with a mouthful of stones in a comic book my father had bought for me. (Before admiring Demosthenes, I had made certain that my father had approved of his politics.) I declaimed, "Is life so dear, or peace so sweet, as to be purchased at the price of chains and slavery? Forbid it, Almighty God! I know not what course others may take, but as for me, give me liberty, or give me death!"

What did I know of life or death? "Give me liberty or give me death," I said over and over through my October days, and my father approved. But a doubt nagged at me. It was all well and good to give up one's own life if one chose to do it, but our loved ones lived in enemy land, our land.

My classmates and I had been taught at school to crouch under the one-foot-by-one-foot wooden writing surface of our desks if an atomic bomb came our way—crouched, our ashes might endure the blast, the falling building, the fireball of the thermal pulse, the intense radiation, the conflagration, and the fallout. We were told to stock up at home on canned foods and to keep matches handy.

Because I thought that since Hiroshima, seventeen years before, all large wars must henceforth be won through the detonation of nuclear weapons, I feared that their poisonous, incinerative power was going to be unleashed on Cuba. I asked questions: "What if there is a nuclear attack on Cuba?" My father hoped that the United States would fire nuclear warheads at the Soviet Union—the dehumanized, and therefore inhuman, monstrous Enemy—and the sooner the better, but not at Cuba. He said, however, that some conventional bombardment and shooting would have to take place in Cuba and that there would be deaths. (Few in exile ever mentioned that there had been civilian casualties in Girón.) My father said that if there was destruction, that was the price that the Cuban people, whom he wanted so badly to save, would have to pay for liberty. He thought, however, that a conventional attack from the United States would quickly accomplish its ends and that deaths would be few.

I was not reassured. The primary activities of war are killing and dying. Moreover, the killing is indiscriminate: bombs shatter the bad and the good, the sympathizers and the opponents of tyrants. I had never experienced war myself—urban terrorism was the worst that La Habana got during the fight against Batista—but our last housekeeper, Olga, had come to us from Jiguaní, Oriente, where she and her children had huddled under their beds at the sound of bombs—and certainly they were good people. Humans were not my only concern. I worried too about the buildings of La Habana that were linked with my experience but so hidden in the past that to lose them from the earth would be to lose them forever.

My mother said to me when we were alone, "Men don't care about the cost of war. Women do. Women worry about preserving life." She looked grievously worried those days. For her too the choices were complicated.

On the other hand, the prospect of the United States' doing nothing to liberate Cuba from its oppressive government was a most dismal one. The world was devoid of logic, I felt. I had constant thoughts of lemmings going over cliffs. My father had once brought me a naturalist comic book with drawings of a migration of hundreds of thousands of determined lemmings through a vast, clean Northern European landscape, and drawings of panicked-eyed lemmings jumping off jagged-edged bluffs and drowning in an ocean. I thought of my species as lemming-like for handing itself over to the gray unlife of Communism, as my father persistently said they were doing. And I thought of my species as lemminglike for considering nuclear war. I could imagine a future with smoky, ruined streets through which small slave bands of emaciated survivors in Dachau tunics wandered with automaton eyes. These visions were attached to both possibilities, Communism and nuclear war, and they did not dissipate with the passing of the missile crisis.

Give me not death, but liberty. I thought that *libertad* was something that Cuba had accomplished before Castro and before Batista, back in the mists of time before the year of my birth. I thought that with the Ten Years' War and the Three Years' War we had not only earned our freedom—and freedom is not something a nation should have to earn—but, I thought, we also had learned how to live it. I thought that the men who called for a new war would know how to make liberty possible in Cuba—once again. It seemed to me that reconstructing a lost freedom probably merited the price in suffering and mortality. I did not know about our history of military men, of corrupt men, of power-hungry men. I did not know that what the men in Miami asked us to believe when they said *libertad* was that if we walked off the edge of the precipice, we would sprout wings; perhaps we would. The chief virtue of *libertad* was that it was a dream. And dreams are necessary, though often dangerous. Our various definitions and betrayals of the dream had kept us busy for a century. The dark-haired woman wearing a red Phrygian cap with a white star walked mute through all our discourse. *"¡Libertad!"* we shouted and refused to be free. *"¡Libertad!"* my father shouted, and he despised the free-speech cacophony of U.S. democracy.

But in October we yearned for freedom, its shapes various as leaves. Although the U.S. and Soviet populations were terrified at the possibility of nuclear war, Cubans on both sides of the Florida Straits, with some exceptions, were not. To us in Miami, the U.S. media appeared hysterical.

For the sake of our independence, our parents or grandparents had fought a devastating three-year war with fire and metal in which three hundred thousand men, women, and children—seventeen percent of our population—had perished. Spain, the Mother Country, preferred to destroy us than to lose us. She forced our people off the land and into reconcentration camps to die of starvation and disease. She shot what livestock she found. It was a scorched-earth war without quarter on either side. No one moved through the emptied countryside but the *mambises,* but increasingly they owned more than a desert: they owned victory. Self-determination had seemed worth the enormous price—still seemed worth the price. We are an all-or- nothing people. We had built a nation upon the suffering of the Three Years' War. Our countryside had become fecund again and our people productive, and we had celebrated the heroes of our war of devastation in song and poetry. Our country called us again. In 1962 political imprisonment, torture, executions, exile, private horrors multiplied by thousands impelled us toward war.

I was born while the nuclear age was still an infant; I knew to be afraid of war in 1962. My father was born in the post-War-of-Independence baby boom. He and his contemporaries were children of individual and national hope, like the fresh, green shoots of sugarcane springing up from burnt-out fields all over Cuba. My father desperately wanted World War III, because he knew only the reconstruction after war, not its new absolute lethalness. Conflagration he wanted, no matter what the cost; Fidel Castro wanted the same thing. Because neither believed in the cost. Fidel Castro sent Khrushchev a message urging him toward a first nuclear strike. Cubans of all stripes possessed a childish faith that our superpower would protect us, our superpower would triumph. Nuclear war could be limited and winnable—even though the superpowers could destroy each other and us.

We Cuban exiles reassured ourselves with the thought that the United States would never use nuclear weapons against Cuba because some of the destructive effects of a nuclear attack on Cuba would reach U.S. territory. Radioactivity would rain down upon Florida in one form or another. If more of us had known about the electromagnetic pulse generated early in a nuclear explosion, we would have been further lulled. A multi-kiloton bomb—a small, tactical bomb—detonated over Cuba might knock out electrical circuitry in much of the United States. Yet a member of the Kennedy cabinet could contemplate it: "Or we're going to decide that this is the time to eliminate the Cuban problem by actually eliminating the island." Why should a great power facing certain doom leave any enemy standing?

If anyone had moved, there would have been a nuclear war. If Khrushchev had fired off a first strike, of course the United States would have retaliated and escalated. But even if the United States had made a first move using only conventional methods of warfare—its invasion of 180,000 men and 1,080 attack sorties—there would have been a nuclear war. The Soviets had deployed six battlefield Luna missile launchers equipped with tactical nuclear warheads along the Cuban coastline. The Lunas had a range of 65 kilometers. The Soviet commander in Cuba had the authority to use them without waiting for Moscow's permission. They almost certainly would have been used against an invading force from the United States—even if fallout would surely poison the Cuba that Soviet forces thus pretended to protect. No one in the United States knew about the trap of the Luna missiles; there was no deterrence to them.

Millions of humans were nearly destroyed by secrets. The Northern Hemisphere was nearly rendered unlivable by secrets. Cubans, Soviets, U.S.ers might have been annihilated—or almost annihilated, survived by small bands of irradiated, vomiting, hemorrhaging, burned, dumb-struck people looking blankly at the charred landscape about them, burdened beyond understanding with a new definition of sovereignty and humanity.

John Kennedy promised never to invade Cuba. After a chaste, face-saving interval, the U.S. began dismantling its Jupiter missiles in Turkey. Without telling Fidel Castro, the Soviets decided to remove their missiles from Cuba. We Cubans stood powerless, watching while the political grown-ups talked in secret signals above our heads. Fidel Castro was enraged; Nikita had taken away the revolution's protection, had wantonly neglected to destroy the large enemy to the north. Fidel Castro would never allow himself to believe in the reality of the gift that had been given him: a lifetime of U.S. protection. My father was enraged, exiled men were enraged.

My father saw the peaceful resolution of the missile crisis as a disaster; therefore, in my life it was. Those Cuban exiles who had clung to their faith in the United States, even after Girón, could now no longer believe that the U.S.ers would do anything. My father had been skeptical since Girón, but the optimism that Miró extracted from his conversations with Kennedy infected my father, who was a pessimist by nature. Although such hopefulness may seem barely possible in men who had suffered betrayal, the two persisted because they needed to believe that they possessed the power of influence. In fact, they did not. The conclusion of October 1962 crushed hope out of both of them. It squeezed the air out of my days. It doomed us to the life of exile from which we had so fervently hoped to escape.

My father believed that Kennedy had committed suicide and doomed his country, that he had capitulated to Communism and had practically given away the United States. My father, therefore, referred derisively to the agreement that ended the crisis as the Kennedy-Khrushchev Pact, an appellation heavy with allusion to the cynical self-advancement of the nonaggression pact between Hitler and Stalin and the cowardice, betrayal, and self-deluded appeasement of the Munich Pact. My father thought that history was repeating itself, but the fact is that for large countries with nuclear armaments, history could never be quite the same.

Now that we have more facts to judge with, it appears that in October 1962 John F. Kennedy followed the only course that could have saved the Northern Hemisphere from destruction. Any overt action by the United States against Cuba during the crisis would have destroyed us. Before I knew about the Lunas, I held the opinion that for the United States to have done nothing about the missiles in Cuba would have been preferable to protesting their presence and being forced into a nonaggression agreement. I now think that to have done nothing to address specifically the presence of the missiles would have been as dangerous as doing too much. Fidel Castro would have continued to exert pressure upon the Soviets to use their nuclear weapons. Exiles would have continued to push for an invasion to overthrow Castro. Perhaps a pretext would have been found for U.S. action against Cuba—possibly a manufactured incident involving the U.S. Naval Base in Guantánamo or a sunken U.S. ship in a re-remembering of the *Maine* (as Robert Kennedy would suggest in an Ex Comm meeting during the crisis). There was the exile corps created by the Kennedy administration in September 1962, Cuban men being trained by the U.S. Army to fight in Cuba. They were to be part of the first battalion to descend in Cuba during a U.S. invasion, they thought. Tactical nuclear warheads would have been detonated over their heads. A Nagasaki at sea would have preceded a nuclear war. We would have been destroyed.

The United States was blind-sided by two enemies—bolder, better players—who were willing to risk all in a sudden endgame. The United States was trapped the moment that the Soviet and Cuban governments began implementing their secret plan to bring nuclear weaponry to Cuba.

I find peace in admitting this to myself after all this time. But we know a lot more now than any of us did then. The disintegration of the Soviet Union has spilled out its secrets. Secrets destroyed my father. He could not take comfort in the fact that for whatever reasons Kennedy made his final choice in October 1962—and they must necessarily have been reasons shaped by incomplete information and an alarmingly flawed character—he made the right decision. He stumbled onto the road that a God that wanted to preserve Its creatures would wish them to take. But my father was beyond comfort, beyond understanding.

Slowly, incrementally, like a victim of water torture, my father went mad—so personally did he take everything, so helpless did he feel to affect anything. To listen to news with him was to listen to a loved one's screams from just outside his torture cell. My mother, who spent twenty-nine years of exile with him, could not understand why anyone would want to mistreat himself this way. He was angry at what Cuba, China, the Soviet Union, or any of the Warsaw Pact nations, or any left-wing guerrilla groups did. He was angry at how U.S. officials reacted, for in his eyes they were always spineless. "They are selling themselves to the Communists!" he shouted as he slapped his knee in anger. Or he shook his head and, touching his fingertips to the forehead that contained the brain that could not conceive what was happening, he exclaimed, "*¡No se concibe!* I don't understand these *americanos*." Then he got on the telephone, either because he initiated the call or because others could not resist the lure of releasing their anger with someone, and he shouted about the event and made dire predictions about the coming end of the world as we knew it.

Painful as it was to witness this, it has been far more painful to experience it. During many years of my life I could not get through a newscast without feeling intense pain. I cursed him who brought me up in such a way that I could not take things in stride, could not pretend that things were unimportant. I had to talk to myself as I watched horrible events unfold. I had to tell myself that the world as we know it will indeed pass, in fact passes constantly, the sorrow and the joy, as everything changes, and that history will see us differently from how we see ourselves: it will put us in perspective, will fit us into proportion with what has gone before and is to come, will look upon us and explain the painful events of the twentieth century as the product of weird, fanatical aberrations—systematic, far-reaching kin of those that clustered around the previous millennium. Foolish century, they will say, and shake their heads. If for humans there are future centuries. Taking the long view brings calm to the lamasery. Unassuaged by wisdom, I take antidepressants.

# IV

*I have said and I am constantly repeating that by our joint effort we must raise a monument to victory and not an obelisk to martyrdom.*

—José Miró Cardona, resignation statment, 18 April 1963

José Miró Cardona officially resigned from the presidency of the Consejo Revolucionario Cubano on 18 April 1963, a date that would add commemorative resonance to his words of pain. My father left his job at the Consejo with Miró, taking with him, Manolo Mariñas says in his eulogy, "only the pen of the virile journalist, favorite weapon of the great gladiator." Before their departure, Miró, my father, and probably others close to Miró produced a document that Mariñas too generously says "saves the honor of anti-Communist Cubans." It could not do that, if that was needed. But Miró's resignation statement did tell the Consejo's story, did articulate truths, though not all truths, that should be recorded, and did allow those connected with its production to walk away with reasserted dignities.

I have searched the document for my father's traces, wondering which sentences' original contours may bear the mark of his hand. Predominant is the betrayed sadness of the disappointed and discarded statesman, a leader more failed than failing. The document is a catalogue of sadness more than of fire. My father preferred to sculpt with fire.

For some time my father had been insisting to Miró, "If you don't resign, I resign." The problem was the U.S. government. As my mother puts it, *"Le daban larga. Lo estaban entreteniendo."* They were stringing Miró along. They had turned a deaf ear to him but would not admit it. They had set up barriers that they sought to portray as channels of communication. My father could not bear the lack of respect toward Miró, toward Cuban

313

exiles. Eventually Miró also could not bear it. The edifice that the Consejo's efforts had built was crumbling all around them.

What we Cubans in Miami had wanted was self-government and self-determination in our own land. Again we made a philosophical blunder. How could a foreign power give us these?

The story of the imminent split between the Consejo and the Kennedy administration began to break in the U.S. press around 16 April. The principal problem, as the Kennedy administration saw it, was that the Consejo was criticizing the U.S. government's policies toward Cuba and the government's treatment of the Consejo itself. There were those on the Consejo who did not favor attacking the United States at all, and certainly not as forcefully as Miró chose to do—whatever good their reticence did them: none of them would ever enter the White House except on public tour.

As always, the United States used dollars as a tool of leverage. They threatened to cut off the Consejo's funding. "We are certainly not going to finance people so they can clobber us," said an unnamed U.S. official to the *New York Times*.

It may seem preposterous now, but Miró expected the United States government to treat the Consejo with a seriousness appropriate to its U.S.-created role of Cuban government-in-exile. Therefore, Miró asked the United States for the same military assistance that Fidel Castro received from the Soviet Union. He sought $50 million with which to finance an exile expedition—a completely exile expedition. Otherwise, he asked for a leading role for Cuban exiles in a U.S. military effort.

Cubans do not grovel, to say the least. The U.S. administration was particularly offended by what they perceived and decried as an "ultimatum" from Miró, and by the Council's desire for influence over U.S.–Cuba policy. The *New York Times* reported: "The feeling in Washington is that the refugees will have to defer to the Administration on matters concerning Cuba. . . ."

We had thought—with certainty after the evidence of Girón—that the Platt Amendment belonged among the dead and buried. Miró asserted in his resignation statement: "I shall never accept as a gift of charity and under conditions an occupied island."

The State Department was familiar with the contents of Miró's resignation statement, and it did not want them to be made public. A 16 April Associated Press wire from Miami quotes "sources close to the council leader" as saying that the U.S. government had threatened to deport Miró if he made his statement public. The "source" was most likely my father, and the AP reporter, Ted Ediger, my father's future boss, who spent much time at Miró's Miami Beach office. Miró was reported to have begun exploring exile in Costa Rica.

In its own preemptive release, the State Department charged: "The statement seeks to discredit several individuals in the Government and to question the good faith and integrity of them, as individuals, and of the United States Government in dealing with the Cuban Revolutionary Council." And well it should. On 9 April the State Department had insisted that the administration still shared "the aim of restoring freedom to the Cuban people." They had a peculiar way of going about it.

During the public disagreement, the *New York Times* published Miró's accusations carefully enclosed within quotation marks, while it presented the administration line frequently without attributive punctuation, as if officials' utterances reflected objective reality. Furthermore, the *Times* attempted to trivialize Miró's disagreements with the government as the possible product of merely personal reversals: "Dr. Miró Cardona's son was among the ransomed prisoners and his personal disappointments are thought to be involved in the present controversy."

I am grateful, however, that the *New York Times* published an English translation of Miró's complete resignation statement on 19 April 1963, devoting a full page to it, eight columns, something inconceivable later, when Cuba had ceased to be important to the United States. Because it takes up an entire newspaper page, I had to photocopy it from the University of

Maryland library's microfilm one small panel at a time. I matched the pieces and pasted and taped them together forming a quilt that threatens to fall apart when I manipulate it. Only flexibility keeps it all from flying apart. The language is less supple; the document published by the *New York Times* is a translation and therefore second-hand—and a strange second-hand at that, for the translation was performed hurriedly by someone who was either not at ease with idiomatic U.S. English or with idiomatic Cuban Spanish.

In an intellectual sense as well, the statement is a quilt. Miró adduces facts, cites international treaties, trusts in the authority of legal precedents. "These, in all their crude reality, are the facts," he says. Miró lays out many more facts than are necessary for his stated audience, the other members of the Consejo. He writes for the wider world, and yet he assumes too much interest, too much knowledge. He piles so many facts into such a short space that he must use shorthand, must assume we all know the background. Yet, sadly, decades later we do not recognize the references unless we are specialists or so determined to understand that we conduct research. Miró and my father wrote not for history but for historians. Ephemeral is our fame.

Miró's statement, specifying dates, describes meetings and other communications with members of the Kennedy administration—incontrovertible facts as far as their occurrence goes but completely debatable as to their content. This principal argument in Miró's depiction of reneging and betrayal by the administration is also its weakest link. Unrecorded conversations are open to interpretation and reinterpretation. And whom would the U.S. press believe—a bitter, sixty-year-old Cuban or a young, handsome U.S. president? Everybody knows we are crazies with our heads on fire. But to those Cubans close to Miró, the facts of the meetings were like uprooted trees in a fast-moving river; my father, like Miró, clung to them for life. For years my father recited the facts, "On 10 April of '62, Kennedy told Miró that what was needed was six divisions. He promised assistance." As he detailed unmet promises his voice got angrier. My father had no defenses, no irony, no distance. He was drowning.

Miró's declaration is that of a man trying to sound reasonable past great pain. He can hardly believe what has happened. He tries to make sense of what seems nonsensical. His pain bleeds through. In eight newspaper columns he reviews the history of Cuba and of U.S. policies toward Cuba between April 1961 and April 1963. In one sentence he summarizes how we experienced this history: "The two years that have passed since the debacle of the 17th of April, 1961, have been really hard and bitter ones for all the Cubans: for the men and women of the underground who were sacrificed; for the brave guerrillas in the mountains; for the proud political prisoners; for the heroic fighters at Girón; for the terror-stricken populations of Cuba; for the bewildered emigrants; for the revolutionary organizations watching their ranks decimated in battle; for the council and for me."

In the document, Girón is "the debacle," "the episode," "the disaster," and "the disastrous experiment." This unqualified, horrified recoiling from the event only begins to shed a weak light on how Miró and his colleagues in the Consejo, Maceo and Varona, all fathers with sons at Girón, may have felt as they searched a few days after the invasion for surviving pieces of the torn brigade in Nicaragua, Guatemala, and the isle of Vieques.

Miró mentions the exile community's political turmoil and the resultant attacks against him briefly, delicately. His articulated pain is always the product of his frustrated efforts for Cuba: "From that moment, with despairing slowness, three more months passed. . . . Overcome with anguish, I left for Washington. . . . All of this interminable process which again ends in desolate frustration. . . ." He sounds exhausted.

Miró is too delicate with the U.S. president. He speaks of him with great dignity, as one national leader speaking of another. He credits Kennedy with "exemplary honesty in a chief executive" for having taken "all the responsibility" for Girón, and

further gives him credit where credit is actually due for personal-
ly seeing to it that funds were given to the widows and orphans
created by the "disastrous experiment." Miró exalts Kennedy's
hope-inspiring, empty, cynical words at the Orange Bowl
Stadium. He reserves direct blame for "the President's collabora-
tors," those silent, unsympathetic bureaucrats who could not
hide behind a screen of lofty promises and resounding words,
those bureaucrats who would have been called to account by
superiors for making commitments the government would not
keep. It was so difficult for Miró to believe that the earnest young
man who had sat with him in the White House would lie. In
these passages I see Miró at work, not my father. My father would
have suggested strongly, in beautiful, often abstract words, but
inescapably, that Kennedy was a lying son of a whore. Neither
my father nor I were made for public office.

John Kennedy said to Miró, "Your destiny is to suffer. Do
not weaken. You have my support and I reiterate my earlier pro-
nouncements. Give the council my most cordial regards." Is it
possible that Miró did not see arrogance in Kennedy's reading
him a destiny that Kennedy had the power to shape? It was alas
an enemy's reading and therefore correct.

Miró attempted to find redemption in suffering for a goal,
and he said so on the eve of the brigade's sentencing, in words
no father should ever say, in words that my father would have
said about me with even more fervent politics and without
prayer: "Prevented from doing my duty as an attorney for the
brigade, I send them a heartfelt salute. Among them is my son.
I am at his side and proud of him. May he accept his fate with
dignity. It is a privilege to suffer and die for one's country. May
God help him."

Miró is so decorous with the U.S. president that he even
keeps his secrets. Besides the disputable facts of official inflec-
tions at meetings with few witnesses, there were also secret facts
to which Miró alludes in his statement, understandings between
the Consejo and the administration. Unprovable, lost facts,

since he does not reveal them. Miró expresses too much hope in the revelatory power of history when he states: "The period from May to October, 1961, was rough at times. We did not hesitate to express our disagreement with the methods and the tactics of the President's collaborators, always—let it be said—in a spirit of cooperation. By the 31st of October of that year, all of our differences had been ironed out and the agreements were put together in one 'agreement,' which history, in its good time, will record." But secrecy is an obstacle to history. Others may not reveal the contents of your past if they prove inconvenient. It is up to you to make them known or to choose well their custodians.

The agreement of October 1961 stipulated the organization of an exile army corps. At his meeting with Kennedy on 10 April 1962, Miró pressed for its establishment. Further, he insisted that age and physical fitness requirements be liberalized so that the corps could come up with the numbers necessary for a proper battalion. The corps was officially created by a call-up from the Consejo on 25 September 1962. The Consejo did not suspect that this was another phantasm. They believed the U.S. administration once more.

In Miami, Miró met with Major General Edward G. Lansdale, whose success in guerrilla warfare in the Philippines would not be repeated in Vietnam, to discuss "aspects of the military problem." The 25 September call-up generated a sense of excitement and impending action. The call to arms asked Cubans to forget their differences, and even their ages, and to enlist as combatants in what was envisioned as an army of liberation, though of course enlistment officially was into the U.S. Army.

At such a sign-up my father was photographed, my father, then fifty-four, a man whose words often stung but who was probably even then unsteady with a pistol, my father who might have been made war minister. My father once said to someone on the telephone, "No, no! It is we the old men who should die for our country. Not the young. The young have to build the future." But it is the young who fight and die in battles and all of us who die in wars.

There was so much urgency from Washington for the special corps recruitment to be carried out that administration officials discussed with Miró in mid-October the possibility of requiring that newly arriving exiles register first with the army before enrolling in the refugee assistance program. Already 240 Cuban men were undergoing military training in a U.S. Army base, presumably to descend upon Cuba when the United States invaded—in response to the presence of missiles, or the shooting down of a U.S. pilot, or Castro's refusal to allow the United Nations to inspect the island to certify the missiles' removal. They would have encountered a doom never experienced in the Western Hemisphere—if they had gone, if the invasion had happened, if the U.S. government had been serious about them.

From 22 October 1962 Miró dates an about-face on the part of the U.S. government so complete and dreadful that he struggles painstakingly—as my father struggled—to understand it. He searches for explanations, weighing more sanguine possibilities, and finally arrives at this terrible moment: "Denying all the arguments, the facts led inexorably to this conclusion: the struggle for Cuba was in the process of being liquidated by the Government." After 22 October, not only were certain actions previously encouraged by the State Department—for instance, commando raids on Cuban installations—censured, but certain activists suspected or known to have been involved in commando actions had their movements restricted to Dade County, Florida. Boats known to be used in anti-Castro raids—two of them the property of the Revolutionary Council—were embargoed and immobilized. Some were confiscated, along with arms. Commandoes began to be hunted down in the waters of the Atlantic and the Caribbean. Miró and my father could barely believe "the most incredible and disconcerting of all the measures adopted: the notice to England to impede or pursue, as the case might be, the Cuban fighters who navigate in the jurisdictional waters of England's possessions in America."

The most insidious change to follow 22 October 1962 was, not surprisingly, a bureaucratic maneuver. Miró's frustrated anger about it is palpable. The administration created an Office of the Coordinator for Cuban Affairs. Whereas before Miró could talk directly with the U.S. attorney general or the president, now all communication between exiles and the administration must take place through the coordinator's office. In fact, all conversations ended there. The coordinator was a wall, not a channel. He was the public bad guy. It was he who was in charge of questioning those accused of commando activity. It was he who dispensed dilatory answers to the Consejo. It was he who introduced and implemented the practice of dispersing all new refugees who signed up for assistance to other, distant areas of the United States, especially to the cold, corn-fed regions of the Midwest where never a Cuban had been seen, creating a diaspora of a diaspora, to break the political back of the Miami exile community, to leach us of strength.

The bad-guy front worked. Even Miró, with all his sophistication, came to say of the office of the coordinator that it had "controlled all, absolutely all of the activities relating to Cuba, since the 22nd of October." The man behind the scrim, the man whose policies the coordinator was implementing, could emerge in spotless raiment to say to the Orange Bowl Stadium crowd, "I can assure you that this flag will be returned . . ." even as he was making it impossible.

*"Nos tomaron el pelo,"* I heard my father say many times, and now my mother, meaning that they, the *yanquis,* took our hair, fooled us. Amid the shifting mirrors and conversations in smoke, elaborate power fantasies were played out on us, on our alien hopes, our foreign bodies. We were importunate and undesirable, only strung along in case we might prove useful. "These, in all their crude reality, are the facts," Miró stated. "The repeated assurances, the constantly renewed promises have been suddenly

liquidated." The source of Cassandra's madness lay in facts: half, in their impotence to stir others to believe and act; half, in the mere possession.

A future had been chosen for us whose destiny it was to suffer. With the notice that all subsequent financial assistance would be cut for those refugees who did not "relocate," came this statement from the coordinator's office: "Each Cuban refugee carries with him the message of the true spirit of the Cubans; his love for freedom and his anxiety to convert the sadness of leaving his home into the inspiration of preparing for a more brilliant future in free countries." The message of the message was inescapable. Permanent exile had been decreed for us.

Struggle as we might, we could not escape a decreed destiny. Thenceforth we would live out our lives as strangers on the earth, subject to others' laws, surrounded by others' customs, threatened by others' plagues, defined as Other by others. We would build cities in foreign lands, raise high the tombs of pharaohs, pour gold into their treasuries. The young among us would develop new-country shells to house our alien hearts. Because we were singers, endlessly we would sing songs of Zion. We would learn too the songs of Babylon.

As Miró knew, life in a nation not one's own is not self-determination. Rather it is a constant challenge to the often contradictory drives to adapt and to be. It tests the limits of our ability to seek or accept education. If we are open to the experience, exile explodes the preconceptions that we bring with us into the land of strangers. With unblinkered eyes we can better see our country, their country, the world and its history. Our sense of relative geography can undergo readjustment: the earth's center is (probably) dense metal, not a nation; of nations there is an ever shifting number that is (currently) less than two hundred but definitely greater than one. (The opposite effect, a hardening of the view that one's nation is the point around which all the galaxies revolve is, of course, also possible.)

Unexpectedly, one can gain insight into biochemistry. It was a popular belief in Cuba that the combination of bananas with milk was poisonous. *"Te puedes pasmar,"* people said ominously, meaning presumably that one might be overcome by a spasmodic seizure. Imagine my *guajiro* father's bewilderment (peasants are supposed to know about these things) when in the United States he encountered advertisements for bowls of Kellogg's Corn Flakes brimming with milk and slices of bananas. The ads' happy families happily dug in, down to the littlest freckled child. We had to conclude that U.S.ers all around us must be eating milk with bananas and surviving.

We change. It is nettlesome, then, for us to live in proximity to people of the territory who, not blessed by exile, still have tubes attached to the front of their eyes. They go their busy way unaware, not seeing us until we almost collide. It is usually we, the exiles, who swerve.

I do not know how he stood it, being so intolerant of slurs against our nationality and nation. My father was needled by people who should have known better even if they were of the territory. At the Miami bureau of the Associated Press, reporters were fond of referring to a propensity for unpunctuality as "Cuban time." My father, who derived as strong a sense of righteousness-in-humility from total, unquestioning obedience to the dictates of his tyrannical god, Chronometer, as ever did medieval monk subduing his flesh to the higher discipline of the spirit upon a cold stone floor, seethed and, out of earshot, imprecated his ignorant coworkers. He tired of telling them, "No, being late is not Cuban time," but he needed a paycheck.

The failure of all attempts to get rid of Fidel Castro meant that we Cuban children were marooned in the U.S. educational system. Sixty-two years had passed since Leonard Wood, U.S. proconsul to an occupied Cuba, set out to eliminate the old Spanish ways of teaching and to establish an educational system modeled on the United States'. He had U.S. textbooks translated literally into Spanish without ever wondering if they would make any sense to Cubans. To Governor Wood, anything Anglo-Saxon was ipso facto better than anything that was otherwise.

Even in 1960 U.S.-managed schooling held for us many dangers, though it would be unfair to fault a Dade County school system that heroically coped with the massive influx of foreign-languaged children that kept arriving at its principals' offices. Dade County had to work with the resources, both material and intellectual, that it had at hand. It was called upon to rise above a dominant U.S. culture that nurtured a most limiting flaw: a contempt toward all things Latin American, accompanied by a singular, dismissive lack of curiosity about us. U.S.ers were neither up to date about Latin Americans nor could they differentiate among us. Brother Andrés, who taught Spanish for the Spanish-speaking (i.e., Español) at Immaculata-La Salle High School told us of a movie he had seen about Teddy Roosevelt and San Juan Hill. The Cubans in the movie were all dressed like stereotypical Mexican agricultural workers, with sarapes and wide-brimmed Mexican-style hats, as in a Western. In *Godfather, Part II,* one of my favorite films, Francis Ford Coppola has a protester in what is supposed to be La Habana—but is more a U.S.er's Havana, and in fact was the Dominican Republic—shout out something that is so perplexing that I have never fully understood it during my several viewings of it. I rewind and review and repeat, and what I can make out is *"¡Valle de la chingada!"* This poetic profanity, or any other containing the word *chingada,* is likely to have been uttered only by a foreign infiltrator; we have a different vocabulary for copulation. When the film *Jurassic Park* opened in 1993, Costa Ricans were appalled to see their land-locked, automobile-congested, and fast-food-franchised cosmopolitan capital city transformed into a backward village by the sea. Universal education is an ideal the industrialized countries have yet to accomplish.

For conscientious exiled children, education presents an unresolvable, fundamental problem: to learn the lessons of the new territory is to become more creatures of that territory and less children of the country that is their parents' obsession. Yet children expected to excel do. Because I am a very fast study, I was guarded about the lessons I was presented, even as I was learning to speak English without a trace of my native accent.

About one school subject I felt that to participate fully was to lose my soul, and that was U.S. history, inaccurately labeled, of course, "American history." Other history study was a pleasure. At Immaculata-La Salle High School, I gladly studied world history, for part of that past, I felt, was my past. Fashionably thin Mrs. Strama, our ninth-grade world history teacher, knew her subject matter well and went to great lengths to make our lessons lively, seldom showing the drain of a pregnancy that made her look increasingly to us like an olive skewered by a toothpick. She even read to her class of Roman Catholic girls excerpts from an action-packed account of the life and deeds of Catherine the Great of Russia that included an unforgettable reference to her dying from having a horse lowered on her.

In tenth grade our half-Cuban classes were forced to study U.S. history. My friend Daisy Pérez and I were particularly resentful and on our guard. We had no interest, we were *cubanas,* we said. But what we really feared was a repeat of past experiences of U.S.ers interpreting history—even ours—through a slanted peephole. Discussion of the so-called "Spanish-American War" drove us crazy. To hear the *yanquis* tell the story, no Cuban ever fought competently for independence. We were free because Teddy Roosevelt and his U.S. men rode their horses roughly up San Juan Hill. What these historical propagandists left out was that the Army of Liberation was on the verge of victory when the United States government saw with displeasure the probability of Cuba's slipping from Spanish control into independence—rather than into U.S. hands, a transfer presumed inevitable since the time of John Quincy Adams. Unable to countenance a Cuba that would not owe the United States its freedom from Spain and therefore, by corollary, its gratitude and submission, President

William McKinley sent U.S. troops to Cuba to impose "order" as defined by U.S. interests.

Another sensitive historical event for Daisy and me was the defeat of the Spanish Armada by the English in 1588, which when taught in the United States, whether in world history or English literature classes, was presented with a disturbingly pro-English slant that sounded to us like gloating. And, after all, those could have been our ancestors on those storm-wracked Spanish ships, and, after all, that was our ancestral land whose power went ever after into decline.

By the time Daisy and I walked into the U.S. history classroom, we had both had separate bouts with the Walter Reed Syndrome. The schools of Cuba taught us, accurately, that it was Carlos Finlay, a Cuban physician, who discovered that yellow fever is transmitted by *Aedes* mosquitos. When we arrived in the Unites States, we were told that some *yanqui* army doctor named Walter Reed had made the discovery. Sometimes Carlos Finlay figured in the story, but always he was relegated to the passive role of dreamer. Dr. Finlay had gone to a party, the scenario went—you know how Cubans like a party—and he had told those gathered that he had had the strangest dream: that yellow fever was transmitted by a mosquito, how odd. Walter Reed was at the party and he—as he was Amuhrrkan and thus possessed greater perspicacity—saw the possibilities that the dream might refer to a reality, and so he set about testing it.

"A dream," Daisy scoffed when we compared our experiences. I suspect that I will always burn with yellow fever.

I reacted to the requirement that I take a course in U.S. history by merely studying what was necessary for each exam. The moment the test was done, I wiped from my mind all memory of its subject. When time came for the final exam, which covered material from most of the course, I actually had to study. I clung to ignorance as to my integrity—most uncharacteristic behavior for a girl who wanted to know everything that did not have to be approached through the Daedalean gate of mathematics.

Would I have preferred for the textbook to have been, as is now fashionable, "relevant" to my experience, and thus to have mentioned that President Thomas Jefferson, after successfully buying Louisiana, had tried to buy Cuba; that John Quincy Adams argued that, in accordance with the "law of nature," Cuba would one day be the United States' as an apple falls off a tree; that during their presidential terms, James Polk (with his secretary of state, future president James Buchanan), the unpopular Franklin Pierce, and the drunkard Ulysses Grant would offer Spain money for us; that Andrew Jackson, Indian fighter and empire builder, drove the Spanish from Florida and dreamed of pressing his effort till he had wrested from them also my island; and that William McKinley would have stolen from us the sovereignty that three hundred thousand of our people had died for? No, these presidential fantasies about my native ground might have been presented with approval, as proofs of the constancy of the United States' lust for our feminine desirability. I might have had to stay home with an illness.

"Immortal América," we sang in Cuba. "Your borders are ties of love of unequaled glory."

The América whose vibrant name I intoned, in the innocence of Cuban childhood, extended from the north of Canada to the southern tip of South America. Our name bound us together in one identity on this vast expanse where humans did not evolve, where everyone came as a foreigner. Our earliest humans crossed longitudes of thought from the foreign soil of Asia more than twenty thousand years ago—that first unrecorded instance in human time when the two isolated halves of earth touched each other. And they radiated through the land, into its tundras, its deciduous forests and grassy plains, its deserts, its mesas, its highlands and tropics, its gemstring islands in a turquoise sea. And other humans came, much later, with their myriad languages, cultures, memories, and night dreams of people who wander. They came from Spain, Portugal, England, France, the Netherlands, Denmark, and Russia to escape the plagues of an Old World or to rid the Old World of the plague of themselves, to search for gold in newness, to spread and praise the words of saviors. Africans were brought, under duress, as slaves; Chinese and East Indians, as indentured workers. In time, people arrived from almost every corner of the world. Many stayed. And we built a New World with economies and social contracts as varied as the hemisphere's topographies and climates, and the boundaries were often not links of love but chasms of suspicion. But we built a new world in very little time, we great mongrel people, we Americans.

My América was one integral continent. The term "continent" will have to do although it is a construct of imprecise minds. Old geography books defined it as "a large land mass not completely surrounded by water," except of course for Australia and Antarctica. As exactly seven wonders were catalogued for the ancient world and the earth's salt water was divided by Renaissance adventurers into seven seas, so has the globe's land mass been partitioned into seven continents by the geopolitical cataloguers. From this list we conclude that there are two Américas, North and South. Geology supports this division—though not that of Europe from Asia. North and South America ride on two developmentally distinct, separately moving tectonic plates. For the convenience of cartographers, who must make details visible on pages of standard size, a third América has been created, the shadow isthmus Central America, geologically part of North America, and except for misfit Panama, culturally linked with Mexico (forming with it the archeological region Meso-America of pre-Columbian glory), yet by the cartographic knife separated off, rendered a disconnected connector. Apart, the lovely Antillean archipelago rides an arc on its own minor plate of geology, independent, like its islands, yet linked to the world that passed and passes through its gateway.

Martin Waldseemüller, the German cartographer who gave us our name, tried to take it back. In 1507 Waldseemüller drew up a map for *Cosmographie introductio,* which, though not exactly a geography of the cosmos, did attempt to embrace the whole earth and welcome its newly discovered expanse. Waldseemüller wrote "America" across the land mass of Brazil, because he believed Amerigo Vespucci to have discovered that area. Controversy raged from the outset. Because Amerigo had been sailing for Portugal, Spain refused to use the designation "America." After all, the Spanish argued, Columbus, or rather Colón, had discovered the new lands, even if he had thought them to be part of the very ancient world of Asia. Probably Waldseemüller meant the name America to apply only to Brazil, but there was a contagious appropriateness to the structure and sound of the neologism that compelled Europeans to apply it to the whole of the recently discovered lands so that it could stand with other fabled conjurations of otherness—Asia, Africa . . . America. There was justice too to the name, for it was Amerigo who first looked upon our pulsating verdancy with awareness that we were the New World. America, then, we were, and not Columbia—or Vineland. "What have I wrought?" the German cartographer upbraided himself, pulling at his hair, weeping into his frayed black sleeves because he was living with a gaggle of scabious scholars in the Vosges. When he published another map in 1516, he pointedly omitted the name America. "There," he thought, "that will put an end to this foolishness."

Then the political stupidity of my compatriots forced me to live among people with blinders who think they see America, but instead they diminish her, my vast, beautiful América.

It took me a few months after arriving as a stranger to understand the assumptions that governed Mrs. Tuttle's second grade classroom at Riverside Elementary School. It was a supposedly temporary classroom, consisting of a small, mostly windowless wooden house outfitted with old-fashioned cast-iron desks bolted to the dark brown floor. It had been transplanted, along with

similar other little houses, to the school's side yard to accommo-
date the unexpected influx of new students. The temporary houses
were still there when I left Miami ten years later. It was not until
1990 that a dazzling new multicolored building was constructed
to replace the old permanence and the perduring ephemerae.

Mrs. Tuttle herself personified the strangeness of the situa-
tion I had suddenly been thrust into. Her hair was as white as
milk—the kind with a layer of creamy yellow butterfat at the
top—and her teeth were stained a stinking medium brown by
the cigarettes she smoked in her white car when she arrived in the
morning and left in the afternoon. I had never before seen such
behavior in a woman who was obviously over sixty years old.

Every day we sang in Mrs. Tuttle's classroom. With Mrs.
Tuttle's explanations, the songs' intended meanings became alarm-
ingly clear. The lyrics tricked me into complicity with the theft of
my continent; they extracted from me a daily betrayal of the coun-
try to which I owed my loyalty. "America the Beautiful" did not
extol the Mexican desert or the Costa Rican varieties of forest or
the young majesty of the Andes—or the rare geology of the Sierra
de los Órganos and the first morning light over the port of
Cabañas, which my father could paint with his tongue but, of
course, we never went to see, never actually went to see with our
eyes. A chasm opened between myself and the children who could
sing such songs with meaning.

For more complicated reasons, the song that most disturbed
me in that dark classroom was one called "America." At first I
looked for myself in it, of course, but eventually, from the diffi-
cult-to-decipher words, which began obscurely, "My country, 'tis
of thee," and from Mrs. Tuttle's cyclopean explication, I had to
accept that the song's subject was the United States. Two lines
were very troubling: "Land where my fathers died, Land of the
Pilgrims' pride. . . ." At first I translated "pilgrims" as *peregrinos,*
wanderers, and thought the line spoke of people like my family
and me. In November I was disenchanted when pictorial repre-
sentations of weird hats, buckles, and muskets appeared in our

classroom. I dismissed the line. That still left me to contend with "Land where my fathers died," which let in a sea of difference between me and the natives of the land. My fathers—ancestors, we were told it was supposed to mean—had not been laid to rest in the United States. My father's family for generations had lived and therefore must have buried its dead in the rich earth of the Cuban countryside. My mother's family, of more recent arrival in Cuba, had found the modestly priced plots of the Cementerio Colón in La Habana a suitable resting place. As horrible, and therefore necessarily distant, a possibility as my father's death was to me, I found it inconceivable that it would take place here, in an alien land, that he would pull a trigger against himself because he was dying in the wrong country.

Because my older compatriots could not find the appropriate meaning of liberty, I have had to live most of my life in a country that does not know the meaning of its name. Amuhrrkah, Amuhrrkah, it is everywhere in U.S. culture. Amuhrrkah, not the world, but the box. "United States," I shout in correction at the television. "United States," I throw back at the newspaper through gritted teeth. Scorpion stings. I have little tolerance for error. I have no emotional distance, few defenses. I want to flee with my husband and my animals to a snug wilderness, far away from the abuse of words. If you let others define you, there may come a time when you will not recognize yourself.

I do not travel well. Travel makes me feel too keenly the familiar vulnerability of alienness.

I do not think that I will ever again attempt to enter the Netherlands. My only visit was a mistake. I had been trying to live literature, responding to Beaudelaire's invitatory catalogue: *Des meubles luisants, polis par les ans . . . Les plus rares fleurs mêlant leurs odeurs . . . Les riches plafonds, Les miroirs profonds. . . .* I had been trying to spend tourist dollars.

I was with my first husband. After our flight from the United States, we had changed planes in London before proceeding to Amsterdam. Once at Amsterdam airport, we got on line at the immigration station. Dutch officials were stamping the passports from the London flight passengers in a quick, mechanical manner that hardly took a thought. A young man with longish wavy hair between yellow and carrot in color was in charge of our post. The man ahead of me had the sort of dark complexion that made me think he must be Indonesian or Sri Lankan. He wore an expensive-looking suit, seemed to be a businessman. When he got up to the counter, the yellow-carrot-haired passport official, rather than stamping his travel documents routinely as he had done with all the others, asked to see his airplane ticket home.

"Racist," I thought to myself. "What a racist."

Then came our turn. We handed the yellow-carrot-haired official our U.S. passports. He looked inside them. He pointed to me and said, "I want to see your ticket home."

I fumbled in my purse for my tickets. My first husband offered his, "Do you want to see mine?"

"No, not yours. Hers," said the yellow-carrot-haired official, pointing at me again.

I produced my ticket. He stamped my passport. I knew the essential difference between my passport and my first husband's passport. Both said "Nationality: U.S.A.," but whereas his had as his place of birth a city in the U.S. Midwest, mine proclaimed, "Place of Birth: Havana, Cuba."

I wanted to be a dam holding back the natural waters from the invented Netherlandish nation so that I could break, flooding and drowning their neat little houses, their polished surfaces, their Calvinist smugness about their predestined election, so that I could drown every last Dutch person, but most of all their gatekeepers who thought their country something to be saved from my Third World contagion, as if their canals did not reek with the corruption of citizens who had allowed their capital city to be turned into a den of vice, a pisspot of whores. It was not for my own protection, I think, that the passport official wanted to keep me out of the melancholy, designated streets where women stood on stoops and inside red-lit windows renting their cunts and forsaking their names, or the ordinary old Dutch squares where a stroll took one past bars advertising themselves with photographs of women's over-painted faces above naked, unnaturally large udders, or the many, many narrow streets where men slinked out of doorways offering drugs for sale. It would have been different, a kindness, if a maternal or paternal official had said solemnly, "No, young lady. You do not want to enter this city. You will be unable to escape a feeling of debasement upon witnessing the market of oblivion and women's flesh." No, I suspect that the young passport official may have thought that I, being Cuban, was seeking the opportunity to take my place with those phantom girls who stood on the sidewalk with their zippers open. It is the height of self-delusion to think that I, who possessed U.S. citizenship, would select humiliation in a little, below-sea-level, linguistically isolated country.

I stepped away from the passport control post and did not know what to do with my rage. Somewhere near an exit, I said to my first husband, "Did you see? Did you see? He wanted to see my ticket and not yours. Goddamn racist country!" I yelled.

I wanted to turn right around and go back to London or go on to France. But I was easily intimidated in those days. My gestures were small. I yelled at the airport. Big deal. To onlookers I was another Amsterdam crazy, another young person on a bad drug trip. But I would have drowned the Dutch in my rage.

Amsterdam Airport was not the first time I had encountered prejudice against my kind. While a student at Barnard College, I sometimes stopped in at a candy shop on Broadway that was run by an elderly German couple. They made fruit-shaped marzipan, candied ginger, Turkish delight coated with powdered sugar, and delicious chocolate truffles. One December day I went in to buy chocolate truffles. Another customer walked in after me, a woman of Upper West Side liberal cast.

That day the elderly German woman felt talkative as she stacked the truffles in the box. "Are you going away during vacation?" she asked me with a heavy accent.

"I'm going to Miami," I said. This generally elicited envy from those stuck in the cold north, but not on this occasion.

"Ach!" said the woman. "Miami used to be so beautiful. We used to go." I realized that she had to be a Jew, a German Jew, and instantaneously I felt I was in the presence of a horrible past. "Yes, Miami was beautiful. But now," she said leaning forward toward me, "now it's full of *Cubans.*"

The other customer stirred uncomfortably as I stood stiff-muscled before the German-Jewish woman wondering if I should run out of the store and leave her standing with the box of candy she was weighing out. I was ashamed. I thought I owed it to myself before the other customer not to seem to be assenting passively to the shop owner's prejudice, which might appear to this Upper West Side woman to be prejudice toward a group not mine. I felt I owed it to my country to announce loudly my nationality and then dramatically reject the German woman's candy and stalk out, proud and honorable before the *yanqui* witness.

But I was a coward. In my early twenties I preferred to go unnoticed through the world. I paid. I left with my box of candy. I put the box in the refrigerator. Eventually, I threw it out with its contents untouched.

My protest consisted of never buying candy from the woman again. I looked angrily into the shop as I passed it on my walks home. Sometimes as a customer opened the door, the smell of chocolate wafted out, but I was not tempted. And how was the old woman to know that one customer was staying away because her nation, her people, had been insulted? I sometimes fantasized about walking back in and telling her what she had done, but I kept silent. The shop owner had had the better of me.

She, who had been summarized, dehumanized, and exiled for her membership in a despised tribe, found the wherewithal to despise my exiled tribe in turn. But I could not hate hers. I could see her as an old woman who was angry because the world had changed in ways she could not control. I could not hate the old woman's people just because she showed contempt for mine. When I was much too young, my mother had tattooed into my consciousness the suffering of the Jews. My fiancé was a Jew. I studied with Jews. I was not a Jew by a mere accident of birth.

Many have gone to Cuba to be strangers among us.

In the upper horizontal field of our national seal, Cuba is depicted as a key on a sea between two equidistant land masses. From the horizon rises a brilliant sun with outspreading rays (maybe the sun is really setting). This depiction of Cuba, Key to the Gulf, hung on the walls of my Cuban classrooms. The symbol's denotation was identified for us but not the curse it signified: that many have wanted, and would want, that key. Cuba, so strategically placed at the doorstep to the New World that its spectacle greeted Columbus soon after his crossing into unsuspected longitudes, has been for those who have sought to control us a port on the way to other, richer countries, Mexico, Peru. Our gold was soon exhausted, but, unlike that other gold-poor country, Costa Rica, we were not allowed to develop quietly into a nation of democratic farmers and shopkeepers. We had our strategic significance and so were vied for and controlled successively by Spain, England, Spain again, and the United States. Pirates raided our coasts.

The Spanish raided our mahogany forests so they could build the Escorial to Philip's battle glory, and they took our cedar and ebony—not bothering to replant in a subservient colony. Then Cuba was found to be fertile in a new way. In the eighteenth century it was discovered that sugarcane fields remained productive in Cuba longer than in the other Caribbean islands. Our economy became fatally linked to that South Seas crop, though we sold the world other products of our natural wealth:

cacao, coffee, palm oil, fruits, timber, nuts, pepper, tortoiseshell (to my shame), and copper (to our patron saint's glory).

Cuba gave the world tobacco too, and therein lies a lesson. To Cuban Indians, tobacco was intoxicating incense for sacred occasions, but the world beyond profaned it and got for its abomination addiction and rotted lungs. Mild Indians seemed a sexual resource to be taken. If with syphilis for Europe they repaid the conquering men, it was only justice; if the old theory is proven false at last, it can be filed with the many other entries in the catalogue of slanders against Cuban sexuality.

Tourists discovered Cuba, and their moral diseases drew them to the subculture of vice that had grown around the harbor in the days when Cuba was a stopping port for the entire Spanish fleet, which it was our job to escort and protect. U.S.ers weaved drunkenly from bar to bar and thought they knew Cuba. They had commerce with whores and thought they knew Cuban women. They frequented roulette tables and dirty shows in clubs owned by U.S. organized crime syndicates and thought this was the life that all Cubans lived.

I was mute, insulted, incredulous when, at nineteen, away from the protection of Miami, I was told by my first husband that Havana had been famous for prostitution. Now I make myself read about the prostitutes and brothels, and it feels as if I were holding my hand over a flame. I read statistics of rage and sadness, measures of a disaster of past and present, a sexually polarized society, the fouling of discarded women, the vigilance of daughters. But what I met away from Miami were laughs and knowing winks, as if offering up the despair of women for foreign men to feed on were funny, as if the stigma on Cuban women were bearable. "I could not go out without a chaperone when I was in high school," I protested feebly. "Most of my friends could not go out without a chaperone."

I don't bother anymore to try to describe the daily lives of Cubans to strangers who cling to their image of Havana as a city of sin—sin to which U.S. and other tourists found so direct and congenial a path. Our ever-venal governments sold, and sell again, the image of Cuba as a whore for tourist dollars (the longed-for *divisas*). And to the brothel and the streets, rolled up with their money, tourists brought and bring their own sick hearts. So much shame as these hearts carry is inadmissible; so much shame seeks projection.

It is a curse to have beautiful beaches. Pray for natural resources hidden under a hellish desert. Those whom Lord-God will taunt he blesses with beauty and a gentle climate: *The plague of work-driven tourists will descend on your land. They will escape from their reality and turn you into a fantasy. They will torture themselves with guilt over the pleasure that creeps into them as they look out on your blue water and breezes caress their hair and their groins, and they will despise you, because my voice will reverberate in their skulls saying, "Cursed is the ground before you. In toil you shall eat its fruit all the days of your life."*

They will shit where they eat the banished fruit of paradise.

From Cuba I already knew U.S.ers. The Río Mar's location in the fashionable suburb of Miramar attracted several as residents. Directly below us, in apartment 233, lived a family from the United States. The middle daughter, Tammy, was my age. There may have been more compatible girls around, but I did not know them; Tammy was my only friend in the building. She had an older brother—alliteratively Tommy, I think—who built model airplanes, and a younger sister called Taffy who was about two and a pain in the neck.

When I was very small, I thought that all people from the United States were blond and blue-eyed. The "T" sibling trio were not counterexamples. Tammy and her brother had dirty blond hair and blue eyes. But they and their mother had skin that must have been olive to begin with in order for it to tan as deeply as it did. Tammy's mother had blue eyes, like her children's, but her hair, which at one time had probably been like theirs, had the mustardy look of dye.

Their stern-looking, heavy-set, black-haired, balding father was not around much. My mother told me that he worked in a gambling casino. It did not occur to me until many years later that I had spent many innocent childhood days playing in the apartment of a man who was probably a member of an organized crime syndicate, for it was the U.S. mob that owned and administered the casinos. He could not have been a very important member of the syndicate. An important gangster, you would think, would be able to swing a view of the sea. Moreover, his apartment, being on the second floor, was directly above the busy car ramp. Or is that a desirable location for a gangster—so that he can see what is coming?

My parents showed remarkably little apprehensiveness—or knowledge—about Tammy's father's probable criminal connections. What concerned them much more was Tammy's wildness. At the ages of six and seven Tammy already had a reputation among the Cuban lobby personnel for doing things that were unthinkable in a Cuban girl. Her physical daring seemed unlimited. She threw herself recklessly into action, turning somersaults in the hallway, roller-skating on the concrete strip in front of the car ramp. We were opposites. My father had convinced me that my body was as fragile as an eggshell. I did not even dare do the things that Cuban girls did.

Tammy fascinated me, and I, her. What most dazzled her about me, I think, were my possessions. "You have so many toys!" she would say with a voice full of the conviction that life had cheated her. Then she would try to get me to part with some of my treasures. She tried to make a deal. She was very bossy, and I am resistant to bossiness. She kept insisting that U.S. children traded things, that it was abnormal for children not to trade. I, on the other hand, liked my things and did not see any reason why I should part with any of them. She finally cajoled me to the point where I agreed to trade my pair of cream-colored barrettes in the shape of cherubs (I had an identical pair in white).

"Well, for that, I can't give you much," said Tammy, assessing the merchandise like a pawnshop owner.

She gave me a pink plastic dust pan. This was a curiosity, for it was very different from the long-handled, right-angled metal dust pans that we used in Cuba. But as soon as I had parted with my cream-colored cherub-shaped barrettes, I regretted my action. I thought about the barrettes all the time. I imagined them in Tammy's hair. Worse, I imagined her destroying them in a few days, as she did with the many toys that she and her siblings brought back from their visits to the United States during Christmas vacation. I took obsessive care of everything I owned; I wanted everything to remain exactly as it had been the day it had come into my life. I pined for my cherub-shaped barrettes. My mother was not sympathetic. She was angry about the exchange.

"You are not to trade anything else," she told me too long after the fact. "If you want something, you know you can ask us for it." Unnecessary admonition—I had no desire to part with anything else that was mine.

I do not remember any other U.S.er kids in the building besides Tammy, Taffy, and Tommy. There was a set of very blond English-speaking siblings, boy and girl, but I was told that they were not from the United States but rather from England or Canada or some such British place. All of the English-speaking children went to the same, separate school. They wore ugly uniforms in a beige that approached brown but was neither beige nor brown; their buses did likewise. I soothed my resentment over their willful separateness with the ugliness they must endure. Later, when I began school in the United States, I realized how inferior the English-speaking children's schooling must have been if their beige-brown school in Cuba followed the U.S. model.

The Cuban children of the Río Mar, on the other hand, went to different schools from one another, which is why it was difficult to make friends in the building. Early mornings, and again after lunch, the disparately uniformed young residents scattered to myriad private schools whose appropriately painted

buses picked up pupils in front of the lobby and the car ramp.
Somehow, when we were in uniform, invisible boundaries went
up among us and we did not talk to children from other schools
as we waited with our adult under the concrete overhang that
jutted from the building's entrance below Tammy's balcony,
sheltering the glass of the lobby. After the revolution, the over-
hang had in it a line of bullet holes that my aunt Nena told me
had been put there during the attempted arrest of a military
officer.

During the twice-daily wait, I examined the various educa-
tional possibilities suggested by the school names painted on the
sides of buses and the divergent aesthetics of the girls' uniforms.
I particularly admired the burgundy uniforms of the Colegio
Mercy, but the school had nuns and rich girls.

My academically demanding Colegio Baldor had white buses
and uniforms that were a cross to bear for my mother (and
housekeeper?): white oxford shoes, crisply starched and pressed
and pleated white shirtdress over white slip. The dress's left breast
pocket carried a red, white, and blue school shield that patrioti-
cally restated the colors of the Cuban flag. The red and blue
details rode also on the sides of the white buses. My parents had
chosen Colegio Baldor simply because the daughters of a
coworker of my mother's were its kindergarten teachers and
because it was not run by nuns, but it turned out to be the right
school for me in ways we could not have foreseen. It tilled well
the ground for the conflicts of my life: it reinforced my father's
example that Cubanness carries with it grave, ineluctable respon-
sibilities, and it taught me English.

The U.S.ers did not keep themselves separate from us only
in educational matters. They led altogether different lives.
Tammy's mother, for example, did not have a job, yet she was
gone the whole day, perhaps at a pool, probably at a country
club, obviously sometimes at a beauty salon. She wore mules—
the kind of high-heeled slippers that Marilyn Monroe sported in
movies—and capri pants. She also wore bright-colored calypso

shirts. She seemed to think that child-rearing was her child-handler's responsibility, for even when she was at home she kept to herself. The only times I saw her in her apartment in the afternoon, she was relaxing in bed and we had to be quiet.

One such afternoon, Tammy's mother was sitting up, reading in bed. Whether because she wanted to annoy her mother or to wrest some attention from her, Tammy decided to show me something in her mother's bathroom, which was connected to the bedroom. I was uneasy about being there, with her mother in the room. But Tammy kept showing me her mother's cosmetics. As usual, despite Baldor's English-language training, Tammy and I conversed in Spanish.

Then I heard Tammy's mother say from her bed, of course, in English, "Tammy, get the girl out of my room."

Like that. "The girl." As if I were a stranger, an urchin who had wandered in off the street, and not her daughter's friend who had a name. Like that. Assuming I would not understand her.

I said to Tammy, *"Vamos."*

And Tammy said to me in Spanish, "No, no, let me show you this."

"Your mother wants us to go," I told Tammy. When she saw that I had understood, she looked down at the floor, and we left.

The girl got out of the *yanqui* bitch's room. And in my own country, no less. "Tammy, get the girl out of my room." I stayed away from Tammy's apartment after that.

Others came to Cuba without lust for plunder. After the revolution, a girl who had been born to a Cuban rebel father and a U.S. mother—a product of exile—joined our second grade class at Baldor. She had not been long in Cuba. She tried very hard, but she still spoke Spanish with a foreign accent. She had blue eyes, dark brown hair, fair skin, and fine bones. She was lovely and nice, but it was obvious that she felt awkward and strange.

One day in late October 1959, the Cuban public was informed that the twin-engine airplane that was carrying Camilo Cienfuegos, chief of staff of the rebel army, along with the pilot and another soldier, had been lost over Cuba. Camilo Cienfuegos, who resembled holy-card images of Christ, had what no one besides Fidel must have, charisma. The peasant-born, plain-spoken Camilo Cienfuegos stood next to his friend and leader, Fidel Castro, and whenever Castro paused and asked, *"¿Voy bien, Camilo?"* Camilo answered, *"Sí, Fidel,"* with a beatific smile. And each time the crowd went wild. The country went wild with celebration when, a couple of days into the supposed search for the missing plane, the false news was disseminated that Camilo lived. No doubt the public jubilation verified for Fidel, the probable author of the disappearance, that he had been on track.

The false rumor reached us at recess. The middle-class girls of Baldor, many marked for exile, exulted all over the yards for the rescued Camilo. We sang the anthem of the revolution in fast, spontaneous rings. We shouted anti-U.S. slogans from inexorable conga lines. It was too much for me. I needed to stand back. I went where the half-Cuban little girl from the United States stood apart from joy, her face wrinkled in distress.

She said plaintively to me, "I wish I was *cubanita!*"

Too often, in too great numbers, we have left Cuba. We have made a habit of exile. Our regnant failures have been made more tolerable by nearby welcoming shores—from which, of course, we could plot and dream of our triumphal return, our righteousness vindicated, our theories translated into law by acclaim, our loved ones unaged, intact the tree-lined streets of our promenades.

Since we developed an idea of ourselves as a nation, Cuba has seen its children leave for exile. The nineteenth century wars of independence created communities of Cubans in New York,

Tampa, Key West. Not only in the United States, but in Mexico and Venezuela—throughout the hemisphere—in Spain, in France, we have often depended on the openness of foreign ports.

Since 1959, a psychotic social experiment has pushed our tendency toward flight to a catastrophic extreme. We have become a dispersed nation, as if the Old Testament contained our story. Though reluctant, we have become accustomed to building tombs and monuments in alien lands. We will tend a perpetual flame for the heroes of Brigade 2506 from Southwest Eighth Street, Miami.

To get away from our homeland we have hurtled in borrowed MiGs, just skimming the waves. Past the armed guardians of Cuba's coasts, with four-in-ten odds against survival (some oceanographers say one-in-ten), we have braved the powerful, unpredictable, deadly Gulf Stream in inner-tube or oil-drum rafts, on pieces of Styrofoam. When the sea swallows us, we rarely leave a trace beyond our relatives' forlorn note that stays tacked up for years at the Cuban Refugee Transit Home in Key West: "Our brother. Should have left through Cojímar May 1991."

Veterans of Girón, who did not want others to be abandoned as they had been abandoned, organized the means of rescue for those stranded in the blinding reflection on the sea and the alien protocols on dry land. And then even that effort was made bitter as new arrivals were labeled "illegal" and held prisoner in a sun-punished Sheol, an instant tent city on a U.S.-leased piece of land on our native island, with the ocean from which they were plucked on one side and Castro's minefield, the world's largest, on the other. There young men mutilated their sound bodies because their minds ached for the empty dreams of hope on which exiles must feed. And new, starved groups took to the sea, and for the first time they were returned whence they came. The sound of our protesting voices might as well have been the buzzing of a bee hummingbird in a hurricane. So the former rescuers, needing to rescue, took to dropping paper messages from the sky above Cuba, wishing to rescue all of Cuba. And some were killed. The son of the *decano* of the Colegio de Periodistas was killed flying above the ocean.

Unable to find hope, we consume ourselves. Decade after decade after decade, we, fortunate ones, wake up each day as exiles with the concerns of exiles, even as we try to lead normal lives— and fail. While we have been away, our country has changed, its alterations accelerated by a ruler who would re-create the world in his own image, razing vegetation that took hundreds of years to grow in order to carry out his latest misbegotten scheme for the chimeric future, because the past, not having been made in his image, is therefore inferior, a blotch, and a taunting challenge to his power. His driving mission is to alter everything, from the physical makeup of his land to the character of his humans. He is a megalomaniacal demiurge with a country for clay.

While we have been away he has changed Cuba's provinces from the traditional six to fourteen. No more the enduring identity of Pinar del Río, Habana, Matanzas, Las Villas, Camagüey, and Oriente. A discussion of location now requires a political decision: do we, for the sake of uniformity of reference, employ Castro's new provincial names? I cannot bring myself to do it.

And save us from demagogic geographical euphemism. He renamed the Isle of Pines, site of our most infamous political prison, the Isle of Youth, in mockery of our history, in denial of his own history as political prisoner and the keeper of more political prisoners than there ever had been in our nation. History dissolves in him.

"There was a time," my father said, his eyes closed, his voice full of nostalgia for what he had not seen, "when the trees of the Isle of Pines were full of little green parakeets." The Cuban conure *(Aratinga euops)* is gone from that place.

Most of what I know about Cuban birds I have read in James Bond's ornithology and U.S. magazines of aviculture; I remember only vaguely the singing of the Cuban countryside as the sun splashed on the flowery vines outside a luncheon *bohío.* I write a book in English, not Spanish. I do not know how the years have transformed my aunt Nena's face. The generation to which she is great-aunt has grown up in Cuba knowing nothing of us or of our time. We did not come to the United States as immigrants. We did not mean to stay. We did not want to convert the sadness of leaving home into a brilliant future in other, free countries. Life in a nation not one's own is not self-determination. Yet I know that I am so altered that I can never again live exclusively in the country of my birth.

José Miró Cardona for decades was a constant smoker of cigarettes, but just as life makes no sense, neither does death, which being of life shares its nature: it was colon cancer that killed him. At least, that was what my father said as he made rare and hurried arrangements to fly to Puerto Rico for the funeral.

I saw Miró for the last time in 1967, just before his schedule and my family's diverged and the Bozas visited an empty, amphibian-surrounded house in Puerto Rico. Fortunately, he had made plans to visit Miami before we left it. He came to a big Sunday dinner of *arroz con mariscos* at our small apartment.

The previous weekend my parents and I had gone to a movie together, something we had not done in years. Sometimes we avoid things for a good reason. The only films I had seen in Miami with my two parents were *The Sound of Music* (watched twice and applauded by my father for its "human" themes); *My Fair Lady* (mildly disapproved of by him for the questionable morality of Alfred P. Doolittle—not forgetting Shaw's socialism); and *Mary Poppins,* Walt Disney's hyperkinetic evisceration of P.L. Travers's magical and powerful heroine (it could not compare with the books, but it was clean, so we went to see it a second time, and all three fell asleep in the theater).

Our 1967 selection, *Dr. Zhivago,* had its dangers. I was nervous. Was Pasternak dissident enough? When the image of Lara's mother's naked back appeared on the screen, I wanted very much to be elsewhere. It did not matter that she lay sick from a suicide attempt and that doctors surrounded her. The space between my father's arm and my arm shrank. I was aware of every breath he took in and exhaled. I did not look at him directly, but I knew he was glowering. At film's end, my father came out of the theater enraged.

"It's pornographic," he said. From the way he looked at my mother I knew that he wanted to blame her, but even he could not do that, so he merely spat upon Flagler Street. "It's inconceivable that they would let a child in," he said pointing to me.

I knew that it would make matters much worse to remind him that the sight of a woman's naked back held neither mystery nor allure for me, that I was fifteen and my body was fully grown. I knew even then that my body was part of the problem.

At the Sunday dinner with Miró, I could tell that my father wanted to make a point because he made an angle with his bony right index finger and thumb, first waving the index finger at the air before him and then pointing it at his temple, like a gun. He said to Miró, "You know I'm always saying that this country is handing itself over completely to the Communists. Last week we saw the film of *Dr. Zhivago* and," he said with increasing anger, "it was Communist propaganda and pornography at the same time. This country is a pigsty."

Miró looked at him amused. He had on him the look we keep for cranks that we remain fond of in spite of their obdurate extremity. "Ah, yes," Miró said, "the fields of flowers, the repeating balalaika theme." He continued to smile benevolently at my father. I could tell that Miró had liked *Zhivago*.

My father, the self-educated fanatic from the Cuban countryside, continued to expound on the film's evil. For the first time I could see my father through the eyes of someone else—someone that my education was preparing me to resemble. Ironically, my father encouraged all my school achievement. He bought me any book I asked for, any serious book, even *The Naked Ape,* about which my mother later admonished me, "Don't let any man know you've read it." And the books with their wide world and the schooling at which I excelled pushed me away from my father, so that it became increasingly difficult for me to be what he wanted me to be: a version of him, an English-fluent mouthpiece.

As I listened to my father speak of pornography and propaganda, I felt shame. Once the shame came to life inside me, it remained, and it grew more intense because I recognized my father's fanaticism in me. Two months before in world history class, Mrs. Strama had burst out laughing at an answer of mine. "Sometimes I think you see the world in black and white," she told me. I do not remember what my ninth grade analysis had been, something about the Soviet Union's secret, self-serving goals in fighting against Germany in World War II. But Mrs. Strama's response stung me, and I played it over and over again in my mind. Because it was true. After my father declared *Dr. Zhivago* pornographic Communist propaganda, I began slowly to become a very different person.

Miró Cardona's Consejo office was located in the rented house in Miami Beach where he and his family lived. In the days before the end of October 1962, it was a place full of people and important activity, somewhat as *El Crisol* had been, but without the special, inky smells. An anxious hope permeated the place from which Miró's son was forcibly absent. The son's young tribe had the run of the building and yard. Miró loved children, and he was indulgent of their noise. He wanted them to express themselves. His wife Ernestina had other, stricter notions of discipline. My father meant for reports of the couple's disagreements to underscore Miró's indulgent saintliness, but he could not fool me, my father, about how he himself really felt about the noise. The kids were too rough for me too.

The commute from Fifth Avenue and Fifth Street in Southwest Miami out to Miami Beach was not an easy one for my father in the beginning of his employment with the Consejo, for he did not have money for a car. Public transportation is always bad in sprawling Miami, but at that time it was nonexistent: bus drivers had gone on strike. Until the resolution of the labor dispute, my father was forced to use extreme ingenuity in a foreign country just to get to work each day. He was startled the first time he was asked by a group of English-speaking strangers where he was going and whether he wanted to share a cab. In his experience, taxicabs were not shared. Quickly, however, he became a habitué of the places where such instant car pools were likely to form. The experience indelibly impressed upon him the importance in Miami of overcoming poverty sufficiently to own an automobile.

"Remember that Miró wants you to call him Tío Pepe. He likes that," my father exhorted me whenever we planned a visit. I knew as I said the name that Tío Pepe as an uncle would inspire admiration and respect but never anger or giggling joy. He would always be kind to me, but we would not search for lizards together, for he was an Important Man. He was to me then an abstract uncle. Abstraction was one of the processes that had come to dominate my exile. It overtook Cuba, the country whose sounds and tastes and exuberantly living things I had known so intimately, and it overtook human relationships. Behind my fanatical urgency for liberation plans to succeed lay a desire for my life to become tangible again.

Miró could not be my uncle the way that Óscar and Rafael had been my uncles. Óscar played with assorted cousins and me hide-and-seek and games of guessing whose hands, kept palm to palm, held a hidden jewel. His expression was ever patient, like a thin bloodhound's. His hair must have turned prematurely gray, for that is the only shade I remember it. He explored with me my grandmother's backyard: the jasmine that hung over the neighbors' wall, Rafael's roses, the shells of snails, and the lizards that eluded not only our fingers but even the grass nooses that we made in order to catch, examine, and then release the bewildered reptiles.

Óscar and I walked around the roots of the big old tree in the corner lot of my grandmother's street. It was the corner just across from the entrance to the Baptist cemetery.

"What kind of tree is it?" I asked.

"I don't know," he answered. We are, none of us, any good at naming trees.

But he reached down under the pile of drying leaves and pulled up the lacy skeleton of a leaf such as those I loved to find pressed in my father's cousin Gloria's old dentistry textbooks. He held it up to the light, that object that was composed of space and the brown, connected memory of a life. I know that it was daytime, but for years I saw the image of Óscar's hand raised beside the tall tree, silvered under a full moon.

Another afternoon Óscar let me sit at the wheel of his powder-blue 1940s Pontiac and blow the horn. Although the engine had not been turned on, I was afraid that I might make the car go accidentally. My uncle thought I was afraid of far too many things, and he was right, but he never saw the thrill I derived through my fear of so much that was ordinary. Óscar did not like to accept ordinariness. He made his own cigarette lighter and put decals on it. Then he put decals on the cigarette pack.

"You run like an old woman!" he criticized, annoying me, wanting me to fling myself at life.

We saw Óscar and his wife Dulce most weekends at my grandmother's house, which my mother and I visited every Saturday and Sunday afternoon and evening while my father worked—or was, at any rate, elsewhere. It was always "my grandmother's house," although, of course, it belonged to her son-in-law Rafael, whose glasses, as owlish as Miró's, heightened the intensity of his gaze. His home office contained sheet after sheet of paint chips that strove to impose taxonomic order onto color. I never tired of looking at them, just as I got as much pleasure from watching the simultaneous order and variety in my Prismacolor pencils as I did from coloring with them. He used the chips to sell his customers Sherwin-Williams paints, for which he was a Cuban representative. Óscar worked for the same company, as a warehouseman.

Rafael made origami birds in his office, and at the beginning of every school year, when my mother and aunt Nena had covered my new books with grocery bag paper, he inscribed the subject and my name on each with elegant calligraphy. I would watch him set up his instruments, pen points like cranes diving toward earth and the blackest ink. I could not get over that blackness. We call it Chinese ink, not India ink as in the United States. *"Tinta china,"* my mother would say, as if the sounds of words contained their meanings. *"Tinta china,"* I would repeat with the reverence I later applied to Beaudelaire.

Two years in a row, Rafael bought me gold earrings when he got his salesman's bonus. My favorites were the golden teardrops with little rubies, which I wore in one of the few pictures I have from my Cuba time, taken when I was seven.

But there was something of the devil in Rafael. Once he came to our apartment for a midday Chinese dinner. My father got plenty of fried wontons from the restaurant because they were my favorite food. *Maripositas chinas,* we call them, little Chinese butterflies. In distributing them, my father put the biggest one with much flourish before me.

"Watch out it doesn't fly off with your plate," my father joked.

I was in the habit in those foolish days of keeping the best for last. I ate around it. I savored the anticipation of allowing myself finally to place it in my mouth and feel its crunch followed by the burst of juicy pork. Suddenly, just as I had finished eating everything else, Rafael's hand darted toward my plate, and before I could scream, he popped my wonton into his mouth. Despite his many kindnesses to me, which my mother listed and which I logically conceded, I did not forgive the theft. Even now, I usually refer to him as The Uncle Who Stole My Wonton. Even now that he has been dead so many years. And Óscar too is dead. And gone too is Miró.

# Memorial

# I

As my father looked down upon her, Cuba, our native land, he saw the ring of turquoise around her and then the sapphire water beyond it turn blood red. In the blood-red water he saw human teeth bobbing, hands sheared by the sharper teeth of sharks, severed feet standing upside down but resolute, still shod in sneakers, sandals, pumps. Beyond the red stain upon the sapphire water, a black, shiny inner tube carried eight comatose bodies through a realm of thirst into worldless shadow.

Hugging the island and the island's island, the blood glowed bright in brown water littered with bruised backs, and brains held in vices, and red-and-blue-bordered envelopes, and old papers paragraphed with laws, and broken, radioactive promises. On the land he saw blasted fruit trees and starving vultures and marasmic people staring from cages out to sea and people spitting on those in cages by the sea and people with guns rattling the bars. In his native province he saw the jungle embrace rusting missile covers. In a vast southern swamp, where thorns tore the skin of young men, he saw a monument to his defeat and to his enemy's victory.

Then the Beast showed himself. He stood, gigantic, on the island; his splayed boots spanned the island east to west, from San Antonio to Maisí. Though the Beast turned his head from right to left, he had already become a man of lead. His black beard was crudely painted, as on a child's coin bank. His olive uniform and visored cap were cast in the style of the young revolution and he had not a wrinkle on him, the man of lead. Conqueror, he kept his hands on his hips, and from other nations, doll men were smiling toward him, nodding when they tipped forward, " Yes! Yes!"

And my father tried to breathe down fire upon the Beast of lead to melt him. For, liquefied, the Beast would roll off the surface of Cuba and into the sea. And when the lead, hissing, hit the water, it would cool and form a layer, afloat but solid, and on this rough, brittle surface exiles would wobble back toward their mother, and her sea would no longer glow red, and for the people of the island the cages would open, and for the exiles there would be an end to the songs of nostalgia.

But his breath could barely supply enough oxygen for his own blood's purposes. It balked in his windpipe, incapable of fire. The time had come to die.

So soon. So soon after.

Through television we millions watched hundreds of thousands of Germans dance on the wall, pour through the wall, tear down the Berlin Wall with their chisels and their will and their rejection of the hated boundary's authority over them. A wall ceased to be a wall. The disintegrating East German government admitted it.

Mikhail Gorbachev, the last general secretary of the Soviet Communist Party, declined the Soviet Union's old prerogative of intervening in Warsaw Pact nations. The Cold War was over. We had won—in principle, by proxy.

On 9 November 1989, the world watched the Berlin Wall become an anachronism, and many shed tears of joy. Within joy, I wept for sorrow: my father would have had to wait very little to see it. Through an abysmal, wasteful sense of timing, he had denied himself an evening of hope. He had died desperate, and then the world had changed more to his liking.

But would he have believed, I asked myself. Would he have accepted the evidence of his eyes—Hungary becoming a multiparty parliamentary state without the swift punishment of Soviet tanks in its streets, this time? Or, out of his habit of distrust, would he have seen the events in Eastern Europe, country after country changing its way of governing without interference from the Soviets, as one more satanic plot of the Soviet Union to persuade the West to let down its guard before a grandiose, irresistible strike? Dualism is a difficult habit to break. Even if he had lived to see the beginning of the disintegration of Communism, he could not have loosened his inner tension. My father was mad beyond life. The Erinyes drive us to the other side with whips of scorpions.

The peacefulness with which Poland, Czechoslovakia, and Hungary made transitions seemed almost unnatural anyway. More than one Cuban saw the bloodshed in Romania and thought to read in it our fate. Riots breaking out throughout the country. The secret police fighting against the people and pro-liberty army factions. That is the model to dread. But no protests can avail while Fidel Castro lives. On the island, dissident groups proliferate and risk and hunger and argue and defy. Exiles map out strategies, review contingencies, dream, and argue—about means, end, time, dialogue or no, embargo or no, Cuba yes and foreign powers no—fixed in our positions, never admitting that we do not know, we simply do not know what will create a better Cuba. Two things we know: Power must not remain in Castro's hands, and he is not going to let go of it while he lives. In the silence of the night, all, especially Fidel Castro, know the first condition for positive change without catastrophe: one death.

During a telephone conversation a couple of years ago, my mother and I discovered that we had nearly identical fantasies about the killing of Fidel Castro. Her first choice was for nature to take him so that there would be no factional fighting. I granted that this would be ideal. But nature is slow, I said. My mother agreed. We each had crafted an alternative scenario: nature not cooperating, someone with the good of Cuba in mind but a terminal disease in body, someone who can get close to Fidel, one of his own, unconnected with exiles or the United States, shoots him (or stabs or poisons or disintegrates him). In my fantasy, the hero is able to withstand the aftermath with detachment because he knows he will soon die one way or the other; in my mother's, he shoots Fidel and immediately shoots himself. She is probably right about that.

I have since reversed one of my basic premises, however. Nature is swift. I'll pin my hope on hemorrhagic dengue.

## II

*I want, when I die,*
*without country, but without master,*
*to have on my slab a bunch*
*of flowers—and a flag!*

—José Martí, *Versos sencillos,* XXV

History is written by the living. At least, my mother and I had the advantage in that. I raged at my father, but I was also mindful that I had a duty to fulfill. I must give my father what he had been denied—a ritual good-bye, a memorial. For this, Kurt and I chose the first anniversary of my father's suicide. As in the previous year, we flew to Miami just after my classes had ended—this time not with terrible news as luggage, but with plans and a mission. We arrived on 18 May.

My mother was incommunicative. She put up walls. She sat on the sofa in a stupor. The silence in which she lived pervaded all our time in the apartment. I dared not ask her the questions I had brought with me: whether she had found my childhood photographs, what years my father had worked at Channel 23.

When we had dinner at La Carreta, on Eighth Street, my mother would not try Kurt's dessert of *tocino del cielo.* "Let me explain. It was Ramiro's favorite dessert," she said pointedly to Kurt. And that was all.

The bloodstain on the bathroom floor had grown fainter. One had to know where to look for the brown shadow in the grout. The right sink support, which had been knocked down by my father's fall, had since been pushed into place. The metal was dented.

On the 19th we woke up to a clear day. We did not tell my mother of our plans. We whispered a lot.

We needed flowers. They should be yellow, I thought, because that was Oshún's color. Or white, for the dead. We walked one block from my mother's apartment to a flower shop with an Anglo name that had been in the same location for the length of our exile. It was dark inside, but the door opened when we pushed on it. A bell rang. A startled thirtyish blond Anglo man came running out to the counter from a back room.

"We wanted to buy some flowers," I explained quickly.

The man looked even more surprised.

"Are you closed?" Kurt asked. "The door was open."

The man was noncommittal.

"Yellow or white preferably," I said with the hope of being helpful.

The man seemed to search in his mind for what "yellow" or "white" or even "flowers" might mean. His mind settled on something. "How about daisies?"

The youthful, sunny innocence of daisies was so ridiculously discordant with my father's personality that I nearly laughed. But they would just be cast into the sea, and my father could usually take a joke.

"Fine," we said. "Yes."

He came out with a dozen large daisies on long stems. The $12 price was high, but at that point we were willing to settle for anything that was not a bullet or a controlled substance.

We left. I was rattled but thankful not to have been gunned down for having tried to buy flowers at a florist's shop on a Saturday morning. We put the flowers in the rented car. We went up to my mother's apartment to get other materials that we needed.

We told my mother that we were going for a drive.

"Would you do me a favor?" she asked. "Would you get some flowers for tomorrow, for Ramiro?"

Kurt and I looked at each other quizzically. "Do you know a good place?" I asked my mother.

"That place down the street doesn't seem to be very good," Kurt said.

"Oh, no, that place is no good. Nobody goes there," my mother said.

She recommended we try a shop on Twelfth Avenue, where an older Cuban man, who was committed to the business of selling flowers, sold us a lovely, varied bouquet, with lilies and freesias and carnations and exotics, for considerably less than our mysterious daisies. He was feeling so cheerful about being in the florist's business that he added more lilies to our bunch, for the hell of it.

Pleased with our purchase and our purchasing experience, Kurt and I walked back to the apartment and put the flowers in my mother's hands. Her cheeks swelled and for a moment she wept. It was her memorial.

As we trimmed the stems and put the flowers in a vase on top of the television set, Kurt led a discussion, which my mother was glad to join, about the quality of the flowers and the bargain of the price. I found speaking difficult. Although my mother's tears had vanished, I did not feel good about leaving her then, though I must. As we headed for the door, she was already on the sofa, apparently in retreat behind her wall; I hoped this time the wall would hold.

I had never been to the Ermita, the shrine to Our Lady of Charity. It now shared the bay with Immaculata–La Salle High School, but during my school years there, a large white stone pietà had faced out to sea instead. Sometimes student couples sneaked out to kiss behind the pietà's tall cement curtain. After my departure from Miami, Monseñor Agustín Román had seen the accomplishment of his dream of building a shrine to our Cuban patroness in the land of exile, a shrine by the sea to a rescuer of those who brave the mutability of the sea.

Several cars were in the parking lot when we arrived at the shrine that early Saturday afternoon. Perhaps my mother and her companions had encountered fewer people on a weekday. But even though we were not alone, from the moment we stepped onto the chapel grounds I experienced a pervasive quiet such as I had never found anywhere else in Miami.

Kurt and I walked to the edge of the water. There were other pilgrims at the edge, sitting in folding chairs and praying perhaps—but not obviously, possibly merely waiting—employing only hushed tones when they spoke, their word-shaping voices drowned by the calm lapping of the water and the blowing of a breeze. Groups formed at distances from one another, granting the others solitude for their contemplations.

Kurt and I sat there at the edge, on the low sea wall, and dangled our feet over Biscayne Bay. The water was clear and shallow. Seaweed danced a slow waltz on bottom sand and on rock. A cormorant perched on a wooden piling. Self-consciously—hoping no one else saw—I threw my bunch of daisies into the water, because my father's flag wreath had wilted before his body was burned. I was glad to see how quickly the current carried the daisies out of view; perhaps so with his ashes. Sponges floated by. Paper plates and a cardboard Pepsi cup bobbed on.

Beginning was difficult. I clutched tightly my hand-written program, my photocopied Oxford Revised Standard Version Bible pages, my Book of Common Prayer. I felt inhibited because I was doing something unusual, and I must speak, though softly, inside a great silence, and I must speak English within the hearing of Cubans at a Cuban monument, and I chose to employ ecumenical and semi-Protestant matter at a Roman Catholic shrine, and I did without clergy upon church property. I feared someone would hear strange, autonomous words and take offense, or that someone with the visual acuity of an eagle and a rare knowledge, for a Cuban, of U.S. Episcopalianism would espy the small, gold-stamped title on the spine of my Book of Common Prayer. I feared we would be thrown out.

Kurt, who knows that I am more neurotic in Miami than anywhere else, gave my shoulder a squeeze. "It's all right," he said, "let's begin." He had not designed the program and did not know exactly what to expect—and he had not even known my father—but he would absolutely play his part; he was my partner, my friend.

We wove my father a memorial with alternating voices. We told of his life and death. We began, of course, with the two accounts, in Deuteronomy 33 and 34, of Yahweh's cruel, arbitrary condemnation of his faithful servant Moses to die alone upon an alien mountain. We then read Isaiah 35, a prophecy of the restoration of Zion. It expressed a dream not unlike my father's, but its hopeful reassurances cut with irony. I selected it because I was angry with God—and because my attention had been drawn to it by Brahms. *He will come and save you. They shall obtain joy and gladness, and sorrow and sighing shall flee away.*

I explicitly recognized the control my father had seized. *Lord, let me know my end and the number of my days.* The power and the frailty of the suicide. *I am worn down by the blows of your hand. Like a moth you eat away all that is dear to us.*

Sea grass rode the water. Two black skimmers grazed the surface. Occasionally, airplanes flew loudly overhead. Clouds obscured the sun and the world became more chill, like steel. In a moment of brightness, a pleasure boat sped by. A fat, pink boy on its deck waved at us frantically, but we would not return his greeting since we were engaged in solemn business. He waved stubbornly on, indignant that we were not waving on demand. In the midst of death, we are in life.

We brought a reminder for my father of my pain and my mother's: *For no man liveth to himself, and no man dieth to himself.* But all we go down to the dust; yet even at the grave we make our song: Alleluia. We brought a balm from the exiled Isaiah: *To comfort all who mourn; to grant those who mourn in Zion—to give them a garland instead of ashes, the oil of gladness instead of mourning. They shall build up the ancient ruins, they shall raise up the former devastations.*

The Bay of Biscay, west to east along its coastal extent in Spain, spawned us—my father's mostly forgotten families, my mother's recently transplanted ones. It was typical of our condition that my father should end in a double displacement, Biscayne Bay, a translated remembering of his ancestral land, beautiful but far even from his real country in the New World. It was a fitting setting, no less, for the telling of his translated story of pained exile by his only descendant, a mourning exile, and her husband from the North. Pain and exile were all that I had been able to associate with my father for decades; they were the stuff of his being, as if he had not dwelt for more than fifty years in his native land. Yet if exile defined him, who had spent a much smaller portion of his life outside his country, it defined me much more.

> *By the waters of Babylon we sat down and wept,*
> *when we remembered you, O Zion. . . .*
> *If I forget you, O Jerusalem,*
> *let my right hand forget its skill.*
> *Let my tongue cleave to the roof of my mouth. . . .*

Kurt's heart leaped with lightness when a little stingray undulated slowly by as I read a passage. I had meant to recite some José Martí from memory—the collected poems that my father had given me had fallen behind other books and could not be found before our trip—but at the seaside I forgot to do it.

When we were finished, we sat silently for a while, and now the silence sounded even deeper than before, since we had been speaking. It seemed to us both that it was time to go. What we had come for had been accomplished. We were at peace, duty done, with the certainty that my father had been thrown into a peaceful place—whatever his state may have been otherwise. Some of the people who had been gazing at the ocean were folding up their chairs. Some new people had come.

We walked to the chapel, which resembles a teepee or a flying saucer or a primitive oven. It rises from a circular base, as befits a shrine to a female. We sat down in the back. The Virgin was represented well; her small statue looked beautiful with

dark skin and a white mantle embroidered with silver. A family
with skin the same color as the Virgin's was tending to her,
arranging a fancy bouquet of yellow flowers in a vase before her,
and neatening the profusion of mostly yellow flowers with
which others had filled cylindrical vases. I liked the seats, tradi-
tional Cuban *taburetes,* chairs made of leather stretched over
wooden frames. But the ugly brown mural overwhelmed the
statue of the Virgin and threatened to come down on us. We
left. In the parking lot we heard the pointless ringing of the 2:20
period bell at Immaculata–La Salle.

When we returned to my mother's apartment, we found that
she had covered almost every inch of the bathroom floor with
narrow ochre throw rugs with insistent brown stripes.

The next day, Kurt and I went back to the Ermita. We saw a
small empty plastic bag being carried swiftly to other parts by
moving water.

My mother detested the bookcase that my father had bought
sometime when I was in seventh or eighth grade or so. It was a
bookcase in his eyes only. To any other observer, the dark grey
metal thing would look like something that belonged in a base-
ment workshop, storing tools. He had bought it without
consultation. One day a man delivered it. My mother took one
look at it and detested it. And detested it for the subsequent
twenty-odd years it made its large presence noticed in the living
room, where such furniture must be placed in a small apart-
ment. My father had probably thought that, being made of
metal, it would be sturdy, but after years of use, the middle part
of the shelves began to sag, and my parents tried some strange
reinforcements of string. My father would not think to purchase
another bookcase; he already had a bookcase. And there the
monstrosity sat, in plain view of visitors, perennially in my
mother's sight.

"I'm going to get rid of these books," my mother said during our visit. "I'm going to give what you don't want to the Colegio. But you take first what you want—and everything that you want. Anything that you think will be useful to you. I want to get rid of this junk thing," the bookcase.

Thus one year after my father's death, my mother gave me, of her own initiative, the inheritance he had not thought to leave me. Excited, I explained to Kurt. Fortunately, there were boxes. I would have taken every book—Kurt and I both have a feverish acquisitiveness about books (and my father's!)—but the boxes, two, set a limit. Selecting was not easy. We packed the chosen and took them to a post office in Northwest, where the postal worker who waited on us with strange decals on her long, long nails was friendly despite our seventy-five-pound burden. The books arrived in Greenbelt before we did; the postal workers there would be glad to see us.

I already had my own, mildewed copy of Hugh Thomas, but I welcomed my father's, although he did not make a mark in it, not even about Thomas's depriving Sorí of his agrarian reform law. There were books of writings by or about Martí, of course. One is full of large *X*'s that my father put through more than a few sayings; I do not know if because he had already used them in speeches or because he violently disagreed with them and he wished to nullify their published existence. When, in the mid-1970s, my father had sent me, without warning, a huge box containing *La enciclopedia de Cuba,* he had retained volume 9 on republican governments, a chronology of events from 1902 till March 1952, for me a very valuable resource—and now I had it. Most useful were Leovigildo Ruiz's Cuban chronologies for 1959, 1960, 1961, and 1967. I wish there were more. Not only is the day-to-day history of a time I saw through the distorting mirror of childhood clarified, but through my father's notations on its pages I can follow his own obsessions and curiosities: SORI, PARDO. Before our visit, my mother had already sent me *Contra toda esperanza* by Armando Valladares,

with my father's proud and pained markings along the margins
of the pages that discussed Alfredito Izaguirre.

After my father's death, I felt old and exhausted.

My mother, not just Carmen but also Madame Butterfly,
broke out of a hard chrysalis. She had two teeth crowned; she
polished her nails. She refurnished her apartment with pleasing
pieces in tones of beige and peach, ridding her life of the exe-
crable, mismatched furniture acquired by my father in strict
accordance with his method of buying the first thing the sales-
man showed him without concern for suitability or aesthetics.

She was a dazed princess released from a forty-seven-year
spell of self-forgetting.

"Don't you find me more talkative?" she asked me by tele-
phone after Kurt and I had returned from our 1990 visit.
"Before, I had to worry about your father's image. Now I say
what I think." Thence a flood of observations, opinions, stories
poured out on me.

"After your father dies, I will see my friends," she had said to
me. And she did see them. Her friend Martha was free at first.
They went shopping and to the theater. Then Martha's parents,
in their nineties, grew totally dependent on her. Deprived of her
companion, my mother too became house-bound. There were
other people of course. But as they got older, they got around
less, or when they did go on an outing with her, they complained
about their ill health and pains and unhappiness. Some died. My
mother had waited so long to see her friends. She could not
accept their decay.

My mother is alone most of the time. Although she some-
times longs for sociability, when people with demands interrupt
her solitude, she is annoyed. She prefers to spend hours each
night with characters from the Spanish-language soaps. She loses

herself in their settings, she says, and those become reality. She is startled back into this world by the final credits.

To my first psychiatrist my first semester of college I expressed fears of what would become of my mother after my father died—his passing, even then, seeming imminent.

"Many women thrive after the death of their husbands. They find an independence they never thought they could have," she averred.

I thought that, not knowing my mother, she simply did not, could not understand.

In July 1990 my mother called to say that she had found a manila envelope that contained the lost photographs of me as a little girl—the one in which I danced the flamenco, the one in which I wore a polka-dotted bow.

## III

*When under the weight of the cross*
*a man resolves to die,*
*he leaves to do good, he does it, and returns*
*as from a bath of light.*

—José Martí, *Versos sencillos,* XXVI

I visited my mother alone in the turning from late September to early October 1991. I wanted to see her, of course, but also to pursue my obsessional research. In the long evenings of her soap operas, I looked through the sign-in book for my father's wake and read the clippings that had been sent to my mother. I saw, among the many expressions of praise and regret, several versions of a terrifying photograph, the last one of my father, taken on 7 May, twelve days before he turned his gun against himself. He is voting in the elections of the Colegio— "His last journalistic activity," says one caption. The other members of the Colegio wear suits and ties; my father is in short sleeves. His right hand holds the ballot over the slit in the ballot box. His gnarly hand, with such long fingers, looks like two hands. It has not shrunk because it is bone. Of what is not bone in his body, much has disappeared, the flesh sucked out. His neck is wrinkles of empty skin. He attempts to smile. This is the worst of all. From that emaciated face with the large eye sockets, the empty, rigid smile looks like a hideous death's-head grin. My father, two weeks before his death, was already a walking skeleton.

Far away from me, without my knowledge, my father's body had been abandoning him in anguished, cryptic exhalations beyond his understanding. I had not been informed. Only one person could have told me and she had said nothing of this.

366

Still seated at the dining table with the photograph in front of me, I struggled to compose my voice. "Papá looked very ill in the last Colegio photograph."

And she answered, "Your father said to me, '*Vieja,* everything hurts me, from my crown to my toenails.'"

"A couple of nights before he killed himself," she also told me, "he had a fever and a cough. The next day his lung specialist said to come in right away. But when the doctor entered the examination room, your father started telling him about how he had had trouble going to the bathroom that morning. And the doctor said, 'I think there's some confusion here.' I had to explain to the doctor about your father's fever."

I forgave him everything—but one. I would not remain more hard-hearted with my father than I would with any other human. I understood his fears: that his illness—real, whether created by body or mind, and causing pervasive pain—would impoverish my mother, exhaust her. He did not say it, but he could have, that we cannot prevent death, only postpone it. He left this world while he could still contribute to it, before his body humiliated his sense of himself. Pain and illness and old age grind us into the dust of death—or worse, if we let them, into a helpless, stinking mockery of life.

But I could not forgive the path that he took out of the world. His collection of medicines provided too many benign opportunities for him to have to shatter my mother's sleep with gunshot, gasps, and blood.

I remembered. The forgetful may find an easy route to forgiveness or indifference. But I did not grant events their death: Girón, my father's shooting.

If you surround a scorpion with a ring of fire, old people used to say, it will sting itself to death.

That November, as I had the previous year, I sought to com-
memorate my father's death on All Souls' Day, which includes in
its generous agenda all the souls of the faithful departed (as
opposed to the unfaithful?), unlike All Saints', which trumpets
the triumph of those who have no need for our prayers. I was
making an attempt—doomed to failure—to be an Episcopalian.
The advertisements in the newspapers indicated an absence of All
Souls' services. I settled for the All Saints' Day evening service at
a tiny Episcopal chapel near our apartment, where for two
months Kurt and I had been restless, skeptical members of the
congregation.

The young priest, mindful of the two correlative observances,
fortunately made the service one of commemoration of all the
dear departed. The adult participants all had suffered losses; the
children too, but they did not yet show the losses' weight. Some
of us wept. We had heard the same readings five days earlier, on
Sunday, but now the words spilled out their special meanings.

The reading from the seventh chapter of Revelation was
almost unbearably painful. In the vision of that John who is iden-
tified forever by the name of the rocky desolation to which the
emperor Domitian exiled him, the blessed in a great multitude
from every nation stand before the throne of God in robes made
white by washing in the blood of sacrifice. They carry palm
branches and praise God and the Lamb.

> And he who sits upon the throne will shelter them with his
> presence. They shall hunger no more, neither thirst any more;
> the sun shall not strike them, nor any scorching heat. And
> God will wipe away every tear from their eyes.

I wanted this peace for my father who had known so little
peace in life, who had made so little peace, but who had needed
peace so desperately that in the end he committed an act of war
against his wife and daughter. And yet because of this violence of

his going, I could not imagine him at rest. *Blessed are those who mourn* was little comfort; I wanted comfort for him: blessed are those who blast their skulls open and widow their wives.

The Prayers of the People is usually the most torpid part of the Episcopal service. But not this time. All present at the service, no more than a dozen, were invited to stand at the altar and there read randomly distributed sections of a list with names of those departed that the congregation at large, present or not, had wished to remember. In most cases we did not get our own. I anticipated a botch, but I was fortunate in my reader's pronunciation of my loved ones' difficult names. Kurt's family names were no easier. Few family names were easy.

For the Eucharist, the priest had decided to be different because we were few. While we remained at the altar, the Eucharistic wafers were passed around on the paten like a dish of cookies at tea. The sharing of the chalice was a complicated affair of handing off, drinking, and wiping the trace of lips. No one managed to follow instructions exactly. One avid churchgoer was so confused that she put the host in her mouth and took it out again.

When the stressful Communion was over, we returned to our seats. Postcommunion—the clearing away of the dishes—was usually the only moment of quiet in that little church. I knelt and closed my eyes.

And I saw, luminous, wearing a white robe, holding a palm branch—my father. To his right was a marble font, and the dense space behind him pulsated, glowing red as with sacred blood or sacred fire. He had recovered from the feebleness of his last days; was again a strong man of sixty. But he looked self-conscious and most uncomfortable in the tunic. He could not have thought it appropriate attire for a man. In the mid-1970s, he had refused to wear a white shirt that a friend had given him because the name Dior, embroidered discreetly in white thread on the pocket, rendered the garment for him somehow feminine. Yet there he stood, before the throne of God—of which I could see but a corner—uncertainly holding the branch of palm (why would a man pick up a palm branch except to shield himself from the noon sun as he stretched out to feel the breeze dry his sweat after a hard morning in the fields?), my suicide father among the blessed. When he perceived my surprise at his state, he said with his forceful voice, impatient, as if he must iterate something to which I had not been listening, "Don't you know that the view from heaven is different from that on earth?"

# Appendix A: Selected Genealogy

## A Visual Aid to Mentioned Relatives*

*Descendants of Hilario Boza Izquierdo*

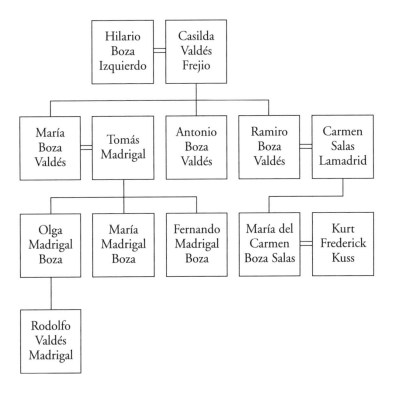

* Omissions should be read as simplification, not disdain.

*Descendants of Manuel Salas San Miguel*

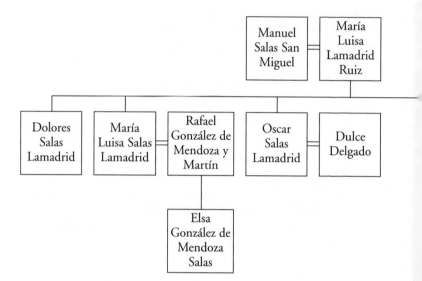

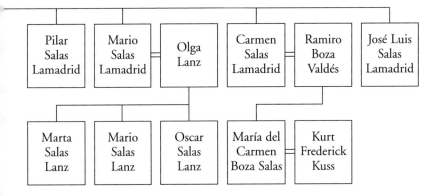

# Appendix B: Chronology

## Elected or Appointed Cuban Administrations and an Intermission

| | |
|---|---|
| Tomás Estrada Palma | 1902–1906 |
| Intervention by the United States under President Theodore Roosevelt | |
| *Provisional Governor:* William Howard Taft | 1906 |
| *Provisional Governor:* Charles E. Magoon | 1906–1909 |
| José Miguel Gómez y Gómez | 1909–1913 |
| Mario García Menocal y Deop | 1913–1921 |
| Alfredo Zayas y Alfonso | 1921–1925 |
| Gerardo Machado y Morales | 1925–1933 |
| Alberto Herrera y Franch | 1933 |
| Carlos Manuel de Céspedes y de Quesada | 1933 |
| Executive Commission *(Pentarchy)* | 1933 |
| Ramón Grau San Martín | 1933–1934 |
| Carlos Hevia y de los Reyes Gavilán | 1934 |
| Carlos Mendieta y Montefur | 1934–1935 |
| José Agripino Barnet y Vinageras | 1935–1936 |
| Miguel Mariano Gómez Arias | 1936 |
| Federico Laredo Bru | 1936–1940 |
| Fulgencio Batista y Zaldívar | 1940–1944 |
| Ramón Grau San Martín | 1944–1948 |
| Carlos Prío Socarrás | 1948–1952 |

# Appendix C

## Fathers and Sons and Sundry Other Public Men Mentioned in the Text

*Artime, Manuel*
Cuban psychiatrist who participated in Brigade 2506 as the Cuban Revolutionary Council's civilian representative.

*Barquín, Ramón*
Major in the Cuban army who planned a coup of young officers against Batista and was betrayed in April 1956.

*Batista y Zaldívar, Fulgencio*
Dictator who began as sergeant stenographer in the Cuban army. He was officially president 1940-1944 and 1952-1958 (in the latter instance by coup d'état) but basically dominated Cuban politics from 1933 on.

*Bosch, Orlando*
Cuban physician who as an exile engaged in sabotage against the Castro government.

*Carbó Morera, Sergio*
Cuban journalist who in 1933 was a member of the pentarchy.

*Carbó y Aniz, Ulises*
Son of Sergio and member of Brigade 2506.

*Céspedes y del Castillo, Carlos Manuel de*
Patriot whose call for independence (Grito de Yara) at his sugar plantation, La Demajagua, in the early hours of 10 October 1868 set off the first Cuban war of independence, known also as the Ten Years' War. He has been dubbed The Father of Our Country.

*Céspedes y de Quesada, Carlos Manuel de*
Son of The Father of Our Country. He served briefly as president of the republic in 1933 after the ouster of Machado and Herrera's one-day presidency.

### Cienfuegos, Camilo
Charismatic, immensely popular chief of staff of the Rebel Army, who disappeared under very suspicious circumstances in October 1959.

### Dorticós Torrado, Osvaldo
Appointed president 17 July 1959 after the resignation of Urrutia. He had been a member of the Communist Party in his youth.

### Fernández Ortega, Eufemio
Adventurer, lawyer, occasional journalist, political gangster, head of the secret police under Prío. He was tried 19 April 1961 and executed 20 April at the fortress of La Cabaña.

### Finlay, Carlos
Cuban physician who discovered that the *Aedes aegypti* mosquito is a vector for yellow fever. This discovery made control of the disease possible. His son, Carlos E. Finlay y Shine, was minister of health in Grau's 1933 government.

### Franca Echarte, Porfirio
Banker who formed part of the pentarchy of 1933.

### García Menocal y Deop, Mario
Conservative president of Cuba from 1913 to 1921. He openly stole his 1916 re-election from the Liberals. Previously, he had had a brilliant career in the Army of Liberation.

### Gómez Ferrer, Juan Gualberto
Cuban journalist and legislator who advocated for Cuban independence, for the abolition of slavery, and for an integrated society that would grant equal rights to all races. His freedom was bought by his slave mother while he was in the womb. Lived 1854–1933.

### Gómez y Gómez, José Miguel
Veteran of all three wars of independence, Liberal leader, and president of the republic from 1909 to 1913. When García Menocal stole the election of 1916 through fraud, José Miguel Gómez led an armed rebellion, for which he was imprisoned. His

son Miguel Mariano Gómez Arias served as president from May through December 1936.

## González Corzo, Rogelio

Under the code name "Francisco" this young engineer organized the anti-Castro underground until he was captured, with Humberto Sorí Marín, in a government raid on 18 March 1961. He was executed at the Cabaña Fortress on 20 April.

## Grau San Martín, Ramón

He represented the Student Directorate's radical platform within the pentarchy of 1933 and then became chief executive. Upon becoming president, he unilaterally abrogated the Platt Amendment. He was forced out of office in 1934 under strong pressure from the U.S. embassy and the military under Batista. He led the Partido Revolucionario Cubano (Auténtico). He was elected president of the republic in 1944 and served a four-year term that was marred by rampant corruption.

## Guiteras Holmes, Antonio

He was appointed minister of government by Grau to the cabinet of 1933, and he won wide popular support for his radical reforms. Upon the ouster of Grau and the imposition of military control by Batista, Guiteras founded Joven Cuba, an organization dedicated to the ouster by force of the government and the establishment of revolutionary reforms. In 1935 he was killed in a long gun battle when several hundred soldiers laid siege to his hiding place.

## Hevia y de los Reyes Gavilán, Carlos

He was trained as an engineer and served as president for thirty-six hours in 1934, between Grau and Mendieta. He was the presidential candidate from the Auténtico party in the 1952 election derailed by Batista's 10 March coup. In 1961 Hevia was a member of the Cuban Revolutionary Council.

## Hornedo Suárez, Alfredo

Wealthy former senator. His Hotel Blanquita and Teatro Blanquita were confiscated by the Castro government.

*Irisarri y Gamio, José Miguel*
Lawyer, member of the 1933 pentarchy.

*Izaguirre Hornedo, Alfredo*
Director-owner of the newspaper *El Crisol.* Nephew of Alfredo Hornedo and father of Alfredo Izaguirre Riva.

*Izaguirre Riva, Alfredo*
Director of *El Crisol* at the age of twenty. After the newspaper was confiscated, he involved himself in clandestine activity against the Castro government and was imprisoned. His death sentence was commuted to thirty years through the intervention of the Inter American Press Association, of which he was the youngest member. In prison he was beaten nearly to death for refusing to do even a moment's forced labor.

*Maceo, Antonio*
The Bronze Titan. Cuban patriot born in Santiago de Cuba in 1845; killed in a surprise attack in Punta Brava on 7 December 1896. With his parents and brothers, he joined the Ten Years' War shortly after its beginning. He protested the treaty that ended it. With Máximo Gómez and José Martí he led the War of Independence (Three Years' War) begun in 1895. He was crucial to the "invasion campaign," which took the war, at first concentrated in the east, all the way through to the west.

*Maceo Mackle, Antonio*
Surgeon, grandson of the Bronze Titan, who was a member of the Cuban Revolutionary Council.

*Maceo Masque (a.k.a. Antonio Maceo, Jr.), Antonio*
Member of Brigade 2506. Son of Dr. Antonio Maceo, the Cuban Revolutionary Council member, and great-grandson of Antonio Maceo, the Bronze Titan.

*Machado y Morales, Gerardo*
President of Cuba from 1925 to 1933. A catastrophic economy, torturous retrenchment, opposition to labor, illegal extension of terms of office, and tyrannical repression inspired creative, determined, and widespread opposition to his regime. He was finally

ousted by the army. The period of his rule is known as *el machadato.*

*Mariñas, Manuel ("Manolo")*
Cuban attorney and journalist who defended Humberto Sorí Marín at his treason trial on 19 April 1961.

*Masferrer, Rolando*
In the 1940s, founder of the Movimiento Socialista Revolucionario (MSR). Senator in the 1950s and head of a private army of thugs, *los tigres.*

*Mendieta, Carlos*
President of Cuba from January 1934 to December 1935. He was put into power through an agreement between U.S. ambassador Jefferson Caffery and Fulgencio Batista. He was little more than Batista's puppet. The general strike of March 1935 and the repression that followed it took place under his presidency.

*Miró Argenter, José*
Chief of staff to Antonio Maceo in the War of Independence. Born in Cataluña. Father of José Miró Cardona.

*Miró Cardona, José*
Law professor at the Universidad de La Habana. In January 1959 he was appointed prime minister by the victorious rebels. He renounced his post on 13 February 1959. In 1960 he obtained political asylum. He served as president of the Cuban Revolutionary Council.

*Miró Torra, José Antonio*
Member of Brigade 2506. Son of José Miró Cardona.

*Morúa Delgado, Martín*
Legislator, president of the Cuban Senate in 1909.

*Oliva, Erneido*
Second in command of Brigade 2506.

*Pardo Llada, José*
Vociferous and vituperative anti-Batista radio journalist who left for the Sierra Maestra. After the triumph of the revolution, he

acted as promoter of the new government and scourge of possible dissenters. He was named head of the government's propagandist radio and television corporation, FIEL. Suddenly, on 25 March 1961, he applied for asylum in Mexico City.

*Pérez San Román, José ("Pepe")*
Commander of Brigade 2506.

*Portela Möller, Guillermo*
Law professor, member of the 1933 pentarchy.

*Prío Socarrás, Carlos*
Last elected president of Cuba, 10 October 1948 to 10 March 1952. He was deposed by Batista with the *Golpe de Marzo*.

*Rivero Díaz, Felipe*
Member of Brigade 2506.

*Rivero, José Ignacio ("Pepín")*
Director-owner of *Diario de la Marina*, one of La Habana's most prestigious newspapers. Lived 1895 to 1944.

*Rodríguez, Carlos Rafael*
Old Communist.

*Román, Monseñor Agustín*
Auxiliary bishop of Miami. The moving force behind the building of the shrine to Our Lady of Charity on Biscayne Bay in Miami.

*Sorí Marín, Humberto*
Advocate-general in the Sierra Maestra. Minister of agriculture after the revolution. He was fired in June 1959. He left the country and in March 1961 he returned to organize the underground. He was captured on 18 March and subsequently killed by firing squad on 20 April.

*Sosa Blanco, Jesús*
Major in Batista's army. His trial on 22 January 1959 at the Sports Palace was televised. He was found guilty at that trial and at the retrial. He was executed by firing squad.

*Urrutia Lleó, Manuel*
First president of Cuba after the revolution. He attempted to resign four times between January and 17 July 1959. The last resignation was accepted. In fact, it was catalyzed by a speech in which Fidel Castro publicly reviled him.

*Valdés, Ramiro*
Head of Castro's political police, the G-2. Later was interior minister.

*Varona y Loredo, Manuel Antonio ("Tony") de*
Prime minister under Prío (1948-50). Member of the Cuban Revolutionary Council. Later founded Junta Patriótica.

# Bibliography

## General

Aeschylus. *Agamemnon.* Translated by Richmond Lattimore. University of Chicago, Aeschylus I. 1953.

Bible, Revised Standard Version.

Fremantle, Francesca, and Chögyam Trungpa, trans. *The Tibetan Book of the Dead: The Great Liberation through Hearing in the Bardo.* Boston: Shambala, 1975.

Henricks, Robert G., trans. *Lao-tzu: Te-Tao Ching.* New York: Ballantine Books, 1989.

Schell, Jonathan. *Fate of the Earth.* New York: Knopf, 1982.

Sophocles. *Ajax.* Translated by John Moore. University of Chicago, Sophocles II. 1957.

Wiesel, Elie. "We Are All Witnesses: An Interview with Elie Wiesel." By Roger Lipsey. *Parabola* 10 (May 1985): 26–33.

## José Martí

All Martí translations are mine.

Martí, José. *Martí: ciudadano y apóstol—su ideario.* Compiled by Homero Muñoz. Miami: author (printed by Editorial AIP), 1968. My father seems to have used his copy as a workbook, as it is replete with brackets and X's. It is inscribed by the compiler.

———. *Páginas escogidas.* Selection and prologue by Alfonso M. Escudero. Madrid: Espasa-Calpe, 1953.

———. *Pensamientos.* Selected by A. Hernández-Catá. Madrid: Atenea, Colección Microcosmos, 1921. This is a treasure I rescued from my father's library in Cuba, a tiny, tapestry-bound and gold-edged volume. It was one of three books I packed in my suitcase.

———. *Poesías completas.* Buenos Aires: Ediciones Antonio Zamora, 1970. I based my translations of José Martí's poetry

385

on the texts appearing in this edition, which was a gift to me from my father.

Massó, José Luis. *Camino de Dos Ríos.* Miami: author (Echevarría Printing), 1966. This is a documentary account of the last days of Martí by a now deceased friend of my father's.

## Cuban History

Báez, Vicente, ed. *La enciclopedia de Cuba,* vols. 6, 9. Madrid: Enciclopedia y Clásicos Cubanos, 1974–75.

Dubois, Jules. *Fidel Castro: Rebel—Liberator or Dictator?* Indianapolis: Bobbs-Merrill, 1959.

Franqui, Carlos. *Retrato de familia con Fidel.* Barcelona: Seix Barral, 1981.

Pérez, Louis A., Jr. *Cuba: Between Reform and Revolution.* New York: Oxford University Press, 1988.

Ruiz, Leovigildo. *Diario de una traición—Cuba: 1959.* Miami: author, 1965. This and the other volumes in the series are very useful chronologies. My father made many annotations in them.

―――. *Diario de una traición—Cuba: 1960.* Miami: author, 1970.

―――. *Diario de una traición—Cuba: 1961.* Miami: author, [Lorie Book Stores?], 1972.

Thomas, Hugh. *Cuba: The Pursuit of Freedom.* New York: Harper and Row, 1971.

Valladares, Armando. *Contra toda esperanza.* Barcelona: Plaza & Janes, 1985.

## Girón and the Cuban Missile Crisis

Blight, James G.; Bruce J. Allyn; and David A. Welch. *Cuba on the Brink: Castro, the Missile Crisis, and the Soviet Collapse.* New York: Pantheon, 1993.

Higgins, Trumbull. *The Perfect Failure: Kennedy, Eisenhower, and the CIA at the Bay of Pigs.* New York: W.W. Norton, 1987.

Johnson, Haynes. *The Bay of Pigs: The Leaders' Story of Brigade 2506.* New York: W.W. Norton, 1964.

Massó, José Luis. *Cuba: 17 de abril.* Mexico City: Editorial Diana, 1962.

Wyden, Peter. *Bay of Pigs: The Untold Story.* New York: Simon and Schuster, 1979.

**Periodicals**

MacPherson, Myra. "The Last Casualty of the Bay of Pigs." *Washington Post,* 17 October 1989, C1.

Mariñas, Manuel G. "Adiós . . . Ramiro Boza." *Diario Las Américas,* 1 June 1989, 7-A.

Miró Cardona, José. "Statement by Dr. Miró Cardona on His Resignation from Cuban Exile Council." *New York Times,* 19 April 1963, 14.